LIFE BEYOND DEATH IN MATTHEW'S GOSPEL
RELIGIOUS METAPHOR OR BODILY REALITY?

BIBLICAL TOOLS AND STUDIES

Edited by

B. DOYLE, G. VAN BELLE, J. VERHEYDEN
K.U.Leuven

Associate Editors

C.T. BEGG, Washington DC – U. BERGES, Bonn – J. FREY, Zürich
C.M. TUCKETT, Oxford – G. VAN OYEN, Louvain-la-Neuve

LIFE BEYOND DEATH IN MATTHEW'S GOSPEL
RELIGIOUS METAPHOR OR BODILY REALITY?

EDITED BY

WIM WEREN, HUUB VAN DE SANDT
AND JOSEPH VERHEYDEN

PEETERS
LEUVEN – PARIS – WALPOLE, MA

2011

Cover:
Τῆς καινῆς Διαθήκης ἅπαντα. Εὐαγγέλιον
Novum Iesu Christi D.N. Testamentum ex bibliotheca regia.
Lutetiae: ex officina Roberti Stephani, 1550. in-folio.
KULeuven, Maurits Sabbebibliotheek, P225.042/F°

Mt 5,3-12

A catalogue record for this book is available from the Library of Congress

ISBN 978-90-429-2518-2
D/2011/0602/86

© 2011, Peeters, Bondgenotenlaan 153, B-3000 Leuven (Belgium)

CONTENTS

Introduction.   IX

PART ONE

GENERAL SCOPE

1. Paul G. Foster, *The Hebrew Bible / LXX and the Development of Ideas on Afterlife in Matthew*   3

2. Tobias Nicklas, *Resurrection in the Gospels of Matthew and Peter: Some Developments*   27

3. Claudia Setzer, *Resurrection in the Gospel of Matthew: Reality and Symbol*   43

4. Kari Syreeni, *Resurrection or Assumption? Matthew's View of the Post-Mortem Vindication of Jesus*.   57

5. J. Andrew Overman, *Matthew and the Fate of Humankind*   79

PART TWO

SPECIFIC TEXTS

6. Dieter Zeller, *The Soul Which Cannot Be Killed by Men (Matt 10:28)*   95

7. Huub van de Sandt, *Eternal Life as a Reward for Choosing the Right Way: The Story of the Rich Young Man (Matt 19:16-30)* . .   107

8. Adelbert Denaux, *The Controversy between Jesus and the Sadducees about the Resurrection (Matt 22:23-33) in the Context of Early Jewish Eschatology*   129

9. Dale C. Allison, *The Scriptural Background of a Matthean Legend: Ezekiel 37, Zechariah 14, and Matthew 27* 153

10. Wim Weren, *Matthew's Stories about Jesus' Burial and Resurrection (27:55-28:20) as the Climax of his Gospel* 189

11. Joseph Verheyden, *The Great Escape: Some Comments on a Controversial Suggestion for Explaining Matt 28:2-4* 201

12. Jürgen Zangenberg, *"Bodily Resurrection" of Jesus in Matthew?* . . 217

BIBLIOGRAPHY 233

INDEX OF SOURCES 257

INDEX OF MODERN AUTHORS 275

INDEX OF SUBJECTS 279

INTRODUCTION

The apostle Paul made the resurrection the centre piece of Christian doctrine as he wrote: "If Christ has not been raised, then our preaching has been in vain and your faith has been in vain" (1Corinthians 15:14). Jesus' resurrection is reported here as a historical event in space and time. The verse highlights that the risen Christ is the core of Christianity and that resurrection is a key theme in the New Testament. What happened on Easter morning? More than two thousand years after the disciples first spread the news of the decisive event in Christian history, believers still ponder over the issue of the resurrection. Books, articles and papers combing the New Testament on this subject battle for attention on the bookshelves.

In 1980, a large tomb containing ten ossuaries was found in the East Talpiot neighbourhood of Jerusalem and recently the claim has been made that this is the tomb of Jesus and several of his family members[1]. Would it be a shattering blow to New Testament instruction about the resurrection of Christ if this was indeed the tomb of Jesus?

Many Christians are not bothered by the Talpiot tomb and its possible implications. They are not shocked, upset or disturbed by the idea that what has been discovered might indeed be the tomb of Jesus as they dispute the idea that Jesus literally rose from the dead. In their opinion, Jesus' resurrection is best understood as a metaphor. Although they consider the resurrection to be profoundly real, they feel it is an error to interpret Gospel reports of a risen Jesus walking and eating literally. The way they see it, Jesus was crucified, died, and was buried and yet rose in the hearts of his disciples. In their view, resurrection should be taken as a figure of speech. The Gospel writers resorted to mythological language to portray Jesus' significance.

For traditional Christians, however, who firmly believe that Jesus rose from the dead physically, the tomb actually being that of Jesus and his family would be big news. The motif of the empty tomb supports their belief in a physical resurrection. Support for this literal interpretation can also be found in Jesus' use of violent metaphors of amputation in Matt 5:29-30

---

1. See S. JACOBOVICI – C. PELLEGRINO, *The Jesus Family Tomb: The Discovery That Will Change History Forever*, San Francisco, Harper, 2007.

and 18:8-9, which suggests there is a bodily continuity between this life and the next. Further proof of the fact that Jesus' teaching implied a belief in a real physical resurrection can be found in the fact that Pilate in having the tomb guarded (Matt 27:64) was bent on the disciples not stealing the body away and then contending that Jesus had been raised from the dead.

The central question of this book is whether Jesus' resurrection is a religious metaphor or a bodily reality. At first sight the choice between these two alternatives might seem unbalanced. It is not a pure antithesis and it would be better to contrast "metaphorical" with "literal" (or "historical"), and "physical" with "spiritual". But interpreting the resurrection in terms of these contrasts, as being either one or the other, is not adequate either. Statements about the resurrection are never meant completely metaphorically or completely literally. They are usually a mix of the two. When applied to Matthew, the statement that "resurrection" is a metaphor covers only half the truth, indicating that Jesus lives on in people's memories, that his name is still honoured and that his cause is continued by his disciples. What is equally important is the message that something has also happened to Jesus himself, namely that, through the agency of God, Jesus, the person himself, comes to participate in a life that is no longer bounded by death.

In order to invite discussion and exchange ideas on this fundamental issue, an expert meeting was organized at the Tilburg School of Humanities in April 2009. In line with the New Testament research programme ("Matthew, James and Didache"), the meeting concentrated on the Gospel of Matthew. The central question what exactly Matthew focuses on at Easter was dealt with in the light of the assumptions of twenty-first century scholars. A great variety of questions came up for review: How does Matthew interpret the concept of resurrection and how does his picture of Jesus' resurrection chime in with other concerns in his Gospel (problems related to God, the community's self-image, the surrounding world and the history of salvation)? How does the story of God raising Jesus from the dead fit in with (other) historical facts? Does Matthew perceive Jesus' resurrection as an event in which the body is also involved? Does he emphasize the bodily aspects of the resurrection of Jesus' followers? What does Matthew mean by "body"? Is resurrection more than a continuation of our temporal existence – more than a coming back to a life identical to our present life? Does it involve a complete transformation of the body into a new and glorious state of being?

The present volume contains the papers presented at the meeting in Tilburg. As the number of invited speakers at the conference was limited, additional contributors were subsequently invited to write essays focusing on a topic that would complement the overall theme. These studies link up with the Gospel of Matthew as well, for it is not our intention to add another volume to the already existing books portraying the historical development of afterlife beliefs in general. It is the Matthean text, the subject of *Life beyond Death in Matthew's Gospel*, which keeps on being highlighted. Naturally, this Gospel can only be understood if it is studied within the framework of other writings, before and after Matthew's book came into circulation.

While the conference itself was held to pay tribute to Professor Wim Weren on the occasion of his being 25 years in office on January 1st, 2009, the publication of these studies coincides with his retirement from the Tilburg chair of New Testament Exegesis in the School of Humanities. This volume is dedicated to him. Wim Weren not only for many years was a successful dean of the former Tilburg Faculty of Theology but he also played a remarkable role in Matthean scholarship. In this field of study, he is probably best known for his contribution to the development of intertextuality by exposing how texts in Matthew gain meaning through their allusions and references to other texts.

This volume is divided into two major sections. *The first section* (Chapters 1-5) deals with the variety and development of ideas and beliefs about the afterlife. It studies the relationship between Matthew's understanding of a post-mortem existence and interpretations of that phenomenon in the Hebrew Bible, the Septuagint, Greco-Roman writings, early Jewish and early Christian literature. By virtue of their broad scope, these essays in addition to their specific content, also provide interesting introductory information.

In chapter 1, *Paul G. Foster* explains special features of Matthew's views of the afterlife in the light of trends in the Hebrew Bible and the Septuagint and as a result of further reflection on life and death in the Judaism of the Second Temple Period. In the Hebrew Bible, texts on the resurrection are extremely scarce; the only unmistakable passage is Dan 12:1-3. The Septuagint offers a slightly more varied picture because the Greek translators sometimes emphasised certain aspects (as in the Psalms, in Isa 26:19 and Job 42:17) and introduced new material, either on bodily resurrection (2 Macc 7) or on the immortality of the souls of the wise (Wis 3:1-10). The afterlife does not play a dominant role in the Dead Sea Scrolls, although a few text fragments have been found that point to the emergence of a belief in bodily resurrection (4Q521; 4QPseudo-Ezekiel). A certain kinship with the Wisdom of Solomon can be perceived in the writings of Philo. The influence of Platonic philosophy is apparent in *De Sacrificiis*, in the immortal state of the soul being referred to, and in the argument that earthly life can have a special quality as a result. The opinions of the Sadducees are diametrically opposed to these views. According to Flavius Josephus, they hold that the soul dies with the body (*Ant.* 18.16). This shows that different positions could be distinguished in Matthew's time. Matthew represents a late stage in the development. He is not directly dependent on a single Jewish source but clearly concurs with the emerging idea of bodily resurrection and links this idea with the prospect that, at the last judgment, the righteous will be rewarded and the wicked punished.

Tobias Nicklas addresses the question of the relationship between Matthew's stories on Jesus' burial and resurrection with similar subjects in the *Gospel of Peter*. Comparing these two texts raises many problems, and divergent views have been defended as to their literary relationship. According to Nicklas, the many parallels can best be explained if we assume that *GosPet* in its current form is a story in which narrative elements from the New Testament Gospels are linked to elements that cannot be found in the New Testament. The Gospels of Matthew and Peter show partly convergent and partly divergent views as regards Jesus' resurrection. Nicklas has made a detailed textual analysis of the story in *GosPet* 34-42, providing an elaborate description of the resurrection of "the Lord" from the point of view of the soldiers guarding the tomb. The guards and the Jewish leaders are direct witnesses of the resurrection whereas, in Matthew's Gospel, this privilege is not even granted to Jesus' disciples. The corporeal aspects of the resurrection are emphasised but, even so, the risen Lord is described as a heavenly figure rather than as someone with a human body. The fact that the soldiers and the elders of the people have seen everything with their own eyes makes it all the more incomprehensible that they have kept silent about their experiences. By doing so, they are guilty of the fact that the Jewish people failed to recognise Jesus as the Son of God. In his analyses, Nicklas also shows various points of contact with other early Jewish and early Christian writings, throwing the distinctive profile of Matthew's stories on Jesus' resurrection into sharper relief.

Claudia Setzer asks how exactly Matthew understood Jesus' resurrection. She argues that in this Gospel resurrection is both reality and symbol. In this matter she prefers the term "symbol" to "metaphor" since a symbol is part of the reality to which it points. In the Jewish bible and even more so in later Jewish sources, there was nothing unusual in combining different images of the afterlife in the same source. Ideas of resurrection, immortality of the soul, or astral immortality are found side by side in the same documents. Most of these ideas are not clearly defined. Since there is – even in the first century C.E. – so much variety in Jewish texts on the afterlife,

Setzer holds that Jesus' resurrection should be regarded as continuous with Jewish expectations. Matthew seems devoted to proving the corporeal reality of Jesus' resurrection to prevent problems for community members. In his time, such a debate over bodily resurrection was real and a factor in separating Matthew's group from other Jewish communities. On the other hand, Matthew surpasses the mere level of corporeality. When not addressing opposition, he shows how Jesus' resurrection moves beyond itself. The phrase "he has been raised" is found three times in the Gospel in a fixed form. It means more than it says. Those who profess the resurrection of the body affirm the goodness of the material world, including the body, as God's creation. It is also a statement about God's power, a performative speech act, similar to the statement "the God who acted at Sinai" or "the God who brought us out of Egypt." Matthew envisages the resurrection of Jesus' body as reality on the one hand, and as a symbol condensing a set of assumptions about God and the world on the other.

Next to the belief in Jesus' (bodily) resurrection, was Matthew also familiar with other conceptualisations of his post-mortem existence? *Kari Syreeni* seeks to answer this question by discussing two recent proposals: a) the argument of Daniel A. Smith that Q and the pre-Markan tradition conceived Jesus' continued existence in terms of assumption; b) Roger David Aus's theory that Mark's empty tomb tradition is influenced by a midrashic use of biblical traditions concerning Moses. In the case of an assumption, the focus lies on the disappearance of the body and the absence of the translated hero, while resurrection involves an appearance of the risen person and his presence. In Mark, these two concepts are combined: in this Gospel, Jesus' resurrection is conceived in terms of an assumption. Q does not speak about Jesus in terms of resurrection, even though a certain idea of his vindication after death is suggested in texts on his return in a new eschatological role. In Q 13:34-35 and 19:42-46, a scenario of disappearance-absence-return is suggested. The conclusion is therefore justified that Q's theology is based on the idea of Jesus' hidden removal and return. According to Syreeni, the assumption theology was quite widespread: apart from Mark and Q, this theology can also be found in the pre-Johannine tradition. David Aus traces the Markan stories about Jesus' burial and the empty tomb tradition back to a midrashic, typological use of various biblical and early Jewish traditions concerning the death and burial of Moses and traditions about the Song of the Well in Num 21:18 and Jacob's well in Gen 29:1-14. It is practically impossible to verify or falsify Aus's detailed hypotheses. Syreeni wonders whether Matthew's story as a whole betrays any knowledge of assumption imagery or Moses typology. Although the first seven chapters and the final passage (Matt 28:16-20) show that the evangelist is familiar with parallels between Moses and Jesus, his book does not contain any clear traces of an assumption theology based on a Moses typology. Instead, he appears to hold a rather orthodox view of the resurrection: he emphasises the corporeal aspects of Jesus' post-mortem existence and perceives the presence of the risen Jesus amidst his disciples mainly in the enduring authority of Jesus' teachings and in his ethical example.

In Matthew's view, those who follow Jesus' example will be rewarded with a next life in the End. But what about the non-Matthean Jews and Gentiles? Do they – the rest of the world – also fit into his eschatological schema? *J. Andrew Overman* investigates who among the many inhabitants of the world would in Matthew's view attain heaven. Most Romans believed there was something after this life. The hereafter was under the control of the high gods who determined man's personal, domestic and political fate. The gods managed one's fortune and chance. Indeed, in Philo of Alexandria and also the scrolls of Qumran, a good and righteous conduct has consequences for one's eternal fate. But are non-Jews, people outside of Palestine, part of the kingdom of heaven? Overman concedes that Matthew's Gospel is at important points parochial, that is, not thinking about the rest of the world but taken up with local issues and instructions to his own community. On the other hand, Matthew's use of the traditions at his disposal reflects a sophisticated level of learning. His shaping of the traditions he has inherited shows him as someone who is aware of the broader, wider world beyond Palestine. Matthew knew about broader developments in his part of the world and his use of Isaiah LXX in Matt 4:15 and 12:18-21 shows how he integrated the rest of the world into his story. In this respect, also his curtailed version of the healing of the centurion's servant, when compared to Luke's, is significant (Matt 8:5-13). And, finally, Matt 24:14 demonstrates that the nations – the rest of the world – play a vital role in his movement and in his eschatological schema. Non-Jews are included, they can have great faith, and they are incorporated in the promises of God if their actions are just and fruit-bearing.

The second section (Chapters. 6-12) moves from the broad topics to specific textual units in Matthew about resurrection, immortality, afterlife and eternal life. Various relevant texts are singled out for particular study.

This section opens with a contribution by *Dieter Zeller*, who investigates the logion in Matt 10:28: "*a.* And do not be afraid of those who kill the body, but cannot kill the soul. *b.* But fear more the One who is able to destroy both the soul and body in Gehenna." This verse consists of two parts. The first part (v. 28a) reflects an anthropology that was current in

Greek philosophy and among Greek-speaking Jews arguing that the soul cannot perish. Zeller shows that not only the Greeks but also Palestinian Jews of the first century C.E. were acquainted with this body-soul dichotomy. The second verse part (v. 28b) conveys the message that God might be inclined to ruin the soul as a deed of punishment. This idea cannot be derived from Greek philosophical tradition and in fact stands in contrast to Greek sensitivity. Thus, although the verse in 10:28 initially seems to be in line with the Greek world view, it has to be interpreted in the perspective of v. 28b: the soul is not presented here as absolutely immortal. The verse in its entirety expresses the idea that somebody who dies falls directly into God's hands. It follows that everyone might be held responsible for the whole of his life on the one hand, but may have confidence in the goodness of God on the other.

Huub van de Sandt explores the Matthean story of the Rich Young Man (Matt 19:16-30). The account consists of three parts and is based upon Mark 10:17-31. Closer examination shows, however, that Matthew has exercised considerable freedom in rewriting Mark's account. He deviates from Mark by linking this episode to the ethical doctrine of the Two Ways, a teaching passed on in the first six chapters of the Didache. After all, the Two Ways doctrine was probably employed in Matt 7:13-27 as well. Matthew's report of Jesus' dialogue with the rich man in 19:16-22 echoes important elements of the Jewish Two Ways instruction. According to Van de Sandt, this also goes for the second and third parts of the story (vv. 23-26. 27-30). In contrast to Mark, Jesus' conversation with the disciples in Matthew simplistically maintains a dualistic pattern in vv. 23-26. Just like the Two Ways pattern in Matt 7:13-14 opened up a series of contrasting alternatives without any nuance in 7:13-27, so the subdivision 19:23-26 appears to be a polarizing piece. The reward in the End focuses on the disciples' eschatological destiny in the third part of the narrative (vv. 27-30). And again, it is the manner in which Matt 7:13-27 deals with the Two Ways (a horrific fate of the wicked and reward of the righteous) that highlights once more Matthew's intention as regards "life" and "death" in this final subdivision. This also explains his insertion of v. 28. The themes of life and death were updated along strictly apocalyptic lines. Adherence to the right way is not motivated by its puny earthly recompense but instead is remunerated by the infinitely greater post-judgment reward.

A book about Matthew's view on life beyond death would be incomplete without an analysis of the passage of Jesus' discussion with the Sadducees on the bodily resurrection (Matt 22:23-33). *Adelbert Denaux* tries to situate this discussion within the wider context of early Jewish views of the afterlife. His results largely correspond to those found by Paul Foster. According to Denaux, there is evidence of an emerging belief in the bodily resurrection of the dead in various sources from before 70 C.E.: in the Hebrew Bible and the Septuagint, in the Dead Sea Scrolls (*On Resurrection*; *Pseudo-Ezekiel*), in the second blessing of the *Amidah*, and in a number of texts in the Pseudepigrapha. There are also texts in which the resurrection is explicitly debated or denied. Denaux analyses the Sadducees' question and Jesus' answer against this background. The Sadducees rely too much on the continuity between life on earth and life in heaven; in the Scriptures, they cannot find any basis for the resurrection or for the idea that God has the power to raise the dead. These assertions are criticised by Jesus. He emphasises that bodily resurrection involves a transformation compared to the earlier earthly existence, indicating discontinuity as well as continuity. Furthermore, Jesus interprets Exod 3:6 as a text that has a deeper meaning and that proves that there is a resurrection. This deeper meaning emerges when the text is understood within its literary context and in the light of texts on God's covenant with the ancestors. Denaux concludes his contribution with the suggestion that Matt 22:23-33 goes back to an incident during the ministry of the historical Jesus and is also rooted in ideas in contemporary Judaism.

According to *Dale Allison*, the story in Matt 27:51b-53 is a legend in which images from Ezek 37:10-14 and Zech 14:4-5 are blended. Pseudo-Ezekiel shows that, as early as in the second century B.C.E., Ezek 37:1-14 was connected to the eschatological reward of the righteous from the people of Israel; Zech 14:4-5 shows that, early on, the Mount of Olives figured as the place of the resurrection. The blending of the images from the two texts also features in the well-known wall painting in the synagogue of Dura Europos from the middle of the third century C.E.. It depicts the dead being resurrected and given a new body against the background of a mountain that is split in two (as a result of an earthquake?). This split mountain plays an important role in the later Christian iconographic tradition. However, on the basis of a large number of texts and traditions, Allison argues convincingly that the conflation of the two Bible texts is of an early date so that Matthew could have derived it from the tradition when he created the legend in 27:51b-53. This legend shows that Matthew held a rather literal view of the resurrection involving a dualistic anthropology that assumed a continued existence of the soul after death, separate from the body (see 10:28; 14:26; 22:29-33). However, since the Gospel contains other images in addition to this view, it must be concluded that Matthew leaves the question as to the exact nature of the resurrection unanswered.

Wim Weren explores how Matthew's stories about Jesus' burial and resurrection (27:55-28:20) relate to the rest of his Gospel. In these stories, lines developed earlier in the book come together. However, they also contain new material, for example, the opponents' allegation that the belief in the resurrection is based on deception. Matthew tries to disprove this claim, but his story about the open grave (28:1-7) is striking as it does not describe how Jesus left his tomb. Why is that? There could hardly have been a more efficacious way to refute the body theft story spread by the opponents. The fact that he fails to give such a description indicates that simply no one could be found who was an eyewitness to Jesus' resurrection. Weren subsequently explores what Matthew understood by "resurrection" and how his picture of Jesus' resurrection fits in with other issues in his Gospel. Resurrection means Jesus' continued presence within his community, in particular with people in distress, whom he calls his brothers and sisters (25:40). From Jesus' interaction with his disciples after his resurrection, Weren infers that Matthew is very close to our idea that the human body stands for the entire person and enables someone to communicate.

Joseph Verheyden looks back at a suggestion that was made in the early 1970s by N. Walter and (independently) by R. Kratz to read Matthew's version of the Empty Tomb story as a rescue miracle ("Befreiungswunder"). The suggestion was critically received in the literature, the main objection being that Matthew does not actually describe the escape or rescue from the tomb. This is true, of course. Yet his version contains a good number of motifs and features of such rescue stories (locking of the door; a guard; the door or gate opened by divine intervention; the victim is absent, but will be met elsewhere). Verheyden analyses these motifs in their relation to the genre and concludes that Matthew has been playing with motifs that are at home in the genre of the rescue miracle, but refuses to take the last step and also describe the resurrection. As a possible explanation, he refers to the irony that characterises much of his version of the empty tomb story: the guard who claim to have seen everything as a matter of fact know nothing; the women whom one might expect to witness the resurrection when meeting with the angel only get information on where they can meet the risen Lord; the reader who might have expected to be granted a description of the resurrection in turn is frustrated.

Jürgen Zangenberg deals with the question of how Matthew portrays the resurrected Jesus. For that purpose he first studies three passages outside the passion narrative which allow short glimpses into how Matthew pictures the existence of persons that were resurrected. The instances 10:28; 14:26 and 22:30 show that resurrection implies some kind of transformation on the part of the resurrected. He then focuses on Jesus' resurrection narratives. The tomb narrative in 27:62-66 and 28:11-15 does not mention precisely how we should imagine the resurrected Jesus. The account suggests that Jesus took his body with him when he rose from the grave, but nowhere is the resurrected Jesus explicitly called "body". In Matt 27:52-53, Matthew describes the appearance of many deceased saints coming out of their graves and refers to "many bodies of the holy ones". There is no mention of transformation, however, and their "bodies" are not different from the bodies they had before. As to Jesus' post-mortal existence (including his resurrection), it is important to establish that Matthew conceptualizes this being in line with Jewish traditions about the death of martyrs whose resurrection consisted in being transported to heaven as an act of vindication. The resurrection directly out of the grave is Jesus' enthronement as a universal ruler who is now able to remain "with you all days" (28:20).

We are indebted to the School of Humanities of Tilburg University (above all to the former Department of Religious Studies) for generously making financial resources available to launch the conference. We would also like to thank the staff at Peeters publishing house for their patience and skill in producing this volume. And, last but not least, we acknowledge our gratitude to Mrs. José Quaedvlieg–de Vaan who assisted us in the process of editing and preparing this volume. She has devoted much of her time to the laborious task of compiling the Bibliography and Indices.

The Editors

PART ONE

GENERAL SCOPE

THE HEBREW BIBLE / LXX AND THE
DEVELOPMENT OF IDEAS ON
AFTERLIFE IN MATTHEW

I. INTRODUCTION

The traditional mantra has been that ideas concerning afterlife are a late development in the evolving religious thought of Israelite and Jewish religion.[1] Thus, representative of mainstream views, Robert Martin-Achard, can open his Anchor Bible Dictionary article on "Resurrection (OT)" with the following statement. "When one reads the OT, one fact is striking: that Israel is attached to life – to this life – and in no way dreams of a marvellous life hereafter"[2]. While there are texts in the Hebrew Bible that relate "death-defying" incidents, these are very much the exception and not the norm. Belief in the possibility of a universal participation in an afterlife state is an unknown concept in the extant records of Israelite religion. Rather, at the point of death there is descent into Sheol, which appears to be a place of darkness, separation from God and of non-existence. While there is some fluidity in the concept of "Sheol" (see further, below) one constant aspect is that it denotes a state where there is separation from God, and consequently at best severely impaired or diminished existence.

---

1. The terms "Israelite" and "Jewish" are used to refer to what is broadly a continuous religious movement with strong nationalistic connections. The term Jewish is used to denote that phase of the movement after the return from exile in the late sixth century B.C.E., when the nation was reconstituted and the rebuilding of the second temple was commissioned with permission of royal edict issued by Cyrus II (Ezra 1:2-4). The Israelite period could be defined as ending with the deportation of the ten northern tribes by the Assyrians in 721 B.C.E. However, since the institutional system of religion in Judah remained relative stable until the exile, for heuristic reasons the label "Israelite" will be retained to describe the religious system until the Babylonian exile in 587 B.C.E. This distinction is important not just for purposes of nomenclature. Rather, in relation to the topic of the afterlife, Persian influences may incipiently re-shape Jewish conceptions of the possibility of post-mortem existence.

2. R. MARTIN-ACHARD, *Resurrection (OT)*, in D.N. FREEDMAN (ed.), *ABD*, Vol. 5, New York, Doubleday, 1992, p. 680.

In the period after the exile, there is a significant shift in Jewish thinking on the topic of the afterlife. It is tempting, and perhaps justifiable, to see some Persian influences perhaps in the form of early Zoroastrian ideas. Eschatological visions of a cosmic renovation of the universe, and the revivification of souls banished to the place of darkness are part of the earliest recoverable concepts of Zoroastrianism[3]. Such an outlook appears to be readily compatible with the very limited statements in the Hebrew Bible concerning Sheol, the place of darkness. However, while there is a possibility that such an influence functioned as a trigger for Jewish reflection on human post-mortem condition, such ideas developed in a Jewish conceptual matrix in a manner that was integrated with the movement's wider theological ideas. Moreover, in subsequent centuries with the spread of Hellenism throughout the Eastern Mediterranean world, Greek influence may also impact Jewish conceptions of afterlife.

This discussion looks primarily at Hebrew Bible and Septuagintal notions of the post-mortem state. General trends within these two corpora of literature are surveyed in the first two sections, along with texts that show alternative perspectives. Two factors assist the selection of the specific texts that are discussed: (i) illustration of some aspect of post-mortem outlook in the Hebrew Bible or Septuagint; (ii) possible background for Matthean perspectives on afterlife. The next collections of texts that are considered are in turn certain Qumran texts, Philonic writings, and the works of Josephus. It is beneficial to consider these texts because they both reveal how ideas of afterlife contained in Jewish scriptures were being interpreted and expanded upon in the late Second Temple period, and specifically for the focus of this study they set the wider literary context for the composition of the Gospel of Matthew, and highlight the major Jewish antecedents in the approximately two centuries prior to the writing of the gospel. In conclusion the study will draw together general trends in the thought concerning the afterlife in Israelite and Jewish religious thought, as well as describing the religious context and possible influences on Matthew's perspective on post-mortem existence.

II. THE POST-MORTEM STATE IN THE HEBREW BIBLE

Within the patriarchal narratives, future hope revolves around the twin aspirations of a long life and plentiful offspring to propagate the family line.

---

3. See W.W. MALANDRA, *Zoroastrianism: Holy Text, Beliefs and Practices*, in *Encyclopedia Iranica* Online Edition, 20 July 2005, available at www.iranicaonline.org.

Thus, the promised blessing given to Abraham for covenant fidelity is that "you shall go to your fathers in peace and be buried at a good old age" (Gen 15:15). This is also coupled with the assurance that his future generations will be blessed with divine provision: "to your descendents I will give this land" (Gen 15:18). Describing the thanatological perspective of the initial promise as contained in Gen 15:15, Westermann observes that,

> Death does not in this case destroy life's "blessed state" (Heilsein), but the blessed state extends right up to death, death in good old age (so too Gen 25:8; cf. Job 5:26). Part of the happy death is to be buried; the return to the earth unites the deceased with his fathers who have returned to it before him.[4]

Thus death is the common lot of all humanity, and divine blessings result in fellowship with the deity during earthly life, promised futurity through progeny, and the provision of prosperity and happiness. The burial practices attested in the patriarchal narratives also appear to speak of the permanence of death. The purchase of the cave of Machpelah in Hebron from Ephron the Hittite, is transferred to Abraham as his property to serve as a place of burial (Gen 23:20). After the appropriate mourning (Gen 23:2), Abraham states his intention to "bury my dead out of my sight" (Gen 23:4), thereby showing some severance of existence between the living and the dead. The story contains no element that suggests that there is any hope for Sarah's future existence. Similarly with Abraham's own death, he is interred in the same site. Abraham is described as having attained a "ripe age", and having been full of years, he is "gathered to his people" (Gen 25:8). Here the story of Abraham's existence is seen to have reached its termination without the aspiration of future life. The same formula is used to describe the death of Isaac (Gen 35:28-29), who is buried in the same location as his parents (Gen 35:27). The death of Jacob is a more elaborate affair, entailing Egyptian embalming processes of forty days duration and a mourning period of seventy days. However, despite Egyptian funerary practices being prominent in the narrative, the related beliefs concerning the afterlife have made no impact. Jacob is transported back to Hebron and buried in the same location as Abraham and Isaac.

While the trio of patriarchs becomes a formulaic way of denoting the deity of the Hebrew Bible, "the God of Abraham, Isaac and Jacob" (cf. Exod 3:6) their death is considered a reality. This perspective is effectively ignored or even inverted in triple tradition material replicated in Matthew's gospel (Matt 22:23-33; Mark 12:18-27; Luke 20:27-40). Jesus uses the formula as a basis for showing that those who enjoyed favourable relationship with

---

4. C. WESTERMANN, *Genesis 12–36: A Commentary* (trans. J.J. SCULLION), Minneapolis, MN, Augsburg, 1985, p. 227.

God, must also have ongoing ontological existence (Matt 22:32). Thus, the Matthean Jesus transforms the notion of the finality of death depicted in the patriarchal narratives into an affirmation of the antithesis of that view. That he could do so, and that such a move is described as being well-received by the crowds, suggests that this was seen as conceptually possible by some of Jesus' contemporaries.

The concept of Sheol is notoriously difficult to pin-down, and has led one scholar to conclude at the end of his study on this place by saying "as somewhere about which we know next to nothing, it is a place with a huge question mark over it"[5]. The term is used in various sections of the Hebrew Bible. It is used four times in the Joseph story (Gen 37:35; 42:38; 44:29.31), to denote metaphorically the bereft state of Jacob when he is told of the alleged death of Joseph, or contemplates the possibility of the death of Benjamin. The physical location of Sheol, when it is mentioned, is consistently described as an underworld. Hence, in graphic judgment and contrary to the normal termination of life, Korah, Dathan, and Abiram are swallowed by the earth while still alive and taken down into the Sheol (Num 16:33). In this way their existence and connection with the living is snuffed out. No reflection is provided on their ontological state, although the implication appears to be that they have ceased to exist in any meaningful way.

References to Sheol are also prominent in Psalms, Proverbs and Job, and occur with repeated use in the prophetic writings of Isaiah and Ezekiel. In the Psalms the following perspectives are provided relating to Sheol. It is the place where there is no recollection of the one consigned to it (Ps 6:6), it is place of silence (Ps 30:18), physical forms are consumed and it takes away meaningful habitation (Ps 48:15), humans are unable to continue living and cannot evade the power of Sheol (Ps 89:48), and human bones are scattered at the mouth of Sheol (Ps 141:7). Therefore, while there is perhaps difficulty in finding language with a suitable degree of sophistication, the authors of the Psalms wish to express the idea that Sheol is the place of non-existence, burial is the gateway to Sheol, and in death eventually all are forgotten and silent. Sheol itself is not a punishment for the wicked, but the common lot of humanity. However, a premature death and the unexpected transfer of a being to Sheol can be understood as divine judgment. Accordingly, Jarick infers "that a post-mortem questioning of the merits or demerits of the departed is not part of the concept of Sheol"[6].

---

5. J. JARICK, *Questioning Sheol*, in S.E. PORTER – M.A. HAYES – D. TOMBS (eds.), *Resurrection* (JSNTSup,186), Sheffield, Sheffield Academic Press, 1999, 22-32, p. 32.
6. JARICK, *Questioning Sheol*, p. 26.

There does, nonetheless, appear to be in certain texts a conceptual conflict between the power of Sheol and the power of God. In a primitive
theology of omnipresence, Ps 139:8 affirms the Lord's presence even in
Sheol. Intercessors in the Psalms declare that the Lord will not abandon
them to Sheol (Ps 16:10). Metaphorically, one can speak the soul being
brought up from Sheol (Ps 30:3; cf. Ps 86:13). Likewise, Jonah praises the
Lord for bringing him back from a post-mortem state when he was in "the
belly of Sheol" (Jonah 2:2). So while Sheol is seen as the normative end of
life state which terminates continued existence, the Lord is seen as being
able to transcend such normative bounds and on occasions to bring back a
soul from the Sheol, or more regularly from circumstance which were considered as leading to Sheol without decisive divine intervention. Apart from
such rare occasions of deliverance from death or near-death circumstances,
the normal expectation is that Sheol is the fate of all people and that human
existence ceases in that domain: "for there is no activity or planning or
knowledge or wisdom in Sheol" (Eccl 9:10). Similar perspectives are found
in prophetic texts where the prospect of Sheol is used either as a taunt
against Babylon (Isa 14:9.11.15), or as part of a lamentation over Pharaoh
and the Egyptians (Ezek 32:21.27).

In contrast to the normative fate of humanity, albeit with exceptional
cases of deliverance from the prospect of non-existence in Sheol, in other
parts of the Hebrew Bible the power of God is depicted as preventing such
a fate. There are two cases of human beings being translated from the
earthly to the heavenly realm: Enoch because of his piety (Gen 5:24), and
Elijah apparently because of fidelity to his prophetic calling (2 Kings 2:1
15). Another mode of escape is through revivification of the recently dead.
This phenomenon occurs on three occasions in connection with the prophetic ministries of Elijah and Elisha (1 Kings 17:17-24; 2 Kings 4:31-37;
13:20-21). While the phenomenon of "translation" involves escape from the
fate of death, it is not a reversal or undoing of the power of death. In relation to the concept of translation Martin-Achard notes,

> The theme of the transfer of the human creature into the heavenly realm was
> well known in antiquity; the technical term used in this regard was the Heb
> verb laqah, which is found in Isa 53:8 where it can have this meaning only
> with difficulty, as well as in Pss 49:16 and 73:24 where one cannot rule out
> that it refers to the "transfer/ascension" of a faithful person[7].

Therefore, the phenomenon of individuals being translated into the heavenly
realm without sharing the common human experience of death is extremely

---

7. MARTIN-ACHARD, *Resurrection (OT)*, p. 681.

rare in the Hebrew Bible. By contrast, while also rare, prophetic healings, which raise the dead, do indeed reverse the power of death. However, these revivification healings are not permanent prophylactics against human mortality, and the texts do not relate any sense of a definitive defeat of death. Both these phenomena have resonances with material in Matthew's gospel. While no individual is translated to the heavenly realm prior to death, the comments about Elijah in relation to John the Baptist (Matt 11:14) and the transfiguration appearance of Elijah (Matt 17:2-13) are dependent upon the acceptance of the reality of the translation account in 2 Kings 2:1-11. However, the expectation of the re-appearance of Elijah may be more dependent on the prophecy in Mal 4:5, than upon the actual account of the translation of the prophet into the heavenly realm. By associating Jesus at his transfiguration with Elijah, Matthew may be making an implicit claim that Jesus likewise belongs to the heavenly realm. This is the implication that Davies and Allison derive from the conversation between the three figures. They suggest "συλ-λαλοῦντες would seem to indicate that Jesus belongs to the same world as Moses and Elijah"[8]. Revivification of the dead occurs in Matthew's gospel in the story of the raising of the synagogue official's daughter (Matt 9:18-26) and during the raising of the holy ones who had died (Matt 27:52-53).

Only two passages in the Hebrew Bible appear to speak of resurrection in a clear manner, although their interpretation is not unambiguous. In the first passage, Isa 26:19, there appears to be the articulation of the hope that the Lord will raise those who have died as martyrs for the sake of his name. However other scholars have suggested that the text is presenting a vision of national restoration through the metaphor of resurrection.[9] Although N.T. Wright mentions this possibility, he asserts that the verse is dealing with the resurrection of faithful individuals. He states, "[t]he original Hebrew refers literally to bodily resurrection, and this is certainly how the verse is taken in the LXX and at Qumran"[10]. However, little is said about the timing or the process of such a resurrection. Given the wider context of this passage in the so-called "Great Apocalypse" of Isa 24–27, where the declaration of an eschatological banquet for all peoples (Isa 25:6) is coupled with a promise that God "will swallow up death for all time" (Isa 25:8), it may be inferred that this post-exilic prophetic vision contemplates the bod-

8. W.D. DAVIES – D.C. ALLISON, JR. *A Critical and Exegetical Commentary on the Gospel according to Saint Matthew*, Vol. 2 (ICC), Edinburgh, T&T Clark, 1991, p. 697.

9. See for instance J. DAY, *The Development of Belief in Life After Death in Ancient Israel*, in J. BARTON – D.J. REIMER (eds.), *Essays in Honour of Rex Mason*, Macon, GA, Mercer University Press, 1996, pp. 231-257.

10. N.T. WRIGHT, *The Resurrection of the Son of God*, Minneapolis, MN, 2003, p. 117.

ily resurrection of faithful martyrs in the eschatological consummation of the ages. Although not tied explicitly to resurrection, Matthew envisages an eschatological banquet for people from the east and the west who join with the patriarchs, but the sons of the kingdom are cast into the outer darkness (Matt 8:11-12). Here are two developments the first of which may have embryonic roots in Isa 24–27. The first is that of a post-mortem hope for all people expressed in terms of an eschatological banquet. The second aspect, which will be considered in more detail, is the transformation of understanding that the place of the dead, Sheol in the Hebrew Bible, is no longer a neutral venue where existence ceases, but has become a place of punishment where a tormented existence continues.

The second text from the Hebrew Bible that envisages resurrection for the faithful is Dan 12:1-3, probably written sometime around the mid 160s B.C.E[11]. The temporal gap between this text and the other texts that have been discussed means that its perspectives have had time to undergo significant evolution. In many ways the treatment of this text would make better sense among the corpus of Jewish intertestamental literature. However, its canonical location in the Hebrew Bible results in it being treated as part of that canonical collection. The promise made is that the dead will awaken, some "to everlasting life", but others "to disgrace and everlasting contempt" (Dan 12:2). The positive aspect of this future existence is expanded upon in Dan 12:3 where either the entire group raised to everlasting life or a subset, depending on who is deemed to have insight and lead many to righteousness, are described as shining brightly as stars of the heaven. It is perhaps beyond the purview of this text to over-differentiate between those who lead others to righteous and those who follow in the path of righteousness. Rather this poetic text promises deliverance for the righteous who suffer martyrdom at the hands of violent oppressors (Dan 11:31-35). The sober caveat issued by Goldingay must be borne in mind

> The meaning of v 2 has been much disputed, partly because its context has not been kept in mind. Its exegesis must be approached via what precedes it, not via the formulated doctrine of resurrection later developed by groups such as the Pharisees and adopted by Christians. Indeed, we must avoid teaching it as a piece of theological "teaching": it is a vision or a flight of imagination, not a "fully developed" belief in resurrection[12].

---

11. In relation to the material in Dan 12:1-3, Collins sees this as part of the fifth compositional stage of the book of Daniel. "Between 167 and 164 B.C.E. the Hebrew chapters 8-12 were added, and chap. 1 was translated to provide a Hebrew frame for the Aramaic chapters." J.J. COLLINS, *Daniel* (Hermeneia), Minneapolis, MN, Fortress, 1993, p. 38.

12. J. GOLDINGAY, *Daniel* (WBC 30), Dallas, Word, 1989, p. 306.

This passage promises that those who "sleep in the land of dust will awake." It is has been observed that the phrase "land of dust" is likely a reference to Sheol, given that the term "dust" is used in parallel to Sheol in Job 17:16[13]. Connections have also been noted between Dan 12:2 and the wording of Isa 26:19. Based upon this closely related language, Nickelsburg states that the "juridical function of resurrection in Isa 26:19 and its place within the context of national restoration support the probability that Daniel is drawing on Isaiah, for Dan 12:1 deals precisely with the judgment and reconstitution of the nation"[14]. It appears that the reality of the persecution and death of many pious Jews who would not conform to the religious demands of Antiochus IV, led to the belief that as they had honoured God by being martyred for their piety, so too God would honour them by returning them to life. In part this was in line with the traditional belief that God's blessing on the righteous was a long and prosperous life. Since, however, their deaths inverted standard Jewish theological expectations of earthly blessings, the articulation of belief in resurrection was an attempt to preserve a belief in a just God, by finding a new means to affirm that he provided abundant life to the faithful. That means was the hope of a return to life in an eschatological future[15]. It is perhaps no coincidence that in a period of Jewish history when apocalyptic expectations were being formed, that the concept of resurrection also began to develop in some sectors of the movement. Matthew's articulation of belief in future resurrection is also closely linked to the apocalyptic eschatology that permeates the gospel[16].

The conventional understanding that Israelite and early Jewish religion, as reflected in the Hebrew Bible, contained little if any belief in post-mortem existence can be seen to be the perspective of the majority of texts that touch upon this issue. In particular, patriarchal narratives and Psalm texts present Sheol as the common fate of all mortal humans, and it is the place where sentient existence ceases. The person who is pious is rewarded with a long and prosperous life, often coupled with the promise of blessings on descendents. The only unambiguous indication of individual resurrection and ongoing existence in the Hebrew Bible is found in Dan 12:2-3, which in that case appears to have been formulated in response to the martyrdom

---

13. G.W.E. NICKELSBURG, *Resurrection, Immortality and Eternal Life in Intertestamental Judaism* (HTS, 26), Cambridge, MA, Harvard University Press, 1972, p. 17; COLLINS, *Daniel*, p. 392.

14. NICKELSBURG, *Resurrection, Immortality and Eternal Life*, p. 18.

15. NICKELSBURG, *Resurrection, Immortality and Eternal Life*, p. 19.

16. See D.C. SIM, *Apocalyptic Eschatology in the Gospel of Matthew* (SNTSMS, 88), Cambridge, Cambridge University Press, 1996, pp. 110-147.

of pious believers, who remained faithful to their understanding of Jewish religion rather than comply with the demands of Antiochus IV. The promise given in Isa 26:19 may also move in this direction, although the meaning of the text is far from clear[17]. However, Blenkinsopp suggests that there may need to be some slight qualification to the view that Israelite religion contained no concept of post-mortem existence. He states that something similar to the outlook of Dan 12:2 can be found at an earlier period. "We detect something of this in the experience of worship here and there in the Psalms (e.g. Ps 73:17. 21-28), in the conviction that Yahveh is God of the living whose gift is life, and the demand for justice as an absolute precondition for faith"[18]. Hence, apart from the single reference in Dan 12:2-3 and a few fleeting and embryonic references to the vague possibility of life beyond the grave, there indeed appears to be an absence of belief in post-mortem existence in the Hebrew Bible. This means that resurrection ideas in Matthew's gospel are likely derived from other sources and reflect a later period in Jewish thought.

III. Afterlife, Resurrection and the Post-mortem State in the Septuagint

Translational choices can often subtly (or at time not too subtly) shift the meaning of an original text. Such changes can be unintended mistakes, or due to the limitations of the semantic fields of various lexemes, or be conscious choices made to conform a text to a different conceptual outlook. While intentionality is hard to determine in the absence of explicit statements concerning the goals of the translator, one may look for recurrent and coherent changes in the ideational world of the base text and how they may be replaced with an alternative perspective[19]. There is, however, a further complexity with the LXX resulting from multiple translators who undertook their work during a lengthy time span. One additional factor which may assist in clarifying the outlook of the compilers of the LXX towards the concept of afterlife is the larger corpus of texts contained in this collection of texts. These have the potential to reveal further developments in Jewish

---

17. As Blenkinsopp notes "[t]hat the first part of this verse has suffered in transmission is fairly obvious". J. BLENKINSOPP, *Isaiah 1-39* (AB, 19), New York, Doubleday, 2000, p. 370.
18. BLENKINSOPP, *Isaiah 1-39*, p. 371.
19. On this highly important yet complex topic, see the helpful discussion of K.H. JOBES – M. SILVA, *Invitation to the Septuagint*, Grand Rapids, MI, Baker Academic, 2000, pp. 86-93.

thinking concerning the post-mortem state at a generally later stage of the
movement than the writings in the Hebrew Bible.

In terms of translational decisions relating to texts dealing with the afterlife in the Hebrew Bible, there are only a few clues relating to shifts in
theological perspectives. In relation to Ps 1:5, Jobes and Silva advance the
following observation:

> Another theological concept that apparently developed within Judaism in the
> Hellenistic period is an eschatology that involved personal resurrection at the
> final judgment. The Greek translation of the Psalms, produced within this
> period, may reflect such a tendency. To cite one possible example, Hebrew Ps
> 1:5 reads, "Therefore the wicked will not *stand* in the judgment," whereas the
> Greek has, "Therefore the wicked will not *arise* in the judgment". The seman-
> tic range of the Hebrew word *qum* includes both arising and standing. The
> Greek verb chosen by the translator, *anistemi*, means specifically "to rise up,"
> and the New Testament writers use it with reference to resurrection[20].

It is questionable how much one can hang on such a subtle alteration,
especially given that the Greek verbal form chosen has a semantic overlap
with the range of meaning encompassed by the Hebrew verb. The emphasis
on bodily resurrection appears to be brought out more clearly in Isa 26:19
(LXX). The text states that ἀναστήσονται οἱ νεκροί καὶ ἐγερθήσονται οἱ ἐν
τοῖς μνημείοις ("the dead shall rise and those that are in tombs shall be
raised"). Speaking of the LXX version, Wright states, "26:19 insists that the
dead will be raised"[21]. A more transparent change is found in the addition
of an expanded comment at the conclusion of Job. The Hebrew text states
"So Job died being old and full of days" (Job 42:17). Such sentiments align
with the traditional expectations of God's blessings upon the righteous, but
there is no sense of post-mortem continuance of being. The LXX adds a
lengthy codicil, the first part of which is significant for this discussion. It
continues Job 42:17 by stating "and he will rise again with those whom the
Lord raises up." Here the text of the LXX articulates an obvious commitment to resurrection and future existence. Although not as clear, passages
such as Deut 18:15; 32:39; and Ps 21:30 (22:29 LXX) have also been seen
as influenced by the same theological trajectory in the Greek translation[22].

More transparent is the development in Jewish thinking pertaining to the
resurrection found in the additional Septuagintal texts. The hopes of the

20. JOBES – SILVA, *Invitation to the Septuagint*, p. 96.
21. WRIGHT, *The Resurrection of the Son of God*, p. 148.
22. See H.C.C. CAVALLIN, *Life After Death: Paul's Argument for the Resurrection of the Dead in 1 Cor 15, Part I. An Enquiry into the Jewish Background*, Lund, CWK Gleerup, 1974, p. 103.

Maccabean martyrs narrated in 2 Macc 7 are replete with confidence in a
future resurrection. Speaking his last words against Antiochus, the second
son cried out "You, you fiend, are making us depart from our present life,
but the King of the universe will resurrect us, who die for the sake of his
laws, to a new eternal life" (2 Macc 7:9). The mother of the seven executed
sons exhorts them with the promise that the Creator will "give back to you
again both your spirit and your life" (2 Macc 7:23). Similarly the youngest
son when rebuking Antiochus for his evil and impiety declares that his
brothers have endured a short pain which "brings everlasting life" since they
"died under God's covenant" (2 Macc 7:36). Goldstein suggests that the
formulation of Jewish belief in resurrection emerged from a theological
dilemma. The standard Jewish outlook was to see torment or punishment
as a result of national or personal disobedience of God and Torah. The
means of ending the punishment was through repentance and renewed
fidelity to the covenant. The theological challenge of the Maccabean crisis
was that piety and repentance led to punishment, whereas infidelity resulted
in avoidance of punishment. This led to the need of reconceptualising ideas
of punishment and reward. As Goldstein presents the problem,

> The standard procedure for hastening the end of a divine punishment was
> confession of sin, repentance, and renewed obedience to the Torah, but Anti-
> ochus' decrees punished with torture and death all acts of repentance and
> obedience to the Torah. If the pious were suffering the climactic phase of
> God's sentence for ancient sin, it would seem that there only course was to
> suffer and die until God's appointed time.[23].

One striking feature of the narrative is the presentation of a double fate in
the afterlife. Thus the fourth son declares to Antiochus that God "promises
that we will be resurrected by him, for you shall have no resurrection unto
life" (2 Macc 7:14). This is similar to Dan 12:2 in speaking of a differentiated
fate, but there is a difference between these texts. In 2 Macc 7:14 the fate of
the impious is not to participate in the resurrected state, whereas in Dan 12:2
such people are "awakened" but to disgrace and contempt. Therefore, the
theology of Maccabees does not entail a punitive resurrected state for the evil,
only an ongoing existence for the faithful. In this regard Matthew appears to
stand closer to the Danielic conception of a dual resurrection either to existence in heavenly realm, or to the unending place of "weeping and gnashing
of teeth" (cf. Matt 8:12). However, Goldstein sees 2 Macc 7:14 as implying
resurrection for Antiochus, but not to the blissful state of "life". He argues,
"the writer is redundant here because he draws on Dan LXX 12:2: Antiochus

---

23. J.A. GOLDSTEIN, *II Maccabees* (AB, 41A), New York, Doubleday, 1983, p. 294.

will have no resurrection unto life because he will awaken from death for eternal contumely and for annihilation"[24]. However, the text may simply speak of no resurrection for Antiochus, instead envisaging his fate as the non-existence of Sheol. The narrative pronounces punishment on Antiochus for his persecution of the brothers. However as the narrative unfolds it appears that it is an earthly judgment in the form of a premature and horrendous death that is envisaged (2 Macc 9) and not some eschatological fate[25]. This narrative should not be construed as presenting a theology of universal resurrection and judgment, rather is seeks to present a response to "a specific unjust situation"[26]. In this sense although ideas of individual resurrection are clearly present, the text makes no claims concerning the universal applicability of resurrection even as a reward for the righteous.

The Wisdom of Solomon appears to envisage an ongoing state of being for the righteous. The expression of afterlife hopes does not present the same level of physicality as 2 Macc 7, which itself may be driven by a desire to portray the physical mutilations inflicted by Antiochus as being undone by God. In contrast to the ideas in 2 Maccabees that respond to the reality of martyrdom, the Wisdom of Solomon is a more considered and philosophically oriented work. In its first section (Wis 1:1–6:21) it presents the notion that the gift of Wisdom is immortality. The text opens by presenting the immoral acts of the wicked as resulting in self-destruction and death. Therefore the author admonishes readers with the following command, "do not court death through a deviant way of life, nor draw down destruction by your own actions" (Wis 1:12). By contrast the intended state of humanity is immortality: "God created man for immortality and made him an image of his own proper being" (Wis 2:23). This intended state is seen as being disrupted the entry of death which was a result of the "devil's envy" (Wis 2:24). A repeated refrain in the text is that "the souls of the just are in God's hand" (Wis 2:1; 3:1). Also as part of Wis 2:1, the text states that "no one has been known to have returned from the grave"[27]. This may represent an outlook that views continued existence not in terms of physical resurrection, but rather as achieved through immortality being given to the souls of the wise. Present trials are seen as a purificatory process. This leads to the comment that,

24. GOLDSTEIN, *II Maccabees*, p. 306

25. As Nickelsburg suggests "Antiochus' judgment will be his terrible death, described in chapter 9." NICKELSBURG, *Resurrection, Immortality and Eternal Life*, p. 95.

26. NICKELSBURG, *Resurrection, Immortality and Eternal Life*, p. 95.

27. It is not entirely clear in Wis 1:16–2:24 when the voice is meant to be that of the author advocating wisdom, and when the words belong to his constructed wicked interlocutor. See D. WINSTON, *The Wisdom of Solomon* (AB, 43), New York, Doubleday, 1978, pp. 9-14; NICKELSBURG, *Resurrection, Immortality and Eternal Life*, p. 67.

> the souls of the just are in God's hand ... for even if in the sight of men they have been punished, their hope is full of immortality; and after a brief chastisement, they will be treated with great kindness, for God has tried them and found them worthy to be his. (Wis 3:1.4-5)

The precise process that leads from the death of the just person to the immortality of the soul is not mapped out. It is more important for the author to assert the certainty of the continued existence of being for the righteous. As Winston describes the perspective of the text, the author "assures his readers that the physical death of the just is in reality only the beginning of a better existence, inasmuch as their souls would enjoy a blissful immortality after a brief period of chastisement"[28].

The major debate that surrounds the perspective of the text on the post-mortem state is whether it has a conception of bodily resurrection. Too often this is construed in terms that are foreign to the text, specifically contrasting a Platonic notion of the pre-existence and eternal continuance of the soul with a supposedly more Jewish notion of physical resurrection. However, in the text the immortal existence of the soul is not an innate property, but a potentiality that can only be given as a divine gift. There is no notion of the soul's pre-existence. The fate of the wicked is cessation of existence. As Puech states, "L'impie pour qui la vie s'arrête au Shéôl, 2,1-3, fera l'expérience de la mort, 2,24b"[29]. So without imposing Platonic notions of the ontological condition of the soul, the exegetical choices appear to be between understanding the outlook of Wisdom as either belief in the immortal but disembodied existence of the souls of the just, or as seeing the language of immortality as also encompassing the conception of the resurrection of the body. Puech, somewhat tentatively suggests that the judgment scene implies a corporeal presence[30]. Wright makes much of this, arguing for a two-stage description of post-mortem events in Wis 3:1-10. Thus 3:1-4 is "a *story* in which the present existence "in the hand of God" is merely the prelude to what is about to happen", whereas "verses 7-10 are describing a *further* event which *follows upon* the state described in verses 1-4"[31]. Despite Wright's wit in berating those who do not accept this two-stage process as unwittingly having "agreed with the wicked in making an alliance with death", he does not account for vv. 5-6 in his schema. This material links the two sections with the souls of the just under-

---

28. WINSTON, *The Wisdom of Solomon*, p. 125.
    29. É. PUECH, *La croyance des Esséniens en la vie future: Immortalité, résurrection, vie éternelle?* Vol. 1: *La résurrection des morts et le contexte scripturaire*, Paris, J. Gabalda, 1993, p. 93.
    30. PUECH, *La croyance des Esséniens en la vie future*, Vol. 1, p. 96.
    31. WRIGHT, *The Resurrection of the Son of God*, p. 167.

going a future time of testing and purification as part of the process that
enables them to exist eternally with God. Nothing in 3:1-10 suggests any
process by which disembodied souls are transformed into an embodied state.
Nor do any of the activities of the souls of the just in the afterlife seem to
require a corporeal existence. It is perhaps safest to observe that this text is
vague concerning the state of immortal existence for the just. It does see
immortal existence as a gift for the wise, and a state from which the wicked
are debarred. To read Wisdom of Solomon as supporting notions of bodily
resurrection is simply to go beyond the limited perspective of the text.

In a section amusingly subtitled "the more Greek the better", Wright
observes "as the Bible was translated into Greek … the notion of resurrection became, it seems, much clearer, so that many passages which might
have been at most ambiguous became clear"[32]. However, translational revision of concepts was perhaps not the most apparent means by which compilers of the LXX introduced the notion of afterlife existence into the Jewish
scriptures. The more obvious way was through including supplementary
texts in the collection, which unambiguous spoke of either the possibility of
bodily resurrection for pious martyrs (2 Macc 7), or of the immortality of
the souls of the just (Wis 1:1–6:21). There is little development in the
regard to the fate of the wicked. In line with Hebrew Bible expectations,
their fate is the cessation of existence. The most significant exception to this
perspective amongst either Hebrew or Greek biblical texts is found in Dan
12:2 where all awake, but in opposition to the fate of the righteous, the evil
ones go away in "disgrace and everlasting contempt."

IV. Perspectives on Afterlife in Qumran Texts

The large corpus of text discovered at Qumran necessitates not only selec-
tivity (although hopefully a broadly representative selection), but also a recognition of the diverse range of perspectives they contain. The manuscripts
discovered at Qumran have been divided broadly into three groups: biblical
manuscripts, as well as sectarian and non-sectarian texts[33]. Since biblical

32. WRIGHT, *The Resurrection of the Son of God*, p. 167.
33. The groupings for Qumran texts are not standardized. VanderKam likewise has three
groups, but he labels these (i) biblical; (ii) apocryphal and pseudepigraphical; and (iii) other
texts. His last group corresponds to what are labeled here as sectarian texts, however whereas
apocryphal texts are here seen as part of biblical texts (since they are included in certain biblical canons) VanderKam places them with pseudepigraphical texts. Here pseudepigraphical
texts, with out apocryphal writings broadly correspond to what is denoted by non-sectarian

perspectives have been surveyed in the previous two sections, here the focus is upon sectarian and non-sectarian texts. Although the classification is not always entirely obvious, generally speaking texts that were produced by the Qumran community to promote their own theology fall into the sectarian category, whereas non-biblical texts that were produced beyond the confines of the community with a wider circulation, yet were read by the sectarians as supportive or compatible with their own ideology fall into the second category. For the purpose of this discussion, taxonomic exactitude although interesting is not entirely important – unless it were to emerge that Matthew's attitude to the afterlife emerged from a particular strand of Second Temple Judaism.

Notwithstanding disquiet concerning a facile identification of the sectarian community with at least some section of the Essene movement, if some connection is allowed then there are at least three bodies of evidence that may assist in trying to determine the group's beliefs concerning the afterlife. These are the texts discovered at the Qumran site, archaeological insights from the cemeteries, and descriptions of the group's beliefs by outsiders. Taking these in reverse order, Josephus provides the following account of Essene beliefs concerning understanding of the immortality of the soul.

> It is a fixed belief of theirs that the body is corruptible and its constituent matter impermanent, but that the soul is immortal and imperishable. Emanating from the finest ether, these souls become entangled, as it were, in the prison-house of the body to which they are dragged down by a sort of natural spell; but once they are released from the bonds of the flesh, then, as though liberated from long servitude, they rejoice and are borne aloft. Sharing the belief of the sons of Greece, they maintain that for virtuous souls there is reserved an abode beyond the ocean. (*B.J.* 2.154-155)

However, here as elsewhere one must question both Josephus' motivation and accuracy in providing this description. Josephus both writes for a largely Hellenistic non-Jewish audience and with the aim of making Jewish beliefs appear more palatable and proximate to Graeco-Roman outlooks. Yet, this description clashes with other reports from non-Essene sources and with perspectives contained in Qumranic texts. By contrast with Josephus, the third century Christian heresiologist, Hippolytus, states of Esssene afterlife beliefs that,

> Now the doctrine of the resurrection has also derived support among these; for they acknowledge both that the flesh will rise again, and that it will be

texts. See J.C. VANDERKAM, *The Dead Sea Scrolls Today*, Grand Rapids, MI, Eerdmans, 2010, pp. 47-96.

immortal, in the same manner as the soul is already imperishable. And they maintain that the soul, when separated in the present life, departs into one place, which is well ventilated and lightsome, where, they say, it rests until judgment. And this locality the Greeks were acquainted with by hearsay, and called it "Isles of the Blessed". (*Ref. Haer.* 9.22)

While both authors see links with what they describe as Greek beliefs, they differ in that Hippolytus attributes to the Essenes a belief in bodily resurrection, whereas Josephus denies that they believed in the continuance of the physical form.

While the estimated number of graves at Qumran is between 1100 and 1200 individual sites of interment, the evidence is limited and does not provide clear insights into specific beliefs in the afterlife. Less than five percent of the graves have been excavated[34]. Apart from those in the southern cemetery, "the graves contained virtually no burial goods or gifts"[35]. In terms of their physical features the graves were uniformly laid out in a north-south orientation. The interment involved the corpses being "apparently wrapped in linen shrouds and some were perhaps placed in wooden coffins … At the bottom of each grave, a niche or "loculus" was dug along the length of the shaft. The body was placed in the loculus, which was sealed by stone slabs or mud bricks. The shaft was then filled with earth"[36]. There is nothing distinctive that distinguishes Qumran burial practice from the wider contemporary Jewish disposal of corpses, nor does the archaeological evidence allow for any secure inferences concerning afterlife beliefs. One must therefore turn to textual evidence to gain insights into ideas about post-mortem existence.

One of the most significant non-sectarian texts which was read at Qumran and in wider Judaism was 1 Enoch[37]. The text has a complex compositional history, with the earliest sections being written prior to the Maccabean period and perhaps as early as the third century, and the final stages being added before the middle of the first century B.C.E[38]. The Similitudes (*1 En.* 37-71), which are generally seen as the latest compositional stage of

---

34. During his archaeological investigation of the site De Vaux excavated only twenty-eight graves. See R. DE VAUX, *Rapport préliminaire sur la deuxième champagne*, in *RB* 61 (1954) 206-236.

35. J. MAGNESS, *The Archaeology of Qumran and the Dead Sea Scrolls*, Grand Rapids, MI, Eerdmans, 2002, p. 168.

36. MAGNESS, *The Archaeology of Qumran and the Dead Sea Scrolls*, p. 168.

37. VanderKam notes that "[a]mong the many fragments found in Cave 4, a relatively large number of manuscripts of Enoch have appeared." VANDERKAM, *The Dead Sea Scrolls Today*, p. 56. In particular see 4Q201-4Q212.

38. G.W.E. NICKELSBURG, *1 Enoch* (Hermeneia), Minneapolis, MN, Fortress, 2001, pp. 25-26.

the work, while not employing resurrection terminology directly, speaks of the "earth", "Sheol" and "hell" giving back what they had previously claimed. Within the wider context this appears to be a reference to a general revivification of the dead, and from amongst them the Messiah or Elect One will select the righteous for salvation.

> And in those days shall the earth also give back that which has been entrusted to it. And Sheol also shall give back that which it has received. And hell shall give back that which it owes. For in those days the Elect One shall arise. And he shall choose the righteous and holy from among them. For the day has drawn nigh that they should be saved. (1 Enoch 51:1-2)

A similar perspective appears to be present in *1 Enoch* 61:5, which describes the return of those who have been destroyed or devoured by desert, beasts or sea-creatures returning on the day of the Elect One. Moreover, this marks a changed mode of existence, for after this return they cannot be destroyed. Yet as Peuch states the details contained in this section are not entirely clear, "l'identité des ressuscités n'est pas claire: s'agit-il de tous les morts, ou des seuls Israélites?" Apart from the uncertainty in identifying the revivified people, it is also unclear whether it is their souls or bodies that are returned from the place of death. This lack of detail aligns the description with other texts from the second or first centuries B.C.E. (such as Dan 12:2), which begin to envisage a post-mortem existence for the righteous that commences in some eschatological period.

Among the texts uniquely known from Qumran, a number seem to express some type of resurrection belief. The Messianic Apocalypse (4Q521) describes a number of aspects of the work of the messiah, including the promise that "he will heal the badly wounded and will make the dead live"[39]. The fragmentary state of the manuscript precludes definitive conclusions. Notwithstanding this, the text seems to suggest that resurrection is an act of God's mercy, which is bestowed upon the righteous through the agency of the messiah[40]. There is no sense, in the extant portion of the text, of the wicked being raised up to face a negative judgment. This, however, may be due to the focus of the text on presenting the works of the messiah on behalf of the righteous.

In its original context the vision of Ezekiel's prophecy over the dry bones (Ezek 37:1-14) appears to be a metaphor for national restoration. The

---

39. For wider question of dating and reconstruction of 4Q521 see É. PUECH, *La Croyance des Esséniens en la Vie Future: Immortalité, Résurrection, Vie Éternelle?* Vol. 2: *Les Données Qumraniennes et Classique*, Paris, J. Gabalda, 1993, pp. 627-692.

40. PUECH, *La croyance des Esséniens en la vie future*, Vol. 2, pp. 686-687.

expanded retelling of this incident, 4QPseudo-Ezekiel[a,b] (4Q385-386),
appears to have transformed this vision in the direction of expressing hope
for individual bodily resurrection. First, instead of the Lord asking Ezekiel
whether the bones can live, it is the prophet who asks the Lord when those
who have loved his name will be rewarded for their loyalty. Consequently
the prophetic vision is seen as responding to a question of theodicy, namely
how God can bring about a just recompense for those who have suffered
for their faithful witness. The vision of Ezek 37 shows the faithful dead
being revivified with reformed bodies, and rising to bless the Lord of Hosts,
"a large crowd of men will rise and bless the Lord who caused them to live"
(4Q385 2.8). Again a text dating from the Hasmonean or perhaps Herodian
period articulates an emerging belief in bodily resurrection. According to
Puech, the brief response placed in God's mouth relates eschatological
events, which encapsulates belief in the resurrection of the just[41].

The Hodayot, or Hymn scroll (1QH), presents a pair of texts that may
portray a belief in the resurrection, although the doxological language may
function at a metaphorical level[42]. On two occasions (1QH xi:19-23; xix:10-
14), the author thanks the Lord for rescue from the place of the dead: "saving my life from the pit, and from Sheol and Abaddon you have lighted me
up" (1QH xi:19; cf. 1QH xi:12). The consequence of having been raised up
is that the hymnist can "take his place with the host of holy ones and can
enter in communion with the congregation of the sons of heaven" (1QH
xi:21-22). For Puech, these words affirm the salvation of the just, and even
if "resurrection" is not directly evoked it is certainly presupposed[43]. Such a
reading of the texts is not without problem, for the author appears to speak
of resurrection and its consequences as a present reality, rather than a future
hope as Puech describes the eschatological dimension of these hymns. As
Nickelsburg describes it, "[t]he point of dispute is whether the use of resurrection language anticipates future glory ... or expresses the belief that
entrance into the community brings one from death to eternal life"[44]. Nickelsburg favours the second alternative on the basis of the genre of the hymns.
In this case the resurrection language is metaphorical, and while it may not

41. PUECH, *La croyance des Esséniens en la vie future*, Vol. 2, pp. 614-615.
42. Acknowledging the presence of metaphorical language Puech states "although depicted
in language full of imagery, the belief in the resurrection of the just is not totally absent from
these texts (1QHodayota xiv, xiii, xix)". See É. PUECH, *Hodayot*, in L.H. SCHIFFMANN – J.C.
VANDERKAM (eds.), *Encyclopedia of the Dead Sea Scrolls*, Vol. 1, Oxford, Oxford University
Press, 2000, p. 368.
43. PUECH, *La croyance des Esséniens en la vie future*, Vol. 2, p. 375.
44. G.W.E. NICKELSBURG, *Resurrection*, in L.H. SCHIFFMANN – J.C. VANDERKAM (eds.),
Encyclopedia of the Dead Sea Scrolls, Vol. 2, Oxford, Oxford University Press, 2000, p. 766.

reveal the specific beliefs of the Qumran community in relation to resurrection, presumably the metaphor works because of wider understanding in contemporary Judaism of "resurrection" in a sense that was not metaphorical for community entrance.

The concept of resurrection is not a major theme in the non-Biblical writings found at Qumran. On the occasions when the concept can be clearly detected it appears either to denote a future eschatological action rewarding the righteous for their faithfulness to the Lord, or to be used metaphorically as part of a realised eschatology that views salvation as being inaugurated through participation in the community. The concept of resurrection shows some development, especially in terms of its metaphorical application. However, the mechanics of resurrection, descriptions of the physical states and consideration of the action in the afterlife apart from praise of the Lord remain undeveloped concepts.

V. PHILO AND THE IMMORTALITY OF THE SOUL

Continuity of being is an idea that can be identified in a number of Philo's writings; however, his discussion of this theme revolves around the concept of the potentiality the soul has for immortality. Although there is not a complete correspondence between the Platonic philosophical system and Philo's perspective on the afterlife, the influence of the former on the latter is self-apparent. However, Puech helpfully summarises what he sees as the key differences in Philo's synthesis of Platonic and Jewish ideas concerning the immortality of the soul.

> Contrairement au système platonicien pour qui seul le monde des idées est source d'immortalité et de bonheur, la pensée philonienne, bien que marquée par cette influence, met constamment l'accent sur la relation personnelle de l'homme avec Dieu. A la limite de la nature mortelle et immortelle, l'homme se doit pratiquer la justice et d'aimer la sagesse pour atteindre cette immortalité bienheureuse[45].

Philo's perspective on the immortality of the soul can be seen in *De Sacrificiis*, where he states that immortality is a divinely imparted gift. Hence Abraham is seen as being added to the company of the people of God, as was Abel, when he left his mortal body through "having received immortality, and having become equal to angels; for the angels are the host of God, being incorporeal and happy souls" (*Sacr.* 2.5). Extracting a general principle

---

45. PUECH, *La croyance des Esséniens en la vie future*, Vol. 1, p. 163.

from this exegetical treatment of the patriarchal stories, Philo argues that "those men who have forsaken human instruction, and having become well-disposed disciples of God, and having arrived at a comprehension of knowledge acquired without labour, have passed over to the immortal and most perfect race of beings" (*Sacr.* 2.7). In this sense, Philo appears to envisage a partially realised immortality for the soul, for those who have attained divine perception in the present life. The corollary of this for those who lack such spiritual insight is that the present life may be viewed as the opposite of life – a type of realised death. Employing Cain as a proto-typical example, Philo states, "for those who die in the company of the pious will receive everlasting life, but everlasting death will be the portion of those who live in the other way" (*Post.*11.39). Therefore, Philo reconceptualises the states of life and death in order to make connections between the state one will enjoy in the afterlife and the understanding that should be given of different individual's state of being in the present life.

Placing Philo within the wider context of late Second Temple Judaism with its emerging conception of life after death, Termini describes his distinctive characteristics.

> In tune with other Judeo-Hellenistic texts from Alexandria, Philo makes no reference to resurrection of the body, and he also de-emphasizes the ideas of hell and a last judgment. In fact, he spiritualizes the very notions of life and death, and minimizes the importance of physical death. A truly authentic life consists in practicing of virtue and in being in communion with God. For this reason the wise man lives already in this life in a kind of immortality, which will take on a perfect form after his death (*Opif.* 154; *QE* 2.39)[46].

Philo's perspective on the afterlife is part of wider Jewish reflection on that topic which had developed over at least the previous two centuries. His conception of post-mortem existence is not conceived in terms of bodily resurrection, but rather envisages the immortal state of the soul, which in some proleptic sense may be realised in the present life. Therefore, Philo stands closer to the outlook contained in the Wisdom of Solomon than that in 2 Maccabees. This is due not only to the Platonic influences which shape his thought, but may reflect the fact that his thinking on the subject has not grown out of the context of martyrdom, where the perception of appropriate divine justice for righteous martyrs is the restoration of their mutilated physical bodies.

---

46. C. TERMINI, *Philo's Thought within the Context of Middle Judaism*, in A. KAMESAR (ed.), *The Cambridge Companion to Philo*, Cambridge, Cambridge University Press, 2009, p. 108.

VI. Josephus and the Portrayal of Sadducean Beliefs

Due to the paucity of Sadducean sources and the apparent extinction of this group with the destruction of the Temple in 70 C.E., information about its views on the afterlife are both secondary and limited. Yet, while detail is missing, those sources that mention Sadducean views on the after-life agree that the position espoused was that of the non-continuance of being after death. Hence the outlook stands in tension with the developments in Jewish theology that either incorporated Platonic notions of the immortality of the soul (but did not uniformly argue for its pre-existence also), as well as those texts that support some adherence to belief in a corporeal resurrection.

In his autobiography, Josephus claims acquaintance with Sadducean beliefs as part of the process of judging which sect of Judaism with which to align himself (*Vita* 1.10). If this claim is reliable, then his statements elsewhere may reveal a degree of personal knowledge of the beliefs of the Sadducees. Specifically in relation to the post-mortem state, Josephus presents the group's ideas very briefly as "the doctrine of the Sadducees is this: that souls die with the bodies" (*Ant.* 18.16). This pithy statement attributes to the Sadducees a denial of any form of belief in ongoing existence either in the form of the immortality of the soul or the resurrection of the body. Elsewhere Josephus gives a slightly expanded description of their outlook. He states, "they also take away the belief of the immortal duration of the soul, and the punishments and rewards in Hades" (*B.J.* 2.165). Although Josephus has allegiance with the Pharisees, this does not appear to have skewed his portrayal of the Sadducean belief concerning the fate of the dead, since what he states is corroborated by other sources (cf. Acts 23:8). What emerges from Josephus' portrayal of Sadducean beliefs is that while the perspective of the Hebrew Bible concerning the existent state of the deceased in Sheol had undergone considerable revision in certain sectors of Jewish thinking in the late Second Temple period, the Sadducees appear to have maintained the traditional perspective contained in biblical texts[47]. Sadducean beliefs provide the strongest link with the actual text of Matthew's gospel in discussing afterlife perspectives. However, the controversy in Matt 22:23-33 defines its own perspective in direct opposition to such Sadducean beliefs. Therefore, Second Temple texts help in understanding the wider

47. See also the discussion on the Sadducean denial of afterlife existence in J.C. VANDERKAM, *An Introduction to Early Judaism*, Grand Rapids, MI, Eerdmans, 2002, pp. 189-190.

contextual matrix in which Matthew's form of afterlife belief emerged, without allowing one to trace lines of direct dependence.

VII. Conclusion: Afterlife in Jewish Sources and Implications for Matthew's Gospel

In contrast to the fairly consistent stance on the afterlife in the Hebrew Bible, there is a remarkable and varied development of ideas on this topic in the Second Temple period. Broadly speaking there appear to be three positions that are detectable, although these evolve throughout the period in different ways, and the development of ideas is often in response to specific situations and challenges without any systematic attempt to articulate a doctrine of afterlife beliefs within Judaism. The concept of Sheol as the location of the deceased and a place where meaningful existence has ceased, appears to retain currency among the Sadducees. Sociologically, it may be tempting to link such steadfast maintenance of the Hebrew Bible's lack of afterlife beliefs with a degree of religious conservatism, as well as the apparent affluence which was content with the suggestion that divine rewards were enjoyed in this life. Such a stance, however, may fail to recognize the religious commitment to this position. Furthermore, Porton notes that Sadducees were noted for the rejection of afterlife in rabbinic sources as a defining religious commitment[48].

Emergent beliefs in continued existence after death generally took one of two major alternatives: either envisaging the disembodied immortal existence of the soul, or the physical resurrection of a recognizable but perhaps transformed or restored body. Interestingly both alternatives drew upon the prior belief that God, being just, would intercede in the most decisive way to preserve the righteous from the ultimate state of separation from the divine presence – death. For Philo, belief in the ongoing existence while dependent on Platonic concepts, married this with Jewish beliefs that God blessed the righteous with existence in his eternal presence. Thus immortality was a differentiated reward for the virtuous soul, not an inherent property it contained. By contrast, belief in resurrection appears to have emerged more directly from the life-negating experience of martyrdom. The theodicy expressed in both Dan 12:2 and 2 Macc 7 presents a belief in the power of

---

48. Porton notes that, "*Abot R. Nat.* A.5 claims that Zadok's followers broke away from Antigonus of Soco over the issue of resurrection: therefore, the evidence suggests that the Sadducees were known for their rejection of the idea of resurrection". G.G. PORTON, *Sadducees*, in D.N. FREEDMAN (ed.), *ABD*, Vol. 5, New York, Doubleday, 1992, p. 892.

God as being superior to that of earthly persecutors. Therefore, the responsive strategy is an inversion of the categories of life and death, with those who die as pious martyrs being promised a qualitatively better life.

Matthew's gospel reflects a later stage of afterlife beliefs with a more developed outlook on the system of reward and punishment. Yet, it draws upon the embryonic notions of physical resurrection, rather than developing the more philosophically indebted ideas of the separate post-mortem existence of the disembodied soul. Whether such an alignment is indicative of the emergence of the Jesus movement in Pharisaic circles, or just reveals that Matthew and fellow believers in Jesus adopted what had become the dominant view by the end of the first century is perhaps ultimately not resolvable. Therefore, in dispute with the Sadducees, the Matthean Jesus unambiguously asserts belief in the resurrection as a future state (Matt 22:28). Moreover, the eschatological judgment involves a universal assembly of all nations with eternal rewards or punishments. Those who are rejected are, according to the Matthean vision, directed to "the eternal fire which has been prepared for the devil and his angels", whereas the righteous enter eternal life (Matt 25:41.46). It appears that the concept of resurrection, which was seen as having utility in comforting martyrs with the assurance that their faithfulness to the law was not in vain, was further enlarged not only to comfort the faithful but also to condemn the wicked. Matthew shows no direct dependence on a single Jewish source for the concept of bodily resurrection. Instead the gospel draws upon the broad development of the concept of the continuance of the physical form in the post-mortem state as a way of advocating the theological belief that God demonstrates his justice towards faithful believers by preserving them to worship him eternally.

University of Edinburgh   PAUL FOSTER
Mound Place
Edinburgh EH1 2LX
UK

RESURRECTION IN THE GOSPELS OF
MATTHEW AND *PETER*:
SOME DEVELOPMENTS

I. Preliminary Remarks

The question of literary dependence between the Gospel according to Matthew and the first pseudo-Petrine text of the so-called Akhmim Codex[1], which was first published in 1892 and is usually considered as the principal witness of the *Gospel according to Peter* (hence abbreviated as *GosPet*), has been answered controversially. While some scholars like J. Denker or H. Koester have claimed the *GosPet's* complete independence from the canonical Gospels[2], others have assessed the *GosPet* to be literary dependent on all four canonical accounts[3]. Moreover, J.D. Crossan has reconstructed a so-called *Cross Gospel* which he interprets as the oldest passion narrative at all[4]. According to him,

---

1. For more information about this manuscript and the texts contained in it cf. T.J. KRAUS – T NICKLAS (eds.), *Das Petrusevangelium und die Petrusapokalypse: Die griechischen Fragmente mit deutscher und englischer Übersetzung* (GCS NF, 11; Neutestamentliche Apokryphen, 1), Berlin – New York, De Gruyter, 2004, pp. 25-53.101-120. Greek texts are quoted from this edition, translations are revised from it. The following contribution concentrates on the first Petrine apocryphon of the codex, usually seen as *GosPet* while the second one is usually interpreted as a revised version of the *Greek Revelation of Peter*, but could also be a witness to the *GosPet*. For more information see T. NICKLAS, *Zwei petrinische Apokryphen im Akhmim-Codex oder eines? Kritische Anmerkungen und Gedanken*, in Apocrypha 16 (2005) 75-96.
2. Cf. J. DENKER, *Die theologiegeschichtliche Stellung des Petrusevangeliums* (Europäische Hochschulschriften, Reihe 23, Band 36), Bern – Frankfurt am Main, Lang, 1975, pp. 56-57: "Das EvPe läßt nicht erkennen, daß es die Redaktionsarbeit der vier kanonischen Evangelien voraussetzt. Eine Abhängigkeit von ihnen konnte darum nicht erwiesen werden". Cf. also H. KOESTER, *Apocryphal and Canonical Gospels*, in HTR 73 (1980) 105-130; IDEM, *Ancient Christian Gospels: Their History and Development*, Philadelphia, PA, Trinity Press International – London, SCM, 1990, pp. 216-240.
3. See, e.g., T.K. HECKEL, *Vom Evangelium des Markus zum viergestaltigen Evangelium* (WUNT, 120), Tübingen, Mohr, 1999, pp. 291-298.
4. See mainly J.D. CROSSAN, *The Cross That Spoke: The Origins of the Passion Narrative*, San Francisco etc., Harper, 1988; IDEM, *Four Other Gospels: Shadows on the Contours of Canon*, Minneapolis, MN, Fortress, 1985, pp. 123-187, and – more recently – IDEM, *The Gospel of Peter and the Canonical Gospels*, in T.J. KRAUS – T. NICKLAS (eds.), *Das Evangelium nach Petrus: Text, Kontexte, Intertexte* (TU, 158), Berlin – New York, De Gruyter, 2007, pp. 117-134.

the *GosPet* can be perceived as a revised version of the *Cross Gospel*. Crossan eventually interprets the present *GosPet*'s analogies to the canonical texts by the fact that the redactor of the *Cross Gospel* may in turn already have known the canonical Gospels. It would take us too far afield to repeat the detailed criticism, which has been raised against Crossan's concept, once again[5]. Yet, the question arises how likely it is that a codex of the 6th or 7th century has passed on an apocryphal writing which finds its sources in a passion narrative of the earliest decades of the Christian era. Furthermore, it must be asked in how far methods like literary criticism and source criticism allow a reliable reconstruction of a text like Crossan's hypothetical *Cross Gospel*.

If we take the idea of "literary dependence" in a broad sense, it seems to me most reasonable to understand at least the Akhmim version of the *Gos-Pet* as dependent on all canonical Gospels (or at least on Matthew, Luke and John). This should be briefly exemplified before I will lead over to the actual topic. To begin with, one problem should be remembered in advance: conclusions concerning literary criticism due to a "synoptic" comparison between the texts of the *GosPet* and the four Gospels of the New Testament are not without problems: what we are comparing is a (probably late) text form of a 6th/7th century codex on the one hand and on the other hand the *critical editions* of the canonical Gospels. In other words, we do not exactly know what happened with the text of the *GosPet* between its (presumable) origin in the mid 2nd century and the transcription of the Akhmim fragment[6]. A look into the earliest extant witness of the text, the very fragmentary P.Oxy. lxi 2949 (early 3rd century?), shows that the text of the *GosPet* has been subject to changes during the centuries of its transmission.

Nevertheless, the multitude of the text's parallels to the Gospel of Matthew, which have already been elaborated by É. Masseux and W.-D. Köhler[7], are quite obvious evidence for the literary dependence between the two texts[8]. However: we do not necessarily have to assume that *GosPet*'s author actually

---

5. See, e.g., the recent overview by P. FOSTER, *The Gospel of Peter*, in: IDEM (ed.), *The Non-Canonical Gospels*, London – New York, Continuum, 2008, 30-42, pp. 38-40.

6. I have developed this argument more detailed in my article T. NICKLAS, *Ein "neutesta-mentliches Apokryphon"? Zum umstrittenen Kanonbezug des sog. "Petrusevangeliums"*, in VigChr 56 (2002) 260-272.

7. Cf. É. MASSAUX, *Influence de l'évangile de saint Matthieu sur la littérature chrétienne avant saint Irénée*, Leuven – Gembloux, Leuven University Press, 1950 (repr. BETL, 75, Leuven, Peeters, 1986), pp. 358-388 and W.-D. KÖHLER, *Die Rezeption des Matthäusevangeliums in der Zeit vor Irenäus* (WUNT, 2/24), Tübingen, Mohr, 1987, pp. 437-448.

8. I regard it as extremely improbable that Matthew could be dependent on the *GosPet*. For this thesis see, however, N. WALTER, *Eine vormatthäische Schilderung der Auferstehung Jesu*, in *NTS* 19 (1972/73) 415-429, who regards at least *GosPet*'s empty tomb stories as more original than Matthew's.

had the Gospel of Matthew (and the other Gospels of the New Testament) lying in front of him on his desk or took at least a regular look into them when he was writing his own text[9]. It seems much more likely that he knew the canonical Gospels (perhaps partly just in oral form) without having them always close at hand[10]. Perhaps Alan Kirk's ideas about a developing early Christian "cultural memory" are helpful here[11]. The canonical Gospels helped to form a certain "pattern" of events, stories, and/or motifs that was connected with Christ's life, ministry, and passion. The author of the *GosPet* created a new story. This story had, however, to fit into this pattern. In other words: in contrast to Tatian, the author of the *GosPet* did not create a "Gospel harmony" like the Diatessaron, but connected narrative elements of the New Testament Gospels with thoughts and motifs that cannot be found in the New Testament. The outcome of this was a new narrative: the *GosPet* that is familiar to us must be interpreted as a text with its own distinct profile[12].

The frame of the narrative presented here has already been dictated by the Gospels of the New Testament (as well as by oral narratives existing simultaneously), but concerning details, the *GosPet* follows its own direction. Due to this fact, the comparison between Matthew's Gospel and *GosPet* is not only rewarding concerning literary history, but also concerning history of theology. The development between both texts' perception of Jesus' resurrection is certainly interesting, but has hardly ever been analysed[13].

In connection with this, scholars often have noted that the *GosPet* describes Jesus' resurrection more drastically and vividly than Matthew (and others) and attributed this to the text's pious interest in miraculous details[14].

---

9. For a similar view see, e.g., H.-J. KLAUCK, *Apokryphe Evangelien*, Stuttgart, Katholisches Bibelwerk, 2002, p. 118.

10. See also R.E. BROWN, *The Gospel of Peter and Canonical Gospel Priority*, in *NTS* 33 (1987) 321-343, and IDEM, *The Death of the Messiah 2* (ABRL), New York – London, Doubleday, 1994, p. 1336.

11. Cf. A. KIRK, *Tradition and Memory in the Gospel of Peter*, in T.J. KRAUS – T. NICKLAS (eds.), *Das Evangelium nach Petrus: Text, Kontexte, Intertexte* (TU, 158), Berlin – New York, De Gruyter, 2007, pp. 135-158.

12. For the position of the *GosPet* in the development of Gospel literature see J. HARTENSTEIN, *Das Petrusevangelium als Evangelium*, in: KRAUS – NICKLAS (eds.), *Evangelium nach Petrus*, pp. 159-181.

13. Regarding the *GosPet*'s resurrection accounts see, however, the recent (but not in all points convincing) contribution of I. VANDEN HOWE, *Het verrijzenisverhaal in het Petrusevangelie*, in G. VAN OYEN – P. KEVERS (eds.), *De apocriefe Jezus*, Leuven, VBS, 2006, pp. 93-121.

14. See, e.g., KLAUCK, *Apokryphe Evangelien*, p. 117, who speaks about *GosPet*'s "ins Wunderbare stilisierte[n] Schilderung der Auferstehung", or G. THEISSEN – A. MERZ, *Der historische Jesus*, Göttingen, Vandenhoeck & Ruprecht, 1996, p. 61, who describe the text as a "phantastische Schilderung der Auferstehung Jesu", while VANDEN HOWE, *Verrijzenisverhaal*, p. 103, characterizes the text "uiterst vreemd" (= "extremely strange").

That cannot be denied completely. Yet, the question arises whether everything has been covered with these few remarks.

In the following paper, I will concentrate on the first Easter narrative of
the *GosPet* (v. 34-42), which describes the Lord's resurrection very explicitly.
Verses 50-57, narrating the annunciation of the resurrection to Mary
Magdalene and her friends (v. 50-51) by an angel, are only analyzed where
they are relevant for the perception of the idea of resurrection.

II. Textual Analyses

Already the fact that the *GosPet* is concerned with the guards at the tomb
shows the closeness of the *GosPet*'s first Easter narrative (v. 34-42) to the
one in Matthew. *GosPet* goes even further than Matthew: it embeds a concise story of the Lord's resurrection in a detailed report about the guards at
the tomb (v. 28-35a.38.43.45-49). Both lines of narration can hardly be
detached from each other, at least in the present edition of the text, where
the resurrection scene (v. 35b-42) is narrated from the soldiers' point of
view. It is striking how much importance the text attaches to the *sensual
perception* of what the soldier on watch and later the complete guard including the centurion and the elders experience:

V. 36: καὶ εἶδον	"and they *saw*"
V. 38: ἰδόντες οὖν οἱ στρατιῶται ἐκεῖνοι	"and so those soldiers *having seen*"
V. 39a: ἃ εἶδον	"what they *had seen*"
V. 39b: πάλιν ὁρῶσιν	"again they *see*"
V. 41: ἤκουον	"And they were *hearing*"
V. 42: ἠκούετο	"was *heard*"

Thus, it could be said that the statements about the witnesses' seeing and
hearing virtually provide the text with rhythm and subdivide it into single
visions and auditions. This already indicates a distinct shift compared to the
respective scene in the Gospel of Matthew: while Matt 28:4 writes that the
guards shook and became like dead men, the *GosPet* states that the guards,
but also the Jewish leaders become more immediate witnesses of the resurrection than even Jesus' disciples.

Nevertheless, the scene can be understood as connected to Matthew: Matt
28:11 states that some of the guards went into the city to report everything
what had happened (ἅπαντα τὰ γενόμενα) to the chief priests. This can just

be referring to Matt 28:1-10. The *GosPet* thus seems to understand Matt 28:4 in a way that the guards experienced the events of Jesus' resurrection. Despite their fear they virtually become a kind of "anti-witnesses" of Jesus' resurrection. They experience in a sensual manner, literally "have first-hand experience" of what is happening at Jesus' tomb, but then impede the further annunciation of the good news. While Matthew's Gospel expresses this only quite indirectly and does not mention whether the guards had any "sensual" perception of the events[15], the *GosPet* emphasizes this fact.

2.1 *Vision 1:*

V. 35-37

Τῇ δὲ νυκτὶ ᾗ ἐπέφωσκεν ἡ κυριακὴ φυλασσόντων τῶν στρατιωτῶν ἀνὰ δύο δύο κατὰ φρούραν, μεγάλη φωνὴ ἐγένετο ἐν τῷ οὐρανῷ ³⁶ καὶ εἶδον ἀνοιχθέντας τοὺς οὐράνους καὶ δύο ἄνδρας κατελθόντας πολὺ φέγγος ἔχοντας καὶ ἐγγίσαντας τῷ τάφῳ. ³⁷ ὁ δὲ λίθος ἐκεῖνος ὁ βεβλημένος ἐπὶ τῇ θύρᾳ ἀφ' ἑαυτοῦ κυλισθεὶς ἐπεχώρησε παρὰ μέρος καὶ ὁ τάφος ἠνοίγη καὶ ἀμφότεροι οἱ νεανίσκοι εἰσῆλθον.

But in the night in which the Lord's day dawned, when the soldiers were safeguarding it two by two in every watch, there was a loud voice in heaven, 36 and they saw that the heavens were opened and that two males who had much radiance had come down from there and approached the sepulchre. 37 But that stone which had been thrust against the door, having rolled by itself, went a distance off the side; the sepulchre was opened, and both the young men entered.

If we compare *GosPet* 35-37 to Matt 28:1-3 word-by-word, it is striking that both texts show mainly disparities: the clearest *verbal* parallel to Matt 28:1 is the use of the verb ἐπιφώσκω.

| *GosPet* 35a: | Τῇ δὲ νυκτὶ ᾗ ἐπέφωσκεν ἡ κυριακή ... |
| Matt 28:1: | Ὀψὲ δὲ σαββάτων, τῇ ἐπιφωσκούσῃ εἰς μίαν σαββάτων |

Besides, the usage of the term κυριακή ("Lord's Day") in the *GosPet* should be noted[16]. Moreover, the *GosPet* obviously situates the events during the night between what we would call Saturday and Sunday. Matt 28:1

---

15. I regard it as quite probable that Matthew does not understand the guards as witnesses of the resurrection, but *GosPet* seems to have understood Matthew in this very manner.

16. There is no evidence of this word in the New Testament Gospels; the earliest Christian witnesses are Rev 1:10, *Did.* 14:1 and Ignatius, *Magn.* 9:1.

speaks of the dawn of the first day of the week. A loud voice in heaven sounds, while two soldiers are safeguarding[17]: none of the four Gospels of the New Testament presents a clear parallel to this motif. Is the reader possibly supposed to remind of Jesus' transfiguration, where a voice *from the cloud* (and a radiant cloud respectively) is mentioned (Mark 9:7 par. Matt 17:5 par. Luke 9:34-35)? The *GosPet* does not narrate *what* the voice in heaven says. Is it possible to merely think of a thunder[18]? How ever it may be: it seems to me very likely that the motif here, like in many apocalyptic texts (cf. in the New Testament, e.g., Rev 1:10.15b; 7:2; 10:4; 12:10; 14:2), functions as a sign that eschatological events will happen. It appears interesting that at least Rev 1:10 presents a comparable combination of "Lord's Day" and "loud voice"[19]. In any case, the motif of the "loud voice" in heaven replaces the "violent earthquake" of Matt 28:2[20]. The latter has not been omitted completely in the *GosPet*, as v. 21 tells that "all the earth was shaken" when the Lord's body touched it at the deposition from the cross. *GosPet* 21, however, might have been developed from Matt 27:51 and 54.

Although the associations between *GosPet* 36 and Matthew are clearly recognizable, one distinction must be mentioned: in contrast to Matthew, *GosPet* describes an opening of heavens, a motif frequent in early Jewish and early Christian literature (Ezek 1:1; Isa 63:19; John 1:51; Acts 7:56; Rev 4:1; *2 Bar* 13:1-2; 22:1). It is often found in scenes of revelation, above all in apocalyptic texts[21] and illustrates the possibility of contact between divine and material world. This idea has to be understood in a very concrete way: in order to be able to descend from heaven, something like the door of a house has to be opened (cf. also *GosPet* 44). Only then, the "other", the material world can be entered[22].

Matthew as well as *GosPet* speak of a descent of one respectively two figures from heaven (Matt 28:2: καταβαίνω; *GosPet* 36: κατέρχομαι). In Matthew's case, it is the angel of the Lord (28:2: ἄγγελος κυρίου), whereas the *GosPet* speaks of "two males" (δύο ἄνδρες). Is it possible that the *GosPet*

---

17. For a correct understanding of the word ἀνὰ δύο δύο cf. L. VAGANAY, *L'Évangile de Pierre* (ÉBib), Paris, Gabalda, 1930, p. 293.

18. For the biblical motif of "thunder" as part of epiphany stories see, e.g., Exod 9:23, 29, 33f.; 19:16, 19; Deut 4:12, 33, 36; 5:22, 23; 1 Sam 2:10; 7:10; 2 Sam 22:14; Job 26:14; 37:4; Rev 8:5; 10:3-4; 11:19; 14:2; 16:18 etc.

19. Cf. also M.G. MARA, *Évangile de Pierre* (SC, 201), Paris, Cerf, 1973, p. 177.

20. Cf. MARA, *Évangile*, p. 177.

21. For more information see F. LENTZEN-DEIS, *Das Motiv der Himmelsöffnung in verschiedenen Gattungen der Umweltliteratur des Neuen Testaments*, in *Bib.* 50 (1969) 301-327.

22. Cf. also Rev 4:1 where the opening of a door allows the seer – the other way round! – to enter heaven.

adopts the perspective of the unbelieving observers here? At least from their point of view these are first of all male figures who descend from heaven. In that case the text would communicate that the present soldiers "see", but do not understand what they see. But probably this interpretation goes a step too far and the text speaks about "two men" because nothing more concrete is necessary in this context.

However, the fact that the *GosPet* never uses the term ἄγγελος, is indeed so remarkable that suppositions were made that these two males might be Moses and Elijah[23] – in this case the text would be referring to the synoptic transfiguration stories. However, there is nothing in the *GosPet* which indicates this identification which also becomes unlikely due to the figures' description: both had "much radiance" (v. 36), and are νεανίσκοι (v. 37)[24]. That is why the obvious interpretation has to be preferred: the passage is about angels, whose figure reminds of males.

Regarding the description of the angels both texts do not show any verbatim contiguity: the attributes πολὺ φέγγος ἔχοντας (*GosPet* 36; cf. also 2 Sam 22:13; Hab 3:4; Ezek 1:4.13.27.28; 10:4; 43:2 LXX) and ἦν δὲ ἡ εἰδέα αὐτοῦ ὡς ἀστραπὴ καὶ τὸ ἔνδυμα αὐτοῦ λευκὸν ὡς χιών (Matt 28:3) remind of traditional descriptions of significant angel-like beings without enabling a concrete identification[25].

Might it be that despite all parallels a theological discrepancy emerges due to the fact that Matthew speaks of the (or just an?) ἄγγελος κυρίου, who is the representative for God's acting per se? Does Matthew express here that it is God Himself who is acting? However, the *GosPet* seems to express the same idea, but in other words. If not already the voice in heaven refers to God, the *GosPet* might imply God's acting in v. 37. While, according to Matt 28:2, the stone which had been thrust against the sepulchre is rolled back by the / an angel of the Lord (ἀπεκύλισεν τὸν λίθον), it "is rolled by itself" according to *GosPet*. Are the passive forms κυλισθείς and ἠνοίγη to be considered as *passiva divina*? Or is this interpretation made impossible by the words ἀφ' ἑαυτοῦ preceding the participle κυλισθείς?

At any rate, the *GosPet* describes the removal of the stone as a miracle. The question is, however, if the apocryphal story is really more miraculous

---

23. Compare the information about older literature (mainly NESTLE) at L. VAGANAY, *Évangile de Pierre*, p. 294.

24. See already the arguments given by VAGANAY, *Évangile de Pierre*, p. 294.

25. Therefore I do not think that speculations about the question, which angels could be meant here, make sense. – Even if it is of lesser importance for our theological concern, it should be noted that both texts describe the angels' movement to the tomb with different verbs: Matt 28:2: προσέρχομαι; *GosPet* 36: ἐγγίζω)

than the Matthean one: is the notion of a stone being rolled "by itself" really "more miraculous" than the idea of an angel rolling the stone and sitting on it (obviously as a sign of triumph)? It might be that the depiction in the more unknown apocryphal text just sounds more unfamiliar to us than the one in the canonical text.

After a short insertion, which reports the reaction of the soldiers to the first vision (v. 38), the text leads over to a second vision + audition: one could say the actual "resurrection scene" of the *GosPet*. This takes place, as the text specially emphasises, not only in front of the actual guard, but also in front of the centurion and the elders of the people.

2.2 Vision / Audition 2:

V. 39-42

Καὶ ἐξηγουμένων αὐτῶν ἃ εἶδον πάλιν ὁρῶσιν ἐξελθόντας ἀπὸ τοῦ τάφου τρεῖς ἄνδρας καὶ τοὺς δύο τὸν ἕνα ὑπορθοῦντας καὶ σταυρὸν ἀκολουθοῦντα αὐτοῖς ⁴⁰ καὶ τῶν μὲν δύο τὴν κεφαλὴν χωροῦσαν μέχρι τοῦ οὐρανοῦ, τοῦ δὲ χειραγω-γουμένου ὑπ᾿ αὐτῶν ὑπερβαίνουσαν τοὺς οὐρανούς. ⁴¹ καὶ φωνῆς ἤκουον ἐκ τῶν οὐρανῶν λεγούσης· ἐκήρυξας τοῖς κοιμωμένοις; ⁴² καὶ ὑπακοὴ ἠκούετο ἀπὸ τοῦ σταυροῦ ὅτι ναί.

And while they were relating what they had seen, again they see three males coming out from the sepulchre, with the two supporting the other one, and a cross following them, 40 and the head of the two reaching unto heaven, but that of the one being led out by hand by them going beyond the heavens. 41 And they were hearing a voice from the heavens saying, 'Have you made proclamation to the fallen-asleep?' 42 And a response was heard from the cross, 'Yes'.

I do not know of any early Christian text narrating Christ's resurrection in a more direct and concrete way than v. 39-42. At the same time, the text, which can be considered the *crucial difference* between the *GosPet* and the Matthean resurrection scenes, raises a number of questions which have not been satisfactorily answered yet. While it is obvious that "the two" are the angels who descended from heaven mentioned a moment ago, and "the one" is the risen "Lord", already here the first difficulties arise:

• Is it sheer coincidence that the "risen Lord" is called "the one" and not Jesus of Nazareth, as e.g. in Mark 16:6? Why does the text call him "the Lord" as in so many other cases? This mysterious manner of depiction could indeed be interpreted in the way that "the one" coming out of the sepulchre does not have any connection to the once living Jesus of Nazareth anymore, that he is possibly an angel-like being, while the body of Jesus may still be in the sepulchre. The description of the risen Lord as "going beyond the heavens" could definitely suggest such an assumption. However, this understanding is made impossible by the fact that the text speaks about a cross following him, i.e. obviously *his* cross (v. 39), which even *after his resurrection* bears close relation to the Risen One.

Another point against it is the (later) statement of the "young man" in the sepulchre (*GosPet* 56), a clear parallel to Matt 28:5. The young man says to Mary Magdalene and her women friends: "Why have you come? Whom do you seek? Not that one who was crucified? He is risen and gone away" (*GosPet* 56). Although the pronoun ἐκεῖνος creates a certain distance, continuity still seems to persist between the "Christ Crucified" and the "risen Lord", who is at the same time regarded as God's minister (*GosPet* 56b).

• What is meant by the depiction that the two angels "*support*" the risen Lord[26]? Must the risen Lord be understood as "powerless", because his δύναμις had forsaken him when he died (v. 19)? Thomas Hieke's interpretation of *GosPet* 19 is helpful here[27]:

> "Der Text hat kein Interesse daran, auch nur den Anschein aufkommen zu lassen, *Gott* hätte den *Kyrios* verlassen. Daher ist die 'Kraft' an dieser Stelle auch nicht Äquivalent für Gott, sondern die Kraft des Herrn (Jesus), die Wunderwerke bewirkt, wie sie so oft im Neuen Testament beschrieben werden".

It is thus easily conceivable that both angels represent some kind of escort of the one who obviously ascends to heaven in triumph. The next parallel of this idea cannot be found in the Gospel of Matthew, but in the third chapter of the *Ascension of Isaiah*: according to this text, the angels Gabriel and Michael will open the tomb on the third day. Christ, the "Beloved", will leave it sitting on their shoulders and afterwards will send out the disciples (cf. also Mark 16:4 in the text form of Codex Bobbiensis [k])[28].

---

26. For the problem of translating the rare verb ὑπορθόω cf. KRAUS – NICKLAS (eds.), *Petrusevangelium und Petrusapokalypse*, 43.

27. T. HIEKE, *Das Petrusevangelium vom Alten Testament her gelesen*, in KRAUS – NICKLAS (eds.), *Evangelium nach Petrus*, pp. 91-115, here p. 106.

28. For a recent discussion of these well-known parallels of *GosPet*'s account see T. NICKLAS, *Angels in Early Christian Narratives of the Resurrection of Jesus: Canonical and Apocryphal Texts*, in F. REITERER – T. NICKLAS – K. SCHÖPFLIN (eds.), *Angels: The Concept of Celestial Beings – Origins, Development and Reception* (ISDCL Yearbook 2007), Berlin – New York, De Gruyter, 2007, pp. 293-311, here pp. 305-308.

• Before we turn to the question how the role of the cross can be understood, the depiction of the risen Lord ought to be examined more carefully:
like the two angels he is characterized as being visible in the shape of a
"male", i.e. being (at least in a certain sense) physical. Yet, there is a difference to the Gospel of Matthew: in contrast to Matt 28:9, one cannot simply clasp his feet and worship him, as it was possible when he was still alive.
Although he remains in the shape of a male, this shape does not only over-
top both angels, but also the heavens (v. 40). Does this mean that the risen
Kyrios is presented as a kind of magnificent angel-like figure here[29]?

This is certainly possible, even though it cannot be proven on the basis
of the present text. In any case, the one who comes out of the sepulchre is
described as already belonging to heavenly spheres[30] even if there is still a
certain continuity to the "crucified Christ". In that case, his size perhaps
just wants to depict his outstanding importance in relation to other heavenly
creatures. An obvious parallel of this thought would be the description of
the "mighty angel" in Rev 10:1-3, who is even more equipped with divine
attributes than the *GosPet*'s risen Lord[31] and has been identified with the
Lord himself since Victorinus of Pettau[32].

Even more close to our text are the descriptions of the Son of God and
Christ in *The Revelation of Elchasaï*[33]. The most important point of contact
might be that this mysterious Jewish-Christian text of the 2nd century,
which only partly survived in quotations of ancient Christian authors,
regards Christ (as well as the Holy Spirit) as male (and respectively female)

---

29. Contrary to FOSTER, *Gospel of Peter*, pp. 36-37, I would not use the term "polymorphy" in connection with the *GosPet*'s resurrection scene. In my understanding "polymorphic
Christology" describes the phenomenon that Christ, like in the *Acts of John*, can be envisioned
simultaneously in different forms. This is clearly not the case here. For a broader discussion of
the terms "polymorphy" and "polymorphic Christology" cf. É. JUNOD, *Polymorphie du Dieu
Sauveur*, in J. RIES (ed.), *Gnosticisme et monde hellénistique* (Publications de l'Institut Orientaliste de Louvain, 27), Louvain-la-Neuve, Institut Orientaliste, 1982, pp. 38-46.

30. For other important angelic figures which are described as "gigantic" see *TestRub* 5:7
or *2 Enoch* 1:2, and 18:1, and the information provided by É. JUNOD, *Évangile de Pierre*, in
F. BOVON – P. GEOLTRAIN (eds.), *Écrits apocryphes chrétiens I* (Bibliothèque de la Pléiade),
Paris, Gallimard, 1997, pp. 241-254, here p. 252.

31. For this connection see also MARA, *Évangile*, p. 183.

32. For a first overview of ancient Christian interpretations of Rev 10 compare W.C.
WEINRICH (ed.), *Revelation* (Ancient Christian Commentary on Scripture NT, XII), Downers
Grove, Ill., 2005, pp. 145-147.

33. For parallels between *GosPet* and the *Revelation of Elchasai* see also F. LAPHAM, *Peter:
The Myth, the Man and the Writings: A Study of Early Petrine Text and Tradition* (JSNTSupp,
239), Sheffield, Academic Press, 2003, p. 31. Lapham, however, is a bit quick in connecting
the different communities in the background of these texts. – For more possible parallels see
MARA, *Évangile*, p. 185.

angel-like figure(s) of indescribable size. Epiphanius of Salamis reports (*pan.* 19:4:1; cf. also Hippolyt, *ref.* 9:13:1-3)[34]:

> "Then he [Elxai] describes Christ as a kind of power, and even gives his dimensions – about ninety-six miles, twenty-four schoena tall, and twenty-four miles, six schoena wide, and similar prodigies about his thickness and feet, and other mythological descriptions".

• Can the risen "Lord" of the *GosPet*, who is linked with the cross by v. 39 and v. 42, be understood, with Maria Grazia Mara, as a kind of "cosmic centre" that connects heaven, earth and netherworld[35]? Due to the differences between the *GosPet* and texts like the *Acts of John* 98:1-6[36] where the cross functions as a kind of cosmic centre, I would be more cautious than Mara. The *Acts of John* distinguish between the "wooden cross", on which Christ is crucified (and which is theologically insignificant for the text), and a cosmic cross of light. The latter is obviously understood as a manifestation of the Lord. As a "boundary post", this cross separates the upper world from the lower world and at the same time offers the opportunity of focusing the rays of light ascending to the upper world. The cross at the border of the two worlds, i.e., the Lord, fills itself with the light of the ones who belong to Christ. The comparison demonstrates the discrepancies of both perceptions quite clearly: even though the cross in the *GosPet* answers instead of the risen Lord, both are definitely different from each other – the cross, which can be understood as the cross on which the "Lord" was crucified, "follows" the three males. Moreover, the text mentions that the head of the risen Lord goes beyond heavens, but it does not give an explicit and synchronous connection between heavenly, earthly and subterranean world.

• But what is the meaning of the cross that follows the risen Lord and answers the question regarding his "Descensus ad inferos" with "Yes"? The talk of a cross that obviously "follows" on its own (here: ἀκολουθέω), is well known from various passages of early Christian literature, in most cases

---

34. Translation: F. WILLIAMS, *The Panarion of Epiphanius of Salamis: Book I (Sects 1-46)* (NHS, 35), Leiden – Boston, Brill, 1987, p. 46. – For an introduction to the *Revelation of Elchasai* cf. L. CIRILLO, *Livre de la révélation d'Elkasaï*, in F. BOVON – P. GEOLTRAIN (eds.), *Écrits apocryphes chrétiens I* (Bibliothèque de la Pléiade), Paris, Gallimard, 1997, pp. 829-872, here pp. 829-838.

35. Cf. MARA, *Évangile*, 183-184, and EADEM, *Il Vangelo di Pietro* (Scritti delle origini cristiane, 30), Bologna, Dehoniane, 2002, pp. 101-102.

36. Text: É. JUNOD – J.-D. KAESTLI, *Acta Iohannis: Praefatio – Textus* (Corpus Christianorum Series Apocryphorum, 1), Turnhout, Brepols, 1983, p. 209.

descriptions of the *parousia*. *Revelation of Peter* 1:6 seems to be particularly important. This text states[37]:

> "For the coming of the Son of God will not be revealed but like lightning which appears from the east to the west. Thus, I will come in a cloud of heaven with great power in my glory *while my cross goes before my face*".

Similar concepts are testified in the Ethiopian version of the *Epistula Apostolorum* (Chapter 16)[38] or in the *Apocalypse of Elijah* 31:15-16[39]. However, in contrast to the mentioned texts, the cross in the *GosPet* does not precede the risen Lord, but follows him.

In all probability, the text understands the answer to the heavenly question as being given by the cross. This has been interpreted in various ways. While J. Denker sees the cross as the "Lord's sign of revelation and triumph over death" (= „Zeichen der Auferstehung und des Triumphes des Herrn über den Tod") and as belonging to "the risen Lord's insignia of power" (= zu den "Insignien der Macht des auferstandenen Herrn" gehörig)[40], J.D. Crossan indicates that, unlike in the mentioned parallels, the cross of the *GosPet* obviously does not function as a sign of triumph or victory[41]. Moreover, the fact that the cross operates independently from the "Lord", follows and does not precede him, has to be taken seriously. Thus, Crossan interprets *GosPet* 39-41 as the description of a scene where the risen Lord delivers the saints from *sheol*[42]. If the passion of the *Cross Gospel*, according to Crossan, depicts Jesus' suffering as the collective suffering of Israel, the resurrection must be understood as the resurrection of Israel's saints. That is why Crossan regards the cross following Jesus as a cruciform procession of Israel's saints who answer in Jesus' name. This explains why the cross (and

---

37. Translation: D.D. BUCHHOLZ, *Your Eyes Will Be Opened: A Study of the Greek (Ethiopic) Apocalypse of Peter* (SBL.DS, 97), Atlanta, Scholars Press, 1988, p. 167.

38. The Ethiopian and the Coptic version of the *EpAp* are differing from each other here. While the Ethiopian version describes the cross as going in front of Christ, the Coptic version speaks only about the "sign of the cross". Cf. J.-N. PÉRÈS, *L'Épître des Apôtres accompagnée du Testament de notre Seigneur et notre Sauveur Jésus Christ* (Apocryphes. Collections de Poche de l'AELAC), Turnhout, Brepols, 1994, p. 75 n. 90.

39. W. SCHRAGE, *Die Elias-Apokalypse* (JSHRZ, V.3), Gütersloh, Gütersloher Verlagshaus, 1980, p. 251, gives even more (and less well-known) parallels: *PsApcJoh* (cod. D, Tischendorf 83), *PsApcDan* (Tischendorf XXXII), Ps-Hippolyt, *De consummatione mundi* 36. See also J. ENGEMANN, *Auf die Parusie Christi hinweisende Darstellungen in der frühchristlichen Kunst*, in *JAC* 19 (1976) 139-156, pp. 146-147.

40. DENKER, *Theologiegeschichtliche Stellung*, p. 98. Interestingly, during the discussion of this paper J. Verheyden expressed the idea that the cross following the Risen Lord could be compared to the later attributes given to Saints (like, e.g., St. Peter's key).

41. Cf. CROSSAN, *Cross That Spoke*, pp. 385-386.

42. Cf. CROSSAN, *Cross That Spoke*, p. 387.

not the Lord) answers the question from heaven. However, Crossan's thesis is not able to explain why the ones who rise together with Jesus are forming a *cruciform* procession and why nothing in the text explicitly supports such an interpretation.

Therefore, the question why it is the cross that answers the heavenly question may be answered with Jan Helderman[43]:

> "Der Auferstandene, selbst voller Herrlichkeit und Triumph, kann die Frage Gottes nicht mehr beantworten, der er die Himmel schon überragt. Das Kreuz teilt nunmehr mit, was in der Unterwelt alles geschehen ist".

At the same time, the cross remains related to the risen Lord: even the *GosPet* would not only speak of the risen Lord's triumph, but also sketch the steady importance of his cross in this situation. So it might be that the explanation of these findings is more close to the notions of the *Revelation of Peter* than Crossan assumes: the leading motive of the text could be that the cross ascends to heaven together with the Lord, because it is needed as a sign of triumph (or identification) during *parousia*. A comparable perception seems to be presupposed in the hymn to Christ in the 6th book of *Sibylline Oracles* (*Or.Sib.* 6:26-27), as it says[44]: "O most blessed wood on which God has hanged spreadly. The earth will not grasp you, no, *you will consider heaven as home*".

• But why does the cross "follow" the risen Lord? I am not able to give a definite answer to this question: might it be that it does not function as the Lord's visible sign of triumph before *parousia*? But perhaps the manner of depiction has simply to do with narrative reasons: the risen Lord must be the first to ascend to heaven (and not his cross), and at the same time the cross must be located on earth to answer the heavenly voices.

• A final aspect has to be touched upon at least: *GosPet* 41 apparently presupposes the notion of a *descensus ad inferos*, but does not specify how this is imagined[45]. Is this motif developed from Matt 27:52-53 narrating the resurrection of "many saints" after Jesus death? There is certainly no

---

43. J. HELDERMAN, *Die Engel bei der Auferstehung und das lebendige Kreuz: Mk 16,3 in k, einem Vergleich unterzogen*, in F. VAN SEGBROECK et al. (eds.), *The Four Gospels 1992* (BETL, 100), Leuven, Leuven University Press-Peeters, 1992, 2321-2342, p. 2334.

44. For this parallel see also VAGANAY, *Évangile de Pierre*, p. 299. Cf. also Ps-Chrysostomus, De cruce et latrone 2,4 (PG 49,413).

45. For a history of the motif of the *descensus ad inferos* see R. GOUNELLE, *La descente du Christ aux enfers: Institutionnalisation d'une croyance* (Collection des Études Augustiniennes, Série Antiquité, 162), Paris, Institut d'Études Augustiniennes, 2000.

clear literary connection between both texts, but both Matthew and the
GosPet show at least a similar pattern of motifs[46]: Jesus' cross and crucifixion
– the resurrection of dead persons – Jesus' resurrection.

But how is this *descensus* understood more concretely? Is it presupposed
that the risen Lord descended to Hades after his death in order to "preach"
to the ones trapped there? How can this descent (and the descending
Lord) be concretely imagined? What is the content of his kerugma? These
questions have to remain more or less open, as the text does not even give
us a hint of an answer, but seems to presuppose that its readers already
understood what is meant. The only thing we can say with certainty
is that the Lord is not simply seen as absolutely passive between his
crucifixion and resurrection. This again presupposes a certain concept of
"corporeality". The crucified Lord *moves* (to other worlds) and *preaches*,
i.e., speaks to others who are dead but must (at least in a certain sense)
be able to *hear* him. All this is not imaginable without at least a certain
"bodily existence".

III. CONCLUSION

Despite all methodological difficulties in dealing with a fragmentary text
surviving only in a late manuscript, the comparison of the tomb narrations
of Matthew and the *GosPet* shows some interesting aspects:

1. The *GosPet* seems to presuppose Matthew's "dramatic" composition
of the resurrection narratives and develops it even further. While Mark
and Luke do not depict the actual event of the resurrection itself, Matthew
and the *GosPet* tell what happens at the tomb before the disciples arrive.
Both versions of the story are linked with the narration about the
guards at the tomb. Even if they do not "look" into the tomb either, both
texts go further than other Gospels in narrating what cannot be described:
they try to express God's eschatological intervention in a historical context.

2. Compared to the Gospel of Matthew, the *GosPet* does not necessarily
present the "more fantastic" or "more miraculous" version of the story. Yet,
the *GosPet*'s large interest in the sensual perception of the events, even for
the opponents, is remarkable. Here, motifs from Matthew are adopted, but
get another direction of impact: although the *GosPet* largely uses anti-Jewish
stereotypes, the text is highly concerned with the question why the Jewish

46. For more information see Dale ALLISON's contribution in this volume.

people did not proselytise in its entirety to Jesus of Nazareth, the "Lord"[47]. This question can be answered with the help of the present resurrection narrative: not only the Roman soldiers provided by Pilate, but also the elders of the people saw and heard what had happened, but concealed everything because of fear of the people and thus prevented the Christianization of Israel.

3. As I was able to demonstrate elsewhere, the *GosPet* shows interest in the "body" or the fleshly existence and the corporal sufferings of the "Lord"[48]. The text also writes of a "visible" and at the same time oversized "bodily existence" of the risen Lord. The primary aim of this description is to portray the risen Lord as a being which now belongs to the heavenly spheres and whose importance exceeds the importance of the angels accompanying him. The text has not directly answered the question to what extent the risen Lord still has to do with the living Jesus of Nazareth. Yet, it seems to be basically in line with the Gospel of Matthew: the risen Lord is obviously accompanied by "his" cross, which is still connected with him. Thus, he can be called the "crucified Christ" even after his resurrection.

4. The Gospel of Matthew speaks of the resurrection of Jesus of Nazareth, but does not broach the issue of the consequences which arise for a possible resurrection of the dead, at least not in its Easter narratives. The *GosPet* implies this in the heavenly question to the cross that follows the risen Lord: the "sermon" to the ones who had passed away can have no other meaning than giving permission to at least some of them to participate in the salvation which has been facilitated by the annunciation of the "Lord". Perhaps even this last idea has its backgrounds in a Matthean text – not in the Matthean tomb stories but in the mysterious passage Matt 27:52-53 speaking about the resurrection of "many saints" after Jesus' crucifixion[49].

Katholisch-Theologische Fakultät   Tobias NICKLAS
Universität Regensburg
D-93040 Regensburg
Germany
tobias.nicklas@theologie.uni-regensburg.de

---

47. Cf. also T. NICKLAS, *Die 'Juden' im Petrusevangelium (PCair 10759): Ein Testfall*, in *NTS* 46 (2000) 206-221.

48. T. NICKLAS, *Die Leiblichkeit der Gepeinigten: Das Evangelium nach Petrus und antike Märtyrerakten*, in J. LEEMANS (ed.), *Martyrdom and Persecution in Late Antique Christianity* (BETL, 241), Leuven, Peeters, 2010, pp. 195-219.

49. English translation of the German original: Evelyn Karl.

RESURRECTION IN THE GOSPEL OF MATTHEW: REALITY AND SYMBOL

Many scholars have attempted to fill the space between the narrative of Jesus' burial and the story of the empty tomb. Discussions of the resurrection of Jesus often make frustrating reading. They often begin with the promise of grappling with historicity, but then rather quickly change shape. They often repair to the abstract, what Wolfhart Pannenberg calls "foggy talk of Easter faith"[1], or become debates about epistemology. In the end, I find wisdom in Dale Allison's statement that "We have restricted access to the past…Some barriers just cannot be crossed"[2]. Even Raymond Brown, who did not shy away from difficult historical questions, did not try to cross the barrier. When he finished his massive two-volume work on the Passion narratives, he was frequently asked if he was ready to tackle the resurrection stories. He replied that he would wait to find out about them "face to face"[3].

If we cannot answer the question, "What really happened?" we can nevertheless address the question of how *Matthew* understands Jesus' resurrection. In Matthew, I will argue, resurrection is *both* reality and symbol. "Symbol" is a better term than "metaphor", because a symbol participates in the reality for which it stands, whereas a metaphor, by definition, is *not* the thing it stands for, but is merely like it.

I. JEWISH EXPECTATIONS OF LIFE AFTER DEATH

I hold with Anthony Saldarini[4] and others that Matthew is still heavily invested in the Jewish community. As someone steeped in Jewish tradition,

---

1. W. PANNENBERG, *Jesus, God and Man*, transl. L.L. Wilkins and D.A. Priebe, Philadelphia, Westminster, ²1977, p. 401.

2. D.C. ALLISON, *Resurrecting Jesus: The Earliest Christian Tradition and Its Interpreters*, New York, T & T Clark, 2005, p. 298.

3. R. BROWN, *The Death of the Messiah: From Gethsemane to the Grave: A Commentary on the Passion Narratives in the Four Gospels*. Vol. 1 (ABRL), New York, Doubleday, 1994, p. xii.

4. A. SALDARINI, *Matthew's Christian-Jewish Community* (CSJH), Chicago, University of Chicago Press, 1994.

Matthew had a pool of ideas about the afterlife from which to draw. The belief in resurrection is not dogma: no such thing exists in first-century Judaism. It is part of a mosaic of related themes about life and death, justice, suffering and God's power.

Some ideas of afterlife and even resurrection are implicit in the Hebrew Bible. Certain terms appear, like *rephaim,* "shades", *Sheol,* "the underworld", and *teraphim,* "household gods", terms that are linked to divination, places of punishment and reward in the afterlife, and ancestral spirits in other ancient Near Eastern languages and cultures. Combined with condemnation of divination and necromancy, these fragments of information suggest a "live" world of the dead in Israelite culture[5]. Occasional shadowy, suggestive images arise, such as David mourning over his son with Bathsheba, saying, "I will go to him, but he will not return to me (1 Sam 12:23)".

Even clearer is the sense that death may be overcome. Three resuscitation stories in 1 Kings 17, 2 Kings 4, and 2 Kings 13 show that death may be reversed. Dramatic images of resurrection appear in Ezekiel 37, where the graphic corporeality of it includes the bones being knit back together, the flesh covering them, and the breath re-entering the body. In Isaiah 26:19, of disputed date, *bodies* will come to life again ("Your dead will live, their bodies will rise again". The Septuagint is a bit less explicit – "the dead shall rise, those in the tombs shall be raised" compared to the dead of the enemy in v. 14, who shall not rise). Isaiah 25:8 promises "God will swallow up death forever". (The Septuagint differs markedly here, "Death has prevailed and swallowed men up, but again the Lord has taken away every tear from every face"). The latest reference, from Daniel 12:2-3, envisions that Michael will appear and the people be delivered; "Many who sleep in the dust of the earth will awake, some to everlasting life and some to eternal abhorrence". It continues with astral immortality. "And the wise shall shine as the brightness of the firmament, and some of the many righteous as the stars forever and ever". These last three references emerge from situations of political turmoil and persecution. Many people quickly dispose of their corporeality by calling them metaphors for national restoration. Metaphors, even poetic ones, only make sense if they express what people think and feel. So these would not make sense to a people with no sense of an afterlife or hope for the defeat of death.

5. See discussion of intimations of afterlife in the Hebrew Bible in my book, *Resurrection of the Body in Early Judaism and Christianity: Doctrine, Community, and Self-definition,* Boston, Brill, 2004, pp. 6-11. I rely heavily on an article by R. FRIEDMAN – S. OVERTON, *Death and Afterlife: The Biblical Silence,* in A.J. AVERY-PECK – J. NEUSNER (eds.), *Judaism in Late Antiquity; Part Four: Death, Life after Death, Resurrection, and the World to Come in the Judaisms of Antiquity* (HO, I. Abt., Bd. 49), Leiden, Brill, 2000, pp. 35-59.

While references to the afterlife and resurrection are occasional and unsystematic, corporeal resurrection seems an indigenous biblical idea. It flows logically from Israel's understanding of a God who creates the material world, who continues to act within its events, and who will triumph over death. Resurrection of the human body, or more generally, God's conquest of death, form a natural part of a powerful "Creation theology", a fundamental prejudice in favour of the created world, including the human being, who is a union of body and soul. God remains involved in the functioning of the created world, and at extraordinary times, acts on it, to rescue, destroy, raise up, and restore.

Belief in resurrection, like other beliefs, is not carefully spelled out or compartmentalized. It often mixes with ideas of immortality of the soul or astral immortality in the same documents. First Enoch, for example, contemporary with 2 Maccabees and Daniel, shows the two ideas side by side, resurrection, "the righteous shall arise", and spiritual immortality, "the spirits of the righteous shall not perish". Most ideas are not defined, since they appear in poetic and apocalyptic material.

Nor does the idea of resurrection arise simply as a response to martyrdom. While it is tempting to say that resurrection of the body develops primarily as a result of martyrdom, the discussion of the Hebrew Bible shows that it is "in the air" long before 2 Maccabees, the first explicit link between resurrection and martyrdom. Its economy makes sense – the body tortured and destroyed is rewarded by being the body raised. Second Maccabees 7 is quite explicit, in the story of the mother and her seven sons, since the mother assures her sons that the God who gave them the body parts will give them back in resurrection.

Yet the implications of the Hebrew Bible suggest the resurrection idea is earlier and more thoroughgoing. Furthermore, as Jan Willem van Henten has argued, it can be linked to the restoration of the Jewish religion and polity. In addition, one could just as easily adjust the scenario to make spiritual immortality the reward for martyrdom, as it is in 4 Maccabees. There martyrdom is about the triumph of reason, "the prize was immortality in endless life" (17:12). Equally reasonable would be the idea that the tortured body is left behind, while the martyr is freed from its pain and weakness. Looking at the whole sweep of belief, martyrdom may be a stimulus to resurrection belief, but is neither its single or primary cause.

I have alluded to the mixed nature of sources on afterlife. The Pharisees, for example, as reported in Josephus, sound as if they believe in a form of resurrection or reincarnation, mixed with some spiritual immortality. Some have suggested Josephus is packaging the descriptions for his Roman audience. But at the same time there is nothing unusual in combining different approaches to afterlife in the same source.

In the Wright-Crossan debates on the historicity of Jesus' resurrection, N.T. Wright has stressed the discontinuity of early Christian belief with Jewish precedent, judging it to be a significant "mutation", inexplicable from elements in Judaism alone. The anomalous nature of the belief thus becomes one of his proofs for its reliability. Although he disagrees with Wright on other points, John D. Crossan agrees with him on the anomaly[6]. Yet there is so much variety in Jewish texts on the afterlife, and no systematic doctrine exists. We should not be surprised to see a fragmentary or mixed understanding of afterlife in any Jewish text. Wright and Crossan also underestimate the generative power of text in Jewish literature. If we consider how a fragmentary verse in Gen 5:24 saying "Enoch walked with God and was not" gives rise to the Enoch literature, or how the vision of Ezekiel 1 generates Merkabah and Hechalot mysticism, meditations on the chariot-throne, it is not difficult to see Jesus' resurrection as continuous with Jewish expectations. It is difficult to see it otherwise. Having considered elements conducive to resurrection belief in the Hebrew Bible, later I will consider material from liturgy and rabbinic literature.

II. CORPOREALITY

In certain ways, Matthew seems deeply invested in proving the corporeality of Jesus' resurrection. Wim Weren has explained the guard story as a careful refutation of the charge that Jesus' body was stolen, a refutation that includes both points and counterpoints. In his literary analysis, Weren shows the interweaving of two competing interpretations based on the idea that Jesus is not in the tomb, one by his followers claiming he has been raised, and a second by those who say the body has been stolen[7]. Weren argues that Matthew may have invented the dissenting argument to forestall problems for community members. I would argue that the strange aside in 28:15 and the hardy presence of the resurrection as a point in Jewish-Christian polemic

---

6. R.B. STEWART (ed.), *The Resurrection of Jesus: John Dominic Crossan and N.T. Wright in Dialogue*, Minneapolis, MN, Fortress, 2006, pp. 18-24.

7. W. J.C. WEREN, *'His Disciples Stole Him Away' (Mt 28, 13): A Rival Interpretation of Jesus' Resurrection*, in R. BIERINGER – V. KOPERSKI – B. LATAIRE (eds.), *Resurrection in the New Testament* (BETL, 165), Leuven, University Press – Peeters, 2002, pp. 147-163. Weren argues that the second may be invented by Matthew to refute possible objections within the community.

argue for disputes with outsiders. In either case, the argument about the stolen body serves the same end; it quiets arguments against the reality of Jesus' bodily resurrection. Gordon Howie has come to a conclusion similar to Weren's, but from a different angle, comparing Matthew's rhetoric to Greco-Roman works where familiar myths are revised and critiqued from a rationalist perspective[8]. He cites examples from as early as the 5th century BCE, showing that stating the counterargument, then refuting it, is a standard method in the rhetorician's handbook.

Some kind of controversy fuels the rhetoric. Several elements combine to show that, for Matthew, this controversy is about the corporeal reality of Jesus' resurrection:

(1) If it were about some kind of spiritual immortality, say, spiritual apotheosis, a vision by the followers, a continuation of Jesus' message or charismatic energy, and the like, no detail about a guard at the tomb or stolen body would apply. The body's absence or presence would not matter, nor would the counterarguments make sense. The tomb would not need to be sealed extra-tight, nor would a guard need bribing to relate a story of theft of Jesus' body, because the tomb would remain untouched.

(2) The language of error or deceit implies a wrong interpretation stemming from an empty tomb. Jesus as a *planos*, deceiver, links to the concern that "the last deception will be worse than the first". Coupled with the sealing of the tomb, deception must refer to the explanation of the corpse and its whereabouts.

(3) Matthew adds particular details to Mark's narrative to prove that it is the correct tomb, and that Jesus' body is not stolen. For example, in Mark, Joseph of Arimithea rolls a stone to seal the grave. In Matthew, it is a "great stone", not easily removed or accidentally dislodged. In Mark, the women "saw" where Jesus was laid, whereas in Matthew, they are "sitting opposite the tomb", so are in increased proximity and are there for some time, so they are better witnesses. Unlike Mark, Matthew begins with a closed tomb, and the readers witness the rolling away of the stone. These are all in addition to the obvious apologetic motifs of the delegation to Pilate and the bribing of the guard.

(4) Matthew shores up the credibility of women's witness vis-à-vis Mark, despite an apparent distaste for the women's discipleship[9]. In general, Matthew evinces little interest or appreciation of Jesus' women disciples or

---

8. J. G. HOWIE, *The Evangelist and the Revisers: Revision and Counter-Revision in Matthew 27 and 28,* in *Hyperboreus* 13 (2007) 209-242.

9. See my article, *Excellent Women: Female Witness to the Resurrection,* in *JBL* 116 (1997) 259-272.

women in any capacity. If we consider the gospels as a whole, up to, but not including the passion narratives, he is the least interested in the women around Jesus. Yet in the story of Jesus' burial and the discovery of the empty tomb, he improves considerably their role from Mark's version. In Mark, they saw where the body was laid (15:46), whereas in Matthew they were sitting across from the tomb, almost as if they too had taken up a guard (27:61). In Mark they come to anoint Jesus' body (16:1). In Matthew they come to *see* the tomb, indicating a witness, including the witness that there is no confusion about which tomb Jesus had occupied (28:1). Matthew adds the words, "Come, see", and "Go, tell" (28:6-7), adding a sense of urgency to the women's commission. In Mark they do not report the empty tomb as instructed, but run away afraid (16:8), whereas in Matthew they show fear *and* joy, and go off to report the empty tomb. More significant, they are the first to meet the risen Jesus, and take hold of his feet, proving he is not a ghost. Matthew amplifies the women's role as guarantors of the credibility of Jesus' burial, the lack of confusion over which tomb was the right tomb, the fact that it was empty, and the physical reality of the risen Jesus. Couched in a gospel that is otherwise indifferent to women, the amplification of the women's witness serves Matthew's purpose of proving the physical truth of Jesus' resurrection.

(5) The arc of Jewish and pagan objection to Jesus' resurrection has a fairly long trajectory, beginning in the gospels. (Interestingly, Paul says the cross is a stumbling block to Jews, but does not mention the resurrection. Nor does he include Jews in the controversy over resurrection in 1Cor 15, nor include resurrection in the controversy with Jewish teachers in Galatians.) Matthew's narrative is the starting point in the trajectory, where there is little reason to doubt his aside, "This story has been spread among Jews to this day". But apologetic touches like the eating of the broiled fish (Luke 24:42-43) or Thomas asking to touch Jesus' side and hands (John 20:27-28) suggest someone questions the veracity of a physical resurrection at an early date. A century later Celsus confirms their apologetic function when he says, "After death he rose again and showed the marks of his punishment and how his hands had been pierced. But who saw this? A hysterical female..." (*Ag. Cel.* 2.55).

Similarly, Mary's question to Jesus in John, when she thinks he is the gardener implies that *someone* says seeing Jesus' body has been moved, "Sir, if you have carried him away, tell me where you have laid him, and I will take him away" (20:15) The apocryphal *Gospel of Peter* describes similar scenes of scribes and Pharisees asking for a guard at the tomb and suppressing the story, but it amplifies even further the Jewish role (they seal the tomb and wait for the guard) and adds details to present an airtight apologetic (they seal the tomb 7 times, see Jesus rise, and admit the truth of the resurrection). Justin shows that the resurrection is still problematic, transmitting the claim that the Jews think Jesus' body was stolen by the disciples to tout his resurrection (*Dial.* 108.2). He also goes to lengths to prove the resurrection from Scripture (32.3-6; 106-108), although his interlocutor Trypho voices no objections, suggesting a continuing debate in his own day.

Jewish and Christian disputes over Jesus' resurrection seem nearly inevitable. Jewish expectations did not include a messiah who would be crucified and die, so they could hardly make sense of one who rose from the dead. Even Celsus understands this: "we are not aware that a Jew would say that the expected Christ would show in himself an example of the resurrection" (*Ag. Cel.* 2.77). Finally, Tertullian refers to Jewish claims that the disciples stole the body to fake the resurrection, and that a gardener removed Jesus' body to avoid crowds trampling his lettuces (*De Spectaculis* 30.6). The continuing vitality of this debate underscores the likelihood that in Matthew's time, such a debate over bodily resurrection was real, and a factor in the separation of Matthew's group from other Jewish communities. One cannot imagine it about any other kind of afterlife, spiritual immortality, personal mystical experiences of the risen Jesus, or the attendant meaning of the event, since the details of the apologetic speak only about a body and its whereabouts.

III. Resurrection as Symbolic

I prefer the term "symbol" to "metaphor" because, as Paul Tillich, cited by Gerd Lüdemann, says, "a symbol participates in the reality of that to which it points"[10]. For example, President Obama is a symbol of America, but he is also continuous with and part of America. Uncle Sam, however, is a metaphor. Whatever the country is, it is not a mythical person in a striped hat. For Matthew, then, resurrection is not either corporeal or symbolic, but is both, and though corporeal, must certainly go beyond that.

As Denaux, Lüdemann and others have pointed out, there is no resurrection *story*[11]. Of the elements of the earliest creed in 1Cor 15:3-7, where

---

10. P. TILLICH, *Symbol und Wirklichkeit* (Kleine Vandenhoeck-Reihe, 151), Göttingen, Vandenhoeck & Ruprecht, 1966, p. 4, cited in G. LÜDEMANN, *Resurrection of Jesus: History, Experience, Theology*, Transl. J. Bowden, Minneapolis, MN, Fortress, 1994, p. 178.

11. A. DENAUX, *Matthew's Story of Jesus' Burial and Resurrection (Mt 27,57–28,20)*, in BIERINGER –KOPERSKI – LATAIRE, *Resurrection in the New Testament*, 123-145, p. 128; LÜDEMANN, *Resurrection of Jesus*, p. 28.

Jesus' death, burial, and resurrection are understood *according to the Scriptures*, followed by appearances, the resurrection is the one element that is not described in the gospels. Why not? Are there no oral traditions that address it? *The Gospel of Peter* feels free to invent or pass on a story of a Jesus emerging from the tomb, followed by a talking cross. The absence of such traditions in the canonical gospels cuts both ways in considering historicity. On the one hand, it suggests no tradition is preserved. No one saw him emerge from the tomb. On the other hand, it argues for reliability for the rest of the narrative, because it proves that the gospel authors are not ready to invent a scene out of whole cloth, even if they believe the event took place.

The absence of a resurrection scene cannot be because of any reticence about supernaturalism on Matthew's part. He expands the Transfiguration story to include dramatic details like Jesus' shining face or the disciples overcome by fear, elements that Allison has pointed out, accompany the Sinai revelation. The empty tomb narrative in Matthew is reminiscent of Sinai, as Matthew adds an angel with a shining face and dazzling clothes, a descent of a powerful figure, and guards shaking with fear[12]. Matthew expands the empty tomb story from Mark, adding an earthquake, and changing Mark's young man into a dazzling angel who descends from heaven. But in spite of his attraction to supernatural elements, he does not supply a story of Jesus emerging from the tomb.

Notably, Matthew's interest in promoting the corporeality of Jesus' resurrection ends with 28:15. The appearance narrative is extremely brief and reticent, and lacks any "proofs" of his embodiment. The eleven "saw" him, which could mean in a vision, a dream, or a mirage. No one touches him, takes hold of him, sees him eat, or any of the other apologetic touches that appear in Luke and John. Matthew provides no material to refute the antagonists of chapters 26 and 27. Presumably the disciples hear him, when he commissions them in v. 18. But the commission takes the form of a prophetic call, similar to the prophets of the Hebrew Bible. Jeremiah, for example, says, "The Word of the Lord came to me saying…" (1:4; 2:1).

The elements of Matthew's narratives that stress the corporeality of Jesus' resurrection seem particularly attached to the polemical material that Weren and Howie delineated. When not addressing opposition, Matthew moves beyond corporeality to the ways in which Jesus' resurrection points beyond itself. Startlingly, Matthew says that some of the eleven disciples doubted,

12. Allison has shown that the Transfiguration and the Jesus' death are nearly twin scenes, using themes of darkness/light, witness by saints/sinners, fear of the witnesses, Jesus confessed as the Son of God. Since the empty tomb scene shows some of these same features, perhaps it forms a sort of third panel in a triptych.

suggesting Jesus' appearance was ambiguous. We are left in nearly as much doubt as at the end of Mark. Did all of the eleven come around to the conviction that they saw Jesus? Did some continue to doubt and fall away? Did they preach even though they were in doubt? Such an opaque and unyielding ending leaves room for the non-corporeal interpretations of Crossan, ("the juice was not turned off"), Lüdemann ("we must stop with the historical Jesus but we may believe that he is also with us as one who is alive now")[13], and De Jonge, ("a continuation of that which had begun before it in response to his person, preaching, and actions")[14].

The resurrection narratives repeat the phrase, "he has been raised (from the dead)". It appears in fixed form three times, including its appearance in the guard story (27:64) in the mouth of the detractors. It qualifies as a speech act, a statement that encompasses a set of values of a certain group. Pamela Eisenbaum shows how "the God who raised Jesus" becomes a performative speech act in Paul and early Christian texts, similar to "the God who brought us out of Egypt"[15]. It is not simply a truth claim, which is assumed, but a new name for God. It is a statement about God's power that implies the hearer's own resurrection. Eisenbaum points out that it is never used apologetically. Thus the repetition in the empty tomb narrative makes a broader statement about God and the world.

Declaring Jesus has been raised means more than it says, because belief in resurrection means more than it says. In my book, *Resurrection of the Body in Early Judaism and Christianity* I discover a constellation of ideas that accompanies belief in resurrection of the body in multiple sources. To sum it up in a few sentences, belief in resurrection of the body carries with it a set of convictions: God is a god of power, who created the world and continues to be interested in the material world he has created. The human body, as part of that creation is fundamentally valuable. The human person is an inextricable combination of body and soul. For justice to be done, resurrection must take place and precede judgment. Those who profess resurrection of the body truly understand the Hebrew Scriptures. People who preach resurrection therefore carry an authority, or legitimacy. I call this a creation theology – a view of the world that affirms the goodness of the material world, including the body, as God's creation, that stems from the

---

13. LÜDEMANN, *Resurrection of Jesus*, p. 183.

14. H.J. DE JONGE, *Visionary Experience and the Historical Origins of Christianity*, in BIERINGER – KOPERSKI – LATAIRE, *Resurrection in the New Testament*, 35-53, p. 49.

15. P. EISENBAUM, *A Speech Act of Faith: The Early Proclamation of the Resurrection of Jesus*, in V. WILES – A. BROWN – G. SNYDER (eds.), *Putting Body and Soul Together: Essays in Honor of Robin Scroggs*, Valley Forge, PA, TPI, 1997, pp 24-45.

Hebrew Bible. I argue that saying "I believe in resurrection of the body" becomes a condensation symbol, or shorthand for this creation theology, a set of assumptions about God and the world.

I became interested in this topic when I noticed the multiple instances where belief in resurrection seemed to be a dividing line between who was in or out of the community. As early as the 50's Paul declares belief in resurrection as the *sine qua non* of the community of believers. He says, "How can some of you say there is no resurrection of the dead? If there is no resurrection of the dead, then Christ has not been raised". For the Pharisees, preaching resurrection distinguishes them and, according to Josephus, contributes to their popularity with the people. The Sadducees, on the other hand, are written off by Jesus as ignorant of the Scriptures and God's power because of their non-belief in Mark and Matthew (Mark 12:18-27; Matt 22:23-33; Luke 20:27-40). The apologist Justin Martyr, writing in the mid-second century, says that those who deny the resurrection do not deserve to be called Christians (*Dial.* 80:3-5). He also coins the term "resurrection of the flesh", which obviates any "spiritualizing" of the process. The rabbis, in the Mishnah fixed in the early third century, similarly reject resurrection – deniers as one of three groups who will not inherit the World to Come (the others are those who deny the divine origin of the Torah and the Epicureans – *m. Sanh.* 10:1; cf. *t. Sanh.* 13:3-5). Since the Mishnah begins by declaring that "All Israel has a share in the World to Come", the rabbis are reading the deniers out of the community. These examples show that the belief in resurrection, like any symbol, reaches beyond itself, becoming a tool to draw the boundaries of communities. I suggest that it is because it carries with it a set of assertions and condenses them into a single symbol.

IV. MATTHEW'S VIEW OF JESUS' RESURRECTION

If these elements are folded into the concept of resurrection and are constitutive of community identity, then Jesus as the one who is raised takes on these elements and projects them outward. He becomes the locus of this creation theology in all its fullness for Matthew's community. "He has been raised" *means* all of the principles elucidated above: Jesus is God's power, the unified human, the promise of justice, the legitimator of the community.

Jesus' resurrection need not be one thing only, or occur in only one mode. As my earlier survey suggests, a mix of ideas may appear alongside each other in the same document without much conflict. Neither Matthew nor anyone else in this period is writing systematic doctrine, but everyone is struggling with the problem of mortality and the apparent triumph of Roman power. Images may appear together which, if pressed to their conclusions, are contradictory, but circle around the same themes of God's power, embrace of the created world and hope for justice. In resurrection, imagination, emotion, and transcendence flow together.

Matthew constructs his empty tomb narrative drawing on a number of themes that infuse biblical and rabbinic traditions: God as a god of power, as Creator of earth, flesh, and stars, as the saviour of Israel, as the enemy of death, as the one who liberates a whole community.

(1) Matthew emphasizes the power of God in his empty tomb story, adding the drama of an earthquake, the angel descending and rolling back the stone, the guards shaking with fear. That resurrection is associated with God's power is demonstrated in nearly every example I came across from the first two centuries. In Jewish liturgy, the early (pre-mishnaic) section that declares God as the "one who gives life to the dead", appears in the *Gevurah* "power" blessing of the central prayer of the *Šemoneh Esreh* "Eighteen" blessings, alongside references to him as the God who sustains the living, frees the captives, brings death and restores life. "Who is like you, O God of power"? appears in its current form. In the conflict story with the Sadducees over the woman with seven consecutive husbands, as we just saw, Jesus claims that the Sadducees' rejection of resurrection shows they understand neither the Scriptures, nor the power of God.

(2) Jesus' resurrection demonstrates that God is Saviour of a whole people. Jon Levenson, in his book, *Resurrection and the Restoration of Israel,* cites rabbinic midrash that show death and resurrection accompany some of the pivotal moments in Israel's history – the *Akedah*, the binding of Isaac, and the giving of the Torah at Sinai, and of course, judgment at the End of Days. In *Pirqe Rabbi Eliezer* 31, for example, Isaac's soul took flight when the sword reached his throat, but returned to his body when the angel stayed Abraham's hand. This proves resurrection is in the Torah, the midrash continues, and ends with Isaac reciting the *mechayeh hametim* blessing, blessing God who raises the dead[16]. The event of the Akedah has communal consequences, as it becomes part of the merit of the Fathers, a spiritual savings account from which later generations may draw. Similarly, the communal event of encountering God at Sinai, as related in *b. Šabb.* 88b, overwhelms the people of Israel so that their souls depart, until God's revivifying dew

---

16. J. LEVENSON, *Resurrection and the Restoration of Israel: The Ultimate Victory of the God of Life*, New Haven, CT, Yale University Press, 2006, pp. 227-228.

brings them back to life[17]. While these references are late, they show the communal nature of the resurrection. The implications of resurrection in biblical and early Judaism are highly social, about a holistic survival embedded in community and memory. This may help us understand the odd statement in Matthew, that the guards at the tomb shook and "became like dead men" – that they too died and were revived at a momentous event in the history of a community.

Similarly, Matthew projects the communal implications of Jesus' resurrection in the charge to announce it to the disciples, and the subsequent mission to bring the gospel to all nations. Wright talks about Jesus' resurrection as a "collaborative eschatology"[18], and refers to Matt 27 in particular as showing an "incorporative Messiahship"[19]. Particularly the events of vv. 51-53, where the dead saints of Israel are restored to life and emerge from their tombs, fit with the notion of resurrection as a communal event, part of the restoration of Israel. It seems to be a two-stage process, where they do not fully emerge until his resurrection.

(3) The "God who raised Jesus", like "the God who acted at Sinai", or "the God who brought us out of Egypt" is the powerful Creator and Sustainer. The struggle against death flows from a biblical attitude that God is the enemy of death, even if he himself is the author of life and death. Levenson shows the Hebrew Bible projects the idea of a Divine Warrior who is victorious over death. Restoration of a whole people by a powerful God, the victorious and sustaining God of life also undergirds resurrection in 1 Maccabees 7.

In conclusion, Matthew understands the resurrection of Jesus on several levels. The corporeal resurrection of Jesus seems inescapable. It comes to the fore particularly when Matthew and his community are faced with opposition to it, either in the form of Jewish objections from outsiders or questions from insiders. Human nature is that we all become more pointed and simplistic when faced with opposition. The nature of a condensation symbol is to show one monochromatic face to the world, but incorporate a range of more nuanced understandings within[20].

Matthew also uses resurrection in a richer, varied, symbolic way. Within the empty tomb and appearance narratives, he incorporates a number of

17. *Ibid.*, p. 226.
18. STEWART, *The Resurrection of Jesus*, p. 31.
19. *Ibid.*, p. 44.
20. A.P. COHEN, *The Symbolic Construction of Community* (Key Ideas), Chichester, Horwood – London, Tavistock, 1985, p. 21.
21. Anthony Cohen says such symbols evoke an emotional response, often draw on a mythic past, and sum up a set of values.

elements. The Divine Warrior who took the side of Israel against his enemy, death, has acted once again. God's power invests the material world, including the body, with significance. The human being cannot be made whole without the body, so the women take hold of Jesus' feet, assuring themselves that he is not a ghost. Like other apocalyptic thinkers, Jesus' victory over death is the beginning of the overturning of powers, both Satanic and worldly, that oppose the righteous, the inauguration of the new age. The mission to the disciples to transform the world implies the transformation is at hand, and is not in heaven, but in the world as they know it. Just as the prophets were called at times of political and historic change, the disciples are summoned. Last, the legitimacy of the believers is summed up in the belief in resurrection, against the doubters, drawing the lines between "us" and "them" quite clearly. Matthew's description of the empty tomb and appearance of Jesus is not only about the fate of Jesus' body, but about a whole set of assertions about a powerful God, his attachment to the material world, and the integrity of a fledgling community.

Manhattan College   Claudia SETZER
Riverdale,
New York City, NY 10471
USA
10471

RESURRECTION OR ASSUMPTION?
MATTHEW'S VIEW OF THE
POST-MORTEM VINDICATION OF JESUS

It is customary to refer to the early Christian belief in the post-mortem vindication of Jesus simply in terms of bodily resurrection. Indeed, mainstream New Testament exegetes often take for granted that this was the only early Christian conception, or in any case the sole "orthodox" explanation for Jesus' continuing existence. When it comes to Matthew, the *prima facie* evidence surely points to a resurrection interpretation of Jesus' post-mortem vindication. Yet some recent Gospel studies alert us to the possibility that Matthew was also acquainted with other conceptualizations of Jesus' post-mortem existence. Since space is limited, I just discuss two fresh surveys of interest for the present theme. The first comes from Daniel A. Smith, who has scrutinized the Markan and Q traditions behind Matthew. The second is from David Roger Aus, an expert in early Jewish and rabbinic traditions and their bearing on the Gospels. Having presented and preliminarily evaluated these two surveys, I will take a closer look at Matthew's final chapters to see whether the Matthean conception of Jesus' post-mortem existence can be understood solely in terms of bodily resurrection.

I. The Assumption of Jesus in Mark and Q According to D.A. Smith

Daniel A. Smith's 2003 article[1] and his later monograph[2] seek to establish the thesis that both Q and the pre-Markan tradition behind the empty tomb narrative conceived of Jesus' post-mortem fate in terms of assumption. If this thesis should prove correct, there is certainly reason to take a closer look

---

1. D.A. Smith, *Revisiting the Empty Tomb: The Post-Mortem Vindication of Jesus in Mark and Q*, in *NT* 45 (2003) 123-137.
2. D.A. Smith, *The Post-Mortem Vindication of Jesus in the Sayings Gospel Q* (Library of New Testament Studies, 338), London, T&T Clark, 2006.

at Matthew, too. Not only were Mark and Q arguably Matthew's main
literary sources; coming from more or less independent traditions, these
sources are likely to cover a considerable range of the earliest Christian
memory of Jesus. Smith distinguishes very carefully between *assumption* and
resurrection as two distinct ways of conceptualizing Jesus' post-mortem survival and vindication. Unfortunately, Smith does not provide one comprehensive definition of these concepts; rather, he repeats his general assessment
of the concepts with minor modifications throughout the monograph. His
"tentative" definition, which hardly becomes much more accurate in the
summary of the book, runs as follows:

> Assumption and resurrection have different views of the fate of the body and
> different theological associations. Assumption involves the disappearance of the
> body, pre- or post-mortem, although … the language of assumption was also
> used euphemistically for someone who had died. Resurrection involves an
> appearance of the resurrected person, rather than the disappearance of the
> body, whether or not the body is thought of as being reconstituted or not.
> Assumption … is associated typically with divine favour and status elevation,
> and consistently in Jewish thought with special eschatological function. With
> resurrection, such ideas – particularly exaltation – are sometimes present, but
> often with special exegetical rationale[3].

The focus here lies on the *disappearance* of the translated body as opposed
to the *appearance* of the risen person. This distinction is anything but clear
in Mark: Mark combined the disappearance of Jesus' body with his promised appearance in Galilee, and the Markan transfiguration story depicted
the visionary appearance of translated Old Testament heroes. Smith also
admits generally that an assumption may be witnessed by those who have
seen the translated person. Thus it may not be advisable to posit too sharp
a distinction between assumption (removal, translation, disappearance) and
resurrection in the mind of Mark or other early Christians. Still, the two
conceptions are not fully interchangeable. One obvious difference worth
stressing is that resurrection tends to be a corporate rather than a merely
individual phenomenon. Thus, while in the Pauline and much of the post-
Pauline tradition Jesus' resurrection is a unique and decisive moment in
salvation history, it is above all the *beginning* (the "first fruit", 1 Cor 15:20)
of general resurrection, or also – less apocalyptically – the mythic centre of
salvation in which the believers are to *participate*. Assumption, by contrast,
is more concerned with the *individual hero's* exceptional status elevation

---

3. SMITH, *Vindication*, p. 52. As examples of "special exegetical rationale" Smith refers
to Rom 1:3-4 (resurrection and exaltation), Rom 8:34 and Acts 2:31-36 (enthronement
theology based on Ps 2).

from a mortal life into the sphere of immortal beings; or alternatively, an immortal being's return to the heavenly realm. Hence – as also the appearance/disappearance distinction suggests – resurrection is often associated with the perceived *presence* of the risen one while assumption rather signals the *absence* of the translated hero. However, these are just ideal types; in practice the distinctions are often blurred.

Concerning the Markan empty tomb story, Smith readily admits that the evangelist's interpretation was in terms of resurrection rather than assumption. That is fair enough, because both the three passion *and* resurrection predictions[4] in chapters 8, 9, and 10, as well as in 14:27-28, together with the words of the young man in the tomb in 16:6 ("He has been raised again [ἠγέρθη])" can hardly be understood otherwise. However, the passion predictions may well be due to Mark's redaction, which would also render most of the young man's message in 16:6-7 redactional (cf. καθὼς εἶπεν ὑμῖν v. 7, referring back to the previous predictions). If the young man's function was only to underline the numinous character of the event and to witness the removal of Jesus' body from the tomb, the narrative is actually a disappearance story, implying assumption rather than resurrection. The motifs of seeking and being embarrassed at not finding the body of the deceased hero are typical of assumption narratives, as is also the role of witnesses. Also, the difficulty with the exhortation to "tell his disciples and Peter" to go to Galilee, a message the women fail to deliver, would vanish at once. Smith refers to Chariton's novel on Chaereas and Callirhoe, where (*Chaer.* 3.3) the former finds his beloved Callirhoe's body missing from her tomb. Although in fact no assumption has taken place, this is how Chaereas immediately interprets the event, even wondering if Callirhoe had been taken away by a divinity or was herself a goddess. Smith concurs with Sjef van Tilborg's and Patrick Chatelion Counet's remark that this "is a text which prototypically determines how ... the disappearance of a body from a grave was interpreted religiously"[5].

The assumption interpretation of the empty tomb narrative is in itself no novelty. The first to suggest it was Elias Bickermann as early as 1924[6]. This view was taken up by Neill Hamilton (1965), who however thought that

---

4. It is customary to speak of the Markan *passion* predictions, which is understandable because the sayings clearly have the passion in focus (as Peter's reaction in 8:32 indicates!). However, the resurrection "after three days" is also predicted in all the sayings.

5. SMITH, *Revisiting*, 129-130, referring to S. VAN TILBORG and P. CHATELION COUNET, *Jesus' Appearances and Disappearances in Luke 24* (Biblical Interpretation, 45), Leiden – Boston – Köln, Brill, 2000, p. 194.

6. E. BICKERMANN, *Das leere Grab*, in *ZNW* 23 (1924) 281-292.

the empty tomb narrative was Mark's own creation and purposefully shaped as "a story of Jesus' translation in resurrection guise"[7]. Smith rejects this hypothesis, which is hard to reconcile with Mark's repeated passion and resurrection predictions as well as with the wording of 16:6.

In her analysis of the Markan empty tomb scene, Adela Yarbro Collins argued for the unified nature of the whole pericope. Like Hamilton, she considered it to be a Markan creation or "fiction" rather than an elaboration of some older tradition[8]. At the same time, she in effect regarded the Markan narrative as an assumption or translation story in the fashion of ancient tales, inspired especially by the importance of the graves of the heroes in the Greco-Roman world[9]. Collins saw no contradiction between assumption and resurrection as far as Mark is concerned: "the author of Mark had interpreted the early Christian proclamation of the resurrection by composing a narrative about the empty tomb"[10]. In other words, Mark simply conceived of Jesus' resurrection in terms of an assumption. Smith refutes this reasoning and sides with Bickermann's hypothesis of an underlying source modified by the evangelist.

In principle, the need to construe a tradition-historical predecessor ought to weaken the force of Smith's interpretation. At the same time it must be noted, first, that the idea of a slight reworking in Mark 16:1-8, in accordance with the redactor's emphases elsewhere in the Gospel and in accord with the Pauline passion-resurrection tradition (1 Cor 15:3-7), is not far-fetched. Secondly, Collins's interpretation shows that this tradition-historical hypothesis is virtually unnecessary – Mark 16:1-8 as it stands can still be read as an assumption story. The question of a possible Markan source or tradition is therefore less decisive on *this* matter[11]. However, while a pre-Markan empty tomb tradition is not necessary for the assumption interpretation, it may prove to be a plausible hypothesis on *other* grounds – and if such a tradition can be made probable (as I think it can), then Smith's hypothesis will readily explain how and why Mark has edited it.

---

7. N.G. HAMILTON, *Resurrection Tradition and the Composition of Mark*, in *JBL* 84 (1965) 415-421, p. 416.

8. A.Y. COLLINS, *The Beginning of the Gospel: Probings of Mark in Context*, Minneapolis, MN, Fortress, 1992, pp. 129-138.

9. COLLINS, *Beginning*, pp. 138-143.

10. COLLINS, *Beginning*, p. 136.

11. SMITH, *Vindication*, p. 164, concedes: "It may be, however, that the question of a pre-Markan disappearance story is moot, because in its present shape – for which Mark of course is responsible – the empty tomb narrative still is more like an assumption story than a resurrection story. Even Mk 16.7 is not entirely out of place here because…an epiphany often serves to conform that an assumption has taken place".

The sayings Gospel Q seems to provide more direct evidence, except of course for the fact that Q itself is a scholarly hypothesis. All modern scholars of Q agree that this Gospel lacks a passion (and consequently resurrection) narrative. It is also widely acknowledged that this lack is not accidental or due to the alleged catechetic *Sitz im Leben* of the material, but is indicative of the theological profile of the Q Gospel[12]. As John Kloppenborg has observed, sayings such as Q 6:22-23 and 11:47-51 interpret Jesus' death as "an instance of the 'typical' – perhaps climactic – prophetic death"[13]. It is not that Q is unaware of Jesus' death on the cross. To the contrary, Q 14:27 ("whoever does not take up his cross and follow me cannot be my disciple") evokes Jesus' shameful death and interprets it as a paradigm of discipleship. This does not mean, however, that there was a pan-Christian "Easter kerygma" which Q presupposes. Jesus' death does not necessarily imply resurrection as the mode of vindication. Kloppenborg remarks that Q displays no signs of applying resurrection language to Jesus, in spite of the fact that Q 11:31-32 speaks of the Queen of the South and the Ninevites as being raised (ἐγερθήσεται, ἀναστήσονται) at the judgment to serve as the accusers of 'this generation'[14]. The traits of Wisdom Christology in Q (cf. Q 7:35, 10:21-22) might also, in Kloppenborg's view, suggest that no special moment of vindication was necessarily needed, since the speaker in Q, being God's Wisdom, already has his authorization from God[15]. However, the document does envisage Jesus in a new post-mortem function as the coming Son of Man, so obviously the Q people had some idea of his vindication after death. Although the precise form of this turn from death to a heavenly figure remains somewhat conjectural, Jesus' lament over Jerusalem in Q 13:34-35 seems to give some clues:

> "Jerusalem, Jerusalem, who kills the prophets and stones those sent to her! How often I wanted to gather your children together, as a hen gathers her nestlings under her wings, but you were not willing! Look, your house is forsaken! …I tell you, you will not see me until [[⟨the time⟩ comes when]] you say, Blessed is the one who comes in the name of the Lord" (Smith, *Vindication*, p. 30, quoting *The Critical Edition of Q*).

---

12. Rightly R. URO, *Apocalyptic Symbolism and Social Identity in Q*, in R. URO (ed.) *Symbols and Strata: Essays on the Sayings Gospel Q* (Publications of the Finnish Exegetical Society, 65), Helsinki, Finnish Exegetical Society – Göttingen, Vandenhoeck & Ruprecht, 1996, 67-118, here p. 111 n. 127: "To argue that Q does not presuppose the Easter stories of the canonical Gospels is not an argument from silence. Q reflects the vindication of Jesus in its own peculiar way…".

13. J.S. KLOPPENBORG VERBIN, *Excavating Q: The History and Setting of the Sayings Gospel*, Minneapolis, MN, Fortress, 2000, p. 373.

14. *Ibid.*, p. 378.

15. *Ibid.*, p. 375.

It is noteworthy that Mark has the same acclamation "Blessed is the one who comes in the name of the Lord" (Ps 117:26 LXX) in his narrative of Jesus' entrance into Jerusalem (Mark 11:1-11). Since there are no traces of an entrance story in Q, the acclamation obviously refers to an eschatological event *after* Jesus' disappearance (through death). Dieter Zeller, in a seminal 1985 essay, interpreted the enigmatic "you will not see me again..." in v. 35b analogously to the description of Elijah in 2 Kings 2:12. There it is stated that Elisha "no longer saw him", a disappearance that encouraged in later tradition the expectation that Elijah would return in a new eschatological role. The disappearance thus invites the imagery of assumption. Kloppenborg finds this a plausible interpretation and suggests that "the Q people may have regarded Jesus' death as death of a just man or a prophet whom God had assumed, pending some future eschatological role"[16].

Daniel Smith's contribution in his 2006 monograph is not only to scrutinize the key passage Q 13:34-35, but also to make a more general case for the significance of assumption theology in early Christianity and to highlight its Jewish and Hellenistic antecedents or parallels. Essentially, Smith confirms Zeller's and Kloppenborg's train of thought concerning the Q passage. He stresses especially the designation of Jesus as "the coming one" (ὁ ἐρχόμενος), a term that Q had already employed in 3:16, where John the Baptist proclaims the coming one, and in 7:19, where John sends his disciples to ask Jesus if he indeed is the coming one or not. The term, then, has unmistakable christological and soteriological connotations in Q. Smith highlights particularly its connecting, assimilating function between Q's Wisdom and Son of Man Christology[17]. The withdrawal of Wisdom corresponds to the removal or disappearance of the earthly Son of Man, and the "coming one" is Jesus both during his earthly ministry and as the heavenly Son of Man.

---

16. *Ibid.*, p. 378.

17. SMITH, *Vindication*, pp. 112-119. One interesting issue that Smith does not discuss in detail is the time aspect of ὁ ἐρχόμενος. The present participle refers in Q 3:16 quite naturally to a person coming (soon) after John, as Matthew's insertion ὀπίσω μου (from Mark) shows. Q 7:19 is more complex (it would seem that Jesus has already *come*), while in Q 13:34-35) Jesus' coming (*parousia*) is still ahead and takes place after his temporal disappearance. Thus the eschatological edge of the designation ὁ ἐρχόμενος unfolds only in the end. In the Markan narrative of Jesus' entrance into Jerusalem the same Psalm (117:26 LXX) as in Q 13:35 (Matt 23:39) is cited, but the reader will understand that "the coming one" is Jesus on his way to Jerusalem. In Matthew the entrance comes before the lament over Jerusalem, so looking back from 23:39 the reader can interpret the entrance as a partial anticipation of the eschatological fulfillment of the Q logion.

Since Q 13:35b suggests a scenario of disappearance-absence-return, Smith examines also two other sets in Q that describe a similar scenario: Q 19:42-46 and 19:12-13.15.23: the return of an absent master, Q 12:39-49 and 17:23-24: the invisibility and sudden appearance of the Son of Man. Although the assumption is never stated *expressis verbis*, the recurring scheme certainly suggests that Q's theology is based on the idea of Jesus' sudden removal and return rather than on his resurrection as the firstborn from the dead as in the Pauline tradition (cf. Rom 8:29; 1 Cor 15:20; Col 1:18). In sum, there is much to suggest that the Q Gospel interpreted the end of Jesus' earthly ministry as a sort of removal or disappearance of a righteous man, a God-sent prophet and an envoy of God's Wisdom. At the same time, the document betrays knowledge of Jesus' death on a cross, so that a pre-mortem assumption à la Enoch or Elijah is precluded.

Smith also discusses early Christian instances of assumption tradition outside Mark and Q, including the ascension of Jesus according to Luke. However, he does not pay attention to the Gospel of John, which certainly makes use of assumption *terminology*[18] and arguably – as I have tried to show elsewhere – even reworks a specific assumption *tradition* concerning Jesus[19]. If

---

18. SMITH, *Vindication*, p. 82 n. 203, notes that the usual verbs for assumption in Hellenistic Jewish writings are μετατίθημι and ἀναλαμβάνω as well as ἁρπάζω (an interesting case is Mark 2:20!). In John none of these verbs is used, but instead we find μεταλαμβάνω (ἐκ τοῦ κόσμου τούτου πρὸς τὸν πατέρα, 13:1) and ὑψόω (mostly in passive, 3:14, 8:28, 12:32.34). In some contexts δοξάζω has a similar tone (12:16.23, 17:1.5). Most notably, the fourth Gospel speaks of Jesus' *disappearance* or his *not being seen / found* any longer (8:21 with 13:33;12:36;14:22).

19. My hypothesis is that John 1–12 is a reworking of an underlying written non-passion layer of material ("the Gospel of glory"), which ended in the divine Word's withdrawal from, and his last appeal to the world at the end of ch. 12. The hypothesis was first put forward in my article, *Incarnatus est? Christ and Community in the Johannine Farewell Discourse*, in J. MRÁZEK – J. ROSKOVEC (eds.), *Testimony and Interpretation: Early Christology in Its Judeo-Christian Milieu*, London – New York, T&T Clark, 2004, pp. 247-263. The next article, *Working in the Daylight: John 9:4-5 and the Question of Johannine "Literary Archaeology"*, in *SEÅ* 70 (2005) 265-279, examined more closely the Johannine redaction in ch. 9 as well as the theme of Jesus' "day work" that belongs to the non-passion layer. In *The Witness of Blood: The Narrative and Ideological Function of the 'Beloved Disciple' in John 13-21*, in A. MUSTAKALLIO – H. LEPPÄ – H. RÄISÄNEN (eds.), *Lux Humana, Lux Aeterna: Essays on Biblical and Related Themes in Honour of Lars Aejmelaeus* (Publications of the Finnish Exegetical Society, 89), Helsinki, Finnish Exegetical Society – Göttingen, Vandenhoeck & Ruprecht, 2005, pp. 164-185, I argue that the Beloved Disciple, introduced in ch. 13, is first and foremost the reliable witness of the passion narrative (including Jesus' corporeal death). In the article, *Testament and Consolation: Reflections on the Literary Form of the Johannine Farewell of Jesus*, in J. PAKKALA – M. NISSINEN (eds.), *Houses Full of Good Things. Essays in Memory of Timo Veijola* (Publications of the Finnish Exegetical Society, 95), Helsinki, Finnish Exegetical Society – Göttingen, Vandenhoeck & Ruprecht, 2008, pp. 573-590, I argue that the main bulk of the first farewell speech in ch. (13-)14 and of the concluding prayer in ch. 17 also belong to the non-passion tradition as an oral sequel to "the Gospel of glory".

we are allowed to add the pre-Johannine tradition to Mark and Q, the conclusion must be that assumption theology was no isolated phenomenon. Quite the contrary, it was surprisingly widespread in the earliest times of the Christian movement.

II. As Moses, So Jesus: Mark's Empty Tomb Tradition According to R.D. Aus

As noted, Adela Yarbro Collins regarded the empty tomb narrative as a Markan creation. This hypothesis challenges the majority view that there was, in addition to general history-of-religion models, an existing Jesus tradition behind Mark's narrative. A recent monograph by Roger David Aus, with the rather exhaustive title, *The Death, Burial, and Resurrection of Jesus, and the Death, Burial, and Translation of Moses in Judaic Tradition* (2008)[20], traces the Markan tradition – and to some extent the canonical Gospel tradition at large – back to a midrashic, typological use of biblical and early Jewish traditions concerning the death of Moses[21]. Considering the importance of Moses typology particularly in Matthew, Aus's observations and hypotheses are interesting indeed. However, we should bear in mind that Matthew's Gospel was not the primary subject of Aus's study.

While dedicating the study to "(a)ll those who, like myself, firmly believe in the resurrection of the dead", Aus is anything but apologetic. Historically, he affirms, the body of Jesus was probably placed by a Jewish servant of the Sanhedrin (that is, neither by a Roman soldier nor a member of the Sanhedrin) in a burying place for criminals. All the disciples and adherents had fled when Jesus was arrested, so nobody knew any longer where Jesus was buried. They may have realized that the likely burial site

---

20. R.D. Aus, *The Death, Burial, and Resurrection of Jesus, and the Death, Burial, and Translation of Moses in Judaic Tradition* (Studies in Judaism), Lanham, University Press of America, 2008.

21. The methodological scope of Aus's study is problematic. The general aim is to elucidate and argue for a Mosaic typology in all and any of the four Gospels (and occasionally in other canonical texts). The analysis proceeds according to an intrinsic parallel chronology, proceeding from efforts to kill Jesus/Moses to the farewell speech of Jesus/Moses, and on to their death, burial, and resurrection/translation. Aus's method tends to produce a maximalist interpretation, where – to put it crudely – *some* Judaic traditions coincide with *some* Gospel accounts. At the same, Aus does suggest detailed tradition-historical routes from Jesus to the Gospels, or from Mosaic traditions to the Jesus narratives. The conglomeration of ideas I present in this paper belongs to the latter category, and Aus makes clear that he is tracing the pre-Markan development.

was among the executed criminals, and therefore they could have seen in Jesus' fate the fulfillment of Isa 53:9, "And they made his grave with the wicked"[22]. If this was the harsh historical reality, how did the first Christians advance a story where Jesus' body was properly buried by a certain "Joseph of Arimathaea, a respected member of the Council and a man who looked forward to the kingdom of God"? And how could they tell that the body was laid "in a tomb cut out of the rock" (Mark 15:42-47)? Quite naturally, according to Aus: they learned it from the Bible, more precisely, from the traditions concerning Moses, the moving water-supplying rock in the wilderness, and the mystery of Moses' burial and death. In addition, the Song of the Well (Num 21:18) played a role in shaping the empty tomb tradition.

The midrashic procedure, as Aus reconstructs it, is rather imaginative[23]. The ideological point of departure was provided by a messianic Moses typology: "As the first redeemer (i.e., Moses), so the final redeemer (i.e., the Messiah)". Thus attention was drawn to the enigmatic burial of Moses in Deut 34:5-6: "There in the land of Moab Moses the servant of the Lord died, as the Lord had said. He was buried in a valley in Moab opposite Beth-peor, but to this day no one knows his burial place". Although some later interpretations read the text against the grain and stressed the public nature of the burial, others focused on the intriguing fact that neither the death nor the burial of Moses was known. This then led to various speculations that in part embellished the sparse mention of Moses' burial: perhaps Moses buried himself, or was buried by angels, or by God himself[24]? In part, the enigmatic notion of Moses' being buried without any person being there to bury him invited an idea which run even more against the canonical version than did the public burial interpretation: Moses was in fact translated directly to God without dying. Among those who were aware of this tradition, and possibly themselves held some such belief, were Philo of Alexandria and Josephus, while the author of *Biblical Antiquities*

---

22. Aus, *Death*, pp. 142-143.

23. For a less imaginative historical-critical survey, see, e.g., M. Myllykoski, *What Happened to the Body of Jesus?*, in I. Dunderberg – C. Tuckett – K. Syreeni (eds.), *Fair Play: Diversity and Conflicts in early Christianity*, Leiden – Boston – Köln, Brill, 2002, pp. 43-82. Myllykoski discusses, among other things, Crossan's suggestion that Jesus was not buried at all and that the figure of Joseph of Arimathea is a total Markan creation. Myllykoski himself finds more historicity behind the burial narrative and the character of Joseph: "I find it likely that the Jewish high priests, powerful men and other members of the Sanhedrin …buried Jesus, like many others who had been crucified routinely in a graveyard of crucified criminals close to the place where he was crucified" (p. 81).

24. Aus, *Death*, p. 160.

(*Pseudo-Philo*) seems to combat this tradition[25]. The clearest passages that render this tradition are found in rabbinic sources[26]. The transfiguration narrative in Mark 9:2-10 suggests that both Moses and Elijah came from heaven to meet Jesus and his company. Elijah was known to have ascended to heaven, and Moses is hardly pictured as coming to the scene from his grave[27]!

Besides the unknown (and, as some of Mark's contemporaries believed, empty) grave, Moses' departure involved another peculiar feature. The well, shaped like a rock, rolled along and accompanied the Israelites on the stations of their forty-year wilderness journey – until it disappeared on the day of Moses' death. According to *Targum Neofiti 1* on Num 21:19-20, the well was "hidden" for the Israelites at the site of Moses' burial, namely, "in the valley which is at the boundary of the Moabites, the top of the height which looks out opposite Beth Jeshimon". Aus remarks that the ancient interpreters had no difficulty with the combination of valley and top of the height, because Deut 34:1.5.6 and Num 21:20 seem to give both places as the site of Moses' death/burial[28]. The site of Moses' death and burial, which according to Deut 34:1 was Pisgah, is in later documents known by several names, often as "a high place" or "a height/heights" or, understood as an Aramaic place name, *Ramatha*. Aus proposes that the person who buried Jesus was named (Joseph of) *Arimathaia* (with a prefixed *aleph* as was common in place names) on grounds of this tradition. Additional proof that the name is derived from the Moses tradition is that all the epithets of Joseph of Arimathea named in Mark 15:43 – "a *respected* member of *the council* who was also himself waiting expectantly for *the kingdom of God*" – occur in the Song of the Well, associated via Pisgah/Ramatha in Num 21:20 with the site of Moses' burial and death. The noun Pisgah, in turn, is rendered as τὸ λελαξευμένον in Num 21:20; 23:14 LXX; Deut 3:17(B); and 3:27, that is, "The Place Hewn out of

---

25. *Ibid.*, pp. 208-216.

26. *Ibid.*, pp. 216-222. At least one of the rabbinic texts (*Sifre* on Deuteronomy) is Tannaitic.

27. *Ibid.*, pp. 216-217. Mark 9 must be a perplexing chapter for anyone who tries to systematize the "New Testament teaching on resurrection". In the story world, the disciples wonder what resurrection from the dead might mean (v. 10). The reader of Mark will also wonder what it means that Elijah has already come (v.13) – the narrative Jesus obviously refers to John the Baptist (as Matthew makes clear), but Elijah as the heavenly figure that appears in the transfiguration narrative is hardly identical with the executed John the Baptist. The identity seems to be of a typological kind (the Baptist is *like* Elijah), but it is difficult to pinpoint precisely in what sense Mark or his tradition meant it.

28. AUS, *Death*, pp. 158-159.

Rock". Thus there was a very old tradition stating that God or the Israelites[29] buried Moses in a tomb hewn out of rock – as Mark 15:46 and Matt
27:60 relate of the tomb provided for Jesus' body by Joseph of Arimathea[30].

The fact that the well/rock in the wilderness inspired Paul (and probably
already his tradition) to a Christological interpretation (1 Cor 10:1-4)[31]
confirms that the early Christians had read this part of their Bible. Aus adds
yet other features to the well tradition that informed the pre-Markan empty
tomb narrative. The well in the wilderness was identified in Judaic tradition
with "Jacob's well", mentioned in Gen 29:1-14. In the Genesis story, the
mouth or opening of the well was covered with a large stone, which could
be rolled away only after "all the flocks were gathered there" (vv. 3.8) –
which gives the impression that all the shepherds from a number of flocks
were needed to move the stone. Gen 29:8 was interpreted as speaking of
three shepherds, and their combined strength was not enough to roll away
the stone. When Jacob alone could move the stone (v. 10), he must therefore have been miraculously strong. For Aus, this is a key to explaining the
Markan empty tomb scene. The three women at the tomb who were unable
to move the large stone and the young man in the tomb, who might be
thought of as having rolled away the stone, correspond to the three shepherds and Jacob[32].

In sum, Aus provides a set of detailed hypotheses to explain the emergence of the empty tomb narrative as an innovative, midrashic use of biblical traditions. Generally speaking, the idea that the formative ideas behind
the empty tomb narrative come from a Jewish Christian rather than a Gentile Christian interpretive activity is to be welcomed. It is, *a priori*, quite
plausible that an early interpretation of the vindication of Jesus' death comes

29. The LXX reads "They buried", meaning the Israelites, whereas the Masoretic text
reads "He buried", meaning God.

30. Aus, *Death*, pp. 168-171.

31. *Ibid.*, pp. 151-155. Aus assumes that Paul received this interpretation from a Palestinian Jewish Christian tradition. I too find a pre-Pauline tradition at least possible, because
Paul's reasoning does not quite fit in the context. If the rock was really the Christ, it would
seem that the Israelites were not only baptized into Moses (v. 2) but received the blessings of
Christ as well – which is obviously more than Paul wished to say. Cf. also the well/living water
theme in John 4 and 7:37-38 as well as the bread of life discourse in John 6. I think, however,
that Aus (p. 153) goes too far in interpreting the blood and water in John 19:34 as an allusion to the wilderness tradition.

32. Aus, *Death*, pp. 180-183. Aus (p. 189) even details his interpretation by quoting
targums and rabbinic texts that deal with the "dew of heaven/ resurrection", a blessing that
Jacob had received on the 14th of Nisan, just before the Passover feast. The miracle at the
well, when Jacob rolled away the stone, took place *on the third day* after the blessing.

from Jewish Christian circles. However, the plausibility of Aus's detailed hypotheses is extremely difficult to assess. The associative chains are long and in practice impossible to verify or falsify. The well/rock traditions seem promising, because there are clear indications in several early Christian texts that this scriptural tradition was reflected upon. The explanation for naming Joseph of Arimathea as the owner of the tomb hewn out of rock is economical, because it too stresses the impact of the well/rock tradition. If one accepts – as I am inclined to do – the historical hypothesis that Jesus was buried in a mass grave for criminals provided by Jewish authorities, then the main options for explaining this name are either a historical reminiscence or some sort of midrashic interpretation of Scripture – and since Mark seems ignorant of even the name of the chief priest at the trial of Jesus, the latter alternative is a real possibility.

However, much of Aus's reconstruction remains in doubt. Scholars with differing methodological preferences will certainly disagree on the plausibility of his overall thesis. As far as the present study is concerned, there is one line of inquiry that permits a critical evaluation of Aus's thesis, namely, to observe whether or not Matthew was aware of any such interpretive traditions as Aus assumes. Of all the Gospel writers, Matthew is likely to be the most conversant with Scriptural traditions and allusions. He would also be expected to appreciate a Moses typology and, recognizing it in his tradition, to enhance rather than suppress it. If Matthew shows awareness of, and even develops the formative traditions that Aus discerns behind the Markan account, this may strengthen the hypothesis; if not, the hypothesis is weakened although not definitely falsified.

III. MATTHEW'S EMPTY TOMB AND RESURRECTION NARRATIVES

As we take a look at Matthew's empty tomb and resurrection narratives, the question is whether the evangelist betrays any knowledge of, or interest in, assumption imagery in general (Smith) and Moses typology in particular (Aus). Matthew's redaction of Mark and the Matthean special tradition are the chief indicators, but it is important also to consider Matthew's story as a whole to see if the overall arrangement complies with a resurrection or assumption imagery and if there is some overarching Moses typology.

In the crucifixion narrative, Matthew follows Mark quite closely while adding or strengthening the scriptural allusions in 27:34 (diff Mark 15:23), 27:35 (diff Mark 15:24), and 27:43 (diff Mark 15:32). Several of the allusions have striking parallels with the speech of the ungodly who oppress the righteous man in Wis 2:10-20, which in turn draws on Isa 52-53 and Ps 22[33]. There is no clear trace of Moses typology in Matthew's crucifixion scene. The most conspicuous reworking is in 27:51-53, which renders a Matthean special tradition. When Jesus had given up his spirit, Matthew follows Mark in telling that "(a)t that moment the curtain of the temple was torn in two from top to bottom". What follows comes from Matthew's own tradition: "The earth shook and the rocks split. The tombs broke open and the bodies of many holy people who had died were raised to life. They came out of the tombs, and after Jesus' resurrection they went into the holy city and appeared to many people". After the inserted passage, Matthew continues roughly as Mark: "When the centurion and those with him who were guarding Jesus saw the earthquake and all that had happened, they were terrified, and exclaimed, 'Surely he was the Son of God!'" In Mark, however, the centurion was alone to comment on Jesus' death, while Matthew has added his companions (the Roman soldiers) and indicates that their response was not simply to the way Jesus died, but specifically to "the earthquake and (all) that had happened (τὰ γενόμενα)".

This latter reworking refers clearly to the earthquake (not mentioned in Mark) and something else that happened at the same time, that is, at least the splitting of the rocks. Whether or not τὰ γενόμενα also refers to the opening of the tombs is less certain, but the expression seems so unspecified and generalizing that I think Matthew somehow wished to include this spectacular event, too, all the more so because the earthquake, the splitting of the rocks and the opening of the tombs obviously go together and form an increasing series of connected events: the earthquake shatters the rocks, and as a result the dead bodies are being "released" from their graves. Naturally the soldiers could not be expected to see the last mentioned event, and still less the appearances of the raised holy ones which took place later. Matthew may nevertheless try to give the impression that the soldiers were witnessing something quite extraordinary and decisive. If this inference is correct, then the placing of the insertion must be original to Matthew's Gospel and is to be interpreted in this context[34]. For our purposes the most important conclu-

---

33. W.D. DAVIES – D.C. ALLISON, Jr., *A Critical and Exegetical Commentary on the Gospel according to Saint Matthew.* Vol. 3 (ICC), Edinburgh, T&T Clark, 1997, p. 609.

34. DAVIES – ALLISON, *Critical*, Vol. 3, p. 634, suspect the words μετὰ τὴν ἔγερσιν αὐτοῦ are an early gloss, but the manuscript evidence for this is rather slender. Others have wondered whether Matthew's tradition did not originally belong with the earthquake in 28:2. In view of the renewed mention of earthquake at Jesus' tomb on the Easter morning, again in the presence of (apparently) Roman guard soldiers (28:2-3), it is not impossible that Matthew's tradition had connected the opening of the tombs with the empty tomb narrative. Such a connection would slightly strengthen Aus's interpretation in that the moving of the stone

sion is that Matthew's special tradition connected Jesus' death and resurrection with a collective mode of resurrection. The legend obviously did not explain what happened to these resurrected people or how this event relates to the general resurrection at the end of time. Nor does Matthew seem to have asked such troubling questions. The legend renders an eschatological sign, not an eschatological doctrine. Generally speaking, this Matthean special tradition and its use by the redactor illustrate the corporate dimension of resurrection belief. Much more than the assumption of a hero or a heavenly messenger, the death and resurrection of Jesus is an event that touches the lives of all his followers – and even the lives of those who preceded him.

The special Matthean tradition also had a story about the guards of the tomb. This apologetic tradition is probably an answer to the allegation of the opponents that the disciples had stolen the body of Jesus (cf. 28:13). The tradition and the allegation itself might be understood in terms of assumption. There is also a detail that might support Aus's hypothesis of an underlying Jacob's well tradition, because the stone at Jesus' tomb seems to be an important element both in the guard story (27:66, σφραγίσαντες τὸν λίθον) and in the angelophany (28:2, ἄγγελος...κυρίου ...προσελθὼν ἀπεκύλισεν τὸν λίθον). The implication seems to be that the guards placed so huge a stone at the tomb that no man alone (and certainly no woman) could roll it away. When the angel removed the stone, an earthquake or a tremble resulted.

However, this detail is hardly significant enough to warrant Matthew's or his tradition's awareness of an alleged pre-Markan tradition. The huge stone is already mentioned in Mark. In the present context in Matthew's Gospel the guard story is obviously meant to serve as a proof for Jesus' bodily resurrection "on the third day" after his death (cf. 27:63.64). Since the previous instance of Matthean special tradition – the opening of the tombs – also points to a resurrection belief, the probability is that the mode of Jesus' vindication in the special tradition here, too, is based on resurrection rather than assumption. Likewise, the special Matthean scene in 28:9-10 with Jesus' appearance to the women who hurried from the tomb would as such be understandable in an assumption story, but its present context makes it unequivocally an appearance of the risen Jesus[35].

---

gains even more prominence and is more directly tied with the tradition of Jacob's blessings as "the dew of resurrection" (AUS, *Death*, pp. 187-194). This is a bit too speculative, however. The latter earthquake in Matthew 28:2 seems to be a minor one (a tremble caused by the moved stone), so there is no necessary connection.

35. The chances are that the scene is Matthew's creation based on Mark's empty tomb narrative. Jesus only repeats the angelic message, so the scene is virtually unnecessary. It is not excluded, however, that Matthew's tradition knew of Jesus' appearance to a group of women.

IV. THE FINAL SCENE: JESUS ON A MOUNTAIN

Thus far, we have not found clear indications of assumption theology in Matthew. Neither have we observed any specific Mosaic typology at work. It remains to be seen whether the last scene with Jesus and the eleven disciples "on a high mountain" can change the picture. It is generally acknowledged that the Matthean "mountain" is heavy with theological symbolism. It is already symptomatic that the several mountains of Jesus' ministry are not named in Matthew – what is important is not the geographical location but the symbolic value. What makes the symbolism of "mountainness" difficult to decode in detail is the fact that the themes connected to the mountain scenes are quite diverse. Indeed, it seems that each and every of the mountain scenes highlights one specific theme associated with the "mountain". What, then, is the unifying symbolism of the mountains of Jesus' testing (4:1-12), basic instructions (4:25-8:1), healing (15:29-31), transformation (17:1-8), and final commissioning (28:16-20)?

Of a number of suggested scholarly interpretations, I find three especially illuminating although their mode of interpretation is quite different. The *ritual* interpretation advanced by K.C. Hanson explores the mountain scenes from the point of view of transformation and status change[36]. In Hanson's view, there is a ritual progression from the mountain of initiation-ordeal (the testing of Jesus, 4:1-12) and the mountain of initial and basic instruction (chs. 5-7) through the mountain of healing (15:29-31) and of epiphany (17:1-8) to the mountain of commissioning (28:16-20). The mountain is an ideal symbol for a rite of passage, as it involves an initial separation from the community ("climbing up"), an intermediary time "on top" where the decisive transformative event takes place in separation from the outer world, and a return ("down") to the community in a new social status. Hanson notes that the missing element in the final commissioning, when compared to the other mountain ascension passages, is that neither Jesus nor the Eleven rejoin society; the scene ends with all of them still together on the mountain. This lack of closure provides the Gospel with an open end: the success of the Eleven is left undeveloped, Jesus remains standing within the community, the future is uncertain except for Jesus' vow of continued presence. Jesus' status as the one to whom all authority has been given is firmly established, but it is uncertain what will become of the newly commissioned apostles. Much of this interpretation is illuminating, but the

---

36. K.C. HANSON, *Transformed on the Mountain: Ritual Analysis and the Gospel of Matthew*, in *Semeia* 67 (1994/1995) 147-170.

closure of the Gospel with a still picture of Jesus and his apostles together
on a mountain needs further clarification. The open end in Matthew's Gospel does not seem to be ritually determined. The status change is obvious
for Jesus' part only, and it is actually just an announcement of the change
that has taken place. The apostles' new role is only envisaged but not realized. Their staying on the mountain with Jesus – "to the end of time", as it
were – contradicts the progressive idea inherent in ritual transformations.

Terence L. Donaldson, in his perceptive study on the mountain symbolism in Matthew, discusses several possible intertextual and thematic interpretations of the final scene. Impressed by the centripetal force of the still
picture, he opts for a *Zion symbolism*: "As one who is greater than the temple, Jesus replaces Zion as the centre of eschatological fulfillment. He is the
one around whom the people are to gather and to whom the Gentiles will
make procession"[37]. There is much to commend this line of interpretation,
and Donaldson is able to connect the Zion theme to some other Matthean
mountain scenes, as well as to interpret the final commission as the sum-
ming up and logical conclusion of the previous scenes. It is also instructive
to note how the Johannine idea of Jesus as the pneumatic replacement of
the temple (John 2:21) – and for that matter, as the replacement of any
mountain of worship (cf. John 4:21) – develops ideas that are found in
Matthew. Thus the Zion imagery is suggestive on a general level, as a symbol for the inviting "centre" of worship (cf. Matthew 11:28: "Come to
me...").

However, on the textual level the Zion imagery is less than obvious. Here
studies that stress the role of *Mosaic typology* in Matthew are needed to complement the picture. The most extensive survey on this topic is by Dale
Allison (1993)[38]. In critiquing Donaldson's interpretation, Allison rightly
points out that there is no reason to play down the Sinai/Horeb motif in
Matthew in order to defend the Zion motif. Already in the Hebrew Bible
Sinai and Zion are clearly associated, as in Ps 89 and Ezek 40, and this
tendency continues in later Jewish tradition. A key text is Isa 2:2-3: "out of
Zion shall come forth Torah"[39]. The final mountain scene in Matthew
recalls first and foremost the mountain of Jesus' programmatic teaching
(chs. 5-7), since it is there that Jesus most clearly delivers "all that I have
commanded you". It is there his surpassing teaching authority is revealed
for the first time (7:28), and it is there Jesus announces the fulfillment of

---

37. T.L. DONALDSON, *Jesus on the Mountain: A Study in Matthean Theology* (JSNTSup,
8), Sheffield, JSOT Press, 1985, p. 185.
38. D. ALLISON, *The New Moses: A Matthean Typology*, Minneapolis, MN, Fortress, 1993.
39. ALLISON, *The New Moses*, 325.

the law and the prophets in a principled way (5:17-20), antithetically vis-à-vis customary Torah teaching (5:21-48), and in a brief summary (7:12). There, Jesus also indicates that obedience to his teaching is required for those who will enter into the promised kingdom (7:13-27). All of this resembles – while overriding – the law-giving at Sinai (Exod 19-23).

Allison makes the interesting observation that the Mosaic allusions pervade particularly the first seven chapters in Matthew, beginning with the birth and infancy stories and until 8:1[40]. Another finding is that the clearest allusions appear approximately in the same order as in the Hebrew Bible. This order is, of course, partly predetermined: in the beginning is birth and infancy, in the end death and burial – though in the case of Moses, his death is not quite certain in the subsequent tradition although it is told in the Hebrew Bible, while in the case of Jesus, the death is quite certain in Matthew but is followed by his resurrection.

That the final scene in Matthew somehow alludes to (the death of) Moses is a relatively common opinion, although not all scholars see a connection[41]. There is an even greater consensus for regarding Dan 7:13-14 LXX, where the Son of Man is given full ἐξουσία, as an essential source of inspiration. Allison concludes that when the elements evidently drawn from Dan 7 and those features that are paralleled in other resurrection narratives are removed, the following elements remain: the mountain, the command to go and disciple the nations, the imperative to observe all Jesus has commanded, and the promise of perpetual divine presence. The mountain motif in itself recalls Moses and the giving of the law (as it did in chs. 5-7), and the three other items are found in God's instructions to Joshua after the death of Moses, Josh 1:1-9 (cf. also Deut 31:23). In addition to these narrative elements, Allison also notes parallels in vocabulary. He infers that Matt 28:16-20, like 1 Chron 22:1-16 and Jer 1:1-10, is "a commissioning narrative with Mosaic associations" [42]. I agree, provided that the analogy is not driven too far[43].

---

40. *Ibid.*

41. One exception is W.S. BAXTER, *Mosaic Imagery in the Gospel of Matthew*, in *Trinity Journal* 20 (1999) 69-83. Baxter seeks to interact with Allison's "important" but "tenuous" work (p. 70 n.4). Although "Matthew's Gospel is speckled with images of Moses" (p. 79), Baxter finds no such image after the last supper. The distinction between Mosaic typology (which Baxter denies to Matthew) and Mosaic imagery seems unclear to me. According to Baxter, Moses typology would demand explicit citation (p. 81) – but is not quoting from the Torah (5:21-48) or introducing the figure of Moses on the mount of transfiguration explicit enough?

42. ALLISON, *The New Moses*, p. 64.

43. An example of over-interpretation is K.L. SPARKS, *Gospel as Conquest: Mosaic Typology in Matthew 28:16-20*, in *CBQ* 68 (2006) 651-663. Sparks observes the same Mosaic allusions as Allison and others, but he makes too much of the perceived antagonism between the brutal conquest of the land by Joshua and the peaceful mission to the nations by the apostles:

Essentially, then, Allison finds in Matthew the same rabbinic maxim as Aus stressed in the pre-Markan tradition: "It follows that Matthew designed his conclusion so as to generate an implicit parallel between Jesus and Moses. Just as the lawgiver, at the close of his life, commissioned Joshua both to go into the land peopled by foreign nations and to observe all the commandments in the law, and then further promised his successor God's abiding presence, so similarly Jesus: at the end of his earthly ministry he told his disciples to go into all the world and teach observance of all the commandments uttered by the new Moses; and then he promised his abiding presence"[44]. Another scholar puts the typological idea in slightly different words, stressing the superiority of Jesus in comparison to the "old" archetype: "Just as on Mount Sinai or Horeb Moses encountered God and received from him the law, so on a mountain during the ministry the disciples had seen the glory of God in the transfigured Jesus and received from him an interpretation of the Law: 'You have heard it said but I say to you'"[45]. I agree that this is a pertinent parallelism, irrespective of how consciously the redactor had planned his Mosaic typology. We cannot know Matthew's mind, but the allusions are there.

V. CONCLUSION: RESURRECTION OR ASSUMPTION –
WHAT'S THE DIFFERENCE?

In the end, it may be somewhat misleading to describe Matthew's Jesus as "the new Moses". The Matthean Christology, as also the canonical Gospels' Christology at large, is throughout a "more-than" Christology[46]: Jesus is *more than* Moses, Elijah, Solomon or any other figure in the Hebrew Bible – or also, *quite other* than these antecedents. As Allison notes, "(t)he first Gospel displays no independent interest in Moses. The man of God's silent yet forcible presence is in servitude to the Messiah"[47]. Since the typology is based on the final type (Christ), rather than the initial one (Moses),

---

"For Matthew, the ultimate 'conquest' of the nations would be accomplished not by sword but by going out, baptizing and teaching" (p. 661). Sparks is not too worried about what he admits may be an over-interpretation: "If Matthew did not intend to make the typological points that I am suggesting here, then I dare say he would wish that he had" (p. 663)!

44. ALLISON, *The New Moses*, p. 266.

45. R.E. BROWN, *The Resurrection in Matthew (27:62-28:20)*, in *Worship* 64 (1990) 157-170, p. 167.

46. I borrow this suggestive term from my Uppsala predecessor Prof. René Kieffer and his article, *"Mer-än"-kristologin hos synoptikerna* (= *"More-than" Christology in the Synoptics*), in *SEÅ* 44 (1979) 134–147.

47. ALLISON, *The New Moses*, p. 275.

the latter remains partial. Also, the final type permits *several* partial proto-
types: the Matthean Christ gathers elements not only from the first redeemer
and law-giver, but even from the Davidic king, the Wisdom of God, and
so on.

Our chief interest here, of course, is whether and how the Mosaic typology illuminates Matthew's conception of the post-mortem vindication of
Jesus. As we have observed, Matthew and probably his special tradition, too,
articulate a rather standard resurrection belief. Aus's ingenious hypothesis
has not been confirmed, but not falsified either. All we can say is that Matthew is well aware of, and actively develops, a Mosaic typology in the early
chapters as well as in the final scene of the Gospel. However, no clear trace
of an assumption Christology has surfaced – unless, then, the Mosaic typology in itself gives reason to doubt that what we see is not all there is. Allison
touches on this possibility in a footnote, as he remarks that if Matthew was
aware of and accepted the tradition concerning Moses' ascension to heaven,
then the parallelism between Moses and Jesus would have been all the more
evident[48]. Since the Markan transfiguration story, which Matthew took
over, suggests that Moses indeed was taken into heaven, it is quite plausible
that Matthew knew of some such tradition. Unfortunately, the Mosaic
typology permits several applications. We might consider forms of simple
parallelism, such as this: Moses was taken into heaven (after or at the time
of his death), and so was Jesus (either in and through resurrection or later
as a separate act as in Luke-Acts). Alternatively, the parallelism might be
more antithetical, for instance: Moses did not die but was translated directly,
whereas Jesus went through death (for the atonement of sins) and was raised
on the third day. And there are more possible nuances. Even if we knew
that Matthew meant some parallelism between Moses and Jesus concerning
the mode of their death/resurrection/assumption, we could not decipher the
precise meaning or purpose of that parallelism[49].

Nevertheless, if we venture *beyond* Matthew's purposes, some conclusions
may be drawn about the actual *function* of his resurrection belief. The final
scene harks back to the beginning of the Gospel, where Jesus is called Immanuel, or "God with us" (1:22-23). Jesus' last words in 28:20 are: "I am with
you always to the end of the age". This is certainly not assumption imagery.
On the face of it, the final scene fulfils many of the ideal aspects of resurrection theology: it is all about divine presence and corporate participation. But

---

48. *Ibid.*, p. 266 n. 320.
49. If one prefers a deconstructionist mode of analysis, one might even conclude that the
mountain of the final commissioning is the burial site of the new Moses – it is there that
Matthew's Jesus remains until the end of the world!

then again, the aspect of presence is brought about through a metaphor, which effectively signals absence as well. The question is, *how* does the Risen One reflect God's presence among his people? Although there is no definite answer, a great deal of this presence must consist in the teaching and the commandments referred to in 28:19. As 23:8 confirms, Jesus' authority is essentially the authority of his teaching. There are other aspects, too – Jesus the law-giver is also the redeemer (1:22) like Moses – but even in 11:25-30 Jesus is first and foremost a teacher (v. 29: μάθετε ἀπ' ἐμοῦ !). In this respect, the mode of post-mortem existence is much the same for Jesus and Moses. The resurrected Jesus is depicted as present, but functionally this means the presence of his teaching, redemptive work and moral example[50]. The translated Moses may be said to be absent – but the law he mediated, the liberation he brought and the example he gave are still present. What is the difference? Matthew may have felt that there is a difference, either in terms of comparison ("more than") or antithesis ("quite unlike"). But even if he did believe so, I doubt that any scholarly method is able to prove him right.

There is no denying that my analysis of Matthew's empty tomb and resurrection narratives has yielded very modest results. The evangelist and his community may have been aware of a variety of resurrection or translation beliefs, but the Gospel text is quite clear about Jesus' bodily resurrection on the third day. Perhaps this obvious conclusion is more interesting than it appears. It is striking that Matthew was so content with the Markan empty tomb narrative – suggestive of a translation story but interpreted as a resurrection story – that he in principle only tied the loose ends that Mark had left (Jesus' appearance to the women to ensure that the disciples received the message, and the promised *rendez-vous* in Galilee) and added the guards from his special tradition. John and Luke narrated Jesus' several appearances to the disciples stressing the material reality of Jesus' resurrection body[51], and Luke even adds the ascension of Jesus to logically complete the story[52]

---

50. It is widely acknowledged that Matthew does not stress the role of the Holy Spirit as the successor of Jesus after the resurrection, despite the trinitarian baptismal formula in 28:19. This is in accord with Matthew's stress on the presence of the resurrected Jesus himself.

51. In comparison with John and Luke, Matthew seems rather disinterested in the bodily nature of the risen Jesus. This may have to do with the metaphorical touch of the final episode, but it is unlikely that Matthew was deliberately demythologizing a realistic view of resurrection.

52. A separate account of Jesus' ascension to heaven would not have been needed in the translation model. Luke's elaborate sequence of resurrection, a liminal period (of forty days, Acts 1:3) and ascension amounts to a *rite of passage* – during and through which the apostles became competent to fulfill their new roles as the messengers of the resurrected Jesus. Luke's solution highlights an inherent logical *difficulty* with the resurrection model, but also the generative, interpretive *possibilities* this model provided.

– but they, too, accepted the basic Markan model. Mark's combination of the Pauline resurrection tradition (1 Cor 15:3-7) and an empty tomb narrative thus became the winning concept. Whatever the precise intent of Matthew's Mosaic typology, his most enduring contribution was to promote this "orthodox" resurrection belief[53].

Åbo Akademi University   Kari SYREENI
Faculty of Theology
Biskopsgatan 16
20500 Åbo
Finland

---

53. I thank my colleagues Risto Uro (Helsinki) and Thomas Kazen (Stockholm) for useful comments on the next-to-final draft of the manuscript. Kazen expressed his general view of the topic in a manner I fully endorse: the issue is exciting – but what a pity that Matthew was such a mainstream theologian!

MATTHEW AND THE FATE OF HUMANKIND

As we know the Greco-Roman world was a world full of gods. And the Roman world thought much and wrote often about death and life beyond death. Of course there were those that rejected the notion of the gods, fate, and that there was anything beyond this life. These voices were minorities, and found most often at or near universities. I have a fifth-century B.C.E. ostracon – black attic ware – from the Athenian agora which contains very simply but nonetheless obstinately, *ATHEOS*, scrawled in Greek, backwards – that is, Atheist. But for most Romans the world was full of domestic, civic, most high gods who played central personal, domestic and political roles for them. To think otherwise was an exception. The gods managed one's fate. They determined who had a good death, how and when we crossed over. The myriad of funerary inscriptions from the Roman period put us in touch with the musings and reality of death and life beyond death in the Roman world. And this vast corpus of material demonstrates for us a broad range and diversity of beliefs and hopes. Many of this genre capture what Burkert referred to as expression of "personal needs" in this life or the next. "I escaped from this evil and found the better"[1]. Many, many more capture simply the average person's thoughts and beliefs about their own death and what may follow. The widespread mystery cults of the Greco-Roman period offered a genre of *Erlösungsreligionen* on a personal level.

While not alone in this point of view Burkert asserted perhaps as vigorously as anyone that "in contrast to Christianity, (these Greco-Roman) mysteries appear both more fragile and more human"[2]. The pathos, the complexity, and range of emotions concerning fate, death, and life without a loved one pepper the funerary remains of our period.

> "The cruel fates have left me sad and old," writes a father whose daughter had died. "I will always be searching for you my darling…Sadly shall I often imagine

---

1. W. Burkert, *Ancient Mystery Cults* (Carl Newell Jackson Lectures), Cambridge, MA., Harvard University Press, 1987, p. 19.
2. *Ibid.*, p. 28.

> your face to comfort myself. My consolation will be that soon I shall see you when my own life is done, and my shadow is joined with yours" (CIL II.3771)[3].

Or simply,

> Death is not the end of life. (Propertius, 4.7)

Or again,

> Here I lie dead and am ashes. Ashes are the Earth. If Earth is a goddess, then I am a goddess and I am not dead. (CIL VI.35887)

Such poignancy is vividly expressed in the words from a Roman funerary inscription from the third-fourth century. A boy of pious parents, one Antonios, had obtained priestly status while still a child only to die at the age of seven. The words posing as those of the deceased boy are clearly those of the parents confronting the reality of cruel fate.

> I performed the mysteries always in august fashion. Now I have left the august sweet life of Helios. Therefore you, *mystai* or friends of whatever kind of life, forget all the august mysteries of life, one after the other; for no one can dissolve the thread spun by the Fates. For I, Antonios the august, lived only seven years and twelve days. (Inscriptiones Graecae XIV, 1449)[4]

The ways in which Romans expressed their thoughts and beliefs about life after death were almost as varied as those beliefs themselves. Most, whether Stoic, farmer, agnostic city dwellers, or eastern Monotheists believed there was something after this. The gods were in control of that. Some, but by no means all, believed there was some correlation between one's life and actions here and where and how one ended up at the close of either their life or the end of time.

An exception here seems to be the ossuaries of Palestine from the Hellenistic and Roman periods magisterially compiled by Rahmani. In examining the inscriptions from the ossuaries one finds little in the way of speculation about the next life, no sardonic comments and in fact very little information outside the family name. They are far more formulaic in this regard, save the occasional brief curse; e.g., "may blindness strike the one who removes these bones"[5].

3. Cf. K. HOPKINS, *Death and Renewal* (Sociological Studies in Roman History, 2), Cambridge, Cambridge University Press, 1983, pp. 227-228.

4. L. MORETTI, *Inscriptiones Graecae Urbis Romae* III (Studi pubblicati dall'Istituto italiano per la storia antica, 28), Rome, Istituto italiano per la storia antica, 1979, inscr. 1169. Burkert briefly touches upon the reluctance some translators have shown in capturing the full force of the inscription's disillusionment.

5. L.Y. RAHMANI, *A Catalogue of Jewish Ossuaries in the Collection of the State of Israel*, Jerusalem, The Israel Antiquities Authority – The Israel Academy of Sciences and Humanities, 1994, p. 197

Philo of Alexandria characteristically captures his happy blend of Jewish, Hellenistic, and Stoic philosophy on this subject in many places. "The good man," he writes, "does not die but departs, in order to show that the soul purified cannot be extinguished and cannot die. The soul departs by way of migration from this earth to heaven and therefore does not undergo the destruction which death appears to bring" (*Her.*, 275-283). Goodness and justice results in the purification which leads the soul to the next life.

At Qumran a range of passages express that community's conviction in the duality that exists in this world between good and evil, light and darkness, and the good and bad ways. Following that path of light and truth impinges directly on one's eternal fate:

> These are the paths in the world: to enlighten the heart of man, straighten out in front of him all the paths of true justice, establish in his heart respect for the precepts of God; it is a spirit of meekness, of patience, generous compassion, eternal goodness, intelligence, understanding, potent wisdom which trusts in all the deeds of God and his abundant mercy…These are the foundations of the spirit of the sons of truth in the world. And the reward for all those who walk in it will be healing, plentiful peace and a long life, fruitful offspring with everlasting blessings, eternal enjoyment with endless life, and a crown of glory with majestic raiment in eternal light. (1QS IV, 2-8)

As we would expect there is a corresponding set of curses for those sons of darkness who have forsaken the true path and practice instead all kinds of impurities. They live an eternity of "unending dread in the everlasting pit, with shame without end – and if that is not bad enough, "all are destroyed" (1QS IV, 11-14).

Here it would appear we are getting closer to the voice of our subject Matthew. He is someone who understands a just path for his adherents. In chapter five, and elsewhere in the Gospel, that way is described in language similar to 1QS IV. Characteristic of the measure of apocalypticism he maintains – which serves as further indication that he is a Second Temple thinker – Matthew believes in a judgment for those who are outside – it would seem particularly leaders or teachers – in his version of the just way taught and expressed through Jesus. And there is an end of time, or the big time, when divine judgment is meted out. Those who did not live according to this way "go to eternal punishment, while the righteous (go) into eternal life" (Matt 25:26).

Like so many of his contemporaries Matthew does believe in heaven. As K. Syreeni has pointed out Matthew has a "polarizing" tendency that comes through when thinking about the next life. This is a fairly consistent feature of his ethic and worldview. Pharisees are excluded in the world to come

according to his way of thinking (5:20; 23:13-15. 27-28). Syreeni noted this
polarizing aspect of Matthean theology is an aspect of his symbolic universe
that seems to pervade his thinking[6]. This is an important insight into Matthew's relations with his contemporaries in Galilee or Damascene Syria.
While this insight into Matthew's ethic and view of others is fundamentally
correct, we should add that the relationship between heaven and earth specifically in Matthew is a bit more nuanced and not as radically polarized as
one might suppose. The terms *heaven* and *earth* are not as polarized as they
might first appear. Matthew's working of the Lord's prayer in 6:10 makes
explicit what is implied in the antitheses of the previous chapter. Of course
in his symbolic universe there is a heaven and earth. But God's kingdom will
merge soon with this earthly reality. And God's θέλημα is enacted on earth
"as it is in heaven". I take Matthew to mean here that the community enacts
principles and values reiterative of the kingdom which is in heaven.

But what I would like to enquire after briefly is the question of just who
is in heaven with Matthew? How does Matthew see the rest of the world
fitting into his eschatological schema? It is an appropriate question to ask
of someone Matthew's vintage. A presumably elite scholar/teacher from Palestine or Syria from the Roman east would be acquainted with philosophical and linguistic developments of the day. Someone who reads and writes
two or three languages and should have had access to some kind of library,
would have a measure of learning that goes beyond halakhic issues related
to Jesus of Nazareth or Matthew's own community. We know, for example,
that Matthew is capable of mingling several sources or traditions when utilizing OT citations. It has been shown definitively that Matthew cites the
Masoretic text, the LXX, and what might be referred to as "extra septuagintal traditions" when utilizing the OT depending on his preferred treatment of the particular OT citation[7]. Matthew's utilization of the traditions
at his disposal reflects a sophisticated level of learning. His supple use and
yet near abiding commitment to the Markan framework and narrative is as
impressive as it is puzzling. His often ever so slight changes in the tradition
he seems to respect deeply can have a substantial effect on the meaning of
that passage or tradition.

For example, his addition of the pronoun αὐτῶν in reference to συναγωγή
(4:23; 9:35; 10:17; 12:9; 13:54; 23:34) well-known at least since Kilpatrick

---

6. K. SYREENI, *Between Heaven and Earth: On the Structure of Matthew's Symbolic Universe*, in *JSNT* 40 (1990) 3-13.
7. W.D. DAVIES – D.C. ALLISON, *A Critical and Exegetical Commentary on the Gospel
According to St. Matthew*. Vol. 2 (ICC), Edinburgh, T&T Clark, 1991, pp. 322-327.

is a seemingly slight modification that has had a substantial impact on our reading of Matthew and his setting[8]. Or take Matthew's deletion of the so-called Strange Exorcist story (Mark 9:38-41 // Luke 9:49-50). This deletion seems provoked by the Matthean rejection of the notion that someone can function as an exorcist for the movement but yet remain outside the group. As Eduard Schweizer said some time ago, "the existence of a genuine (Christian) exorcist who does not 'follow us,' that is not a member of the Matthean community, is unthinkable to Matthew"[9]. In 12:30 Matthew does retain a version of the original conclusion to this story, though that is all: "he who is not with me is against me and he who does not gather with me scatters". Here we can see Matthew's editorial process at work as he carefully and subtly shapes the traditions he has inherited. However, his summarizing logion which is now about sins against the Holy Spirit in Matt 12:31-32 completely changes the force of the earlier Q and Markan pericope.

But Matthew's editing of this material allows us to see he leans toward allowing that someone can be a member of a broadly defined group of believers or followers of Jesus yet not specifically part of Matthew's own church or gathering. These passages and others that betray Matthew's hand reveal he is thoughtful about boundaries, about community membership, and who is ultimately a part of the commonwealth of heaven. Matthew's narrative seems to emphasize Galilee. Jesus does not leave Galilee except for his journey to Jerusalem and those from outside Galilee actually come to Galilee to see Jesus, not the other way around[10]. This too is an interesting insight into Matthean boundary maintenance but requires a longer look than we can afford here. But, while Matthew demonstrates a focus on Galilee when retelling the pattern of Jesus' movements in the region, he also reveals an awareness of the broader, wider world beyond Palestine which we would expect to find in someone of Matthew's social standing. Matthew's concentration on Galilee when compared to the other Gospel writers and his near obsessive focus on his local competition usually summarized in the artificial hybridization of "the scribes and Pharisees", could lull us into thinking he is far too parochial a thinker to be reflecting on the οἰκουμένη or πάντα τὰ ἔθνη and their relation to his story. This would be a mistake.

So indeed Matthew is a scribe trained for the kingdom of heaven. He works with texts and traditions closely and in nuanced ways. And he has a

---

8. G.D. KILPATRICK, *The Origins of the Gospel According to St. Matthew*, Oxford, Oxford University Press, 1946, p. 110.

9. *Matthäus und seine Gemeinde* (SBS, 71), Stuttgart, Katholisches Bibelwerk, 1974, p. 115.

10. J.A. OVERMAN, *Matthew's Gospel and Formative Judaism: The Social World of the Matthean Community*, Minneapolis, MN, Fortress, 1990, p. 126.

range of texts at his disposal as well, as we know. As a trained scholar and part of that very small literate percentage of the ancient world Matthew would have been aware also of some of the thoughts and developments extant in the wider Roman world relative to our theme. Are people beyond Matthew's community, and people beyond his realm or locality, part of Matthew's vision? Are non-Jews, non-Matthean Jews, people outside of Palestine part of Matthew's thinking and ultimately part of his kingdom of/in heaven? Such a question, we can be confident, was part of Matthew's thought-world.

While this may seem a simple question it is complicated I think by the state and history of Matthean studies. This is so because so much of Matthean studies has focused on two apparently quite distinct categories – Jews and Gentiles. The range of reasons for this is many. The salvation –history scheme so popular earlier in the last century and still operative in many circles sets our question up in this manner. Matthew's interest, according to some, is in a new Israel, a true Israel, or a new people, that is ostensibly Gentile but acknowledges Matthew's language and imagery grounded in historic Israel. This dichotomy and juxtaposition, or often apparently polarized categories in Matthean studies, is punctuated by the all too familiar competing texts of Matthew 10:5 and the closing of the Gospel, 28:19-20. These two texts, along with a few others, have been debated and utilized to try to determine the following question: is Matthew's community Jewish and does it remain Jewish while in some limited sense open to Gentiles, or does his story lead to a rejection of historic Israel and a mission and embrace of the broader Gentile world?

These debates continue for good reason. In the end the Gospel of Matthew does not lend itself to some of the simple categorizations we have proposed over the last century. Matthew's story contains what appear to be contradictory passages. The entire story and every particular verse cannot be fully or even adequately explained in the terms and categories we have proposed. I think that also Matthew himself and his immediate milieu are responsible for some of this confusion. Matthew's Gospel is at important points parochial. By that I mean he focuses on local issues that give us the sense he is not thinking about the rest of the world. For this reason the closing of the Gospel has caught many interpreters off guard. It shouldn't end that way, or it ought to be a textual variant resulting from later Patristic meddling. Matthew's attention to quite specific halakhic issues, his ongoing, and at points tiresome, *Auseinandersetzung* with local Jewish leaders, and his instructions to his own community, especially in chapter eighteen, are all parochial, local issues. And his language when he engages these local issues is where he is at his harshest. These parts of the Gospel do not lead the interpreter to believe that Matthew is thinking very far outside of his box – beyond his particular locale. But I would suggest there are parts of his Gospel that are far less parochial, and suggest a broader and more systemic approach to a question that circulated widely among Roman *literati*. For these reasons we have yet to find a way, a language, or a philosophy which adequately captures Matthew's point-of-view on the question of the fate of humanity – that is the rest of the world – in his story.

For someone with Matthew's training it is reasonable to assume that he knew about broader developments in his part of the world – political and philosophical, literary and historical, as noted earlier. Through Greek historiography and philosophy Rome inherited a worldview that overtime they extolled. In philosophy and politics, but in material statements and urbanization as well, Rome made manifest that the world was one, it was connected, and most of the time from their point of view, they ran it[11]. As is widely recognized Stoic philosophy influenced most of the literate population – (and even quasi-literate because of the influence of Stoic orality) and made as a central tenant the essential and also political unity of the world and humankind[12]. The mid-second century B.C.E. Greek captive turned historian Polybius is one of the first Roman writers to give voice to the cosmopolitanism the Romans championed after the defeat of Carthage. In his prologue he announces perhaps the controlling theme of his work:

> There can surely be nobody so petty or apathetic in his outlook that he has no desire to discover by what means and under what system of government the Romans succeeded in less than fifty-three years in bringing under their rule almost the whole inhabited world (οἰκουμένη), an achievement which is without parallel in human history (*Histories*, 1.1).

---

11. On Roman globalization or *cosmopolitanism* R.B. HITCHNER, *Globalization avant la Lettre: Globalization and the History of the Roman Empire*, in *New Global Studies* 2 (2008) 1-16; R. MORTLEY, *The Idea of Universal History from Hellenistic Philosophy to Early Christian Historiography* (Texts and Studies in Religion, 67), Lewiston, NY, Edwin Mellen, 1996; C. EDWARDS – G. WOOLF (eds.), *Rome the Cosmopolis*, Cambridge, Cambridge University Press, 2003; on the material world carrying a coherant and pervasive message about unity across the empire P. ZANKER, *The Power of Images in the Age of Augustus*, Ann Arbor, University of Michigan Press, 1988; H. HÄNLEIN-SCHÄFER, *Die Iconographie des Genius Augusti im Kapital- und Hauskult der frühen Kaiserzeit*, in A.M. SMALL (ed.), *Subject and Ruler: The Cult of the Ruling Power in Classical Antiquity* (Journal of Roman Archaeology. Supplementary Series, 17), Ann Arbor, JRA, 1996, pp. 73-98; and C. EDWARDS, *Incorporating the Alien: The Art of Conquest*, in *Rome the Cosmopolis*, pp. 44-70, to mention a few.

12. L. HILL, *The Two Republicae of the Roman Stoics: Can a Cosmopolite be a Patriot?* in *Citizenship Studies* 4 (2000) 65-79; G. REYDAMS-SCHILS, *The Roman Stoics: Self, Responsibility, and Affection*, Chicago, University of Chicago Press, 2005, pp. 83-114.

For Polybius and others like him the affairs of Italy and Africa are now inextricably connected to the affairs of Greece and Asia. The unity and connectedness of the world may well have been part of his charge as a hired historian of Rome's Eastern-Asian conquest and incorporation, as Walbank has observed. Even so that does not make Polybius incorrect[13]. The so-called Roman Greek East emerged as a particularly important region and player in the Roman codification of this worldview. Belief in a connected or organic whole to human affairs emerged with force in the Roman worldview driven especially by developments and acquisitions in the East. Communities across the Roman East were inevitably caught up in these developments.

One hundred years later Cicero continues this theme that is at once Stoic, and therefore common, but also now codified Roman thought and rhetoric.

> We are all born of justice...by nature. That is clear if you examine the common *bonds* among human beings. There is no similarity, no likeness of one thing to another, so great as the likeness we all share (*De Legibus* 1.28-29).

The notion of a universal community is fundamental for Cicero and his peers. They are *cosmopoliteis*, citizens of the world. The ground of that universal community he refers to as justice. Cicero also acknowledges levels of human bonds and connectedness. There is a grand level of human fellowship among the entire race which makes us one. But there are more parochial links between people involving race, language, city-states, shrines, colonnades, streets, circles of acquaintances and still close friends, and family bonds. We start "from the unrestricted fellowship of the human race and arrive at smaller and confined groups" (1.53)[14].

Philo too, is a closer contemporary of Matthew, who in many respects stood in the philosophical and political train of Cicero and other cosmopoliteis of the day. The unity and ecumenical nature of the world is something obvious to him:

> God possesses all things but needs nothing; while the good man, though he possesses nothing in the proper sense, not even himself, partakes of the precious things of God so far as he is capable. And that is but natural, for he is a world citizen (κοσμοπολίτης), and therefore not on the roll of any city of human habitation in the world; rightly so because he has received no mere piece of land but the whole world (ὅλον τον κόσμον) as his portion (*Moses I*, 156-157)[15].

---

13. F.W. WALBANK, *Polybius*, Berkeley, University of California Press, 1972, p. 42.

14. REYDAMS-SCHILS, *The Roman Stoics*, pp. 77-78; I wish to thank Andy Ver Steegh for numerous helpful and spirited contributions on this topic.

15. C. ROETZEL, *OIKOUMENE and the Limits of Pluralism in Alexandrian Judaism and Paul*, in J.A. OVERMAN – R.S. MACLENNAN (eds.), *Diaspora Jews and Judaism*, Atlanta, Scholars Press, 1992, p. 175.

In the view of a very wide array of Roman writers Rome herself became the political embodiment of this philosophical worldview. Rome was expert at structuring this conviction into its daily life and iconography. There were those who were slow to apprehend this message. For them there was the Roman victory and even monuments to Roman prevalence over them[16]. Such material and architectural expressions could be found in just about any a major city and unmistakably in any metropolis. The striking architectural uniformity of the imperial cult in the East is a material feature of this iconographic unity and cosmopolitanism. Dio states as much when he describes the evolution and spread of the Roman imperial cult from Asia Minor where he claimed it began and then spread from there around the Empire (Dio, 50.20.6). The unifying force of the cult and consistent shape ritually in the East is a significant aspect of the enduring impact of S. Price's work on imperial control and imprint upon the Greek East[17]. The Sebesteion and *Ethnē* reliefs from Aphrodisias come to mind as a example of Roman political expression of the breadth and yet unity of the *oikoumenē* in their day[18]. The Roman empire gave political embodiment to a philosophy that had been widespread for some time.

This too was Matthew's world. So where does the rest of the world, people who know little about synagogues, purity laws, or discipleship with Jesus fit in? As with Cicero there are levels of relationships and issues Matthew confronts. Global issues are there but they do not set the table or necessarily guide the agenda. They must be measured along with other issues that maybe local or parochial, but by no means less important.

Matthew's use and interpretations of Isaiah is a suggestive component in his fashioning how the rest of the world fits into his story. Wim Weren and others have shown us in convincing detail Matthew's sophisticated and nuanced use of Isaiah. He can use the MT text, the LXX, he may prefer an extant targumic version of Isaiah, and he can write his own septuagintal version. Professor Weren showed this definitely in his article on Matthew's use of Isa 5: 1-7 in the Parable of the Tenants (Matt 21:33-46)[19].

---

16. Most recently M. BEARD, *The Roman Triumph*, Cambridge, MA., Harvard University Press – London, Belknap Press, 2007.

17. S. PRICE, *Rituals and Power: The Roman Imperial Cult in Asia Minor*, Cambridge, Cambridge University Press, 1984. So also H. HÄNLEIN-SCHÄFER, *Veneratio Augusti. Eine Studie zu den Tempeln des ersten römischen Kaisers* (Archaeologica, 39), Rome, Bretschneider, 1985 and the uniformity that existed across the empire already in the Augustan period with respect to the architecture of the imperial cult buildings.

18. R.R.R. SMITH, *The Imperial Reliefs from the Sebasteion at Aphrodisias*, in *JRS* 77 (1987) 88-138.

19. W. WEREN, *The Use of Isaiah 5,1-7 in the Parable of the Tenants (Mark 12,1-12; Matthew 21,33-46)*, in *Bib* 79 (1998) 1-26.

Matthew signals this penchant early on when he uses Isaiah's description of Galilee in 4:15, found also in I Macc, as being *of the* ἐθνῶν, thereby drawing attention to the northern tribal region of Galilee. This region had been a hotly disputed area at least since the Hasmoneans and the second century B.C.E. when some inhabitants underwent forced circumcision. The region, referred to by some as Iturea, continued to be unruly and of crucial military and political importance from the time of Sulla or Crassus until it was pacified under Augustus and Herod. The region erupted again with unrest at the outbreak of the first Jewish revolt. It was from precisely this region that Augustus secured the infamous lost Roman standards from the Parthians which had loomed so large in the Roman collective psyche[20]. As is well known only Matthew utilizes this passage from Isaiah. And it was also precisely in this small but crucial spot that Matthew placed his well-crafted Petrine confession in 16:13-20. Was Galilee – Upper Galilee a non-Jewish area? The answer is, somewhat, or marginally so. It was mixed in some sense. It remained Iturean in certain places but was part of the Kingdom of the Agrippas at the time of the Gospel. But this region was in the midst of significant urban and military development during the time of Jesus and the Flavian period – very likely the time of Matthew's Gospel. To our best knowledge the region was mixed through the course of the entire first century[21].

Another Matthean Isaiahism of considerable import is found in 12:18-21. Matthew's careful modification of LXX Isaiah is noteworthy. He utilizes LXX Isaiah often and deftly. As Seeligmann showed some time ago the LXX, but especially LXX Isaiah, has been modified with a view toward the wider world – toward the οἰκουμένη[22]. Over a third of all references to this term in the LXX are found in Isaiah. His modifications and what appear to

20. G. SAMPSON, *The Defeat of Rome in the East: Crassus, the Parthians, and the Disastrous Battle of Carrhae, 53 BC*, Philadelphia, PA, Casemate, 2008, pp. 114-148; J.A. OVERMAN, *Between Rome and Parthia: Galilee and the Implications of Empire*, in Z. ROGERS (ed.), *A Wandering Galilean: Essays in Honour of Sean Freyne*, Leiden, Brill, 2009, pp. 279-300.
    21. A very informative survey of the region is offered in J.F. WILSON, *Caesarea Philippi: Banias, the Lost City of Pan*, London, Tauris, 2004, pp. 1-37; M. HARTAL, *The Land of the Itureans: Archaeology and History of the Northern Golan in the Hellenistic, Roman and Byzantine Periods* (Golan Studies, 2), Qazrin, Golan Research Institute, 2005.
    22. I.L. SEELIGMANN, *The Septuagint Version of Isaiah: A Discussion of Its Problems* (Mededeelingen en verhandelingen van het Vooraziatisch-Egyptisch Genootschap "Ex Oriente Lux", 9), Leiden, Brill, 1948; see also J.W. OLLEY, *Righteousness in the Septuagint of Isaiah: A Contextual Study* (Society of Biblical Literature Septuagint and Cognate Studies, 8), Missoula, Scholars Press, 1978. More recent scholarship has demonstrated that contrary to earlier opinions the Greek of the LXX was commonplace and dialects written off as Hebraisms at an earlier time were in fact fully intelligible to a broader audience. M. HARL (ed.), *La Bible d'Alexandrie. La Genèse*, Paris, Cerf, 1986; cf. ROETZEL, *OIKOUMENE*, pp. 164-165.

be philosophical and theological predilections led some scholars to accuse the translator of gross incompetence. Rather this shows LXX Isaiah's familiarity and engagement with a broader and pervasive Hellenistic milieu. LXX Isaiah interacted with this and other concepts that characterized the learned Hellenistic circles of which Matthew was a part. One clear feature of that circle was an awareness of the breadth and the connectedness of that world. Matthew has drawn upon that LXX tradition.

Matthew's use of Isa 42:1-4 in 12:18-21 is a central passage in glimpsing his view of the wider world. This Isaiah passage which fits his cosmopolitan philosophy with respect to the *Ethnē*, barely fits the criterion for a Matthean fulfillment citation. The citation is supposedly related to the warning "not to make him known" in 12:16. The Isaiah passage does not illuminate this issue in any manner. Matthew has utilized this passage in the middle of the Gospel to signal again the Matthean Jew's awareness of the place and role of the *oikoumenē* in his story. His treatment of the LXX and MT in this instance is most interesting. He has followed the MT in some places, improved upon the LXX in others, and done his own crafting (or utilized "non-Septuagintal traditions") in others. The evocative passage, "until he leads justice to victory" comes from an independent source or is his hand, and he then returns to the LXX text to conclude the quote emphasizing the involvement and inclusion of the rest of the world, the ἔθνη. The Isaiah passage fits too well into his worldview not to be utilized. He has his own favorite construction of this text and was compelled to use it. The immediate context of this passage follows the Pharisees' determination that they had to find a way to "destroy" Jesus (12:14). But, unlike other texts from earlier Jesus movements or communities, the Matthean citation of Isaiah is not accompanied by a denunciation of Israel much less Jews[23]. It is a well-fashioned reminder of the place of the *Ethnē*, the nations, in the Matthean worldview.

Matthew's scaled down version of the healing of the Centurion's servant, when compared to Luke, is also significant (Matt 8:5-12). Matthew combined the healing story with an apocalyptic logion found in Luke 13:28-29. The presence of faith in a Gentile Centurion does not in Matthew's view mean faith does not exist in Israel – as some have suggested. That the nations roundabout are included in Matthew's thought and plan as he understands Jesus' teaching does not therefore mean Israel is rejected. This is a false dichotomy which has informed too much Matthean scholarship.

---

23. An editorial nuance unfortunately overlooked by Flusser. D. FLUSSER, *Two Anti-Jewish Montages in Matthew*, in ID., *Judaism and the Origins of Christianity*, Jerusalem, Magnes, 1988, pp. 552-560.

This man's faith is great and he captures the authority of Jesus decisively. The "sons of the kingdom," whom we meet elsewhere, are or can be cast out. This Q passage does not fit seamlessly into Matthew chapter eight, but he has utilized this passage here, though it would have made more sense in chapters 24-26. But even here we do not see a rejection of Israel. The so-called "sons of the kingdom" may be all people in Israel, but more likely refers to leaders or presumptuous Jews in Palestine who in Jesus', or Q's, or Matthew's view assume too easily what their ultimate fate is.

Two brief observations which bear upon our topic. Matt 24:9b is an interesting case in point. In 10:17-22 Matthew is following Mark concerning the persecution and hatred followers of Jesus will have to endure. "They will be hated *by all* because of my name" (Matt 10:22 // Mark 13:13 // Luke 21:17). But in 24:9b Matthew finds a way to utilize this logion again. Here he inserts his phrase πάντων τῶν ἐθνῶν. "You will be hated *by all nations* because of my name". Here we have another subtle modification by Matthew that reminds us that the story he is telling is also a global story engaging the whole world.

Finally also in chapter twenty-four, 24:14, we have a Matthean addition addressing his theme of the relationship between his story and his people or community on one hand, and the *oikoumenē* on the other. He begins in 24:13 citing Mark 13:13: "he who endures to the end will be saved". But Matt 24:14 has been fashioned by Matthew: "and this gospel / message of the kingdom will be preached throughout the whole world (ἐν ὅλῃ τῇ οἰκουμένῃ), as a testimony to all nations (πᾶσιν τοῖς ἔθνεσιν); and then the end will come". The nations, the rest of the world, the *oikoumene*, (used explicitly here by Matthew in 24:14), play a vital role in his movement and in his eschatological schema.

There is relatively little indication they figure prominently in his community now. But he is aware that his community and his story of Jesus is transpiring on a world stage. And the rest of the world is figured into this story by Matthew at several key junctures. As the rest of the world is tied to Rome's decisions and fate, so *the nations* are tied to the drama that transpired in Jesus and continues with parochial or local modifications in the Matthean community[24].

---

24. My own view is that more work can be done on the presence of a similar *cosmopolitanism* in early rabbinic literature. Here we may find some interesting and striking parallels with Matthew. Such a connection was briefly explored by D. Flusser in suggestive ways. See his *Johanan ben Zakkai and Matthew*, in ID., *Judaism*, pp. 490-493. Connections with Matthew and traditions about Johanan b. Zakkai are obvious in several ways and deserve exploration; Matthew's, Josephus's, and Johanan b. Zakkai's treatment of the destruction of

The nations, cosmopolis or *inhabited world*, are part of Matthew's story and they are included in the eschatological drama and decision making. They too must live justly and bear fruit in the manner Matthew has stated numerous times throughout the Gospel. Matthew's passages touching upon the nations seem rather undogmatic. That is, non-Jews are included, they can have great faith, and they are incorporated in the promises of God based on Matthew's use of Isaiah. There are few restrictions placed on *the Nations* and their participation in the-world to-come seems to depend on their actions being just and fruit- bearing. It is equally important to note that in the mention or inclusion of the *Ethnē* in Matthew's story and in his depiction of the eschatological fate of history, there is no corresponding negation of Jews or Israel. That has often been inferred by interpreters but Matthew is not Acts or a host of second–fourth century early Christian anti-Jewish writers.

When we consider where Matthew is living, when we see his access to sources or manuscripts, and when we acknowledge the elite stratum of society Matthew inhabits, it is unlikely that he would not be aware of the political and philosophical *oikoumenē* that now inhabits and controls his part of the Roman Greek East. The Matthean community is "a light to the world" (5:14-16). The rest of the world is involved in this cosmic drama and they have an opportunity to learn the way of righteousness and bear fruit as Matthew's Jesus has instructed. Matthew knows, as do many other writers drawn from the canons of early Jewish and Christian communities, that, to quote Cicero, "there is a fellowship in the world which is extremely widespread. For this reason there exists a law of the nations (*ius gentium*), which while not always the same as the civil law, is followed by all people" (*On Duties* 3.69). Matthew's *panta ta ethnē* have the opportunity to follow what for Matthew is God's law which leads to life. Cicero confessed that we do not fully understand the law that unites humanity. In the same section of *On Duties* Cicero utilizing characteristic Stoic language concludes that "We do not have a firm and lifelike figure of true law and genuine justice; we make use of shadows and sketches. I wish we would follow even those; for they are drawn from the best examples of nature and truth". Matthew asserts that for both Jew and non-Jew the way of justice and mercy was made a great deal firmer and more lifelike in the teaching, actions, and interpretations of Jesus. This is the universal law the Matthean community follows in contrast to their local leaders and which the world also may follow.

Jerusalem, the use of Hos 6:6 in *'Abot R. Nat* and Matthew as a post-destruction apologetic for life without the Temple, or traces of the development of a post-70 early rabbinic school are all promising areas of Matthean convergence with traditions associated with Johanan b. Zakkai.

The discussions about Jews and Gentiles in Matthew have often suffered from operating with these categories in rather narrow terms. It is an understatement to say both figure prominently in his Gospel. Matthew demonstrates considerable interest in *panta ta ethnē* and yet writes as a Jew largely to Jews in a post-70 Palestinian setting. And both of these groups or inadequate categories are part of the eschatological drama captured in his Gospel. We have to acknowledge that he has little interest in dispensing with either group or category. In the world in which he lives how could he? And his story in truth does not support such an either-or construction. We are still looking for a language that can hold together the broad, cosmopolitan construction of "the rest of the world," which Matthew has worked into his story in important and potent ways, together with his particular community in Palestine that is at odds with the local Jewish leadership in the harshest of terms and images. Both are part of his story and both must be held together as we think about Matthew's theology and the eschatological fate of both of these groups.

Macalester College   J. Andrew OVERMAN
1600 Grand Avenue,
Saint Paul, MN 55105
USA

PART TWO

SPECIFIC TEXTS

THE SOUL THAT CANNOT BE KILLED
BY MEN (MATT 10:28)*

When I was asked by the editors to contribute something to the present volume on "resurrection / immortality / eternal life in Matthew as reflecting Greco-Roman anthropological thought", the only passage that came to mind was Matt 10:28:

> And do not be afraid of those who kill the body, but cannot kill the soul.
> But fear more the One who is able to destroy both the soul and body in Gehenna.

The eschatological representations of the First Gospel – it seems to me – are deeply imbued with Jewish apocalypticism, as is likewise the case in the second half of our verse. Here, God is implied in the anony-mous "One" as a judge who can destroy both body and soul in hell. This does not sound like Greek philosophy. But does the first half of v. 28 nev-ertheless betray the influence of "Greco-Roman anthropological thought"?

I. SOURCE CRITICISM

First of all, where does this logion come from? Does it exhibit Matthean style? Its parallel in Luke 12:4-5 indicates that it originates from the source Q. In Luke it belongs to a cluster of sayings that extends from Luke 12:2 to 12:9 and is concerned with fearless confession. If we connect this with Luke 12:11-12 = Matt 10:19-20, the confession is situated in Jewish syn-agogues. The cluster can be analyzed more precisely as follows: Luke 12:4-7 form a subunit connected by the catchword "to fear". The latter appears twice[1] in the thematic antithetical 2nd person plural Imperatives of

---

* I am grateful to Rev. Anthony Pateman for revising my English, and to the editors for adapting the text to the formal rules and for introducing Greek fonts.

1. The repetitions in Luke 12:5a.d are usually considered a Lucan embellishment. The subdivisions of the verses follow F. NEIRYNCK, *Q-Synopsis: The Double Tradition Passages in Greek* (SNTA, 13), Leuven, University Press – Peeters, 1988.

12:4bc.5bc, and is resumed in v. 7b as consequence after a paradox (rhetorical question v. 6a / statement v. 6b) with a conclusion *a minori ad
maius* in v. 7a[2]. Matthew integrated the whole complex of sayings into his
missionary discourse in chapter 10.

Matthew's formulation of the admonition is more concise. Only he
employs the body and soul dichotomy, while Luke uses a more vague cir-
cumscription: the killers kill the body, but after that can do nothing more.
In the second half, Luke seems to avoid the un-Greek diction of "killing
the soul". He speaks of the one who, after he has killed[3], has the authority
to cast into hell[4]. Thus, for most exegetes, Matthew attests to the more
original sounding of Q[5], all the more so because he shares the Semitic equa-
tion of ψυχή with "life" in other passages (2:20 = Special M; 6:25 = Q;
10:39 = Q; 16:25-26 = Mark; 20:28 = Mark). Elsewhere, he follows the
biblical usage of ψυχή for the inner self, not explicitly distinguished from
the body (22:37 = Mark; 26:38 = Mark, the quotation in 12:18, so also
the Special M-passage in 11:29). Moreover, Luke apparently expressed his
bias in favour of individual retribution after death[6], while Matthew/Q presupposes Jewish dogmatics: body and soul must be reunited in the general
resurrection, before being judged by God[7], when both can be condemned

---

2. Whether the whole composition of v. 4-7, which has structural parallels in Q 12:22-
31, goes back to the historical Jesus is discussed in my *Die weisheitlichen Mahnsprüche bei
den Synoptikern* (FB, 17), Würzburg, Echter, [2]1983, pp. 95-96.100-101. Cf. U. LUZ, *Das
Evangelium nach Matthäus* (EKKNT, I/2), Zürich – Braunschweig – Neukirchen-Vluyn,
Benziger – Neukirchener Verlag, 1990, p. 124; J. SCHLOSSER, *Le logion de Mt 10,28 par. Lc
12,4-5*, in F. VAN SEGBROECK – C.M. TUCKETT – G. VAN BELLE – J. VERHEYDEN (eds.),
The Four Gospels 1992. Festschrift Frans Neirynck (BETL, 100), Leuven, University Press –
Peeters, 1992, 621-631, pp. 629-631; M. EBNER, *Jesus – ein Weisheitslehrer?: Synoptische
Weisheitslogien im Traditionsprozess* (Herders Biblische Studien, 15), Freiburg, Herder, 1998,
pp. 296-301.

3. Who is doing the killing? Obviously not God, but the phrase could be misunderstood
in this way.

4. In Matt 5:29 "to throw (simplex) the whole body into hell" seems to be ordinary language. See Mark 9:45.47 "being thrown into hell".

5. S. SCHULZ, *Q Die Spruchquelle der Evangelisten*, Zürich, Theologischer Verlag, 1972,
pp. 157-158; SCHLOSSER, *Logion*, pp. 623-625; P. HOFFMANN – CH. HEIL, *Die Spruchquelle
Q*, Darmstadt, Wiss. Buchgesellschaft – Leuven, Peeters, 2002, p. 76 following the Critical
edition of Q by J.M. Robinson – P. Hoffmann – J.S. Kloppenborg Verbin, Minneapolis,
Fortress – Leuven, Peeters, 2000; H.T. FLEDDERMANN, *Q: A Reconstruction and Commentary*
(Biblical Tools and Studies, 1), Leuven, Peeters, 2005, pp. 568-571.

6. Cf. J. DUPONT, *Die individuelle Eschatologie im Lukasevangelium und in der Apostelgeschichte*, in P. HOFFMANN (ed.), *Orientierung an Jesus*, Freiburg, Herder, 1973, 37-47,
p. 41.

7. This is illustrated by the allegory of the blind and the lame Apocr. Ezek., frg. 1 (JSHRZ
V, pp. 52-53); cf. the similar dialogue between Antoninus and Rabbi in *b. Sanh.* 91ab (Bill.
1, p. 581; 4, p. 1110).

to eternal destruction in the fire. It does not seem plausible, therefore, that it was Matthew who introduced the body-soul terminology to sharpen the antithetical parallelism. While it is true that Matthew writes in good Greek, there is no evidence that he also directly propagates Greek ideas. Should we thus conclude that the body-soul terminology was already current in the Syrian/Palestinian milieu where Q was composed, or was even found on the lips of the historical Jesus?

II. Form and Typical Situation

The logion consists of two parallel clauses in the vetitive resp. in the imperative mood. They are opposed to each other. The opposition is explained by a participle modifying the object of fear. Because of this explanatory element, I have treated Matt 10:28 elsewhere as a sapiential admonition[8], although the addressee is in the plural, not in the singular as in the traditional wisdom sayings. The second person plural even seems characteristic of the admonitions of Jesus who forms a community of followers. These admonitions are often enlarged by rhetorical questions (here v. 29-31), adding further plausibility to the request. While this kind of admonition can be situated in Jesus' instruction of potential and actual followers, the typical situation for our logion is more specific: the addressees who can call God their father (cf. v. 29b) are being prepared for possible martyrdom at the hands of man. We call this kind of speech "Martyriumsparänese". One of its favourite topics is precisely the opposition "fear of men" vs. "fear of God"[9].The motifs of the paraenesis for martyrs can appear in the actual description of their martyrdom. There, they argue against the judge and the persecuting ruler respectively as they were instructed beforehand. These narrative texts focusing on the dialogue between the ruler and the sage ready for martyrdom, were recently grouped together in a study by G. Holtz.[10] It is a pity, however, that she concentrated on Jewish and Gospel texts only and omitted classical literature. Let us now turn to the history of the motif in Matt 10:28a where we will explore two approaches, one Jewish and one classical-Hellenistic.

8. In my monograph Zeller, *Mahnsprüche*, p. 95.
9. Zeller, *Mahnsprüche*, pp. 97-98 with examples from 1Enoch 92-104 and 2 and 4 Maccabees.
10. G. Holtz, *Der Herrscher und der Weise im Gespräch: Studien zu Form, Funktion und Situation der neutestamentlichen Verhörgespräche und der Gespräche zwischen jüdischen Weisen und Fremdherrschern* (ANTZ, 6), Berlin, Institut Kirche und Judentum, 1996.

III. The Immunity of the Martyr and Its Anthropological Foundation (Jewish Sources)

The encouragement not to fear persecution or the death inflicted by human subjects is sometimes motivated by the limitation of such unjust attacks: they concern only "this life". This motif is also reflected from time to time in the passion narratives[11]. Thus Isaiah being sawed by his adversaries says to his torturer:

> You cannot take from me more than the skin of my body (*Ascen. Isa.* 5:10, basically Jewish).

In 2 Macc 6:30, the old Eleazar is beaten to death. But the dichotomy of body and soul allows a differentiation:

> [...] I am enduring terrible sufferings in my body under this beating, but in my soul I am glad to suffer these things because I fear him [God].

Only the body is the object of the torturer's lashes; they have no impact on the soul. The soul opens a space of freedom in which Eleazar can accept martyrdom willingly. This body-soul dualism is absent, however, from the famous chap. 7 of the book, in which the sufferings of the seven brothers are described. The second of brothers addresses king Antiochus:

> You accursed wretch, you dismiss us from this present life, but the king of the universe will raise us up to an everlasting renewal of life (2 Macc 7:9).

While here the compensation for the physical life taken unjustly is eschatological resurrection, 4 Maccabees – repeating the story with Hellenistic concepts – is interested in an immediate being with God for the martyrs. Though the author is acquainted in psychological terms with the dichotomy of body and soul (cf. 1:20.28), his solution is not quite the same as that of Matt 10:28. Since he sometimes uses ψυχή in its OT sense of "life" (6:29; and parallel to "blood" in 13:20), the martyrs can say that the tyrant "destroys"[12] or even "kills" (9:7 θανατόω) their life. Nevertheless, he cannot damage their Self (9:7 personal pronoun). He only thinks

---

11. Cf. Holtz, *Ibid.,* p. 314; she speaks of "das Motiv der Ohnmacht des Herrschers", sometimes combined with the god-given authorization to execute the martyr. Cf. also D. Zeller, *Jesus und die Philosophen vor dem Richter (zu Joh 19,8-11),* in Id., *Neues Testament und hellenistische Umwelt* (BBB, 150), Hamburg, Philo, 2006, 123-127, p. 126.

12. Cf. 11:7 πορθέω (t.c.) said of "men"; 9:25 ἀναρρήγνυμι, less dramatic 12:20 ἀποδίδωμι (text not certain).

he can (13:14)[13]. It is only in a later addition (10:4) that corporal punishment is set in contrast with the executioners' incapacity to touch the soul. But the soul is not immortal in itself. It is only after their expiatory death that the children and their mother "receive holy and immortal souls from God" (18:23). Eternal agony of the soul, however, awaits those who do not respect the commandment of God (13:15).

As we see, the eschatology of 4 Maccabees is more spiritualized than Matt 10:28. It lacks the terminological precision of Matt 10:28a. The case is similar to the *Wisdom of Solomon*, the first chapters of which raise the problem of the early death of the just man caused by the evildoers. The solution here consists in denying death completely as far as the pious is concerned.

> The souls of the just are in the hand of God, and torture will not touch them (3:1).

This includes a certain immortality (3:4), though the bodily dimensions are left obscure. Since the corruptible body already burdens the soul in this life (9:15), it does not play a role in the heavenly rest. Again, the soul does not own immortality by itself. Man does not even possess the soul. It is a loan that God breathes into the body (15:11), and it is reclaimed at the end (15:8). It is only when it is sheltered in the hand of God that it acquires the incorruptibility for which human beings were destined from the beginning (2:23).

These writings do not resign themselves to the triumph of violence and injustice. A life devoted to God cannot end by the stroke of a sword. Either it is gratified by a future resurrection of the body, or there is an element that survives the destruction of physical life. For Greek-speaking Jews, this was the soul. While it is true that Wisdom and 4 Maccabees often use ψυχή in a holistic sense, at the moment of death the soul alone guarantees continuity into an afterlife. What is amazing is the fact that this is said most clearly in a text coming from a Palestinian milieu: Matt 10:28.

IV. The Immunity of the Philosopher and Its Anthropological Foundation (Pagan Sources)

Do we encounter the idea of the soul's immortality, used in a forensic setting, in still older, non-Jewish sources? The argument that the judge is

---

13. I leave aside the question whether ψυχαί in 13:13 means "lives" (plural as in 9:7) or "souls" – so H.-J. KLAUCK, *4. Makkabäerbuch* (JSHRZ III, Lfg. 6), Gütersloh, Mohn, 1989, p. 738 with note 13. In my view, it makes good sense that the brothers who received their lives from God now consecrate themselves with their body to this same Creator.

not able to destroy the true self of the martyr has its remote roots in a famous dictum of Socrates in Plato's *Apology* 30c. Earlier on, the philosopher had explained his service to the Athenians in the name of the god. If they were to kill such an important man they would damage themselves more than him. Applied to Socrates' accusers this means,

> In no respect would either Meletus or Anytus do me harm – they would not be able to do so – because I do not think it legitimate that a better man is harmed by a worse one.

Some perhaps consider death, exile or loss of honour to be a serious injury, but Socrates does not think so. Only an unjustified accusation is such an evil. Here it is not the soul that is indestructible, but the moral quality of Socrates. To do harm (in Greek βλάπτειν as in 4 Macc 9:7) is taken in the sense of "to make worse". Socrates' adversaries are not able (οὐ δύνασθαι as in Matt 10:28) to do this. His statement is quoted in later tradition, be it pagan or Christian, to mark the limits of human disposition over other people[14]. Epictetus, *Diss.* 1.29.16 insists in the fact that it is only the poor body of Socrates that suffers prison and poisoning. In the same vein, the philosopher Anaxarchus reacts against the king of Cyprus who wants him to be beaten with clubs of iron.

> Crush the sack of Anaxarchus, you will not crush Anaxarchus (himself).

This too became a widely spread utterance[15]. Thus, the container is distinguished from the content: the personality.

But we are still lacking a reference to the soul as representing the true self which cannot be touched. For this reason we will explore another Platonic dialogue, namely the *Phaedo*, to see why Socrates can face death without grumbling. In the last hours before taking the poison he develops his doctrine of the soul's immortality. Like Jesus, he wants to allay the anxiety of his disciples (cf. 77e, 84b-e). He finally does this by arguing that the soul cannot perish (106a-d), although its post-mortal destiny depends on the degree it purified itself from the body during lifetime[16]. Among earlier philosophers,

---

14. Cf. Epictetus, *Diss.* 1.29.18; 2.2.15; 3.23.21; Maximus of Tyrus 12.8.1; applied to Fortune: Epictetus, *Ench.* 53.4; Plutarch, *Mor.* 475e. Once again, the forensic situation is evident in the allusion in Justin, *1 Apol.* 2.4; 45.6 and Clement of Alexandria, *Strom.* 4.11.80.4.

15. Cf. Diogenes Laertius 9.59; Philo, *Prob.* 109 and *Prov.* 2.11; Origenes, *Contra Celsum* 7.53. In an epigram, Diogenes Laertius 9.28 applies the motif to the philosopher Zeno of Elea.

16. Therefore, the Greek conception of the immortality of the soul should not be played off against the Biblical one as "naturhaft". Not only Plato, but also the rabbis proceed from a heavenly origin of the soul. In both cases, human decisions during life have an impact in the soul's state after death.

the Pythagoreans[17] in particular formulated the idea of the soul's immortality, combined with a doctrine of its transmigration into other bodies. They projected the mythical underworld into heaven. The soul that loved a good life on earth would return to its astral seat (Plato, *Tim.* 42b). The hope that the soul dying would be liberated from the body and dwell with the stars or would be received in the ether was relatively popular among intellectuals of imperial times, as grave inscriptions attest[18].

Let us return to the topic of the inviolability of the philosopher confronted with his judge. This argument is formulated in body-soul terminology by Philostratus in the speech of the accused Apollonius of Tyana before the emperor. In his *Vita Apollonii* 8.5, the philosopher is acquitted, but the emperor wants to retain him for a private meeting. Apollonius asks for the opportunity to accuse his accusers in his turn.

> If not, send someone who catches my body, because it is impossible (to catch) the soul[19].

The fact that this anthropology was current among Greek-speaking Jews, is best illustrated by the addition in 4 Macc 10:4 (see above). It is also represented by the *Testament of Job*, originally written in Greek, in which Job 2:6 (God gives Job into the hands of Satan under the condition of sparing his life) is interpreted thus: Satan can treat Job's body as he pleases but with respect to his soul, God gave him no power (20:3)[20]. We can only speculate how and when this dualism of body and soul also invaded Palestinian Judaism. Apocalyptic writings like *1 Enoch* use the term "souls", but also "spirits" for the bearer of human identity after death[21]. It seems that the Jews of the homeland in the first century C.E. were acquainted with the body-soul dichotomy. Like the Greeks and the Greek pseudepigrapha[22] they speak of death as the separation of body and soul (cf. *4 Ezra* 7:78). Perhaps the

---

17. Alcmaeon of Croton following Aristotle, *De Anima* I 2 405a 29-33.

18. Cf. P. HOFFMANN, *Die Toten in Christus: eine religionsgeschichtliche und exegetische Untersuchung zur paulinischen Eschatologie* (NTAbh NF, 2), Münster, Aschendorff, 1966, pp. 44-57; more recently I. PERES, *Griechische Grabinschriften und neutestamentliche Eschatologie* (WUNT, 157), Tübingen, Mohr Siebeck, 2003, e.g. pp. 198-200 showing the inscription for Aelianus of Sabini, 1/2nd cent. CE.

19. The text goes on: The emperor will not even catch his body, because Apollonius vanished. In a similar way the Jewish-Christian *Apocalypse of Elijah* 34,6.33-36; 35,4-6 denies to the Antichrist not only the disposal of the soul, but also of the bodies of the martyrs because of their resurrection.

20. Cf. further Pseudo-Phocylides 105: The souls (parallel "spirit" 106.108) remain uninjured in those passing away.

21. Cf. E. BRANDENBURGER, *Fleisch und Geist: Paulus und die dualistische Weisheit* (WMANT, 29), Neukirchen-Vluyn, Neukirchener Verlag, 1968, pp. 60-62.

22. Cf. E. SCHWEIZER, σῶμα κτλ, in *ThWNT* 7 (1964) 1024-1091, pp. 1047,40-1048,6.

Pharisaic Hasidim, disillusioned to a degree in their expectation of an immi-
nent resurrection (Dan 12:2-3), took refuge in this model to answer the
question about the final destiny of the martyrs[23]. The soul – wherever it is
localized – becomes an important link between physical dissolution and resurrection. Our passage is not interested in an intermediary state but pays only
attention to an element that escapes the brutality of men. In the end it turns
out that this element is not sufficient; the soul has to be completed by the
body. God acts with the whole human being[24].

V. Not a Greek Element: The Ruin of the Soul

In Matt 10:28a, the soul cannot be killed by men, but it is certainly not
immortal as v. 28b shows. After reunion with the body, God can destroy both
in hell. Following Plato, the soul delivered from the body can be transferred
into other incarnations. As we have seen already, our admonition presupposes
that the soul receives a new body. Not only because both elements are called
to account in God's judgment[25], but also because they are necessary to enjoy
eternal life or to suffer eternal death. This everlasting punishment is here
described as "ruin". It is presupposed that the soul – of the just or of the bad
man – outlasts death, but in God's judgment human beings reincorporated
in a general resurrection can be condemned to destruction that concerns both
components. The Greeks, on the other hand, and especially the Orphics, were
also aware of physical tortures of the soul in the hereafter (cf. e.g. Plato,
Phaedo 113d-114b), but they would not define this as "ruin of the soul". This
would constitute an oxymoron. Philo uses the metaphor of "death of the soul"
in the context of a "realized eschatology" designating loss of virtue or the
immediate consequences of immoral action. In my opinion, it cannot be
derived directly from Greek philosophical tradition[26].

---

23. That the Pharisees also had their martyrs is proved by the notice of Josephus, *Ant.*
13.380-383; *B.J.* 1.97-98, 113.
24. J. Gnilka, *Das Matthäusevangelium* (HThKNT, 1/1), Freiburg – Basel – Wien,
Herder, 1986, pp. 387-388 writes: "Die vulgarisierte hellenistische Anthropologie hat es
ermöglicht, die Seele als die Zeit zwischen Tod und Endgericht überbrückendes anthropolo-
gisches Kontinuum zu denken, aber es bleibt eine Unausgeglichenheit, insofern für den Semi-
ten eine leiblose Existenz eigentlich eine Unexistenz ist".
25. Cf. the texts in note 7.
26. See my essay *The Life and Death of the Soul in Philo of Alexandria*, in *The Studia
Philonica Annual* 7 (1995) 19-55. More optimistic, E. Wasserman, *The Death of the Soul in
Romans 7: Sin, Death, and the Law in Light of Hellenistic Moral Psychology* (WUNT 2/256),
Tübingen, Mohr Siebeck, 2008 connects the concept more closely with the "illnesses of the
soul" in platonic and stoic philosophy.

We can infer that a ruination of the soul as a result of God's action particularly contradicts Greek sensitivities. On the other hand, the idea is conceivable in Jewish-Palestinian sources[27]. In the latter, God is the almighty Creator and Judge who is not bound by metaphysical laws, but realizes his will and the sanctions connected with it in great sovereignty. In an anecdote[28], the famous rabbi Johanan ben Zakkai acknowledges his fear of appearing after death before this heavenly king. Compared with a king of flesh and blood, God can inflict more frightening measures of punishment. His killing means eternal death. Thus, there might be a Greek origin for the topic of the immunity of the wise man against the doom of death, expressed by the inability of men to kill the soul. The idea, however, had already penetrated the Jewish mind in the Diaspora and at home. The sequel in Matt 10:28b is shocking for Greek thinking. The author does not shrink from affirming a paradox, not to say a contradiction: The soul that cannot be killed by men, is destroyed by God. It is not imagined as instantaneous annihilation, but as an ongoing process (cf. Mark 9:48) to enhance the frightening effect on the listener. This, however, is not the place to evaluate the threatening apocalyptic imagery used by the logion[29]. We have to concentrate on the first part of the verse and to ask what its function is and what its truth could be.

VI. Some Hermeneutical Reflections

Matt 10:28 envisages an extreme situation, the doom of physical destruction. How can we accept it without denying our faith? Since modern psychology – if it still uses the concept of soul – presumes a narrow unity of feeling and action between body and soul, an attitude as described in 2 Macc 6:30 – heavy external pain together with inner joy – looks quite improbable. The speaker of our logion, however, uses a philosophical model, the indestructibility of the soul, to suggest the possibility of distance from the overwhelming experience from outside. For one moment he accepts the world-view of some cultivated Greeks, because it offers courage and consolation. But the permanency of the soul is not his final solution. In the continuation,

---

27. Cf. SCHLOSSER, *Logion,* p. 624.

28. *B. Berakot* 28b, cf. Bill. 1, p. 581.

29. For the development of the doctrine of hell, see H. RÄISÄNEN, *The Rise of Christian Beliefs: The Thought World of Early Christians,* Minneapolis, Fortress, 2010, pp. 121-124. Cf. his critical reflections in *Matthäus und die Hölle: Von Wirkungsgeschichte zur ethischen Kritik,* in M. MAYORDOMO (ed.), *Die prägende Kraft der Texte: Hermeneutik und Wirkungsgeschichte des Neuen Testaments* (SBS, 199), Stuttgart, Kath. Bibelwerk, 2005, pp. 103-124.

the anthropological argument is topped by a theological one. The first half of our verse does not stand on its own, but has to be interpreted via the second half[30]. The soul may be withheld from the deadly grip of men, but it does not warrant life in a definite sense. This depends on God's decision and gift alone.

Naturally, one might also consider both parts of the verse as complementary. The immortality of the soul then appears as a prerequisite for the final act. Individual eschatology and universal eschatology fit together[31], but it is difficult to get both elements into a system. Not only is there a plain contradiction regarding the immortality of the soul, there is no reflection on the how and where the soul passes the interim period. And finally, it was the "delay of the parousia" – a wholly unsystematic factor – that favoured the career of the concept of the soul's immortality. It had to fill the gap to the resurrection as it disappeared further and further into an undefined future.

If the first half of our verse is ultimately based on the Greek idea of the immortality of the soul, it can hardly be exploited dogmatically to support the general conviction that something in the human being lives on at the moment of death. In spite of "near-death-experiences", life without a bodily substratum hardly seems possible. It is not just part of a man that dies but the human subject as such. If the soul, according to Aristotle[32], is the principle of living, it does not make sense to turn the soul into an independent living being. We cannot just take over the worldview of ancient authors, be it Plato or "Matthew".

We can follow the intention of the saying, nevertheless. Firstly, brutality against people like the martyrs should not have the last word in society. Our text is even convinced that it will not. Secondly, death is no way out of human responsibility. With the image of the Bible, one might say that the dying person falls directly into the hands of God[33]. This can mean that when confronted with God one is held responsible for the whole of life or – as in Wis 3:1 and Luke 23:46 – that one confidently returns life to its origin. Our saying is aware of the ambiguity of the "hands of God". They

---

30. Cf. G. DAUTZENBERG, *Sein Leben bewahren: Psyché in den Herrenworten der Evangelien* (SANT, 14), München, Kösel, 1966, 138-153, p. 148.

31. Theological attempts to reconcile the philosophical idea of the soul's immortality with the biblical idea of the resurrection are discussed by H. SONNEMANS, *Seele: Unsterblichkeit, Auferstehung: zur griechischen und christlichen Anthropologie und Eschatologie* (Freiburger theologische Studien, 128), Freiburg – Basel – Wien, Herder, 1984.

32. *De Anima* II 4 415b 8.

33. Cf. the words of Eleazar in 2 Macc 6:26: "Whether I live or die I shall not escape the hands of the Almighty."

are sheltering hands (v. 28a), but also hands that punish (v. 28b). The hermeneutical question is whether we can go so far as to objectify these representations. Christian confidence is not life insurance. But why should the followers of Jesus stand less firmly before the worldly authorities than a Socrates or their master himself? In any event, their confidence is not based on an ontological quality of the soul, but on the goodness of the Creator who can make something out of broken pieces, even out of nothing.

Johannes Gutenberg-Universität Mainz   Dieter ZELLER
Weilburger Tal 10
65199 Wiesbaden
Germany

ETERNAL LIFE AS A REWARD FOR
CHOOSING THE RIGHT WAY:
THE STORY OF THE RICH YOUNG MAN
(MATT 19:16-30)

The story of the encounter between Jesus and the rich young man in conjunction with the comments on this event in Matt 19:16-30 make up a literary unit[1]. In 19:16 a new character is introduced and the unit ends with a change of genre in 20:1. Moreover, the unit's beginning and ending are marked by inclusion of the phrase "eternal life" in 19:16 and 19:29. Two themes, wealth (19:21.22.23.24.27.29) and eternal life (19:16.17.29), permeate and pervade the section's content.

The account consists of three parts[2]. In the first subsection (19:16-22) someone asks Jesus what he must do to have eternal life. Jesus tells him to keep the commandments and specifies which ones. The young man claims he has observed them and Jesus instructs him to sell his possessions, give the money to the poor, and follow him. Then the man goes away sad. The second and third subsections render Jesus' discussions with his disciples. He first (vv. 23-26) instructs his disciples about wealth by emphasizing that it will be as impossible for someone who is rich to enter the kingdom as for a camel to go through the eye of a needle. The disciples ask whether anyone can be saved and Jesus replies that God is able to do everything. The third subsection (vv. 27-30) contrasts the rich man's refusal to sell his wealth with

1. W. CARTER, *Households and Discipleship: A Study of Matthew 19-20* (JSNTSup, 103), Sheffield, JSOT, 1994; D.J. HARRINGTON, *The Gospel of Matthew* (SP, 1), Collegeville, MN, Liturgical Press, 1991, p. 277; D. PATTE, *The Gospel according to Matthew: A Structural Commentary on Matthew's Faith*, Philadelphia, Fortress, 1987, pp. 268-74; F.W. BEARE, *The Gospel according to Matthew*, Oxford, Blackwell, 1981, pp. 393-401; P. BONNARD, *L'Évangile selon Saint Matthieu* (CNT, 1), Genève, Labor et Fides, ³2002, p. 286.
2. See e.g. W.D. DAVIES and D.C. ALLISON, *A Critical and Exegetical Commentary on the Gospel according to Saint Matthew*. Vol. 3 (ICC), London – New York, T&T Clark, 1997, p. 38; W. CARTER, *Matthew and the Margins: A Sociopolitical and Religious Reading* (The Bible and Liberation Series), Maryknoll, NY, Orbis, 2000, p. 387; U. LUZ, *Das Evangelium nach Matthäus*, 3. Teilband, Mt 18-25 (EKKNT, 1/3), Zürich, Benziger Verlag – Neukirchen-Vluyn, Neukirchener Verlag, 1997, p. 120.

the disciples' response of leaving family and possessions. Peter asks what he and the other disciples who have left everything and followed Jesus will receive as their reward. Jesus' answer functions to reassure the audience of the appropriateness and significance of abandoning wealth by following him. He clarifies their eschatological destiny: their reward will be realized in the age to come when true loyalty and proper worth are revealed.

With the exception of v. 28, the Matthean version of the story as a whole is based upon Mark 10:17-31. Both accounts evidence the basic idea of a fundamental contrast between possessions and property in this life and the treasures of the coming kingdom. Closer examination shows however that Matthew has exercised considerable freedom in rewriting Mark's account. The story of the rich young man opens with the question in Matt 19:16: "What good deed must I do to have eternal life?" The first usage of the word "life" (ζωή) in Matthew's Gospel is found in Matt 7:13-14 where there is mention of an easy way "that leads to destruction" and a hard way "that leads to life (ἡ ἀπάγουσα εἰς τὴν ζωήν)". The antithetical parallelism describes two ways and the choice is between these alternatives. The metaphor of the Two Ways is usually employed to refer to responses to God's law and in Matt 7:13-27 it refers to reactions to Jesus' explanation of the law in the preceding part of the Sermon on the Mount. It recalls the beginning of a teaching of the Two Ways section passed on in the first six chapters of the Didache which also details two contrasting moral ways serving as a framework for the subsequent exposition of two sets of opposing ethical characteristics or antagonistic groups of people associated with the way of life (Did 1–4) and the way of death (Did 5), respectively[3].

In considering the elements related to afterlife in Matt 19:16-30, this paper might examine the connection between wordings like "eternal life" (v. 16), "life" (v. 17), "treasure in heaven" (v. 21), "enter the Kingdom of Heaven / Kingdom of God" (vv. 23. 24), "to be saved" (v. 25), and "inherit eternal life" (19:29). Most of these terms, expressions and phrases are found in the Markan counterpart (10:17-31) too and thus do not specifically characterize this episode in Matthew. Yet if Matthew significantly changed the content and profile of Mark's story it might be interesting to investigate

---

3. Further, see below. See also H. VAN DE SANDT – D. FLUSSER, *The Didache: Its Jewish Sources and Its Place in Early Judaism and Christianity* (CRINT, 3/5), Assen, Van Gorcum – Minneapolis, Fortress, 2002, pp. 55-237; W. RORDORF – A. TUILIER, *La Doctrine des douze Apôtres (Didachè)* (SC, 248 bis), Paris, Cerf, [2]1998, pp. 22-34; K. NIEDERWIMMER, *Die Didache* (KAV, 1), Göttingen, Vandenhoeck & Ruprecht, [2]1993, pp. 48-64 and 83-158; English Translation: *The Didache* (Hermeneia), Minneapolis, MN, Fortress, 1998, pp. 30-41 and 59-124.

some of his important alterations and ask how these are related to his ideas about afterlife.

In the following pages I therefore draw attention to some genuine puzzles which emerge when comparing Matt 19:16-30 to the parallel text in Mark 10:17-31. Why did Matthew for example add the love command in v. 19? Why did he call attention to the man's youthfulness (v. 20) or, perhaps better, why did Matthew change Mark's "all these I have observed from my youth" (suggesting that the man is no longer a youth) into "The young man said to him, 'all these I have observed'" (v. 20)? Why has Matthew omitted the Markan verse in which not only the rich but people in general are said to have difficulties entering God's kingdom (Mark 10:24)? And, finally, why did Matthew insert v. 28 which is not in Mark? Why was he keen on emphasizing the eschaton here? And why are the Twelve presented here as judging Israel?

Determining the precise provenance of any specific element or expression within Matthew is difficult, since there are usually many possibilities. Yet we believe that in particular the Two Ways teaching can shed light on Matthew's redactional activity in our pericope. After all, there is widespread scholarly consensus that there are important agreements between Matthew's Sermon on the Mount and the Two Ways (*section I*)[4].

---

4. The presence of the Two Ways motif in this Matthean passage has led scholars to argue for Matt 7:13-14 as the source of Did 1:1; see PH. SCHAFF, *The Oldest Church Manual, Called the Teaching of the Twelve Apostles*, New York, Funk & Wagnalls, [2]1886, p. 18 (on top); J. MUILENBURG, *The Literary Relations of the Epistle of Barnabas and the Teaching of the Twelve Apostles*, Marburg, n.p., 1929, p. 73; F.E. VOKES, *The Riddle of the Didache: Fact or Fiction, Heresy or Catholicism?* (The Church Historical Society, 32), London, SPCK – New York, Macmillan, 1938, p. 19. We have shown conversely that Matt 7:12-14 has traits of a pre-Matthean tradition closely affiliated with some form of Did 1:1-2; see VAN DE SANDT – FLUSSER, *The Didache*, pp. 193-204. Moreover, there is common recognition that elements in Matt 5:17-48 closely agree with items in the Two Ways; for the close agreement between Matt 5:17-48 and Did 3:1-6 see F.X. FUNK, *Doctrina duodecim Apostolorum: Canones Apostolorum ecclesiastici ac reliquae doctrinae de duabus viis expositiones veteres*, Tübingen, Laupp, 1887, p. 12; L. GOPPELT, *Christentum und Judentum im ersten und zweiten Jahrhundert* (BFCT, II, 55), Gütersloh, Bertelsmann, 1954, p. 187; H. LILJE, *Die Lehre der zwölf Apostel: Eine Kirchenordnung des ersten christlichen Jahrhunderts*, Hamburg, Furche-Verlag, 1956, pp. 51-52; ST. GIET, *L'Énigme de la Didachè* (Publications de la Faculté des Lettres de l'université de Strasbourg, 149), Paris, Ophrys,1970, pp. 158-160; C.N. JEFFORD, *The Sayings of Jesus in the Teaching of the Twelve Apostles* (VCSup, 11), Leiden – New York – København – Köln, Brill, 1989, pp. 65-67; H.D. BETZ, *The Sermon on the Mount: A Commentary on the Sermon on the Mount, Including the Sermon on the Plain (Matthew 5:3-7:27 and Luke 6:20-49)* (Hermeneia), Minneapolis, MN, Fortress, 1995, p. 219; G. BORNKAMM, *Der Aufbau der Bergpredigt*, in *NTS* 24 (1978) 419-432, p. 432; D. FLUSSER, *A Rabbinic Parallel to the Sermon on the Mount*, in D. FLUSSER, *Judaism and the Origins of Christianity* (collected articles), Jerusalem, Magnes, 1988, 494-508, pp. 497-499. 504-505; ID., *Die Tora in der Bergpredigt*, in H. KREMERS (ed.), *Juden und Christen lesen dieselbe Bibel* (Duisburger Hochschulbeiträge, 2), Duisburg, Braun, 1973, 102-113, pp. 106-09 and notes. 11-12; VAN DE SANDT – FLUSSER, *The Didache*, pp. 225-234.

This fact legitimates further research. Matthew's acquaintance with the Two Ways at least suggests the possibility that he read the Markan version of the rich man's story in a similar vein. In order to show this we will first investigate Matthew's report of Jesus' dialogue with the rich young man (vv. 16-22) and ascertain that his portrait of this event echoes important elements of the Jewish Two Ways instruction (*section II*). We will note next that Matthew's version of Jesus' conversation with the disciples in the second part (vv. 23-26) simplistically maintains a dualistic pattern. Just like the Two Ways pattern in Matt 7:13-14 opened up a series of contrasting alternatives without any nuance in 7:13-27, so the subdivision 19:23-26 appears to be a polarising part (*section III*). Finally, we come to the reward in the End (vv. 27-30) focusing on the disciples' eschatological destiny (*section IV*). And again, it is the manner in which Matt 7:13-27 deals with the Two Ways that highlights once more Matthew's intention with "life" and "death" in this final subdivision.

I. THE WAY OF LIFE IN THE SERMON ON THE MOUNT

Matthew's first usage of "life" (ζωή) to contrast "destruction" (ἀπώλεια) in 7:13-14 suggests that the question in Matt 19:16 concerns the young man's eschatological fate:

> Enter by the narrow gate (στενὴ πύλη); for the gate (ἡ πύλη) is wide and the way is easy, that leads to destruction (ἡ ὁδὸς ἡ ἀπάγουσα εἰς τὴν ἀπώλειαν), and those who enter by it are many. For the gate (ἡ πύλη) is narrow and the way (ἡ ὁδός) is hard, that leads to life (ἡ ἀπάγουσα εἰς τὴν ζωήν), and those who find it are few. (Matt 7:13-14)

It is difficult to retrieve a coherent image of this logion presenting the motif of the Two Ways in combination with the theme of the Two Gates. The confusion can be explained, however, when we consider the two divergent topics of the Two Ways and Two Gates to represent two different stages in the history of our saying. This observation is substantiated by the evidence in Luke 13:23-24:

> And someone said to him: "Lord, will those who are saved be few?" And he said to them, "Strive to enter by the narrow door (διὰ τῆς στενῆς θύρας); for many, I tell you, will seek to enter and will not be able."

Because these verses show close affinities to Matt 7:13-14, both Matthew and Luke might have drawn on the common Q source. Many scholars argue that Luke has preserved this Q logion more faithfully than Matthew[5]. If the tradition is retained in a more authentic form in Luke 13:23-24, the Two Ways motif as presented in Matthew appears to seriously interfere with the structural pattern of the statement about the gates. It might be appropriate therefore to assume this motif has been added to the logion at a later stage. In that case Matthew has adapted and expanded the original gate saying by the inclusion of the Two Ways emphasis in 7:13c[6].

The Two Ways tradition ranges across a variety of Christian documents from the first five centuries, including Didache 1-6, Doctrina, Letter of Barnabas 18-20 and some five later writings[7]. Each of these constitutes an independent witness to an ancient Two Ways tradition in which the basic pattern is essentially the same, particularly the appearance of the two ways (one of life and one of death) and the presence of a double catalogue of virtues and vices in which each of the ways consists. The close resemblances between the different versions of the Two Ways are generally explained in modern research by their – direct or indirect – dependence upon an earlier Jewish Two Ways document which is no longer extant. The late David Flusser and I recently attempted to reconstruct this original teaching. Because this source was in Greek, it may also be called the Greek Two Ways[8]. For our purposes it is important to establish that this (hypothetical) version generally reflects the wording of the Two Ways in the Didache, except for the Christianised sections 1:3b–2:1 and 6:2-3[9]. In this paper, therefore, the Christian Didache will be followed excluding those parts and details differing from the hypothesized Greek Two Ways.

5. T.W. MANSON, *The Sayings of Jesus as Recorded in the Gospels according to St. Matthew and St. Luke*, London, SCM, 1949, p. 175; J. DUPONT, *Les Béatitudes 1: Le problème littéraire* (ÉBib), Bruges, Abbaye de Saint-André – Louvain, Nauwelaerts, 1969, p. 95; J. JEREMIAS, *Neutestamentliche Theologie* 1: *Die Verkündigung Jesu*, Gütersloh, Mohn, 1971, p. 28, note 19; ID., πύλη, πυλών, in *TWNT* 6, 920-27, pp. 922-923; F. MUSSNER, *Das 'Gleichnis' vom gestrengten Mahlherrn (Lk 13,22-30): Ein Beitrag zum Redaktionsverfahren und zur Theologie des Lukas*, in *TTZ* 65 (1956) 129-143, pp. 131-132.

6. See U. LUZ, *Das Evangelium nach Matthäus*, 1 Teilband, Mt 1-7 (EKKNT, 1/1), Zürich, Benziger Verlag – Neukirchen-Vluyn, Neukirchener Verlag, 1985, pp. 296-397; DAVIES – ALLISON, *Matthew*, vol. 1 (1988), p. 696.

7. As represented by the Apostolic Church Order, the Epitome of the Canons of the Holy Apostles, the Arabic Life of Shenute, the Ps.-Athanasian Syntagma Doctrinae, and the Fides CCCXVIII Patrum.

8. For the above information and a reconstruction of the Greek Two Ways, see VAN DE SANDT – FLUSSER, *The Didache*, pp. 112-139.

9. In Barnabas and the Doctrina Apostolorum there are no passages that parallel the materials in Did 1:3a-2:1 and Did 6:2-3. For further details on the establishment of an earlier form of the Two Ways and its versions in early Christian literature, see VAN DE SANDT – FLUSSER, *The Didache*, pp. 55-80; 238-270.

In the Two Ways instruction the Way of Life (ὁδὸς τῆς ζωῆς) is characterized firstly by a fusion of the commandments of divine and altruistic love and a subsequent directive "do not yourself do to another what you would not want done to you"[10]. The definition of the right way of life in the Greek Two Ways thus includes love of God, love of one's neighbour, and the Golden Rule. The latter two precepts of this triad in fact indicate a single governing principle appearing here in two forms, namely the verse in Leviticus and the subsequent Golden Rule[11]. Having quoted these two great rules, the Two Ways then proceeds to describe the path of life itself: "the interpretation of these words is …" (1:3a)[12]. The subsequent section in the reconstructed Two Ways contains a list of precepts which cover the essentials of the second half of the Decalogue (2:2-7)[13].

Within first-century Christian circles the doctrine of the Two Ways was employed in pre-baptismal instruction[14]. This is explicitly stated in Did 7:1

---

10. This latter rule is not only reflected in the Two Ways 1:2c but is frequently found throughout Jewish, Christian, and Hellenistic sources. About the so-called "Golden Rule", see A. DIHLE, *Die Goldene Regel: Eine Einführung in die Geschichte der antiken und frühchristlichen Vulgärethik* (Studienhefte zur Altertumswissenschaft, 7), Göttingen, Vandenhoeck & Ruprecht, 1962; P.S. ALEXANDER, *Jesus and the Golden Rule*, in J.H. CHARLESWORTH – L.L. JOHNS (eds.), *Hillel and Jesus: Comparative Studies of Two Major Religious Leaders*, Minneapolis, MN, Fortress, 1997, pp. 363-388.

11. Surely this maxim is to be considered synonymous with the love command in Lev 19:18. SEE W. BACHER, *Die Agada der Tannaiten*. Vol. 1, Strassburg, Trübner, 1884; repr. Berlin, De Gruyter, 1965-1966, p. 4: "Dieses Wort" (the Golden Rule) "ist nichts anderes, als die negative Ausdrucksweise für das biblische: 'Liebe deinen Nächsten wie dich selbst' (Lev. 19,18)". For additional references, see D.C. SIM, *The Gospel of Matthew and Christian Judaism: The History and Social Setting of the Matthean Community* (Studies of the New Testament and Its World), Edinburgh, T&T Clark, 1998, p. 128, note 56. This assumption is supported by *Tg. Ps-J.* on Lev 19:18. Here the Golden Rule is attached to the altruistic love commandment by paraphrasing the comparative pronoun כמוך with the following clause: 'so that what is hateful to you, you shall not do to him.' The commandment to love one's neighbour as oneself is explained in *Tg. Ps-J.* on Lev 19:34 in the same way, that is, as a reference to the Golden Rule in its negative form.

12. It is quite like Hillel who in his famous reply to the pagan who inquired about a pithy summary of Judaism, is reported to have appended to the Golden Rule: "the rest is interpretation" (*b. Šabb* 31a); See VAN DE SANDT – FLUSSER, *The Didache*, pp. 158-160.

13. Already in the Hebrew Bible the image of the Two Ways was used to portray the call of God's Torah: Deut 11:26; Jer 21:8 etc. See U. LUCK, *Die Frage nach dem Guten: Zu Mt 19,16–30 und Par.*, in W. SCHRAGE (ed.), *Studien zum Text und zur Ethik des Neuen Testaments*, Berlin – New York, De Gruyter, 1986, pp. 282-297. In the Second Temple period there is a close affinity between the ideas and ethical principles in the reconstructed Greek tractate of the Two Ways and the views in the early Derekh Erets doctrine. Oral tracts with subjects concerning Derekh Erets existed as early as the second century C.E. and part of these writings reflect the teachings of pious Jews on moral behaviour. See VAN DE SANDT – FLUSSER, *The Didache*, pp. 165-179.

14. By this I do not mean, however, that the use of the Two Ways teaching was solely restricted to catechetical instruction prior to baptism. That it was used otherwise as well is shown by its insertion into the Letter of Barnabas, which was written to baptized Christians.

in a verse that directly follows the rendering of the Two Ways section: "Concerning baptism, baptize as follows: after having previously said these things (ταῦτα πάντα προειπόντες), baptize" (7:1). The candidate who applied for baptism was instructed in the ethical catechesis as contained in the Two Ways tradition[15]. It is also possible that the supposed life situation *(Sitz im Leben)* of the Two Ways tradition used by Matthew – that is the setting of the Two Ways before it was introduced into the present context of the Gospel – might have been a catechetical situation, perhaps even an instruction for neophytes[16].

We return to the Sermon on the Mount in order to establish that it is even more likely that material from the Two Ways was used to supplement the original gate saying in Matt 7:13-14 when we realize that Matthew – unlike Mark and Luke – has placed this statement in close proximity to the principle of loving one's neighbour. The middle section of the Sermon on the Mount opens and closes with references to "the Law and the Prophets" (5:17 and 7:12). In 7:12 this main body of the Sermon is brought to a close by a positive formulation of the Golden Rule: "So whatever you wish that men would do to you, do so to them; for this is the Law and the Prophets". Matthew perceives the Golden Rule as an eminent summary and decisive climax of the preceding demands, prohibitions, and ethical discussion in 5:17–7:12[17]. The ensuing phrase in 7:12c ("for this is the Law and the Prophets") indicates that the Golden Rule can serve as an underlying principle of "the Law and the Prophets". Examining the Sermon on the Mount as a whole, one notices that the Two Ways motif (7:13-14) and the positive formulation of the Golden Rule directly connected to it (7:12) are the essential scope and climax of the foregoing rules of conduct for believers. The image of the Way of Life is used as expressing the call of the Torah. Interestingly, the same elements, the double love commandment, i.e., love of God and love of neighbour, and the Golden Rule serve as the essential components of the Way of Life in the Greek Two Ways.

---

15. As late as in fourth-century Egypt the Two Ways manual was used as a pre-baptismal teaching and a basic instruction about Christian life to neophytes. See VAN DE SANDT – FLUSSER, *The Didache*, pp. 86-89.

16. G. BRAUMANN, *Zum Traditionsgeschichtlichen Problem der Seligpreisungen Mt V 3-12*, in *NovT* 4 (1960) 253-260, pp. 259-260; W. POPKES, *Die Gerechtigkeitstradition im Matthäus-Evangelium*, in *ZNW* 80 (1989) 1-23, p. 17.

17. G.N. STANTON, *A Gospel for a New People: Studies in Matthew*, Edinburgh, T&T Clark, 1992; reprinted, 1993, pp. 303-304; R.A. GUELICH, *The Sermon on the Mount: A Foundation for Understanding*, Waco, TX, Word Publishing, ²1983, pp. 360-363 and 379-381; BETZ, *The Sermon on the Mount*, p. 518; See also K. SYREENI, *The Making of the Sermon on the Mount: A Procedural Analysis of Matthew's Redactorial Activity* 1: *Methodology & Compositional Analysis* (Annales Academiae Scientiarum Fennicae Diss., 44), Helsinki, Suomalainen Tiedeakatemia, 1987, pp. 158-160 and 173-180; SIM, *The Gospel of Matthew*, pp. 127-130.

II. THE WAY OF LIFE IN MATTHEW 19:16-22

The core topics of Matt 19:16-30, wealth and kingdom, recall Jesus' teaching in the Antitheses of the Sermon on the Mount about the commandments (5:17-48), about being perfect (5:48) and about poverty and treasure in heaven (6:19-21). The impossibility of serving both God and the mammon (6:24) is concretely demonstrated in 19:16-30[18]. In contrast to "laying up treasures on earth" which are perishable and can be stolen (6:19), one should "have treasure in heaven". And there is more. The story of the rich young man in 19:16-30 not only is a narrative illustration of important portions of the Sermon on the Mount but, like the Sermon, may have been inspired by the Two Ways as well. This is shown by the changes Matthew makes to his Markan source. A first indication suggesting an image of a way or road is found right at the beginning of Jesus' dialogue with the rich man. Matthew has the man ask: "Teacher, what good deed must I do, to have eternal life? (ἵνα σχῶ ζωὴν αἰώνιον)" (19:16)[19]. The rich man seems to be thinking that it might be possible to obtain eternal life in the same way he acquired his possessions. Matthew has Jesus reply in v. 17 by replacing the man's wording of "to have" (ἵνα σχῶ) with "to enter" (εἰσελθεῖν) and "eternal life" (ζωὴ αἰώνιον) by just "life" (ζωή): "If you wish to enter life (εἰς τὴν ζωὴν εἰσελθεῖν), keep the commandments". This revision is redactional and seems to reflect the attempt to conceive the question within the framework of the Two Ways. It "transfers the man from the market to the road and implies that he must make a pilgrimage instead of a purchase"[20].

Another remarkable change in comparison to Mark is Matthew's transformation of the man into a young man in v. 20. Matthew drops the phrase "from my youth" (ἐκ νεότητός μου) in Mark 10:20 and labels him "the young man" (ὁ νεανίσκος) twice (19:20.22). In Luke 18:18 the young man is called a "ruler" (ἄρχων) which may be considered another hint of his being mature in age. Why has Matthew altered the man's age? Only in the first Gospel is the rich man said to be "young". The latter term is perhaps related to the word τέλειος in Matt 19:21 which in addition to meaning "perfect" also signifies "mature, grown up," so that the story is about a

---

18. DAVIES – ALLISON, *Matthew*, vol. 3, p. 63.

19. Interestingly, this question is found in Luke twice. One occurrence is found of course in the parallel account in Luke 18:18 where the ruler asks "what must I do to inherit eternal life?" (τί ποιήσας ζωὴν αἰώνιον κληρονομήσω;) and the other is articulated – with the very same words – by a lawyer (νομικός) in 10:25.

20. DAVIES – ALLISON, *Matthew*, vol. 3, p. 43.

young man growing up[21]. But there is also another possibility. Matthew may have identified the questioner as a "young man" so as to emphasize the instruction needed to enter a new life. We have seen that the Two Ways often served as a basic catechetical instruction preceding the ritual of baptism. The supposed *Sitz-im-Leben* of the teaching used by Matthew was a catechetical situation, perhaps even an instruction for neophytes[22]. Because Matthew was interested in the conditions for admission in the community he compared the rich man to a convert and calls him "young"[23].

Additional alterations introduced in Mark's version of the story betray Two Ways traits as well. In 19:17b there is a direct connection between entering life and keeping the commandments. As for the sequence of the commandments, Matthew evidently depends on Mark except for the commandment "you shall not defraud" which is lacking in Matthew. He probably knew that this commandment was not found in the Decalogue. Also Matthew's formulation of the commandments – having the negative οὐ followed by a second person future indicative instead of μή followed by an aorist subjunctive – varies from Mark's wording. He did not assimilate the rendering of Scripture here to the LXX[24] but instead adapted Mark's phrasing of the commandments to "with which he was familiar and which suited him here"[25]. In his usage of the negative οὐ followed by a second person future indicative Matthew may have fallen back on the Two Ways wording that exhibits the same phraseology.

21. W.R.G. LOADER, *Jesus' Attitude towards the Law: A Study of the Gospels* (WUNT, 2/97), Tübingen, Mohr Siebeck, 1997, p. 226; See also LU7, *Das Evangelium nach Matthäus*, vol. 3, pp. 123 and 145; E. YARNOLD, *Τέλειος in St. Matthew's Gospel*, in F.L. CROSS (ed.), *Studia Evangelica IV* (TU, 102), Berlin, Akademie-Verlag, 1968, 269-273, p. 272.

22. Among the Therapeutes described by Philo of Alexandria in his *On the Contemplative Life* there was a category of men called νέοι who served at table but were not slaves (nr. 72). Pierre Geoltrain translates this term νέοι by "novices" because "nous avons vu" (*Contempl. Life* nr. 67) "que certains Thérapeutes ont grandi 'dès leur jeune âge' dans la vie contemplative". See P. GEOLTRAIN, *Le traité de la vie contemplative de Philon d'Alexandrie: Introduction, traduction et notes* (Semitica, 10), Paris, Librairie d'Amérique et d'Orient Adrien-Maisonneuve, 1960, p. 43 (traduction) and p. 58 (notes).

23. See P. BONNARD, *L'Évangile selon Saint Matthieu* (CNT, 1), Genève, Labor et Fides, ⁴2002, p. 288: "ce mot est peut-être une allusion aux catéchumènes de l'Église matthéenne". This view might be substantiated by the aorist participle προσελθών ("having approached") in v. 16 as its Hebrew counterpart, the verb קרב ("to approach"), has a technical meaning in the Community Rule of Qumran expressing the arrival of candidates for initiation. See S. LÉGASSE, *L'appel du riche (Marc 10,17-31 et parallèles): Contribution à l'étude des fondements scripturaires de l'état religieux* (VS), Paris, Beauchesne, 1966, pp. 196-198.

24. As proposed by DAVIES – ALLISON, *Matthew*, vol. 3, pp. 40 and 44; LUZ, *Das Evangelium nach Matthäus*, vol. 3, p. 122; J. GNILKA, *Das Matthäusevangelium* (HTKNT, 1/2), vol. 2, Freiburg – Basel – Wien, Herder, 1988, p. 162.

25. M.J.J. MENKEN, *Matthew's Bible: The Old Testament Text of the Evangelist* (BETL, 173), Leuven, University Press – Peeters, 2004, pp. 211-212.

More important is the adjustment in Matt 19:18-19. Jesus instructs the questioner to keep the second table of the Decalogue in order to enter life. The link between 'life' and commandments was quite common in Jewish tradition[26]. Matt 19:18-19 might thus reflect traces of a common catechism, a view that is substantiated by the article τό preceding the Decalogue commands in Matt 19:18. When Matthew, deviating from Mark 10:19 (and Luke 18:20), appends this τό he as much as says he is reproducing extant (catechetical) material[27]. At variance with Mark, Matthew attaches the summary command of Lev 19:18 as well. The commands from the second table of the Decalogue are associated with neighbourly love: "You shall not kill, You shall not commit adultery, You shall not steal, You shall not bear false witness, Honour your father and mother, and, You shall love your neighbour as yourself" (v. 18b-19). By stressing the triad of life (v. 16 and again in v. 17), the second table of the Decalogue (vv. 18b-19a), and the principle of neighbourly love (v. 19b) Matthew's version of the rich man's episode reflects a substantial part of the Two Ways teaching.[28] For we have seen that the reconstructed Way of Life is defined first by a fusion of the commandments of divine and altruistic love, the subsequent Golden Rule and a list of precepts covering the second table of the Ten Commandments in Did 2:2-7[29]. By

26. See Deut 30:15-20; Lev 18:5; Prov 6:23; Mal 2:4-5; Bar 3:9; Ps Sol 14:2; Rom 7:10; 4 Ezra 14:30; *m. 'Abot* 2:7; cf. DAVIES – ALLISON, *Matthew*, vol. 3, p. 43. Moreover, in addition to the double love commandment and the single commandment to love one's neighbour (or its variant version in the Golden Rule) also the second table of the Decalogue was thought of as covering the whole Torah as well. The Decalogue kept an honoured place until the end of the first century. For more information, see F.E. VOKES, *The Ten Commandments in the New Testament and in First Century Judaism*, in *SE* 5 (1968) 146-154; K. BERGER, *Die Gesetzesauslegung Jesu: Ihr historischer Hintergrund im Judentum und im Alten Testament*, vol. 1 (WMANT, 40/1), Neukirchen, Neukirchener Verlag, 1972, pp. 258-361; Y. AMIR, *Die Zehn Gebote bei Philon von Alexandrien*, in ID., *Die Hellenistische Gestalt des Judentums bei Philon von Alexandrien* (Forschungen zum Jüdisch-Christlichen Dialog, 5), Neukirchen-Vluyn, Neukirchener Verlag d. Erziehungsvereins, 1983, pp. 131-163; K.-W. NIEBUHR, *Gesetz und Paränese: Katechismusartige Weisungsreihen in der frühjüdischen Literatur* (WUNT, 2/28), Tübingen, Mohr, 1987, pp. 63-66. In addition, also the second table of the Decalogue was commonly seen as summarizing the essentials of the Law as may be derived from instances in Pseudo-Phocylides, *Sentences* 3-7 and Rom 13:8-10.

27. See GNILKA, *Das Matthäusevangelium*, vol. 2, p. 164; BONNARD, *L'Évangile selon Saint Matthieu*, p. 288.

28. See for example also C.N. JEFFORD, *The Sayings of Jesus in the Teaching of the Twelve Apostles* (VCSup, 11), Leiden, Brill, 1989, pp. 54-56.62; A.J.P. GARROW, *The Gospel of Matthew's Dependence on the Didache* (JSNTSup, 254), London – New York, T&T Clark, 2004, pp. 240-241 and 247-248.

29. The second table of the Decalogue has nevertheless been expanded with specific elements, including pederasty, magic, sorcery, abortion, and infanticide. The command to "honour your father and mother" seems out of place as it belongs to the first table of the Decalogue. Apparently there were traditional divisions which assigned this precept to the

introducing this material by the article τό he was able to recall the whole of the familiar instruction about the Way of Life.

The term "perfect"(τέλειος) in the clause "if you wish to be perfect" (v. 21) has no Markan counterpart and, apart from the additional occurrence in Matt 5:48, it is not found in the Gospels. In Matt 5:48 it serves to conclude 5:21-48, a pericope which presents examples of what it means to abide by a "greater righteousness". Jesus' requirement in 5:20 that the disciples' righteousness must be "greater" (πλεῖον) than that of the scribes and Pharisees[30] is echoed in 5:48: "You, therefore, must be perfect (τέλειοι), as your heavenly Father is perfect (τέλειος)". The charge in Matt 19:21 corresponds to the greater righteousness announced in Matt 5:20, implying that more Torah must be done than the legal minimum[31]. Following Jesus requires observing the commandments and, conversely, there can be no true observing of the commandments if they are not kept in accordance with their explanation by Jesus[32]. Since the word τέλειος ("perfect") is lacking in the other Gospels it is surprising to find it in the Didache twice. In Did 1:4 the phrase "and you will be perfect" occurs in a non-retaliation context and in Did 6:2a those who are able to carry the "whole yoke of the Lord" are called "perfect". As seen above, we believe Did 1:3b–2:1 and 6:2-3 to be later Christian additions to a basic Two Ways tradition[33]. On the other hand, the repeated occurrence of the term "perfect" in precisely those Matthean contexts which display a close association with the Two Ways may indicate that Matthew was acquainted with a copy of the Two Ways which included Did 6:2-3.

second table; cf. S. Eli. Rab., Chap. 7 (= M. FRIEDMANN [Ish-Shalom] [ed.], Pseudo-Seder Eliahu Zuta [Derech Ereç und Pirkê R. Eliezer], Vienna, n.p., 1904; reprinted [and, in addition, Seder Eliahu Rabba and Seder Eliahu Zuta] Jerusalem, Wahrmann, 1969, p. 35) and Pseudo-Phocylides, Sentences, vv. 3-8.

30. See GUELICH, The Sermon on the Mount, pp. 135 and 156; LUZ, Das Evangelium nach Matthäus, vol. 1, p. 230; J.P. MEIER, Law and History in Matthew's Gospel: A Redactional Study of Mt. 5:17-48 (AnBib, 71), Rome, Biblical Institute Press, 1976, pp. 116-119; DAVIES – ALLISON, Matthew, vol. 1, p. 501.

31. DAVIES – ALLISON, Matthew, vol. 3, p. 46; CARTER, Households and Discipleship, p. 117; LUZ, Das Evangelium nach Matthäus, vol. 3, pp. 46 and 123-125; GNILKA, Das Matthäusevangelium, vol. 2, p. 165.

32. See also W.J.C. WEREN, The Ideal Community according the Matthew, James, and the Didache, in H. VAN DE SANDT – J. ZANGENBERG (eds.), Matthew, James and Didache: Three Related Documents in Their Jewish and Christian Settings (Symposium Series, 45), Atlanta, SBL, 2008, 177-200, p. 189; M. KONRADT, The Love Command in Matthew, James, and the Didache, in VAN DE SANDT – ZANGENBERG (eds.), Matthew, James and Didache, 271-288, pp. 274-278.

33. See also H. VAN DE SANDT, The Didache Redefining its Jewish Identity in View of Gentiles Joining the Community, in A. HOUTMAN – A. DE JONG – M. MISSET-VAN DE WEG (eds.), Empsychoi Logoi: Religious Innovations in Antiquity (AJEC, 73), Leiden – Boston, Brill, 2008, 246-265, pp. 248-253.

We can draw the conclusion, then, that the Two Ways teaching sheds light on the story of the rich young man in Matt 19:16-22 in two respects. First, it is clear that observance of the second table of the Decalogue in vv. 18-19 does not suffice to be qualified for eternal life. In Matthew the rich man asks: "What do I still lack" (v. 20b)? Obviously the speaker believes he has faithfully observed the law but in spite of his obedience Matthew shows him to be aware of his failure to enter life. Matthew has Jesus reply in v. 21: "If you wish to be perfect (τέλειος), then go, sell all your possessions and give to the poor". This higher ethical standard is not an additional requirement but the concrete enactment of the command to love one's neighbour. This brings us to the second point. There appears to be an important distinction between keeping Torah within a normal Jewish framework of expectations (vv. 18-19) and keeping Torah as defined by the love command (vv. 18-22)[34]. In Matthew, the emphasis on obedience to the second half of the Decalogue is far from simply a quantitative demand for compliance with every commandment; it is a requirement to live out all the implications of loving one's neighbour. Of course, Matthew's presentation varies from the pattern in the Two Ways tradition since he relies significantly on Mark's Gospel and largely follows his word order. Yet, by adding the love commandment to the second part of the Decalogue Matthew indicates that rather than considering all injunctions of the Torah of equal weight, he prioritizes values. In Matthew and the Two Ways the love commandment is the primary interpretative key to the Decalogue commandments[35]. The law is subordinated to a single dominant perspective through which all the other commandments and directives are interpreted.

III. The Way of Death in Matthew 19:23-26

It is important to establish that in describing Jesus' general statement about the rich in vv. 23-26 Matthew still depends upon Mark. He follows

---

34. This is not the same as saying that we are dealing here with two kinds of Judaism, the traditional type keeping the commandments, and the 'perfect' type that involves following Jesus; see D.J. HARRINGTON, *The Rich Young Man in Matthew 19,16-22: Another Way to God for Jews?* in F. VAN SEGBROECK – C.M. TUCKETT – G. VAN BELLE – J. VERHEYDEN (eds.), *The Four Gospels 1992*, vol. 2, Leuven, University Press – Peeters, 1992, pp. 1425-1432. In my opinion this distinction cannot be maintained since the one variety cannot lead to salvation apart from the other.

35. As seen above, the diverse precepts in the Sermon in Matt 5:17–7:12 and the Way of Life in Did 1:2-4:14 are organized by and subsumed under the love command (Matt 7:12 and Did 1:2).

Mark's narrative closely and preserves the same solution: ultimately only God makes salvation possible (v. 26). In v. 23 Matthew largely agrees with the phraseology of Mark 10:23 where Jesus turns from the rich man to his disciples commenting on what has just happened: "And Jesus said to his disciples, 'Truly, I say to you, it will be hard for a rich man to enter the kingdom of heaven'". The next verse in Mark, however, is not found in Matthew: "And the disciples were amazed at his words. But Jesus said to them again, 'Children, how hard is it to enter the kingdom of God!'" It is significant that after 19:23 Matthew has omitted the wide-ranging statement of Mark 10:24. Whereas Mark has changed the subject from the rich man to all men, Matthew keeps the discussion on the subject of riches and the kingdom[36].

According to Matthew, one lives either by God's values or by those based on wealth. A similar dualistic trend is found in Matt 7:13-14 where the Two Ways theme sets the stage for the contrasting replies to Jesus' Sermon on the Mount that follow in the final section (7:13-27). The Two Ways represent the dualistic trend of answering Jesus' call for acceptance of his words. The deeds or behaviour of the false prophets (7:15-23) offers a polarity of good trees and virtuous fruit (good natures generating good deeds) with bad trees and evil fruit (bad natures producing bad deeds). This subject continues through vv. 21-23, mentioning those who do the will of the Father as opposed to those who do not. Also, in the subsequent parable of the two builders (7:24-27) the antithesis is between those hearing and practising the words of Jesus and those hearing but not practising them.[37]

For the sake of his wealth the rich man rejected Jesus' offer of eternal life by walking the right path. He preferred walking the Way of Death and destruction into the fires of hell. The call for voluntary poverty in Matt 19:21 was not answered in v. 22. While according to Matt 19:23 it was hard for the rich to enter the kingdom, it has become almost unachievable in the next verse: "Again I tell you, it is easier for a camel to go through the eye of a needle than for a rich man to enter the kingdom of God". The disciples however still miss the point as they were astounded and asked "who then can be saved" (19:25)? They give the impression that they still believe that those with high social status and wealth were divinely favoured and

36. See also C. COULOT, *La structuration de la péricope de l'homme riche et ses différentes lectures (Mc 10, 17-31; Mt 19, 16-30; Lc 18, 18-30)*, in RSR 56 (1982) 240-252, p. 249.

37. Matthew opens a general drift of two opposing paradigms by presenting the Two Ways (7:13-14), contrasting the way which leads to destruction with the way which leads to life. The ways expounded upon here correlate with the positive and negative examples of the concluding units.

seem to regard wealth as a sign of divine support (Deut 8:11-20; 28:1-14, esp. 11). Instead of seeing wealth and prosperity as a power which forces a rich man to choose between God and his possessions, between treasure in heaven and treasure on earth, they conceptualized prosperity and wealth as marks of divine favour. Yet, by calling the rich man to sell his possessions in 19:21 Jesus has rejected this view[38].

Just like in 7:13-27, Matthew has Jesus employ the Two Ways dichotomy in 19:23-26 and he does so, again, by articulating a response to Jesus' teaching in 7:13-14. The image of the two paths of death and life is applied in terms of a behavioural contrast between the wealthy and others[39]. In the Markan parallel verse (10:21) Jesus looks at the man and loves him. In Matthew there is no mention of Jesus' love for the rich young man. After all, this man has forfeited life (see also 16:26) since when given the choice he opted for mammon. Where the rich man fails, Peter and others succeed. This reward is not expected in this mortal life but as an eschatological good to be realized in immortality.

IV. ESCHATOLOGICAL LIFE AS A REWARD IN MATT 19:27-30

In order to convince the young rich man to convert from the way of death to the way of life Matthew uses economic and heavenly language. The final benefit and blessing is referred to by the words "life" (v. 17), "treasure

---

38. W. CARTER, *Matthew and the Margins: A Sociopolitical and Religious Reading* (The Bible and Liberation Series), Maryknoll, NY, Orbis, 2000, pp. 390-391; see also DAVIES–ALLISON, *Matthew*, vol. 3, p. 53. The Two Ways also contains complaints against the wealthy. The characteristics of those who follow the Way of Death in the lengthy list of the Two Ways 5:2 includes people who "do not show mercy to a poor person, who are not distressed by [the plight of] the oppressed, ..., who reject the needy person, who oppress the person who is distressed, [who are] defenders of the rich [and] unjust judges of the poor".

39. Interestingly, the narrow eye of the needle in Matt 19:24 has been associated with the narrow way of 7:13-14 on several occasions. See for example Clement of Alexandria, *Quis dives salvetur*, 26:7: "the camel which passes through a straight and narrow way (διὰ στενῆς ὁδοῦ καὶ τεθλιμμένης) sooner than the rich man". For the Greek text see O. STÄHLIN – L. FRÜCHTEL (eds.), *Clemens Alexandrinus*, vol 3: *Stromata Buch VII und VIII, Excerpta ex Theodoto, Eclogae propheticae, Quis dives salvetur, Fragmente*, Berlin, Akademie-Verlag, ²1970, p. 177. And in Origen, *Contra Celsum*, 6.16 it says: "If Celsus were honest and had read the Gospels without hatred and hostility, he would carefully have considered why it is a camel, the animal which is crooked by its natural constitution, which he compared to a rich man, and what he who said that the way leading to life is narrow and strait (στενὴν φάσκοντι εἶναι καὶ τεθλιμμένην τὴν ὁδὸν τὴν ἀπάγουσαν εἰς τὴν ζωήν) meant by the narrow eye of the needle". For the Greek text see M. BORRET, *Origène: Contre Celse*, vol. 3: livres V et VI (SC, 147), Paris, Cerf, 1969, p. 218 and for the English translation compare H. CHADWICK, *Origen: Contra Celsum*, Cambridge, University Press, 1953; reprinted 1965, p. 329.

in heaven" (v. 21), "to be perfect" (v. 21), "enter the Kingdom of Heaven / Kingdom of God" (vv. 23.24), "to be saved" (v. 25), and "inherit eternal life" (19:29)[40]. The theme of eternal life is also found in verses of the parallel synoptic accounts (Mark 10:17; Luke 18:18), but in the Matthean section this element is especially highlighted both by Jesus' conditional response to the young man (v. 17) and by the general statement that all who (πᾶς ὅστις) follow Jesus will inherit eternal life in v. 29[41].

Peter, picking up on Jesus' promise to the rich man of "treasure in heaven" (19:21), asks in Matt 19:27 about the disciples' future and eschatological reward. For in contrast to the rich man, they were not trapped by wealth. Jesus responds in vv. 28-30. Let's turn to verse 29 first. Jesus declares that they will inherit eternal life which lies entirely in the future. The verse affirms eschatological fortune for all faithful followers: "And every one who has left houses or brothers or sisters or father or mother or children or lands, for my name's sake, will receive a hundredfold, and inherit eternal life". Deviating from Mark 10:30a-c ("there is no one who will not receive a hundredfold now in this time, houses and brothers and sisters and mothers and children and lands, with persecutions"), Matthew keeps the audience's attention on the future. In Mark there was a distinction between rewards with persecution "now in this time" (v. 30a-c), and eternal life "in the age to come" (v. 30d). Matthew puts all the rewards into the age to come.

Jesus starts responding to Peter however in the preceding v. 28 which offers an even more radical difference from Mark as it presents a lengthy statement lacking in Mark:

(a) Jesus said to them, "Truly, I say to you, at the regeneration (ἐν τῇ παλιγγενεσίᾳ),
(b) when the Son of Man shall sit on his glorious throne,
(c) you (ὑμεῖς) who have followed me will also sit on twelve thrones, judging the twelve tribes of Israel".

As a result of this Matthean insertion the Twelve are singled out from the rest of Jesus' followers. Important questions prompted by this verse are: Where does this verse come from? What does παλιγγενεσία mean? And why did Matthew add this verse to this third section?

The Twelve are rewarded here with the special privilege of sitting on twelve thrones and judging the twelve tribes of Israel (v. 28c). Moreover,

---

40. CARTER, *Households and Discipleship*, p. 117.
41. F.W. BURNETT, *Παλιγγενεσία in Matt. 19:28: A Window on the Matthean Community?*, in *JSNT* 17 (1983) 60-72, p. 63.

it is noteworthy that by adding this clause 28c Matthew generates a clear distinction between the Twelve (note the emphatic ὑμεῖς in 19:28) and everyone else (καὶ πᾶς ὅστις in v. 29) who became a disciple[42]. For our purposes it is significant to see that v. 28c displays some similarity with the wording of Luke 22:30b although the latter clause is found in a completely different context:

> [(Luke 22:29) And I assign to you, as my Father assigned to me, a kingdom]
> (30a) that you may eat (ἵνα ἔσθητε) and drink (πίνητε) at my table in my kingdom,
> (30b) and sit on (καθήσεσθε) thrones judging the twelve tribes of Israel.

In Luke 22:30 the sitting upon thrones is rather artificially connected with the dining at the eschatological table. First, from grammatical point of view the formulation of the promises in Luke rather abruptly shifts from a present conjunctive (ἔσθητε and πίνητε) to a future indicative (καθήσεσθε). Second, the images represented by the two phrases do not quite fit together since the disciples are first lying down at a table (30a; see also v. 27) and then sit on thrones (30b)[43]. It thus appears that initially Luke 22:30b circulated independently, that is, without 30a. Moreover, the close affinity of the promise in Luke 22:30b with Matt 19:28c and its absence in Mark lead one to conclude that this saying probably derives from the Q source. Both Matthew and Luke might then have provided this Q-logion with an introduction of their own (Matt 28a.b and Luke 22:29-30a).

It is thus difficult to escape the impression that Matt 19:28c combines the traditional saying about the judging of the Twelve in v. 28c with the wording of vv. 28a.b. The phrases in 19:28a.b are found in Matthew only and evidence heavy redaction. Matthew probably intended to highlight the eschatological nature of the function promised to the Twelve in 19:28c. And this brings us to some observations on our second question regarding "the regeneration". The temporal phrase ἐν τῇ παλιγγενεσίᾳ ("at the regeneration" in v. 28a) is coupled with the return of the Son of Man to exercise judgment in v. 28b. Its wording is closely related to statements like:

---

42. "The promised function of ruling" ('judging' might however be more appropriate here – see below) "has nothing to do with inheriting eternal life as a reward for discipleship; it is an eschatological promise of the Risen Jesus to the Twelve, apparently as a glorious 'bonus' to them. The second way 19:28 interrupts the flow of the traditional emphasis of the pericope is that the Twelve are singled out as a group from the rest of Jesus' followers": BURNETT, Παλιγγενεσία in Matt. 19:28, p. 63.

43. See J. DUPONT, Le logion des douze trônes (Mt 19,28; Lc 22,28-30), in Bib 45 (1964) 355-392, pp. 356-363.

The Son of Man will send his angels, and they will gather out of his kingdom all causes of sin and all evildoers, and throw them into the furnace of fire; there men will weep and gnash their teeth. Then the righteous will shine like the sun in the kingdom of their Father. He who has ears, let him hear (Matt 13:41-43);

and

For the Son of Man is to come with his angels in the glory of his Father, and then he will repay every man for what he has done (Matt 16:27);

and

When the Son of Man comes in his glory, and all the angels with him, then he will sit on his glorious throne. Before him will be gathered all the nations, … (Matt 25:31-32a)

Since the images above are very close to the portrayal in Matt 19:28b ("when the Son of Man shall sit on his glorious throne") the latter instance must also be a description of the Last Judgment when the Son of Man will preside over the final verdict[44]. Matthew frequently points toward the return of the "Son of Man" to complete God's purposes, to exercise judgment, and establish God's reign (10:23; 24:27-31.36-44; 25:31-46; 26:64). The phrase ἐν τῇ παλιγγενεσίᾳ seems thus to be synonymous with the clause "in the age to come" (ἐν τῷ αἰῶνι τῷ ἐρχομένῳ) in Mark 10:30 and is therefore to be translated as "at the regeneration", i.e., "at the new birth of the world". The idea of a new world succeeding the existing one at the parousia of Jesus in Matt 19:28 is sometimes thought of as a renovation of the present world order in a changed earth[45], sometimes as a new world order which replaces the present world after its destruction at the eschaton[46]. In any case, Jesus' response focuses on the End, on the disciples' eschatological fortune at the Last Judgment[47].

44. DUPONT, *Le logion des douze thrônes*, pp. 364-368. 377-378.
45. So e.g. E. SCHWEIZER, *The Good News according to Matthew*, London, SPCK, 1978, pp. 389-390; BURNETT, *Παλιγγενεσία in Matt. 19:28*, p. 65; W. SCHENK, *Die Sprache des Matthäus*, Göttingen, Vanderhoeck & Ruprecht, 1987, p.18.
46. The term παλιγγενεσία expresses the idea of cosmic destruction and regeneration which the new age will bring; so D.C. SIM, *The Meaning of παλιγγενεσία in Matthew 19.28*, in *JSNT* 50 (1993) 3-12, p. 5; GNILKA, *Das Matthäusevangelium*, vol. 2, p. 172; T.W. MANSON, *The Sayings of Jesus*, London, SCM Press, 1949, pp. 216-217; BEARE, *The Gospel according to Matthew*, p. 398; A.H. MACNEILE, *The Gospel according to St Matthew*, London, Macmillan, 1915, p. 281; W.C. ALLEN, *A Critical and Exegetical Commentary on the Gospel according to St Matthew* (ICC), Edinburgh, T&T Clark, 1907, p. 212.
47. J.D.M. DERRETT, *PALINGENESIA (Matthew 19.18)*, in *JSNT* 20 (1984) 51-58 argues that the word's true meaning is "resurrection". See also LUZ, *Das Evangelium nach Matthäus*, vol. 3, p. 129.

The traditional image of the Twelve sitting on thrones judging the twelve tribes of Israel apparently appealed to Matthew. But why did Matthew insert this verse 28 in his third section of the rich man's episode? In order to understand this we must turn to Matt 7:13-27 again since that passage closely parallels 19:23-30. We noted above that 7:13-27 offers the Two Ways (7:13-14) as interpreting two mutually exclusive ways of answering Jesus' call. The subsection stresses the importance of man making a fundamental choice between different types of right and wrong behaviour. Moreover, in addition to the two ways of behaving, the passage also shows the horrific fate of the wicked and the reward of the righteous. The admonitions and warnings demonstrate that "life" and "death" can be reached by vindication and condemnation through judgment.

Matt 7:13-27 may be divided into two parts. After the initial passage with the Matthean Two Ways emphasis in vv. 13-14, the community is warned in 7:15-23 against false prophets who are hard to identify. But since a good tree bears good fruit and a bad tree bad fruit, the disciples can discern these disguised false prophets by their practices and lifestyle. In 7:19 the Matthean Jesus depicts their fate at the final judgment. The tree that bears bad fruit will be cut down for firewood[48]. This is followed by the solemn declaration of a primary criterion of divine judgment in 7:21: "Not everyone who says to me, 'Lord, Lord,' will enter the kingdom of heaven, but only the one who does the will of my Father in heaven". Although the false prophets confess Jesus as Lord, prophesy in his name and perform other mighty works, Matthew has Jesus radically dismiss them with the words from Ps 6:9 as "workers of lawlessness" ($\dot\alpha\nu o\mu\acute\iota\alpha$). They fail to do the will of the Father.

The subsequent passage in 7:24-27 sets out stark alternatives again. Two brief scenes illustrate two contrasting responses to Jesus' teaching and the corresponding eschatological destinies. He who hears Jesus' words and obeys them is compared to a wise man who built his house upon a rock. On the other hand, he who hears Jesus' words and does not obey them is compared to a foolish man who built his house upon the sand. The first house built on the solid foundation (that is, those who hear and follow the teachings of Jesus) will survive the overwhelming and threatening storm and flood, that is, eschatological judgment[49], whereas the latter (those who hear but do not

48. John the Baptist had previously employed this image of judgment in Matt 3:10 against the Pharisees and Sadducees. In Matthew everyone, whether disciples, Pharisees and Sadducees, are judged by one law.

49. See DAVIES – ALLISON, *Matthew*, vol. 1, pp. 721-722; LUZ, *Das Evangelium nach Matthäus*, vol. 1, pp. 537-538; J. GNILKA, *Das Matthäusevangelium*, vol. 1 (HTKNT, 1/1), Freiburg, Herder, 1986, p. 282; W. WIEFEL, *Das Evangelium nach Matthäus* (THKNT, 1), Leipzig, Evangelische Verlagsanstalt, 1998, p. 156; F.V. FILSON, *A Commentary on the Gospel According to St. Matthew* (BNTC), London, ²1971, p. 108.

follow Jesus' teachings) will be entirely shattered. The Way of Life and the Way of Death as metaphor in Matt 7:13-14 have been given an eschatological orientation. Closely related to the ethics of the Greek Two Ways, Jesus is the one who definitively interprets the law so that his words provide the basis for "life" (5:21-48; 7:24-27; 12:1-14)[50].

The warnings against false prophets and the foolish builder in Matthew 7:13-27 sets stringent observation of the Torah in accordance with Jesus' exposition as the preeminent principle that will be employed in the final judgment to determine whether people can or cannot enter God's kingdom. A similar Two Ways interpretation seems to be presupposed in Matt 19:27-30 as the themes of life and death have been updated along strictly apocalyptic lines. By his present conduct, by following (ἀκολουθήσαντές) Jesus, that is, by carrying out the ethical mandates provided, man can become worthy of eternal life. Matthew does not use the word "life" in the meaning of a happy, long life on earth. Obedience to the right way is not determined by its puny earthly reward but instead is remunerated by the infinitely greater post-judgment reward. With respect to the approaching End, the word "life" comes to indicate divine exoneration and acquittal contrary to conviction and being found guilty. For Matthew life (ζωή) was an eschatological rather than biological, physical or natural term. It is the promise of compensation as opposed to the punishment of "eternal fire" in Matt 18:8 and the "hell of fire" in 18:9:

> And if your hand or your foot causes you to sin, cut it off and throw it away; it is better for you to enter life (εἰσελθεῖν εἰς τὴν ζωήν) maimed or lame than with two hands or two feet to be thrown into the eternal fire. And if your eye causes you to sin, pluck it out and throw it away; it is better for you to enter life (εἰς τὴν ζωὴν εἰσελθεῖν) with one eye than with two eyes to be thrown into the hell of fire (Matt 18:8-9)

The verses demand radical sacrifice in order to avoid the causes which lead an individual to sin. It is better to live without the hand, foot, or eye which caused one to stumble than to be thrown into hell with them[51].

In Matt 19:27 Peter asks for a reward for the Twelve who "have left everything and followed" Jesus. Since following Jesus (ὑμεῖς οἱ ἀκολουθήσαντες μοι) involved complete fulfilment of the Torah's requirements in accordance

---

50. The Sermon in Q probably concluded with two units which Matthew has taken up in his closing section. The first passage (Matt 7:15-23) concerned good and bad fruit (cf. Luke 6:43-44), a pair of opposites which Matthew creatively incorporated into his warning about false prophets and connected with the final judgment as well (Matt 7:15-23). The second and final unit deals with the wise and the foolish builders (reflected in Luke 6:47-49) which was retained, albeit in an adapted form again, in Matt 7:24-27.

51. These verses are a doublet of Matt 5:29-30 but, interestingly, the clause "enter into life" of Matt 18:8-9 is absent in Matt 5:29-30. Both passages, Matt 5:29-30 and 18:8-9, probably draw upon Mark 9:43-47.

with Jesus' exposition, the Twelve were to become his deputies and assistants in judging the twelve tribes of Israel[52]. The explanation of the Torah which Jesus received directly from the Father[53] – and was obeyed by the Twelve – will be used at Judgment day[54]. Israel will be judged by the Twelve at the consummation[55].

V. Conclusion

Subtle matters of style and content suggest the usage of a Two Ways tradition behind the Matthean form of the episode. Matt 19:16-22 has a close relationship with a version of the Two Ways. Of course it is not an easy task to determine the exact shape of the Two Ways used by Matthew. He probably altered the original form of the material in a manner that was consistent with the format in Mark. Moreover, if one takes the examples one by one some of them may emerge as accidental agreements. When all instances are considered in combination, however, the general case for dependence of our Matthean episode upon a form of the Two Ways seems strong.

Although Matthew was loyal to the tradition he inherited from Mark, he needed to retell the story of the rich man in light of the experience of his own Christian community where the Two Ways probably belonged to the usual catechesis before Baptism. Matthew envisaged a role for the Two Ways in this

---

52. DUPONT, *Le logion des douze thrônes*, p. 378; FILSON, *Gospel According to St. Matthew*, p. 210. Jesus was the judge who authoritatively interprets Torah. In the Antitheses of Matt 5:21-48 Jesus seems to use the controlling clause "but I say to you" to expound the demands of Torah and in Matt 11:27 the power to disclose "these things" to infants is delivered to the Son so as to reveal the Father to whom he chooses.

53. See DAVIES – ALLISON, *Saint Matthew*, vol. 2, pp. 275.280; B.TH. VIVIANO, *Study as Worship: Aboth and the New Testament* (SJLA, 26), Leiden, Brill, 1978, p. 188; C. DEUTSCH, *Hidden Wisdom and the Easy Yoke: Wisdom, Torah and Discipleship in Matthew 11.25-30* (JSNTSup, 18), Sheffield, Sheffield Academic Press, 1987, p. 33.

54. "The theme of judgment, and with it the application of Torah, is never far from Matthew's thinking. The disciples, already commissioned to bind and loose on earth (16:16; 18:18), will share his role in the future"; LOADER, *Jesus' Attitude towards the Law*, p. 227.

55. DUPONT, *Le logion des douze thrônes*, pp. 370-81; GNILKA, *Das Matthäusevangelium*, vol. 2, pp. 171-172; DERRETT, *PALINGENESIA*, pp. 53-54. Others have the term κρίνοντες refer to the function of ruling in the new age. They associate the sitting on the twelve thrones with the governing. In that case the twelve disciples would enter into God's kingly power by themselves becoming leaders. If so, it might be "that for Matthew and his tradition, κρίνοντες had the range of the Hebrew šāpat. In this case, the sitting on the throne designates the exercise of authority over a period of time". See DAVIES–ALLISON, *Matthew*, vol. 3, p. 55; see also BURNETT, Παλιγγενεσία *in Matt. 19:28*, pp. 62-63; R.H. MOUNCE, *Matthew* (NIBC, 1), Peabody-Carlisle, Hendrickson – Paternoster Press 1991, p. 185. The judgment explanation, however, seems to be more appropriate to our episode's content.

narrative because he and his intended readers – all baptized followers of Jesus – might have been reminded of their initiation into the Matthean community by reading Mark's story of discipleship, wealth and eternal life. For this reason Matthew even emphasizes the rich man's youth. The assumption that Matthew read Mark in light of the Two Ways explains other phenomena in our episode as well. It elucidates Matthew's specific arrangement of various themes in vv. 16-22, that is, the question about life, the second half of the Decalogue, the addition of the love command and the reference to perfection. Moreover, it also clarifies why Matthew left out most of Mark 10:24 and inserted the eschatological roles of Jesus and the Twelve in Matt 19:28.

While the traditional Two Ways shows no real interest in eschatology, it takes on new overtones in Matthew. "Life" is named as the specific reward for those who rigorously strive for a higher righteousness. In the Rich Man's episode Matthew applies the conceptual tool of a choice between life and death by drawing a sharp contrast between voluntary poverty and wealth. Wealthy people cannot enter eternal life (vv. 16-22. 23-27). Only when one observes the rulings of the right Way, "Life" becomes "eternal life" which lies entirely in the future.

The incentive for doing right or wrong in Matthew is reward-based[56]. His eschatology is directed at achieving ethical behaviour by people keeping the commandments and attaining righteousness through that behaviour. Condemnation serves as a hortatory tool to extort moral behaviour from Matthew's community. Matthew is far less concerned with the systematization of the details of hell and the afterlife than he is with using every possible means to urge the living to behave properly. He gives no indication that individual persons, whether as a whole or in part, will be transferred to heaven or hell at death and rejects any immediate disposal to bliss or misery after death. When people die they do not move on to dwell in some in-between place or a given intermediate state. They remain dead until they are raised (14:2; 17:9; 28:7). Matthew expects one single total resurrection before the Judgment at the End. All will "live again" but before resurrection can occur, the "Day of Judgment" must arrive. Choosing the right way leads to eternal life!

Tilburg University   Huub VAN DE SANDT
School of Humanities
PO Box 90153
5000 LE Tilburg
The Netherlands

---

56. See J. CLARK-SOLES, *Death and the Afterlife in the New Testament*, New York – London, T&T Clark, 2006, p. 177.

THE CONTROVERSY BETWEEN JESUS AND THE SADDUCEES ABOUT THE RESURRECTION (MATT 22:23-33) IN THE CONTEXT OF EARLY JEWISH ESCHATOLOGY

The controversy about the resurrection is the only episode in which the synoptic tradition has transmitted a direct confrontation between Jesus of Nazareth and the Sadducees, one of the "schools" composing the rich variety of Judaism in the Second Temple period. Jesus' dealings with other groups such as the Pharisees and the Herodians have received much more attention from the Evangelists. The fact that the synoptic writers did in fact narrate the discussion of Jesus with the Sadducees, is all the more remarkable when one realizes that after the fall of Jerusalem (70 C.E.), the Sadducees definitively lost their leading role in Jewish society. It is even more remarkable when the story is a creation of the early Christian community, as a number of scholars assert. There must have been a reason why the tradition of Jesus' discussion with the Sadducees has been preserved and transmitted in the synoptic tradition. One reason might be the issue that they discussed: the possibility of a bodily resurrection of the dead. The reason why the Sadducees are mentioned here is because they deny the resurrection. The discussion is not about the more general question of the afterlife. It concerns a specific form of belief in afterlife, namely the bodily resurrection of the dead. With J.H. Charlesworth, we agree that the term resurrection (ἀνάστασις) "denotes the concept of God's raising the body and soul after death (meant literally) to a new and eternal life (not a return to mortal existence)". He adds that the notion of resurrection should not be confused with the Hellenistic concept of the immortality of the soul, which seems to be espoused in the Wisdom of Solomon (3:1–4:16)[1].

---

1. J.H. CHARLESWORTH, *Where Does the Concept of Resurrection Appear and How Do We Know That?*, in J.H. CHARLESWORTH (ed.), *Resurrection: The Origin and Future of a Biblical Doctrine* (Faith and Scholarship Colloquies Series), New York – London, Continuum –

In this paper we want to undertake a close reading of the pericope, mainly in its Matthean form (Matt 22:23-33), in order to unravel the meaning and relevance of the passage. Our study will deal (I) with the larger context of the discussion about afterlife in the early Judaism, (II) with the structure of the text unit, (III) with the question of the Sadducees, (IV) the answer of Jesus, and finally (V) with the tradition-historical place of the text unit.

I. RESURRECTION IN EARLY JUDAISM

In order to understand the discussion between Jesus and the Sadducees, one should have a general view of the diversity of opinions concerning the future of the dead in early Judaism[2].

It is well known that the Hebrew Bible scarcely directly refers to the concept of the resurrection of the dead. It seems that Israel was more attached to the present life as a gift of God and did not dream of a marvel-

---

Clark, 2006, 1-21, p. 2. The author makes a useful distinction between different categories of "resurrection" language: resurrection of a nation (Ezek 37:1-12), raising of a group from disenfranchisement (1QH^{a}16:5-6), raising of the individual from social disenfranchisement (1QH^{a}16), from personal embarrassment (1QH^{a}10:9-14), from the sickbed to health (1QH^{a}17:4-12; Mark 5:21-43), from inactivity to do God's will (1QH^{a}14:29-30), from despondency due to consciousness of sin (11QPsa 19:10-11), from ignorance to divinely revealed knowledge (1QH^{a}19:12-14), from meaninglessness in this world to a realizing eschatology: experiencing the End time in the present (1QH^{a}11:19-20), or both now and in the future (1QS 4:6-8; John 5: 25); raising of Christ from Sheol (*descensus ad inferos*) (*Odes of Solomon* 42:11), raising an apocalyptist into heaven (2 *Enoch* 1:8; 2 Cor 12:1-3; Rev 4:1), a spiritual raising up or awakening of an individual (Eph 5:14); raising of the individual from death to mortal life (1 Kings 17:17-24; 2 Kings 4:31-37; 13:20-21; John 11); and finally the raising of the individual from death to eternal life. The latter concept is the classic resurrection belief.

2. See the surveys of G.F. MOORE, *Judaism in the First Centuries of the Christian Era.* Vol. 2 (1930), New York, Schocken Books, 1971, pp. 377-395 (eschatology); J. BONSIRVEN, *Le Judaïsme Palestinien au temps de Jésus-Christ: Sa théologie. I. La théologie dogmatique* (Bibliothèque de théologie historique), Paris, G. Beauchesne & Fils, 1934, pp. 468-485 (la résurrection). 486-503 (le jugement). 504-526 (la rétribution definitive: la récompense). 527-541 (la rétribution definitive: le châtiment); G.W.E. NICKELSBURG, *Resurrection, Immortality, and Eternal Life in Intertestamental Judaism* (HTS, 26), Cambridge, MA, Harvard University Press, 1972; H.C.C. CAVALLIN, *Life after Death: Paul's Argument for the Resurrection of the Dead in 1 Cor 15. Part 1. An Enquiry into the Jewish Background* (ConBNT, 7), Lund, Gleerup, 1974; O. SCHWANKL, *Die Sadduzäerfrage (Mk. 12,18-27 par.): Eine exegetisch-theologische Studie zur Auferstehungserwartung* (BBB, 66), Frankfurt am Main, Athenäum, 1987, pp. 142-292; R. MARTIN-ACHARD – G.W.E. NICKELSBURG, *Resurrection*, in D.N. FREEDMAN (ed.), *ABD*, Vol. 5, New York, Doubleday, 1992, pp. 681-691.

lous life after death. It was generally believed that the dead dwelled in Sheol, "a vast underground region, dark and dusty". The dead were forgotten (Ps 88:13; Qoh 3:19-21; 9:5-10) and had "no contact with the world of the living and still less with the living God"[3]. There were some exceptions to this common destiny. Some exemplary individuals were taken up into heaven (the assumption of Enoch in Gen 5:24, and Elijah in 2 Kings 2:1-15). There were also healings in which dead persons came back to life on earth (1 Kings 17:17-24; 2 Kings 4:31-37; 13:20-21). The prophets also used the image of a resurrection to evoke the restoration of Israel (Hos 6:1-3; Isa 26:19) and of Judah (Ezek 37:1-14).

The only text of the Hebrew Bible (MT) which clearly envisages the resurrection of the dead is Dan 12:2-3 (composed some time during the Maccabean Revolt 167-164 B.C.E):

2a And many of those who sleep in the land of dust shall awake:
 b some to everlasting life,
 c and others to everlasting reproach and derision.
3a But those who instruct in wisdom shall shine like the shining of the firmament.
 b And those who turn the multitudes to righteousness, like the stars forever and ever.

Dan LXX

2 καὶ πολλοὶ τῶν καθευδόντων ἐν τῷ πλάτει τῆς γῆς ἀναστήσονται,
οἱ μὲν εἰς ζωὴν αἰώνιον, οἱ δὲ εἰς ὀνειδισμόν,
οἱ δὲ εἰς διασπορὰν καὶ αἰσχύνην αἰώνιον.
3 καὶ οἱ συνιέντες φανοῦσιν ὡς φωστῆρες τοῦ οὐρανοῦ
καὶ οἱ κατισχύοντες τοὺς λόγους μου ὡσεὶ τὰ ἄστρα τοῦ οὐρανοῦ εἰς τὸν αἰῶνα
τοῦ αἰῶνος.

Dan Th.

2 καὶ πολλοὶ τῶν καθευδόντων ἐν γῆς χώματι ἐξεγερθήσονται,
οἱ μὲν εἰς ζωὴν αἰώνιον καὶ οὗτοι εἰς ὀνειδισμὸν καὶ εἰς αἰσχύνην αἰώνιον.
3 καὶ οἱ συνιέντες ἐκλάμψουσιν ὡς ἡ λαμπρότης τοῦ στερεώματος
καὶ ἀπὸ τῶν δικαίων τῶν πολλῶν ὡς οἱ ἀστέρες εἰς τοὺς αἰῶνας καὶ ἔτι.

In this text, the elements necessary to speak of a resurrection are present: the people mentioned are really dead (רבים מישני אדמת־עפר "many of those who sleep in the land of the dust"); a mention of their resurrection (יקיצו "they shall awake"); a resurrection which does not mean a

---

3. MARTIN-ACHARD – NICKELSBURG, *Resurrection*, pp. 680-681; R. MARTIN-ACHARD, *De la mort à la résurrection d'après l'Ancien Testament* (Bibliothèque théologique), Neuchâtel, Delachaux et Niestlé, 1956.

return to earthly life but to "everlasting life" (לחיי עולם). The resurrection is not universal (not all, but many). The resurrection takes place in the future (although it is not clear when this future takes place). It concerns the good (2b) and the bad (2c), who receive a different 'reward' or 'punishment' accordingly. The quality of the good has to do with wisdom (3a) and righteousness (3b). Their resurrected existence is compared with the radiance of the firmament and the stars. The author uses metaphorical language in order to describe the modus of existence of the risen righteous; he possibly thinks of a transformation or maybe even an exaltation in a heavenly world, or an 'astral immortalization', which might imply a transformation into angelic existence (cp. Dan 8:10). The usage of the elements of the firmament and the stars may have brought later readers to the idea about an existence in heaven, and the risen body as a luminous body that is comparable to the stars[4].

Other texts in the Hebrew Bible, such as the "Isaianic Apocalypse" (Isa 24-27, esp. 25:8; 26:19) and Ezekiel's vision of the valley of dry bones (Ezek 37), have been invoked as testimonies of belief in the bodily resurrection. The highly poetic language of Isa 24-27, however, is rather hailing the future glory of the people of Israel than describing the resurrection of the dead. And even when Ezek 37 has from very early times been interpreted as a portrayal of the future resurrection of the dead[5], the text is in fact describing – in a highly symbolic and metaphorical fashion – how God will bring his people from the national extinction of the exile to a glorious national restoration in their own land[6].

---

4. Cf. C.D. ELLEDGE, *Resurrection of the Dead: Exploring Our Earliest Evidence Today*, in CHARLESWORTH, *Resurrection*, 22-52, p. 28: "Daniel may well have understood the resurrection of the deceased body ... as a supernatural transformation of the deceased body into a new and star-like existence in the heavenly world". He points to other early Jewish traditions of that kind: *Similitudes of Enoch* (= *1 En.*) 58:2-3; *Pss of Sol.* 3:12; *2 Ezra* 7:97; *2 Bar.*); CHARLESWORTH, *Resurrection*, pp. 12-13 points out that in some apocalypses the stars are angels (cf. *1 En.* 90:21; 18:15). Moreover, according to Charlesworth, *1 En.* 22-27, which antedates 200 B.C.E., gives a still earlier evidence of the concept of resurrection in early Judaism. Yet, it seems that Daniel is far clearer than its Enochic predecessor, according to Elledge (p. 28). See already PLATO, *Timaeus* 41d-42b (360 B.C.E.): "And having made it he divided the whole mixture into souls equal in number to the stars, and assigned each soul to a star; ... He who lived well during his appointed time was to return and dwell in his native star, and there he would have a blessed and congenial existence".

5. E.g. in 4 Macc. 18:17; *Apocr. Ezek.*; *Sib.Or.* 2.221-226; 4Q385 frag. 2; the schools of Hillel and Shammai (*Gen. Rab.* 14:5; *Lev. Rab.* 14:9), *Liv.Pro.* 3.11-12; *Barn.* 12:1; *Apoc. Pet.* 4.7-9; Tertullian, *Resurrection* 29-30.

6. Cf. ELLEDGE, *Resurrection of the Dead*, pp. 25-26.

Evidence of belief in the resurrection can be found in the Septuagint, the Bible of Greek speaking Jews in Hellenistic times. One should distinguish between books that have a Hebrew counterpart in the MT and books that occur only in the LXX and, therefore, not in the MT. To the first group belong Isa 26:19[7]; Ps 1:5[8]; Job 14:14; 19:25-27; 42:17[9]; and Ezek 37[10], which display a more pointed eschatological language including eschatological resurrection. It is disputed whether this is due to a free interpretation of the translator (eschatologization) or to a presumed different Hebrew *Vorlage*[11]. To the second group belong the historical writings describing the Maccabean revolt against the attempts of Antiochus IV to hellenize the Jews living in Israel. The book of 2 Maccabees (probably composed before 63 B.C.E) clearly attests the martyrs' belief in a future bodily resurrection of the righteous (7:9.11.14.25.29.36; 12:43-46; 14:37-46). Three of the brothers contrast their murder by Antiochus with God's bringing them back to life. Their resurrection to life is seen as a rescue from death and God's vindication (7:9.11.14):

---

7. Isa 26:19 LXX ἀναστήσονται οἱ νεκροί, καὶ ἐγερθήσονται οἱ ἐν τοῖς μνημείοις, καὶ εὐφρανθήσονται οἱ ἐν τῇ γῇ· ἡ γὰρ δρόσος ἡ παρὰ σοῦ ἴαμα αὐτοῖς ἐστιν, ἡ δὲ γῆ τῶν ἀσεβῶν πεσεῖται. "The dead shall rise, and those who are in the tombs shall be raised and those who are in the earth shall rejoice; for the dew from you is healing to them, but the land of the impious shall fall" (transl. A. Pietersma – B.C. Wright). See A. HOGETERP, *Expectations of the End: A Comparative Traditio-Historical Study of Eschatological, Apocalyptic and Messianic Ideas in the Dead Sea Scrolls and the New Testament* (STDJ, 83), Leiden, Brill, 2009, pp. 258-259.

8. Ps 1:5 LXX: 5 διὰ τοῦτο οὐκ ἀναστήσονται ἀσεβεῖς ἐν κρίσει οὐδὲ ἁμαρτωλοὶ ἐν βουλῇ δικαίων· 6 ὅτι γινώσκει κύριος ὁδὸν δικαίων, καὶ ὁδὸς ἀσεβῶν ἀπολεῖται. "5 Therefore the impious will not rise up in judgment, nor sinners in the council of the righteous, 6 because the Lord knows the way of the righteous and the way of the sinners will perish". See HOGETERP, *Expectations of the End*, pp. 261-262.

9. Job 14:14 LXX: ἐὰν γὰρ ἀποθάνῃ ἄνθρωπος, ζήσεται συντελέσας ἡμέρας τοῦ βίου αὐτοῦ· ὑπομενῶ, ἕως ἂν πάλιν γένωμαι. "For if a person dies, then would live again, when he has completed the days of his life, I would endure until I would be born again"; 19:25-27: 25 οἶδα γὰρ ὅτι ἀέναός ἐστιν ὁ ἐκλύειν με μέλλων ἐπὶ γῆς. 26 ἀναστήσαι τὸ δέρμα μου τὸ ἀνατλῶν ταῦτα· παρὰ γὰρ κυρίου ταῦτά μοι συνετελέσθη, 27 ἃ ἐγὼ ἐμαυτῷ συνεπίσταμαι, ἃ ὁ ὀφθαλμός μου ἑόρακεν καὶ οὐκ ἄλλος· πάντα δέ μοι συντετέλεσται ἐν κόλπῳ. "25 To be sure, I know that he who is about to undo me on earth is everlasting. 26 May my skin, which patiently endures these things, rise up; for these things have been accomplished on me by the Lord – 27 things I am conscious of in myself, things my eye has seen and no other, and all of them have come to an end for me in my bosom"; 42:17αα: γέγραπται δὲ αὐτὸν πάλιν ἀναστήσεσθαι μεθ' ὧν ὁ κύριος ἀνίστησιν. "And it is written that he will rise again with those the Lord raises up". See HOGETERP, *Expectations of the End*, pp. 262-264.

10. See HOGETERP, *Expectations of the End*, pp. 259-261.

11. *Ibid.*, pp. 257-265.

9 ... Σὺ μέν, ἀλάστωρ, ἐκ τοῦ παρόντος ἡμᾶς ζῆν ἀπολύεις,
ὁ δὲ τοῦ κόσμου βασιλεὺς ἀποθανόντας ἡμᾶς ὑπὲρ τῶν αὐτοῦ νόμων
εἰς αἰώνιον ἀναβίωσιν ζωῆς ἡμᾶς ἀναστήσει.
11 ... Ἐξ οὐρανοῦ ταῦτα κέκτημαι
καὶ διὰ τοὺς αὐτοῦ νόμους ὑπερορῶ ταῦτα
καὶ παρ' αὐτοῦ ταῦτα πάλιν ἐλπίζω κομίσασθαι·
14 ... Αἱρετὸν μεταλλάσσοντας ὑπ' ἀνθρώπων
τὰς ὑπὸ τοῦ θεοῦ προσδοκᾶν ἐλπίδας πάλιν ἀναστήσεσθαι ὑπ' αὐτοῦ·
σοὶ μὲν γὰρ ἀνάστασις εἰς ζωὴν οὐκ ἔσται.

9 You accused wretch, you dismiss us from this present life,
but the King of the universe *will raise us up to an everlasting renewal of life*,
because we have died for his laws.
11 From heaven I got these (tongue and hands)
and because of his laws I disdain them
and from him I hope to get them back again.
14 It is desirable that those who die at the hands of human beings
should cherish the *hope* that God gives *of being raised by him again*.
But for you there will be no *resurrection to life*!

Interestingly, the author refers to the theology of creation by understand-ing the resurrection as a 'recreation' of the physical body. Moreover, his faith in the bodily resurrection is an answer to a theodicy question: how can God allow evil and suffering in the world, even for those who have been faithful to him (6:12-17)?

Since the discovery and the publication of the Qumran manuscripts, at least two non-sectarian texts give clear evidence of a belief in the resur-rection of the dead of the righteous at the end of times[12]. This is not much in comparison to the more than 500 non-biblical manuscripts in Qumran, and despite the fact that some of these texts clearly express the

---

12. See CHARLESWORTH, *Where Does the Concept of Resurrection Appear*, pp. 14-15; ELLEDGE, *Resurrection of the Dead*, pp. 32-35. There is some discussion whether these texts really express the community's view, since they were not written by members of the community (non-sectarian Qumran texts). For a general presentation, see É. PUECH, *La croyance des Esséniens en la vie future: Immortalité, résurrection, vie éternelle? Histoire d'une croyance dans le judaïsme ancien. 1. La résurrection des morts et le contexte scripturaire* (ÉBib, 21), Paris, Lecoffre – Gabalda, 1993; H. LICHTENBERGER, *Auferstehung in den Qumranfunden*, in F. AVEMARIE – H. LICHTENBERGER (eds.), *Auferstehung – Resur-rection* (WUNT, 135), Tübingen, Mohr Siebeck, 2001, pp 79-91; HOGETERP, *Expectations of the End*, pp. 247-334 ('Resurrection of the Dead in the Dead Sea Scrolls and the New Testament'). Hogeterp (pp. 266-269, 274-276, 281-284) points to three other non-sectarian texts in which the concept of afterlife might also imply resurrection: 4Q245 (*Pseudo-Daniel*[c]), 4Q548 (*Visons of Amram*[f] *ar*), and 4Q434a (*Grace after Meals*). See also his nuanced discussion of the so-called sectarian texts of Qumran (pp. 285-292).

hope for *post mortem* salvation[13]. One Qumran text (palaeographically dated in the early first century B.C.E), *On Resurrection*, also called the *Messianic Apocalypse* (4Q521), presents the resurrection of the dead as one of the many signs that will inaugurate the eschatological salvation for Israel; it will be a part of the great reversal that will turn the suffering of the righteous into glory: "[For] he shall heal the slain ones, and bring life (יחיה) (to) the dead ones (ומתים), (and) bear joyful news (to) the Poor Ones" (4Q521 2 ii + 4 line 12). This is the only pre-Christian text that mentions both the Messiah (in line 1) and the resurrection (in line 12) within the same fragment (4Q521 2 ii + 4). God, either directly or through his Messiah, will raise the righteous as an act of justice. The author uses the perspective of the future resurrection as a rhetorical means to exhort the readers to persist seeking God in difficult times. It may be inferred from another fragment of the same composition that the author does not yet envisage a general resurrection but only the resurrection of the dead of God's people (4Q521 7 6: "He who gives life [will rais]e the dead of his people, ויק[ים המחיה את מתי עמו)[14].

The second Qumran text is *Pseudo-Ezekiel^{a-e}* (4Q385-388,391). The manuscripts are palaeographically dated to the late second century B.C.E. (4Q391) and to the second half of the first century B.C.E. (4Q385, 4Q385b, 4Q386, 4Q388, 4Q385c) respectively[15]. The author of these fragments proves to be a creative interpreter of Scripture in that he rewrites many of the visions of the prophet Ezekiel, among which the vision of the valley of dry bones (Ezek 37). He also seems to be concerned with the question of theodicy: how God will reward the faithful for their righteousness. He lets the prophet boldly pose the question to God:

> I have seen many in Israel who love your name and walk on the paths of righteousness. When will these things happen? And how will they be rewarded for their loyalty?

---

13. Cf. LICHTENBERGER, *Auferstehung in den Qumranfunden*, p. 91: "Die auffälligste Tatsache ist wohl, daß von den über 500 in Qumran gefundenen nichtbiblischen Handschriften nur zwei oder drei explizite Aussagen über Totenauferstehung machten … Der Tenor der Texte aber läßt keinen Zweifel daran, daß die qumran-essenische Gemeinschaft auch über den Tod des einzelnen hinaus an eine Teilhabe am Heil glaubte, auch wenn die dies nicht mit dem Gedanken der leiblichen Auferstehung von den Toten in Verbindung brachte".

14. Hebrew texts from É. PUECH, *Qumrân grotte 4. XVIII: Textes hébreux (4Q521-4Q528, 4Q576-4Q579)* (DJD, 25), Oxford, Clarendon Press, 1997, pp. 10 and 23.

15. D. DIMANT, *Qumran Cave 4. XXI: Parabiblical Texts, Part 4: Pseudo-Prophetic Texts* (DJD, 30), Oxford, Clarendon Press, 2001, p. 16.

God answers in referring to Ezek 37:

> And he said, "Son of man, prophesy over the bones and say 'May a bone con-
> nect with its bone and a joint with its joint.'" And so happened.
> And he said a second time, "Prophesy, and sinews will grow on them and they
> will be covered with skin all over." And so it happened.
> And again he said, "Prophesy over the four winds and they will live and *a large
> crowd of men will rise and bless the LORD of Hosts who cause them to live...*"
> And I said, "O Lord, when will these things be?" (4Q385, fragment 2)

Obviously, the author understands Ezek 37 as a prophecy about a literal
bodily resurrection. He does not speak of the transformation of dead bodies,
but of their physical reconstitution (comp. 2 Macc). His interpretation of
the resurrection of the dead, however, is not a substitute for the so-called
original meaning of Ezek 37, namely, the restoration of Israel. 4Q385 and
4Q386 exhibit an apocalyptic vision which places the resurrection of the
righteous within the larger setting of the eschatological restoration of God's
people in the land of Israel[16]. *Pseudo-Ezekiel* might also illustrate how resurrection hope emerged in Jewish thinking, namely, as part of the emergence
of apocalypticism through a quite radical intensification of beliefs that were
already latently present in prophetic literature. This involved a more literal
understanding of certain symbolic and poetic notions present in the prophetic writings[17]. Other texts seems to provide a similar tendency: Dan 12
might be inspired by Isa 26:19, *On Resurrection* by Isa 61 and other texts,
and 1 Cor 15:54 by Isa 25-26 and Hos 13:14. Hence, it should not be
surprising that the synoptic tradition, which we study in this paper (Mark
12:18-27 par. Matt 22:23-33; Luke 20:27-40), defends the resurrection
hope through a radicalized reading of Exod 3:6[18].

---

16. A. HOGETERP, *Resurrection and Biblical Tradition: Pseudo-Ezekiel Reconsidered*, in
Bib 89 (2008) 59-69. The author even asks whether this early interpretation of Ezek 37
does not invite the modern reader to be prudent with a too one-sided interpretation of the
prophetic text: "Perhaps the biblical text already provides a point of departure for the intertwined occurrence of resurrection and restoration, for the symbolic imagery of revivification
not only occurs in Ezekiel 37,1-10, but also recurs in the interpretative section, in Ezek
37,12-13" (p. 69). Indeed, Ezek 37 uses an 'image' (resurrection) to describe a future 'reality' (the restoration of Israel). The choice of this image, and not other possible images,
implies a certain knowledge of and reflection on the notion of bodily resurrection in the
mind of the author.

17. So P.D. HANSON, *The Dawn of Apocalyptic*, Philadelphia, PA, Fortress, 1975.

18. Cf. ELLEDGE, *Resurrection of the Dead*, pp. 35-36. 1QpHab VII 7-8 is another
example of intensifying a prophetic vision (Hab 2:3) in the sense of eschatology: "Its interpretation: the final age will be extended and go beyond all that the prophets say, because
the mysteries of God are wonderful" (F. GARCÍA MARTÍNEZ – E.J.C. TIGCHELAAR, *The Dead
Sea Scrolls Study Edition*, Vol 1, Leiden – Grand Rapids, MI, Brill – Eerdmans, ²2000,
p. 17).

Another possible testimony of the belief in the resurrection of the dead is the second benediction of the *Amidah* (*Eighteen Benedictions*). This is a liturgical text that was recorded in the rabbinic tradition but antedates 70 C.E., having profound parallels with the above mentioned text of Qumran 4 Q521[19]. The text – in its Palestinian formulation – interestingly links the resurrection to the power of God, similarly to what Jesus does in Matt 22:29:

> Mighty Thou art – humbling the haughty,
> Powerful – calling to judgment the arrogant,
> Eternal – preserving the dead,
> Causing the wind to bow and the dew to fall,
> Sustaining the living, resurrecting the dead (*měhayeh hamētîm*),
> O, cause our salvation to sprout in the twinkling of an eye!
> Blessed art thou, O Lord, who resurrects the dead (*měhayeh hamētîm*)[20].

The texts quoted above prove that belief in the bodily resurrection of the dead is attested to several times (though altogether not often) before 70 C.E. in different sources such as the MT (Daniel), the LXX (Isa 26:19; Ps 1:5; Job 14:14; 19:25-27; 42:17; 2 Maccabees), the Dead Sea Scrolls (*On Resurrection, Pseudo-Ezekiel*), as well as in Jewish liturgy (*Amidah*). Casey Elledge also lists nine examples of texts in the Pseudepigrapha (written between c. 200 B.C.E. – c. 100 C.E.) that mention the bodily resurrection of the dead: *1 Enoch* (2nd cent. B.C.E. – 1st cent C.E.), *Testaments of the Twelve Patriarchs* (2nd cent. B.C.E.), *Psalms of Solomon* (1st cent. B.C.E.), Pseudo-Philo, *Biblical Antiquities* (also known as *Liber Antiquitatum Biblicarum* = L.A.B.) (1ste cent. C.E.), *4 Ezra* (late 1st cent. C.E.), *2 Baruch* (early 2nd cent. C.E.), *Pseudo-Phocylides* (1st cent. B.C.E. – 1st cent. C.E.), *Life of*

---

19. Cf. S. HULTGREN, *1Q521, the Second Benediction of the* Tefilla, *the* Hăsîdîm, *and the Development of Royal Messianism*, in *RevQ* 91 (2008) 313-340; ID., *4Q521 and Luke's Magnificat and Benedictus*, in F. GARCÍA MARTÍNEZ (ed.), *Echoes from the Caves: Qumran and the New Testament* (STDS, 85), Leiden, Brill, 2009, 119-132, pp. 125-126: "Both texts affirm that God is the one who gives (or will give) life to the dead. Both texts speak of God as the one who heals (or will heal) the sick or the wounded. Both texts speak of God as the one who upholds the weak, although with different words". The second benediction calls God the "upholder of those who fall". 4Q521 2 II 8 calls God the one "who raises up those who are bowed down". Finally, as we have noted that 4Q521 contains allusions to 1 Sam 2:1-10, so we note that the second benediction does also (cf. ממית ומחיה in the second benediction with the same expression in 1 Sam 2:6)".

20. Translation in CHARLESWORTH, *Where Does the Concept of Resurrection Appear*, p. 15, referring to J. HEINEMANN, *Prayer in the Talmud* (SJ, 9), Berlin, De Gruyter, 1977, pp. 26-27. Charlesworth adds: "Most likely, in synagogues and the temple, Pharisees and other Jews chanted the second benediction, perhaps in a form similar to the old Palestinian rite quoted above. It is also likely that Paul was familiar with a similar form of the *Amidah*". Might the same be said of Jesus?

Adam and Eve (= L.A.E., 1st cent. C.E.), *Lives of the Prophets* (1st cent. C.E.)[21].
This literary evidence is substantial, though not overwhelming[22].

21. ELLEDGE, *Resurrection of the Dead*, p. 47. We have added the dates given in J.H. CHARLES-
WORTH (ed.), *The Old Testament Pseudepigrapha*, 2 Vols., London, Darton, Longman & Todd,
1983-1985 (from now on abbreviated as *OTP* 1 and 2). Elledge does not give precise references.
We complement: *1 En.* 22-27 (esp. 22:13: resurrection of the spirits of the wicked) and 92-105
(esp. 103:3.7: resurrection of the spirits); *Pss. of Sol.* 3, 13, 14, 15 (esp. 3:11-12: 11 ἡ ἀπώλεια τοῦ
ἁμαρτωλοῦ εἰς τὸν αἰῶνα, καὶ οὐ μνησθήσεται, ὅταν ἐπισκέπτηται δικαίους. 12 αὕτη ἡ μερὶς τῶν
ἁματωλῶν εἰς τὸν αἰῶνα· οἱ δὲ φοβούμενοι τὸν κύριον ἀναστήσονται εἰς ζωὴν αἰώνιον, καὶ ἡ ζωὴ
αὐτῶν ἐν φωτὶ κυρίου καὶ οὐκ ἐκλείψει ἔτι); *4 Ezra* 7:32 ("The earth shall give up those who are
asleep in it, and the dust those who dwell silently in it; and the chambers shall give up the souls
which have been committed to them"; 7:37 ("Then the Most High will say to the nations that
have been raised from the dead, 'Look now, and understand whom you have denied, whom you
have not served, whose commandments you have despised!'"); *2 Bar.* 30:1; 42:8; 51:10 ("For in
the heights of that world will they [the righteous] dwell and they will be made like the angels and
equal to the stars"); Ps.-Phoc., *Sentences*, 97-115 (the Jewish poet juxtaposes the resurrection from
the dead [103-104], immortality of the soul [105-108,111,115], and divinization [104] without
explaining how they fit together); *L.A.E.* 41:2-3: "And the Lord said to him [Adam], 'I told you
that *you are dust and to dust you shall return*. Now I promise to you the resurrection; I shall raise
you on the last day in the resurrection with every man of your seed'"; *Liv. Pro.* 2:15 ("And in the
resurrection the ark will be the first to be resurrected and will come out of the rock and be placed
on Mount Sinai, and all the saints will be gathered to it there as they await the Lord and flee from
the enemy who wishes to destroy them"); 3:11-12 (about Ezekiel: "When the people was being
destroyed by its enemies, he went to the [enemy] leaders and, terrified by the prodigies, they ceased.
He used to say this to them: 'Are we lost? Has our hope perished?' and in the wonder of the dead
bones he persuaded them that there is hope for Israel both here and in the coming [age]").
     For the relevant passages in the *Testaments of the Twelve Patriarchs* (*T. Sim.* 6:7: "Then I shall
arise in joy, and I shall bless the Most High, because of his marvelous [works]"; *T. Jud.* 25:1: "And
after these things, Abraham and Isaac and Jacob shall arise unto life"; 25:4: "And those who die
in sorrow shall arise in joy … And those who die because of the Lord shall be awakened unto life";
T. Zeb. 10:1-4:"And now, my children, do not sorrow that I am dying nor grieve that I am per-
ishing. For I shall arise again in your midst as a ruler in the midst of his sons … But as for now,
I am going away into my rest, as my fathers", and *T. Benj.* 10:6-10: "Then you will see Enoch,
Noah, and Shem, and Abraham and Isaac and Jacob standing on the right hand in gladness. Then
we also shall arise, each [of us] over our tribe, worshipping the king of heavens … Then also all
shall rise, some unto glory and some unto shame. And the Lord will judge Israel first concerning
[her] iniquity against him. And then he shall judge all the nations"); see H.W. HOLLANDER – M.
DE JONGE, *The Testaments of the Twelve Patriarchs: A Commentary* (SVTP, 8), Leiden, Brill, 1985,
pp. 61-63; C.D. ELLEDGE, *The Resurrection Passages in the Testaments of the Twelve Patriarchs:
Hope for Israel in Early Judaism and Christianity*, in CHARLESWORTH, *Resurrection*, pp. 79-103.
     For *Pseudo-Philo* (L.A.B.) (3:10: "But when the years appointed for the world have been
fulfilled, then the light will cease and the darkness will fade away. And I will bring the dead to
life and raise up those who are sleeping from the earth"; 19:12-13: to Moses God says: "And
I will raise up you and your fathers from the land of Egypt in which you sleep and you will
come together and dwell in the immortal dwelling place that is not subject to time"; 25:7:
"And who knows that if you tell the truth to us, even if you die now, nevertheless God will
have mercy on you when he will resurrect the dead?"), see D.J. HARRINGTON, *Afterlife Expectations in Pseudo-Philo, 4 Ezra and 2 Baruch, and Their Implications for the New Testament*, in R.
BIERINGER –V. KOPERSKI – B. LATAIRE (eds), *Resurrection in the New Testament* (BETL, 165),
Leuven – Paris – Dudley, MA, Peeters, 2002, pp. 21-34.
     22. We do not discuss here the epigraphic evidence which can be found on tomb inscrip-
tions. See CAVALLIN, *Life after Death*, pp. 99-101, 166-170; P.W. VAN DER HORST, *Ancient*

At that time, however, there was "no single Jewish doctrine about life after death … there is rather a great variety and pluralism of ideas both about the end of the world history and about death and about which follows the death of the individual person"[23]. In the Jewish literary sources, resurrection (of the body) and immortality (of the soul) are combined, juxtaposed, harmonized or systematized (e.g., an intermediate state of the soul between death and the final resurrection of the body). The newness of the life after death is expressed in different ways and the time when the new life of the righteous (and the punishment of the wicked) commences is also varied[24].

Even so, there are also voices which explicitly deny the resurrection or call it into question (e.g. Job 14:7-12; Eccl 3:19-21; 9:3-5; Sir 10:11; 30:17; 38:21-23). Flavius Josephus' reports on the three great philosophical schools of early Judaism (the Pharisees, Sadducees and Essenes) allege that the first and the third movements accepted an afterlife of some type, while the Sadducees clearly rejected any form of life after death: they denied both the survival of the soul and the possibility of retribution in Hades (see a long description in *Jewish War* 2.119-166; and an abbreviated presentation in *Jewish Antiquities* 18.11-25)[25]. Flavius Josephus summarizes the Pharisaic position about life after death in three points: "(1) every soul is immortal; (2) only that of the good, however, passes into another body[26]; (3) whereas

---

Jewish Epitaphs: An Introductory Survey of a Millennium of Jewish Funerary Epigraphy (200 B.C.E. -700 C.E.) (CBET, 2), Kampen, Pharos, 1991, pp. 114-126; PUECH, *La croyance des Esséniens en la vie future*, pp. 82-99; J.S. PARK, *Conceptions of Afterlife in Jewish Inscriptions: With Special Reference to Pauline Literature* (WUNT, 122), Tübingen, Mohr, 2000.

23. CAVALLIN, *Life after Death*, p. 199. Hence, it is an oversimplification to oppose a 'Jewish doctrine of the resurrection of the dead' against a 'Greek doctrine about the immortality of the soul'.

24. *Ibid.*, p. 199: "immediately after death, sometimes on the Last Day or in an eschatological future which is not precisely defined".

25. See a discussion of F. Josephus' description in J. LE MOYNE, *Les Sadducéens* (ÉBib), Paris, Gabalda, 1972, pp. 27-63; E. SCHÜRER, *The History of the Jewish People in the Age of Jesus Christ (175 B.C. – A.D. 135): A New English Version Revised and Edited*, ed. G. Vermes – F. Millar – M. Black, Vol. 2, Edinburgh, Clark, 1979, pp. 381-415 (Pharisees and Sadducees), 555-590 (Essenes); S. MASON, *Flavius Josephus on the Pharisees: A Composition-Critical Study*, Boston – Leiden, Brill, 2001, pp. 156-170. 297-300.

26. According to F. Josephus, the "Pharisees believed in something like *metempsychosis*, the transmigration of the soul out of one body at death into a different body in the future (cf. Plato, *Phaedo* 70c-d, 72a)" (cf. ELLEDGE, *Resurrection of the Dead*, p. 38). One could ask whether Josephus attributes to the Pharisees a form of 'reincarnation', in order to adapt his presentation to the Hellenistic main stream concept of his time. Some would speak of a misrepresentation of the Jewish doctrine of resurrection by appropriating Greek reincarnation terminology for it (so Elledge, *Resurrection of the Dead*, pp. 37-39), others are more positive (so MASON, *Flavius Josephus on the Pharisees*, 161-170, p. 169: "at a time when many different views of the afterlife were circulating in the Graeco-Roman world, Josephus added to the list a Jewish theory of resurrection by appropriating for it the language of reincarnation").

the wicked suffer endless punishment" (*War* 2.163)[27]. The Sadducees, however, rejected (ἀναιροῦσιν) all these three points: "As for the persistence of the soul after death, penalties in the underworld, and rewards: they will have none of them" (*War* 2.165). The Essenes accept the (1) immortality of the soul and (3) the everlasting punishment of the wicked (*War* 2.154-158). Pharisees and Essenes had a fairly similar view of immortality, with only one difference: according to the Essenes, after death, the souls of the good do not enter a new body, but go to an idyllic heavenly place. Josephus' own view on the afterlife is very similar to that of the Pharisees and the Essenes (see *War* 2.157; 3.372-375; *Ant.* 17.349-354). He also claims that the doctrines of an afterlife and final judgment are taught in the Mosaic Law[28], an idea which is also expressed in the Mishna (*m. Sanh.* 10:1)[29].

Josephus' description of the position of the Sadducees is confirmed by the New Testament (Mark 12:28 parr.; Acts 4:2; 23:8) and by rabbinic sources (*b. Sanh.* 90a-92b; *Tanhuma Bereshit* 5)[30]. In these texts, their attitude is described, above all, as a negation of the resurrection of the dead and, according to Acts 23:8, even as a negation of belief in angels and spirits. A. Saldarini rightly remarks: "The testimony of all the sources that the Sadducees did not believe in resurrection, afterlife and judgment fits the other things we know about them and is historically reliable and convincing"[31]. The reasons for

---

27. *War* 2.163: (1) ψυχήν τε πᾶσαν μὲν ἄφθαρτον, (2) μεταβαίνειν δὲ εἰς ἕτερον σῶμα τὴν τῶν ἀγαθῶν μόνην, (3) τὰς δὲ τῶν φαύλων ἀιδίῳ τιμωρίᾳ κολάζεσθαι. See the parallel description of the Pharisaic position in *Ant.* 18.14: "That souls have an immortal power is a conviction among them, and subterranean punishments and rewards come to those whose conduct in life had been either of virtue or vice; for some, eternal imprisonment is prepared but for others, freedom to live again (ἀναβιοῦν)". The Sadducees are said to reject the Pharisaic belief: "They hold that the soul perishes along (συναφανίζει) with the body" (*Ant.* 18.16).

28. Cf. *Against Apion* 2.217-8.: "For those who live in accordance with our laws (τοῖς νομίμως βιοῦσι) the prize is not silver or gold ... No, each individual, relying on the witness of his own conscience and the lawgiver's prophecy, confirmed by the sure testimony of God, is firmly persuaded that to those who observe the laws (τοῖς τοὺς νόμους διαφυλάξαι) and, if they must needs die for them, willingly meet death (προθύμως ἀποθανοῦσι), God has granted a renewed existence (δέδωκεν ὁ θεὸς γενέσθαι πάλιν) and in the revolution [of the ages] (ἐκ περιτροπῆς) the gift of a better life (βίον ἀμείνω λαβεῖν)". (transl. Thackeray)

29. *m. Sanh.* 10:1: "All Israelites have a share in the world to come, for it is written, *Thy people also shall be all righteous, they shall inherit the land for ever; the branch of my planting, the work of my hands that I may be glorified* [Isa 60:21]. And these are they that have no share in the world to come: he who says that there is no resurrection of the dead prescribed in the Law,..." (transl. Danby). H. DANBY, *The Mishnah*, Oxford, University Press, 1977, p. 397, notes that "prescribed in the Law" is omitted by some mss.

30. See a discussion of the rabbinic evidence about the negation of the resurrection by the Sadducees in LE MOYNE, *Les Sadducéens*, pp. 169-174.

31. A.J. SALDARINI, *Pharisees, Scribes and Sadducees in Palestinian Society: A Sociological Approach*, Grand Rapids, MI, Cambridge, U.K., Eerdmans – Livonia, MI, Dove Booksellers, 1988, p. 304.

their rejection of belief in the resurrection should probably be sought in their conservatism and their social status: they did not want to introduce the new idea of resurrection because it could not be proven from the Torah in its literal sense. Furthermore, their aristocratic lifestyle was more orientated towards inner world matters than towards questions about life after death[32].

II. STRUCTURE OF MATT 22:23-33

The structure of the text unit is obvious[33]. The dialogue between the Sadducees and Jesus is enclosed within a narrative introduction (v. 23a-b) and a narrative conclusion (v. 33). It consists of two parts: the question of the Sadducees (vv. 23-28) and Jesus' response (vv. 29-32). Each part is subdivided into three parts. The Sadducees' intervention consists of (1) a quotation of the Torah, more specifically the levirate law (v. 24); a practical case (v. 25-27), and a question (v. 28). Jesus' answer contains (1) a rhetorical rebuke: the way the Sadducees deal with the issue of the resurrection shows their ignorance of Scripture and of the power of God (v. 29); (2) a first reason why they are mistaken: the levirate law is inapplicable to the resurrection because the condition of the risen person is different from that of the person on earth as the result of a transformation (v. 30); the second reason why they are mistaken is (3) that they do not understand the nature of God as it is revealed in Scripture (v. 31-32). The whole discussion turns around the possibility of bodily resurrection. The response to the question depends on the way one interprets Scripture and the way one understands the mystery of God. There is a hermeneutical and a theological dimension[34]. In what follows, we will concentrate on the content of the opposite views and arguments of the two characters of the story as well as the historic plausibility of the controversy in light of early Jewish evidence. Viewed from this angle, Matthew's text is very near to Mark's text, which was his source for telling this story. Hence, here we need

---

32. Cf. LE MOYNE, *Les Sadducéens*, pp. 167-175.357-364; CAVALLIN, *Life after Death*, p. 194; SCHÜRER, *History*, p. 411: "In this rejection of the Pharisaic legal tradition, the Sadducees represented an older viewpoint: they stood by the written Torah. For them, none of the subsequent development was binding. Their religious outlook was similarly very conservative … They rejected belief in bodily resurrection and in reward in a life to come, and indeed any kind of personal survival whatsoever".

33. W.D. DAVIES – D.C. ALLISON, Jr., *A Critical and Exegetical Commentary on the Gospel According to Saint Matthew. III. Commentary on Matthew XIX-XXVIII* (ICC), Edinburgh, T&T Clark, 1997, p. 221.

34. Cf. J.G. JANZEN, *Resurrection and Hermeneutics: On Exodus 3.6 in Mark 12.26*, in *JSNT* 23 (1985) 43-58.

not focus on the differences between the two, for which we refer to the commentaries. It is also obvious that the narrative introduction (v. 29a-c) and conclusion (v. 33) are of less interest – except for the characterization of the Sadducees –, because they are certainly part of the narrator's text, and not acts or sayings of Jesus which are the focus of our attention.

III. THE QUESTION OF THE SADDUCEES

From the very beginning, the synoptics make it clear that the reason why they introduce the Sadducees is because they say that there is no resurrection (of the dead) (μὴ εἶναι ἀνάστασιν) (Matt 22:23 parr.). This initial qualification offers the reader a key on how to understand the discussion between the two opponents of the controversy. In this first characterization of Jesus' opponents, it is remarkable that the synoptics use the noun ἀνάστασις without qualification (comp. Matt 22:28 parr.). Matthew only qualifies the noun in 22:31 (τῶν νεκρῶν) (Mark and Luke have a verbal form in the parallel text). This implies that the readers were used to understanding the unqualified substantive as referring to bodily resurrection. One should not assume that this usage is only possible in Christian resurrection language, since the author of 2 Maccabees praises 'noble Ioudas' for bringing a sin offering for the fallen comrades: "In doing this he acted very well and honourably, taking account of the resurrection (ὑπὲρ ἀναστάσεως διαλογιζόμενος)" (12:43). And from what follows it is clear that he refers to the bodily resurrection: "For if he were not expecting that those who had fallen would rise again (εἰ μὴ γὰρ τοὺς προπεπτωκότας ἀναστῆναι προσεδόκα), it would have been superfluous and foolish to pray for the dead" (12:44). This example shows that in certain circles of pious Jews, observing the Law and the customs of the fathers, belief in the bodily resurrection was accepted in such a manner that one could refer to it by the unqualified noun ἀνάστασις. The same might be true for the phrase ἐν τῇ ἀναστάσει (without qualification) in Matt 22:28 parr. and 22:30, meaning "in the resurrected condition (of the just)"[35]. Although the phrase occurs in Luke 14:14 (with qualification ἐν τῇ ἀναστάσει τῶν δικαίων) and John 11:24 (ἐν τῇ ἀναστάσει ἐν τῇ ἐσχάτῃ ἡμέρᾳ), it is also found in Jewish writings such as *Lives of the Prophets* 2:15 (first century C.E.)[36] and *t. Sanh.* 13:5 (*bithiyyat hammētîm*).

35. Transl. DAVIES – ALLISON, *Matthew. III*, p. 227.
36. Greek text in C.C. TORREY, *The Lives of the Prophets: Greek Text and Translation*, Philadelphia, Society of Biblical Literature, 1946, p. 22: καὶ ἐν τῇ ἀναστάσει πρώτη ἡ κιβωτὸς ἀναστήσεται καὶ ἐξελεύσεται ἐκ τῆς πέτρας καὶ τεθήσεται ἐν ὄρει Σινᾶ. "And in the resurrec-

The narrator presents the controversy as a result of the initiative of the Sadducees, who provide an example of a widow who, after the death of each husband, was successively married to seven brothers. The Sadducees come to Jesus (προσῆλθον) and address him in his quality of "teacher" (διδάσκαλε) in an attempt to disqualify him as one. As stated, the Sadducees' intervention consists of (1) a quotation of the Torah, more specifically the levirate law (v. 24), (2) a practical case (v. 25-27), and (3) a question (v. 28). The whole intervention is orientated towards the final question: "In the resurrection then, whose wife of the seven will she be? For all had (married) her". The (ironic) point of the question is only understandable in the light of the practical and yet extremely hypothetical case, which is put before the attention of the teacher, namely, the woman, who marries the seven brothers, finally dies childless. This strange case, however, is a possible result of the fulfilment of a casuistic provision of the Torah concerning the levirate marriage. The quotation in Matthew (and Mark) is a free combination of the levirate law in Deut 25:5 with a concrete example in Gen 38:8[37]. The purpose of their question is to argue that the belief in the general resurrection contradicts the law, because it would imply that the resurrected woman would have seven husbands in the afterlife (polyandry), according to the provision of the law. The only way to survive death is by "raising up seed" (v. 23: ἀναστήσει σπέρμα), and not by the "resurrection of the dead" (v. 31: ἀνάστασις τῶν νεκρῶν)!

This argument is in agreement with the evidence that proponents of the 'new' doctrine tried to argue that resurrection is taught in the Law[38]. To the benefit of the Sadducees one must say that asking for a scriptural warrant for a 'new' doctrine is a theologically sound approach. Moreover, the Sadducees' way of questioning Jesus displays great rhetorical skill, they make use of the

tion the ark will be the first to be resurrected and will come out of the rock and be placed on Mount Sinai" (transl. D.R.A. Hare).

37. Deut 25:5 LXX: Ἐὰν δὲ κατοικῶσιν ἀδελφοὶ ἐπὶ τὸ αὐτὸ καὶ ἀποθάνῃ εἷς ἐξ αὐτῶν, σπέρμα δὲ μὴ ᾖ αὐτῷ, οὐκ ἔσται ἡ γυνὴ τοῦ τεθνηκότος ἔξω ἀνδρὶ μὴ ἐγγίζοντι· ὁ ἀδελφὸς τοῦ ἀνδρὸς αὐτῆς εἰσελεύσεται πρὸς αὐτὴν καὶ λήμψεται αὐτὴν ἑαυτῷ γυναῖκα καὶ συνοικήσει αὐτῇ; Gen 38:8: καὶ γάμβρευσαι αὐτὴν καὶ ἀνάστησον σπέρμα τῷ ἀδελφῷ σου. The most interesting difference between Matt and Mark is that Matt uses the simple verbal form ἀναστήσει σπέρμα instead of the composite verb in Mark 12:18 ἐξαναστήσῃ. According to M.J.J. Menken (*Matthew's Bible: The Old Testament Text of the Evangelist* [BETL, 123], Leuven, Peeters, 2004, p. 214), this is not due to Mathew's use of the LXX, but to his own editorial skills: "By using ἀναστήσει, Matthew creates a suitable play on words: the ἀνάστασις of offspring for the dead brother is irrelevant in relation to the eschatological ἀνάστασις of the dead. So Matthew's choice of the verb in v. 24 can be adequately explained by his linguistic habit and the context in which he used the word".

38. See notes 28 and 29. For a full discussion of the later rabbinic attempts to prove the resurrection from Scripture surveyed in *b. Sanh.* 90b-92a, see SCHWANKL, *Die Sadduzäerfrage*, 1987a, pp. 275-281.

144   A. DENAUX

rhetorical devices of *auctoritas* (appeal on the authority of the Law, v. 23), *narratio* (vv. 25-27), and *reductio ad absurdum* (v. 28)[39]. The presupposition of their argument is that they think that bodily resurrection would imply that the earthly human relationships would be transferred without much change to one's present status: e.g., marriage bonds and sexual relations are continued in heaven. They think in terms of simple and unqualified continuity between the two modes of existence, on earth and in heaven. There is a more serious difficulty behind their question: if God cannot guarantee posterity to a dead man who has fulfilled the levirate law – he himself dies childless and also his brothers –, how one can hope that God will or can raise up the dead man himself[40]? Hence, their question "has two facets, one having to do with scriptural warrant and one having to do with divine will and power. That is, the issue is at once hermeneutical and theological"[41].

IV. JESUS' RESPONSE

Jesus' response also shows a rhetorical strategy: it is introduced by a general reproach (*argumentum ad hominem*) (v. 29), then, it is followed by an argument of rejection (*correctio*) (v. 30), and an affirmative argument based on Scripture (recourse on *auctoritas*) (v. 31-32)[42]. Jesus opens with a direct reproach to his opponents, pointing to their error (πλανᾶσθε)[43] and lack of knowledge (μὴ εἰδόντες). By mentioning the object of their error and ignorance, he announces the two key words in the following argument: (the interpretation of) Scripture (τὰς γραφὰς) and (the theological issue of) the power of God (δύναμιν τοῦ θεοῦ) (Matt 22:29).

The first argument deals with the 'how' of the resurrection (22:30). Jesus corrects the view of the Sadducees, who simply transfer their inner-worldly condition to the afterlife: sexual intercourse within marriage, – oriented towards procreation as a means to overcome mortality and perishability –,

---

39. Cf. O. SCHWANKL, *Die Sadduzäerfrage (Mk 12.18-27) und die Auferstehungserwartung Jesu*, in *Wissenschaft und Weisheit* 50 (1987) 81-92, p. 84.

40. Cf. B.R. TRICK, *Death, Covenants, and the Proof of Resurrection in Mark 12:18-27*, in *NovT* 49 (2007) 232-256, p. 238 thinks that the Sadducees follow the Jewish exegetical principle *qal wahomer* (lesser-to-greater logic): "1) if the natural 'raising up' of childbirth has failed, how much more so will the more difficult 'raising up' of resurrection, and 2) if the means for 'raising up' provided by the Torah have failed, how much more so will a 'raising up' that is not ordained by Torah".

41. Cf. JANZEN, *Resurrection and Hermeneutics*, p. 48.

42. Cf. SCHWANKL, *Die Sadduzäerfrage*, 1987b, p. 85.

43. Matthew sharpens the question of Mark 12:24 (οὐ διὰ τοῦτο πλανᾶσθε ...) into a direct reproach.

is no longer needed in the world to come (οὔτε γαμοῦσιν οὔτε γαμίζονται: "(Men) neither marry nor are (women) given in marriage"[44]). Instead, the dead will undergo a transformation: their bodies will be transformed into a kind of angelic existence, because angels are immortal beings and do not marry (ἀλλ᾽ ὡς ἄγγελοι ἐν τῷ οὐρανῷ εἰσιν)[45]. Therefore, Jesus counters his opponents by affirming that the relation between the earthly and risen existence involves continuity and discontinuity. There is continuity in the sense of identity. The risen person is the same person as the one who lived on earth. Yet, the conditions of the risen person are different: his body is transformed into an exalted, imperishable body in a modality comparable to that of angels (discontinuity). According to Bradley Trick, behind the Sadducees' perceived conflict between the resurrection and the levirate marriage law lies a misunderstanding of Scripture: "Since the levirate marriage law requires that death annuls the covenantal bond of marriage, none of the woman's prior marital relationships would continue into the resurrected state"[46]. Jesus' view that in the afterlife humans will be transformed into an angelic state is not new: the conceptions of astral immortality and an angelic existence in the afterlife are well attested in Jewish writings before him. William Davies and Dale Allison have collected evidence for the following items[47]: the thought that eschatological destiny will be angelic is found in several sources[48]; angels and stars were already closely associated with each other. Angels were often thought of as stars[49]; astral immortality, which was the dominant conception of afterlife in the post-classical Greek world, entered Jewish thinking[50]. Therefore, the inference that humans would become like angels was easily conceivable.

44. Transl. DAVIES – ALLISON, *Matthew*. Vol. III, p. 227.
45. *Ibid.*, p. 229: "As sex was largely thought of as serving the purpose of procreation, not pleasure, and as angels were thought of as deathless, intercourse for them was unnecessary and would only have been self-indulgence. So too shall it then be for the righteous who, upon gaining eternal life, will no longer need to reproduce".
46. Cf. TRICK, *Death, Covenants, and the Proof of Resurrection*, p. 254.
47. DAVIES – ALLISON, *Matthew*. Vol. III, pp. 227-229.
48. *Ibid.*, p. 228, footnote 47: "Wisd 5.5 (assuming that 'sons of God' are angels); 4QSb 4.25 ('you [shall be] as an angel of the Presence' – in a blessing of priests); 4Q511 fr. 35; *1 En.* 104:1-6: *2 Bar.* 51:5 (the saints will be changed 'into the splendor of angels'). 51.10: ('And they shall be made like angels, and be made equal to stars'); *T. Isaac* 4.43-48. It seems likely that the exaltation of Enoch in *1 En.* 70-71 and of the speaker of 4 QMᵃ are 'angelifications' of human figures (cf. *2 En.* 22:4-11); ... Philo, *Sacr* 1:5 depicts Abraham as now being 'equal to angels' – and precisely because he has overcome death".
49. Cf. Judg 5:20; Job 28:7; Dan 8:10; *1 En.* 43:1-4; 86:1-6; 90:20-27; *2 En.* 29; *T. Sol.* 20:14-17; L.A.B. 32:15; *Jos. Asen.* 14. (Rev 1:20; 9:1; 12:4).
50. Cf. Dan 12:2-3; *1 En.* 104:2-7; 4 Macc. 17:5; *2 Bar.* 51:10: "And they shall be made like angels, and be made equal to stars"; L.A.B. 33:5; *As. Mos.* 10:9; *CIJ* 2:43-44, no. 788.

The second argument deals with the "that" of the resurrection (vv. 31-32). Jesus now counters the Sadducees' argument that the doctrine of resurrection is not grounded in the Torah and is, therefore, inacceptable. He also refers to a Torah text, Exod 3:6, passing by other texts from Scripture that are more explicit (e.g. Dan 12:2), hence, accommodating the approach of his opponents. Since there is no evidence of the use of Exod 3:6 as proof for the resurrection in both early Jewish and early Christian literature[51], Jesus stands alone in the choice of this proof text, not however in the way that he chooses to interpret the text. The introductory question in Matt 22:31, "Have you not read that was spoken to you by God, saying", is less precise than in Mark 12:26 which refers to the "book of Moses, in the account about the bush". Some doubt whether the dropping of 'Moses' has any theological import[52], yet, it might point to Jesus' theocentrism: he has a direct knowledge of God's will in the Torah, without needing any human authoritative mediation in bringing or interpreting God's will. By adding "for you", the Matthean Jesus personalizes the issue. The divine word in Exod 3:6 is addressed directly to the Sadducees, who are also descendants of Abraham, Isaac and Jacob, their ancestors, whose sterility and childlessness were removed by the power of God (Gen 17:17-19: Abraham and Sarah; Gen 29:31; 30:22-23: Jacob and Rachel).

Quite a few scholars have found Jesus' scriptural argument unconvincing, at least according to contemporary exegetical standards. At the most the argument would imply a continued existence after death and hence an interim state[53]. The present tense of the emphatic divine pronouncement (ἐγώ εἰμι) supposes that Abraham, Isaac and Jacob cannot have ceased to be, even when they were already dead at that time[54]. Yet, the force of Jesus' argument cannot be understood by looking at an isolated verse (Exod 3:6), but to the verse in its context. F. Dreyfus has convincingly shown that the

---

51. Cf. J.P. MEIER, *The Debate on the Resurrection of the Dead: An Incident From the Ministry of the Historical Jesus?*, in *JSNT* 77 (2000) 8-14, pp. 10-11. SCHWANKL, *Die Sadduzäerfrage*, 1987a, p. 278, gives a list of 17 discussions in *b. Sanh* 90b-92b in which 22 OT texts are quoted. Exod 3:6 is lacking.

52. Cf. DAVIES – ALLISON, *Matthew*. Vol. III, p. 230, n. 71.

53. Cf. TRICK, *Death, Covenants, and the Proof of Resurrection*, p. 234: "Jesus' argument does not actually seem to prove anything, but if it does prove anything, it seems to prove immortality, not resurrection". Davies and Allison (n. 33, p. 230), remark that both an interim state and resurrection are not mutually exclusive and are sometimes combined (e. g. *1 En.* 20:8 and 22:1-14; 60:8 and 62:15; 2 Macc. 7:9 and 36; *4 Ezra* 7; Josephus, *War* 3.374 [characterizing the Pharisees]).

54. The MT has no verb (so Mark), the LXX does (so Matt). However, Matthew edits Mark without recurrence to the LXX, because in many cases, he inserts a verb where Mark has an ellipsis (cf. MENKEN, *Matthew's Bible*, p. 215).

revelation formula "The God of Abraham, the God of Isaac, the God of Jacob" in Exod 3:6 (comp. 3:15.16; 4:5) does not focus on the relation of the ancestors to God, but on the relation of God to the ancestors. The phrase is used in contexts where God is seen as the One, who protects and saves individuals or his people and shows them his grace and mercy (e.g. *Jubilees* 45:3). The phrase is related to "the God of our fathers" (3 Macc. 7:16) or "God of X" (e.g. Judith 9:11), which means help, support, protection, saviour[55]. We have already pointed to the second of the *Eighteen Benedictions*, which praises the powerful God, who raises the dead. Remarkably, the first benediction also contains a phrase, which Jesus uses in his argument with the Sadducees:

> Blessed are thou, O Lord, our God and God of our fathers,
> *God of Abraham, God of Isaac, and God of Jacob*,
> Great, mighty and awesome God,
> God Most High, creator of heaven and earth,
> Our shield and shield of our fathers, our refuge in every generation,
> Blessed art thou, O Lord, shield of Abraham[56].

Moreover, the phrase is linked to the covenant (and the promises), which God made with the ancestors and their descendants (e.g. Exod 2:24 and 3:6.15.16; *As. Mos.* 3:9)[57].

J.G. Janzen has pointed to the hermeneutical assumption implied in the use of the phrase, namely, "the identification of some kind of analogy between the situations of the ancestors and those of the later exegetes". This assumption is not only put into practice by Jesus but by the narrator of Exodus 3 himself. The promises of posterity spoken to the ancestors are reinterpreted by the narrator of Exodus by extending God's saving power

---

55. Cf. F. DREYFUS, *L'argument scripturaire de Jésus en faveur de la résurrection des morts*, in *RB* 66 (1959) 213-224. *Jubilees* 45:3 (between 161-140 B.C.E.): "And now let the Lord, the God of Israel, be blessed, the God of Abraham and the God of Isaac, who did not withhold his mercy and his kindness from his servant Jacob" (transl. O.S. Wintermute, in *OTP* 2, p. 136); 3 Macc. 7:16 (earlier part of the 1st century B.C.E.): "giving thanks to the God of their fathers, the everlasting savior of Israel" (transl. H. Anderson, in *OTP* 2, p. 529); Judith 9:11: "but you are a God of the lowly, you are the helper of the inferior, the supporter of the weak, the shelterer of the desperate, the savior of the hopeless. 12 Yes, yes, God of my father and God of the inheritance of Israel, ... 14 ... that you are God, God of all power and strength, and that there is no one other than your shielding the race of Israel" (transl. A. Pietersma – B.C. Wright).

56. Translation HEINEMANN, *Prayer in the Talmud*, p. 26, n. 16.

57. *As. Mos.* 3:9 (1st century C.E.): "God of Abraham, God of Isaac, and God of Jacob, remember your covenant which you made with them, and the oath which you swore to them by yourself, that their seed would never fail from the land which you have given them" (transl. J. Priest in *OTP* I, p. 928). The phrase is explicitly connected with the idea of the covenant and with the promise of a lasting posterity.

to the situation of the Exodus generation. In the immediately preceding context, the narrator writes: "God heard their groaning [of the Israelites in their slavery] and he remembered his covenant with Abraham, with Isaac and with Jacob" (Exod 2:24). Thereafter follows the story of God's self-revelation in the burning bush and Moses' call to bring his people out of the slavery in Egypt (Exod 3:1-15). Jesus' application of Exod 3:6 to the issue of the death and resurrection of individuals (and, hence, to the general resurrection at the end of times) may be understood as another extension and intensification of the original meaning of Exod 3:6[58]. His interpretation implies continuity and discontinuity. The continuity lies in the creative and saving power of God and his faithfulness to his covenant promises. The discontinuity lies in the different situations of need in which God intervenes: the barrenness of the ancestors, the slavery of his people, and the mortality of humans. The Sadducees are neither able to understand Jesus' proof from Scripture, nor do they accept his point of view, because they are stuck to the literal sense of the text, as are many modern scholars. Biblical authors, apocalyptic writers, and Jesus himself apply different hermeneutics in interpreting Biblical texts, which are subject to ongoing interpretation, application and intensification[59]. They are not afraid of seeing a fuller sense in biblical texts than a literal one, as they progressively reveal the mystery of God's dealing with human beings[60].

Therefore, the God of the covenant cannot be a God of the dead but of living people. As B.R. Trick pointedly remarks: "God's faithfulness to his covenant implies the patriarchs' continuing existence since the patriarchs' death would have released God from his covenantal obligations"[61]. And he explains: "If … death annuls a covenantal bond, then the fact that God initiates the Exodus out of Egypt on the basis of his covenant with the patriarchs must imply that they are still alive to God. In fact, the Exodus

58. Cf. JANZEN, *Resurrection and Hermeneutics*, pp. 44-46.
59. See what we said on Pseudo-Ezekiel and footnotes 17 and 18.
60. Cf. DREYFUS, *L'argument scripturaire de Jésus*, p. 221-222: to the objection that Jesus forces the literal sense of Exod 3:6, Dreyfus answers: "Mais nous pensons que l'on est ici devant un cas particulièrement net de sens plénier: c'est-à-dire d'un cas où un développement ultérieur de la révélation fait percevoir une profondeur du texte que l'auteur n'a pas perçue, bien qu'elle y fût implicitement contenue … le progrès de la révélation a précisément consisté à faire découvrir à Israël que la mort est un échec et une faillite même quand elle frappe le vieillard comblé de jours et assuré d'une nombreuse descendance. Elle est le mal par excellence dont tous les malheurs et les souffrances de l'existence ne sont qu'un avant-goût. A cette lumière, la mort des Patriarches, même après une longue vie de bonheur, si elle est le dernier mot de leur histoire, apparaît comme une faillite des promesses de Dieu garanties par l'Alliance, et dont le nom de Dieu d'Abraham, d'Isaac et de Jacob est le symbole".
61. TRICK, *Death, Covenants, and the Proof of Resurrection*, p. 236.

story itself demonstrates God's desire and power to fulfil his promise to give the land of Canaan to the patriarchs and their descendants, a promise whose fulfilment will ultimately require resurrection. The Sadducees have therefore also misunderstood God's power"[62]. The idea that the righteous as well as the patriarchs "live unto God", was known in certain Jewish circles, as seen for example in 4 Macc 7:18 and 16:24[63].

According to Otto Schwankl, from a semantic point of view, there are two main categories implied in the story: life and relationship[64]. The topic 'life' is treated in an antithetical way, both positively (resurrection) and negatively (die, dead)[65]. The topic 'relationship' plays on two levels: the bond of marriage and the covenant with God. The first bond, that of marriage, is similarly dealt with in an oppositional way: the whole issue is whether one has or does not have a husband, a wife and children[66] and ends with the question: "Whose wife of the seven will she be?". The first part of the story displays an obstinate attempt to establish relationships, which finally does not succeed. The second bond is the covenant between God and human beings. In the story, the two categories flow together and define each other mutually: life is essentially seen as a relationship; death is understood as a lack of relationships. Similarly, the question of resurrection is put in terms of relationship. What is the primary and founding relationship, which makes resurrection possible and thinkable? For the Sadducees, the founding

---

62. *Ibid.*, p. 254.

63. 4 Macc. 7:18-19: ἀλλ' ὅσοι τῆς εὐσεβείας προνοοῦσιν ἐξ ὅλης καρδίας, οὗτοι μόνοι δύνανται κρατεῖν τῶν τῆς σαρκὸς παθῶν 19 πιστεύοντες ὅτι θεῷ οὐκ ἀποθνῄσκουσιν, ὥσπερ οὐδὲ οἱ πατριάρχαι ἡμῶν Αβρααμ καὶ Ισαακ καὶ Ιακωβ, ἀλλὰ ζῶσιν τῷ θεῷ. "Only those who with all their heart make piety their first concern are able to conquer the passions of the flesh, 19 believing that to God they do not die, as our patriarchs Abraham, Isaac, and Jacob died not, but live to God" (transl. H. Anderson in *OTP* 2, p. 553); 4 Macc. 16: 24-25: Διὰ τούτων τῶν λόγων ἡ ἑπταμήτωρ ἕνα ἕκαστον τῶν υἱῶν παρακαλοῦσα ἀποθανεῖν ἔπεισεν μᾶλλον ἢ παραβῆναι τὴν ἐντολὴν τοῦ θεοῦ, 25 ἔτι δὲ καὶ ταῦτα εἰδότες ὅτι οἱ διὰ τὸν θεὸν ἀποθνῄσκοντες ζῶσιν τῷ θεῷ ὥσπερ Αβρααμ καὶ Ισαακ καὶ Ιακωβ καὶ πάντες οἱ πατριάρχαι. "With these words the mother and the seven exhorted each one and persuaded them to die rather than transgress the commandments of God, 25 and they knew full well themselves that those who die for the sake of God live unto God, as do Abraham and Isaac and Jacob and all the patriarchs" (transl. H. Anderson in *OTP* 2, p. 562). 4 Macc. is written outside Palestine between 63 B.C.E. and 70 C.E., or more specifically: between 18 and 55 C.E. (so E. Bickermann and H. Anderson, in *OTP* 2, p. 534).

64. For what follows, see SCHWANKL, *Die Sadduzäerfrage*, 1987b, pp. 85-87.

65. Positive vv. 23b: resurrection; 23f: raise up; 25a: were (= lived); 28a: resurrection; 30a: resurrection; 31a: resurrection; 32b: living, versus negative 24c: dies; 25b: died; 26a likewise (= died); 27: died; 31a: dead; 32b: dead.

66. Positive: 24e: marry his wife; 24f raise up descendants; 25b: married; 26a: likewise (= married), versus negative: 24c: dies; 24d: not having children; 25b-c: died, having no descendants; 26a-c: likewise (= died, having no descendants); 27: died; 28b: whose wife of the seven will she be?

relationship is of sociological nature and finds its highest expression in marriage. The marriage bond, however, cannot be the basis of resurrection and is even incompatible with it. Jesus puts the marriage bond into perspective and points to another, more essential relationship: the relationship between God and humanity, as is shown in the covenant between God and the ancestors Abraham, Isaac and Jacob. The covenantal relationship between God and humanity is stronger than the bond of marriage and cannot even be destroyed by death.

V. THE *SITZ IM LEBEN JESU* OF THE STORY

The question whether the synoptic story of Jesus' debate with the Sadducees preserves an actual incident that took place during Jesus' historical ministry has received divergent answers. Scholars like R. Bultmann and A.J. Hultgren thought that the story was a creation of the early Church[67]. Others, like R. Pesch and O. Schwankl, thought that the story has preserved something of an incident from the ministry of the historical Jesus[68]. J.P. Meier, the well known author of *The Marginal Jew*, has supported the latter view in a paper some ten years ago[69]. He first observes that even the proponents of an early Christian origin accept that Mark, who has the oldest version of the story, is dependent on pre-Markan tradition. Furthermore, when applying the so-called criteria of discontinuity and coherence to the story, Meier thinks that they argue for a basic historicity of Jesus' debate with the Sadducees. The discontinuity of Jesus' behaviour with either Judaism or early Christianity can be shown in four points: (1) there is a tendency of the synoptic tradition to multiply dispute stories involving Pharisees, but not Sadducees; (2) the topics usually handled in dispute stories are not dealing with the law of levirate and sexual activity after the general resurrection; hence, Jesus' dispute with the Sadducees is atypical; (3) the way, in which the question of the general resurrection is treated and grounded, is different from the way that early Christian writers saw Jesus' own resurrection as the efficient and/or exemplary cause of the future resurrection of believers; (4)

---

67. R. BULTMANN, *Die Geschichte der synoptischen Tradition* (FRLANT, 12), Göttingen, Vandenhoeck & Ruprecht, [8]1970, p. 25; A.J. HULTGREN, *Jesus and His Adversaries: The Form and Function of the Conflict Stories in the Synoptic Tradition*, Augsburg, MN, Augsburg Publishing House, 1979, pp. 132-131.

68. R. PESCH, *Das Markusevangelium. II. Teil: Kommentar zu Kap. 8,27-16,20* (HTKNT, 2/2), Freiburg, Herder, 1977, p. 235: SCHWANKL, *Die Sadduzäerfrage*, 1987b, pp. 88-90.

69. MEIER, *The Debate on the Resurrection of the Dead*.

the text of Scripture, on which Jesus bases his argument in favour of the resurrection, i.e. Exod 3:6, is absent from Jewish discussions – before or after Jesus – which try to give a scriptural warrant to the belief in the resurrection (cf. *b. Sanh* 90a-92b). On the other hand, "while the general resurrection was not a direct topic of Jesus' preaching, it does cohere with and is implied by some of his eschatological pronouncements"[70].

We can fully agree with these arguments. We even may say that the evidence brought in this paper strengthens the argument of coherence: Jesus' way of behaving coheres with the general picture we have of him as someone who has a view of life exclusively centred on the one living God and his kingdom. His fundamental statement and attitude is that belief in God and his creative power is impossible without belief in the resurrection. Furthermore, the authoritative way he uses and interprets Scripture in order to explain the reality and the saving will of God coheres with this general image. Moreover, the evidence we have collected concerning the emergence of the belief in the general resurrection, the language and the arguments used thereby, and the variety of opinions in early Judaism concerning this doctrine (the Sadducees being the well known opponents to the doctrine), offers a fitting context for an incident such as narrated in the synoptic tradition. There is nothing in the story that sounds impossible during the time and in the context that Jesus lived and worked. The way Jesus behaves is marked by continuity and discontinuity. On the one hand, his attitude is fully rooted in the life and faith of contemporary Judaism in which he takes a stand. On the other hand, as someone, who has a special bond with his heavenly Father, he affirms the ongoing development of the eschatological doctrine in an original and authoritative way, over and against the priestly authorities of his time.

Tilburg University   Adelbert DENAUX
School of Theology
PO Box 90153
5000 LE Tilburg
The Netherlands

---

70. *Ibid.*, p. 24, referring to Matt 8:11 par.; Luke 14:14; Matt 11:21-24 par.; Matt 12:41-42 par.; Mark 9:43-47 par.; Mark 14:25.

THE SCRIPTURAL BACKGROUND OF A MATTHEAN LEGEND: EZEKIEL 37, ZECHARIAH 14, AND MATTHEW 27

Matt 27:51b-53 reads as follows: "The earth shook, and the rocks were split, and the tombs were opened, and many bodies of the saints who had fallen asleep were raised, and coming out of the tombs (after his resurrection) they entered the holy city and appeared to many." Until recent times, most commentators on this enigmatic passage, unique to the First Gospel, paid scant heed to its possible background in the Jewish Bible[1]. Other questions were to the fore. Did the tombs open on Friday or on Sunday? When exactly did the dead come back to life? Had they lived in olden times or died only recently? Can we name any of them? What did their resurrection have to do with Jesus' descent into the realm of the dead? Did they ascend with him before Pentecost? Or did they remain abroad thereafter for quite some time? Did they eventually return to their graves, there to await a second resurrection at the last trump?[2].

Over the previous one hundred years or so, as more and more scholars have come to view Matthew's story as a legend, most of these questions have ceased to be asked. Other matters have garnered attention; and theological and literary issues, not historical concerns, now dominate the commentaries. This has led to much reflection on the possible intertextuality of Matt

---

1. Commentators who say nothing on the matter include HILARY of POITIERS, *Comm. Matt ad loc.* (SC, 258), ed. J. Doignon, Paris, Cerf, 1979, p. 256; JEROME, *Comm. Matt ad loc.* (SC, 259), ed. É. Bonnard, Paris, Cerf, 1979, pp. 300-302; JOHN CALVIN, *Commentary on a Harmony of the Evangelists, Matthew, Mark, and Luke*, vol. 3, Grand Rapids, MI, Eerdmans, 1972, pp. 211-213; M. POOLE, *Annotations on the Holy Bible*, 3 vols., London, Henry G. Bohn, 1846, 3:141-42; W. NAST, *A Commentary on the Gospels of Matthew and Mark: Critical, Doctrinal, and Homiletical*, Cincinnati, Poe & Hitchcock, 1864, p. 624; J. WELLHAUSEN, *Das Evangelium Matthaei*, Berlin, Georg Reimer, 1914, p. 140; W. GRUND-MANN, *Das Evangelien nach Matthäus* (THNT, 1), Berlin, Evangelische Verlagsanstalt, 1968, pp. 561-563.

2. For these issues see D.C. ALLISON, Jr., *Matt 27:51-53 and the Descent ad inferos*, in P. LAMPE – M. MAYORDOMO – M. SATO (eds.), *Neutestamentliche Exegese im Dialog: Hermeneutik – Wirkungsgeschichte – Matthäusevangelium*, Neukirchen, Neukirchener Verlag, 2008, pp. 335-355.

27:51b-53. Many are now persuaded that the passage draws upon the language of Ezek 37, especially v. 12 ("I am going to open your graves, and bring you up from your graves, O my people; and I will bring you back to the land of Israel")[3]. A lesser number has found the primary intertext to be rather Zech 14:4-5, or argued that both Zechariah and Ezekiel have influenced Matthew's text[4]. Still others have perceived echoes of 2 Sam 22:7-8;

3. See, e.g., D.I. BLOCK, *The Book of Ezekiel: Chapters 25-48*, Grand Rapids, MI, Eerdmans, 1998, p. 389; G.J. BROOKE, *Ezekiel in Some Qumran and New Testament Texts*, in J.T. BARRERA – L.V. MONTANER (eds.), *The Madrid Qumran Congress: Proceedings of the International Congress on the Dead Sea Scrolls Madrid 18-21 March, 1991* (STDJ, 11), 2 vols., Leiden, Brill – Madrid, Editorial Complutense, 1992, 1:332; R.E. BROWN, *The Death of the Messiah: From Gethsemane to the Grave: A Commentary on the Passion Narratives*, 2 vols., New York, Doubleday, 1994, 2:1123, 1140; G.W. BUCHANAN, *The Gospel of Matthew*, 2 vols., Lewiston – Queenston – Lampeter, Mellen Biblical Press, 1996, 2:1014-15; J. GRASSI, *Ezekiel XXXVII.1-14 and the New Testament*, in *NTS* 11 (1965) 163; R.H. GUNDRY, *Matthew: A Commentary on His Handbook for a Mixed Church under Persecution*, Grand Rapids, MI, Eerdmans, 1994, p. 576; D.J. HARRINGTON, *The Gospel of Matthew* (SP, 1), Collegeville, MN, Liturgical Press – Michael Glazier, 1992, p. 403; J.P. MEIER, *Matthew* (NTM, 3), Wilmington, DE, Michael Glazier, 1980, p. 352; A. MELLO, *Évangile selon Saint Matthieu: Commentaire midrashique et narratif* (LD, 179), Paris: Cerf, 1999, p. 485; B. PARAMBI, *The Discipleship of the Women in the Gospel according to Matthew: An Exegetical Theological Study of Matt 27:51b-56, 57-61 and 28:1-10* (Tesi Gregoriana Serie Teologia, 94), Rome, Gregorian University Press, 2002, pp. 117-118; D.J. PAUL, *'Untypische' Texte im Matthäus? Studien zu Charakter, Funktion und Bedeutung einer Textgruppe des Matthäischen Sonderguts* (NTAbh, 50), Münster, Aschendorff, 2004, p. 100; M. RIEBL, *Auferstehung Jesu in der Stunde seines Todes? Zur Botschaft von Mt 27,51b-53* (SBS), Stuttgart, Katholisches Bibelwerk,1978, pp. 47-48, 61; W. SCHENK, *Der Passionsbericht nach Markus: Untersuchungen zur Überlieferungsgeschichte der Passionstraditionen*, Gütersloh, Gütersloher Verlagshaus Mohn, 1974, pp. 75-76; E. SCHWEIZER, *The Good News according to Matthew*, Atlanta: John Knox, 1975, p. 515; D.P. SENIOR, *The Death of Jesus and the Resurrection of the Holy Ones (Mt 27:51-53)*, in *CBQ* 38 (1976), pp. 312-329; ID., *The Death of God's Son and the Beginning of the New Age*, in A. LACOMARA (ed.), *The Language of the Cross*, Chicago, Franciscan Herald Press, 1977, pp. 31-59; ID., *The Passion According to Matthew: A Redactional Study* (BETL, 29), Louvain, University Press, 1975, pp. 319-320; K. WENGST, *Ostern – Ein wirkliches Gleichnis, eine wahre Geschichte: Zum neutestamentlichen Zeugnis von der Auferweckung Jesu*, Munich, Chr. Kaiser, 1991, pp. 96-97; B.F. WITHERINGTON, III, *Matthew* (Smyth & Helwys Bible Commentary), Macon, GA, Smyth & Helwys, 2006, p. 521 ("possibly"). U. LUZ, *Das Evangelium nach Matthäus*, 4 vols. (EKK, 1/1-4), Düsseldorf – Zürich, Benzinger – Neukirchen-Vluyn, Neukirchener Verlag, 1990-2002, 4:567, recognizes the influence of LXX Ezek 37:12-13 but downplays its significance.

4. E.g., D.C. ALLISON, Jr., *The End of the Ages Has Come: An Early Interpretation of the Death and Resurrection of Jesus* (Studies on the New Testament and Its World), Edinburgh, T. & T. Clark, 1987, pp. 42-46; R.D. AUS, *Samuel, Saul and Jesus: Three Early Palestinian Jewish Christian Haggadoth* (SFSHJ, 105), Atlanta, Scholars Press, 1994, pp. 117-120 (Aus also finds traditions about 1 Sam 28 in the background); M.C. BLACK, *The Rejected and Slain Messiah Who is Coming with His Angels: The Messianic Exegesis of Zechariah 9-14 in the Passion Narratives*, PhD Thesis, Emory University, Ann Arbor, MI, University Microfilms, 1991, pp. 222-226; F.D. BRUNER, *Matthew: A Commentary. Volume 2: The Churchbook. Matthew 13-28*, Grand Rapids, MI – Cambridge, UK, Eerdmans, 2004, p. 762; P. FIEDLER, *Das Matthäusevangelium* (TKNT, 1), Stuttgart, Kohlhammer, 2006, p. 418; J. GNILKA, *Das Matthäusevangelium*, 2 vols. (HTKNT, 1/1-2), Freiburg, Herder, 1986-1988, 2:477 ("vielleicht" for Zechariah); D.M. GURTNER, *The*

Isa 26:19; or Dan 12:2-3[5]. One scholar has suggested that the chief influence is an extra-canonical text, *1 En.* 93:6[6].

In the following pages, I shall leave to the side discussion of *1 Enoch*, Daniel, Isaiah, and 2 Samuel, to which the secondary literature directs only occasional attention. I will concentrate instead on the relationship, first, between Ezek 37 and Matthew's curious episode of the revived saints and, second, between that episode and Zech 14:4-5.

I. EZEKIEL 37

Ezek 37 famously recounts a vision in a plain or broad valley full of dry bones. After the Lord tells the seer to prophesy to those bones, so that they will live again, Ezekiel hears a rattling. The bones then come together, whereupon they are covered with sinews, flesh, and skin, after which the creative breath of God enters into them and they come to life: "they lived, and stood on their feet, a vast multitude" (37:10). Vv. 11-14 identify the bones with Israel and foresee that God will bring the people, who now lie in the grave, back to the land.

Torn Veil: Matthew's Exposition of the Death of Jesus (SNTSMS, 139), Cambridge, Cambridge University Press, 2007, pp. 146-151; J. MORGENSTERN, *The King-God*, in *VT* 10 (1960) 181; C.M. MOSS, The *Zechariah Tradition and the Gospel of Matthew* (BZNW, 156), Berlin – New York, De Gruyter, 2008, pp. 197-201. Although K. STENDAHL, *Matthew*, in M. BLACK – H. H. ROWLEY (eds.), *Peake's Commentary on the Bible*, Sunbury-on-Thames Middlesex, Nelson, 1962, p. 797, does not cite Zech 14:4-5, he does, in his commentary on Matt 27:51-53, observe that the resurrection "was expected to take place at Jerusalem when the Mount of Olives split in two," an event that Zech 14:4-5 foretells. Cf. SCHWEIZER, *Matthew*, p. 515.

5. J. NOLLAND, *The Gospel of Matthew: A Commentary on the Greek Text*, Grand Rapids, MI – Cambridge, UK, Eerdmans, 2005, pp. 1204, 1214, 1216-1217, appears to find influence from all three of these as well as from Ezek 37; Zech 14:4-5; and Dan 12:2-3. Cf. N.T. WRIGHT, *The Resurrection of the Son of God*, Minneapolis, Fortress, 2003, pp. 633-634; he sees allusions to Isaiah, Ezekiel, Daniel, and perhaps Zechariah. Already ALBERTUS MAGNUS, *Super Mt cap. XV-XXVIII ad loc.* Opera Omnia 21/2, ed. B. Schmidt, Münster, Aschendorf, 1987, p. 649, cites Ezekiel, Zechariah, and Isaiah. For A. WINKLHOFER, *Corpora Sanctorum (Mt 27,51ff)*, in *TQ* 133 (1953) 30-67, Isa 26:19; Ezek 37:12; Dan 12:2 and perhaps even additional texts (Isa 2:19; Nah 1:6; Zeph 3:8) are in the background. SENIOR, *Passion*, p. 320, regards the possibility of allusion to Dan 12:2-3 as "tantalizing". Cf. H. GROTIUS, *Operum theologicarum*, vol. 2, part 1, Amsterdam, Joannis Blaev, 1679, p. 276, and J. SCHMID, *Das Evangelium nach Matthäus* (RNT,1), Regensburg, Friedrich Pustet, 1965, p. 374. The structural similarity between part of Matt 27:52 (πολλὰ σώματα τῶν κεκοιμημένων ἁγίων ἠγέρθησαν) and Dan 12:3 (πολλοὶ τῶν καθευδόντων . . . ἀναστήσονται) is indeed intriguing; the vocabulary, however, is not the same. J. GILL, *Gill's Commentary*, 6 vols., Grand Rapids, MI, Baker, 1980, 5:297, observes the possible parallel with Isaiah.

6. See R.L. TROXEL, *Matt 27.51-54 Reconsidered: Its Role in the Passion Narrative, Meaning and Origin*, in *NTS* 48 (2002) 41-47. GURTNER, *Torn Veil*, p. 149, n. 53, and NOLLAND, *Matthew*, p. 1216, n. 486, offer criticism.

Most modern scholars, like Origen and Jerome long before them[7], hold that Ezekiel's vision was originally a symbolic prophecy about the future resuscitation of the house of Israel: God's people will soon leave the land of exile, Babylon, and return to the land of promise[8]. From an early time, however, many understood Ezek 37:1-14 to be more than a promise about the end of exile and a return to the land: they understood the section to prophesy eschatological return from the grave[9]. So-called *Pseudo-Ezekiel*, composed at the latest in the second century B.C.E. and preserved in Hebrew fragments from Qumran, probably — although this has been debated — interprets the resurrection in Ezek 37 as a reward for the righteous dead of Israel, who will someday return to life[10]. Similarly, Papyrus 967 of the LXX, from the second or

7. ORIGEN *apud* METHODIUS, *Res.* 3.9 (GCS, 27), ed. G.N. Bonwetsch, Leipzig, Hinrichs, 1917, pp. 401-403; JEROME, *Comm. Ezek* 11 ad 37:1-14 (CCSL, 75), ed. Fr. Glorie, Turnhout, Brepols, 1964, pp. 510-522.

8. Cf. R. Judah b. Ilai in *b. Sanh.* 92b: Ezekiel's vision was but a parable. Other rabbis in *b. Sanh.* 92b understand the resurrection literally but think of it as already accomplished: some came back to life and then died again (cf. 90b; Tg. Ps.-J. Exod 13:17; Tg. Cant 7:10; *Eccl Rab.* 3.15.1; *Cant Rab.* 7:9; etc.).

9. In addition to what follows see Rev 11:11; *1 Clem.* 50:4; *Apocalypse of Peter* 4; JUSTIN, *Apol.* 52 (PTS, 38), ed. M. Marcovich, Berlin, De Gruyter, p. 194; IRENAEUS, *Haer.* 5.15.1; THEODORET OF CYRUS, *Quaest. Gen* 54, ed. R.C. HILL, p. 114. Jewish sources include *Liv. Proph. Ezek.* 3:12; *Mek.* on Exod 20:7; *Sifre* Deut 306; *Tanh.* BUBER Wayyeshev 9:8; *y. Šeqal.* 47c (3:3); *y. Šabb.* 3c (1:3); *y. Kil.* 32c (9:3); *y. Ketub.* 35b (12:3); *b. Šabb.* 152b; *b. Ta'an.* 2b; Pal. Tg. Ezekiel 37 (see A. DÍEZ-MACHO, *Un Segundo fragmento del Targum Palestinese a los Profetas*, in *Bib* 39 (1958)198-205); *Gen Rab.* 13:6; 14:5; 96:5; *Lev Rab.* 14:9; *Deut Rab.* 7:6; *Pirqe R. El.* 33; *Ma'aseh Daniel*, ed. A. Jellinek, Leipzig, F. Niles, 5:128. According to G.W. NICKELSBURG, *1 Enoch 1: A Commentary on the Book of 1 Enoch, Chapters 1-36; 81-108* (Hermeneia), Minneapolis, Fortress, 2001, p. 315, *1 En.* 25:6 may borrow from Ezek 37:5, 7-10 and refer to the resurrection. TERTULLIAN, *Res.* 30-31 (CSEL, 47), ed. A. Kroymann, Vindobanae, Tempsky, 1906, pp. 67-70, argues for a literal interpretation, attributing an allegorical interpretation to "the Jews". The margin of the Peshitta at the beginning of Ezekiel 37 has: "Concerning the resurrection of the dead". Cf. LXX Q^mg: νεκρῶν ἀναβίωσις. For the position that the eschatological resurrection of the dead is implicit in Ezek 37 see É. PUECH, *La croyance des Esséniens en la vie future: Immortalité, résurrection, vie éternelle? Histoire d'une croyance dans le Judaïsme ancien*, 2 vols. (ÉBib, 21-22), Paris, Gabalda, 1993, 1, pp. 49-52; also the interesting argument to this effect by B. LANG, *Street Theater, Raising the Dead, and the Zoroastrian Connection in Ezekiel's Prophecy*, in J. LUST (ed.), *Ezekiel and His Book: Textual and Literary Criticism and their Interrelation* (BETL, 74), Leuven, Leuven University Press – Peeters, 1986, pp. 307-314.

10. So D. DIMANT, *Resurrection, Restoration, and Time-Curtailing in Qumran, Early Judaism, and Christianity*, in *RevQ* 19 (2000) 527-548; F. GARCÍA MARTÍNEZ, *The Apocalyptic Interpretation of Ezekiel in the Dead Sea Scrolls*, in F. GARCÍA MARTÍNEZ – M. VERVENNE (eds.), with the collaboration of B. Doyle, *Interpreting Translation: Studies on the LXX and Ezekiel in Honour of Johan Lust* (BETL, 142), Leuven – Paris – Dudley, MA, Leuven University Press – Peeters, 2005, pp. 163-176; A.L.A. HOGETERP, *Resurrection and Biblical Tradition: Pseudo-Ezekiel Reconsidered*, in *Bib* 89 (2008) 59-69. For another view see J. TROMP, *"Can These Bones Live?" Ezekiel 37:1-14 and Eschatological Resurrection*, in H.J. DE JONGE – J. TROMP (eds.), *The Book of Ezekiel and Its Influence*, Aldershot – Burlington, VT, Ashgate, 2007, pp. 61-78. On the difficult

early third century C.E., places Ezek 37 after chapter 39, which makes the vision of dry bones follow the destruction of Gog (39:1-20) and Israel's return to the land (39:21-29) and come right before the vision of the new temple and polity (40:1-48:35), which might well have encouraged readers to think of eschatological resurrection: if Ezekiel has already recounted the return to the land, must not the vision of bones have to do with something else?[11]. The *Apocryphon of Ezekiel*, written before the end of the first century C.E., and known only through quotations, contained among other things a parable about the reunion of body and soul at the resurrection. That it circulated under Ezekiel's name strongly implies that someone, because of Ezek 37, thought of him as a prophet of the resurrection[12]. *Sib. Or.* 2:221-26, which could well belong to an originally Jewish work (of uncertain date)[13], uses the language of Ezek 37:1-10 to describe the bodies that will be raised at the judgment[14]. The same is probably true of *Sib. Or.* 4.179-82, which is a pre-Christian Jewish text[15], as well as perhaps 4 Macc 18:17 and *Liv. Proph. Ezek* 13[16].

---

problem of exactly what fragments belonged to *Pseudo-Ezekiel* see M. BRADY, *Biblical Interpretation in the 'Pseudo-Ezekiel' Fragments (4Q383-391) from Cave Four*, in M. HENZE (ed.), *Biblical Interpretation at Qumran*, Grand Rapids, MI – Cambridge, UK, Eerdmans, 2005, pp. 88-109.

11. See further J. LUST, *Ezekiel 36-40 in the Oldest Greek Manuscript*, in *CBQ* 43 (1981) 517-533; ID., *Ezekiel's Utopian Expectations*, in A. HILHORST – É. PUECH – E.J.C. TIGCHELAAR (eds.), *Flores Florentino: Dead Sea Scrolls and Other Jewish Studies in Honour of Florentino García Martínez* (JSJSup, 122), Leiden, Brill, 2007, pp. 403-19; and S. S. SCATOLINI APÓSTOLO, *Ezek 36, 37, 38, and 39 in Papyrus 967 as Pre-Text for Re-Reading Ezekiel*, in GARCÍA MARTÍNEZ – VERVENNE, *Interpreting Translation*, pp. 331-357.

12. The most important study is J.R. MUELLER, *The Five Fragments of the Apocryphon of Ezekiel: A Critical Study* (JSPSSup, 5), Sheffield, Sheffield Academic Press, 1994; see esp. pp. 38-47, 78-100, 168-71. For the plausible conjecture that the Apocryphon of Ezekiel is part of the same document as Qumran's Pseudo-Ezekiel see B.G. WRIGHT, *The Apocryphon of Ezekiel and 4QPseudo-Ezekiel*, in L.H. SCHIFFMAN – E. TOV – J.C. VANDERKAM (eds.), *The Dead Sea Scrolls: Fifty Years After Their Discovery 1947–1997. Proceedings of the Jerusalem Congress, July 20–26, 1997*, Jerusalem, Israel Exploration Society in cooperation with the Shrine of the Book, Israel Museum, 2000, pp. 462–480. If so, it would dispel all doubt as to whether Pseudo-Ezekiel foresees a literal resurrection from the dead.

13. So J.J. COLLINS, *The Sibylline Oracles*, in J.H. CHARLESWORTH (ed.), *The Old Testament Pseudepigraph*, 2 vols., Garden City, New York, Doubleday, 1983, 1:330-32.

14. "Then the heavenly one will give souls and breath and voice to the dead and bones fastened with all kinds of joinings... flesh and sinews and veins and skin about the flesh, and the former hairs. Bodies of humans, made solid in heavenly manner, breath and set in motion, will be raised on a single day."

15. "When everything is already dusty ashes, and God puts to sleep the unspeakable fire, even as he kindled it, God himself will again fashion the bones and ashes of men and he will raise up mortals again as they were before."

16. 4 Macc 18:17: the slain priest, Eleazar, "affirmed the word of Ezekiel, 'Will these dry bones live?'" *Liv. Proph. Ezek* 13: "In the wonder of the dead bones he persuaded them that there is hope for Israel both here and in the coming (age)." Although sometimes cited in this connection, Sir 49:8 is probably irrelevant.

These materials suffice to establish the likelihood that the interpretation of Ezek 37:1-14 in terms of the eschatological resurrection of the dead was not just known in pre-Christian times but probably well known. It may even be reflected in the LXX. The MT for Dan 12:2 prophesies the following: "Many of those who sleep in the dust of the earth shall awake, some to everlasting life, and some to shame and everlasting contempt". The Hebrew word here rendered "dust" is עפר. Unexpectedly, the LXX turns this into πλάτος, which is the equivalent not of עפר but of רחב, the adjectival sense of which is "wide" or "broad." So the LXX seems to be saying that those who sleep in the broad earth or land (ἐν τῷ πλάτει τῆς γῆς) will rise up.

The explanation for this departure from the MT is far from obvious. It occurs, however, that just as MT Dan 12:2 seems to draw upon Isa 26:19[17], so may LXX Dan 12:2 allude to Ezek 37:1-14. For the vision of dry bones is set in the midst of העקבה (vv. 1-2), and the word, העקב, traditionally rendered into English as "valley" (so e.g. KJV, RSV, NRSV), refers to a broad alluvial river basin[18]. In LXX Ezek 3:22-23; 8:4; and 37:1-2, העקב actually becomes πεδίον, whose first meaning is "plain" (LSJ, s.v.). So one wonders whether the translator's odd insertion of πλάτος into LXX Dan 12:2 assumes that the resurrection will take place in a broad, flat expanse, an idea that would presumably derive from Ezek 37:1-2.

Whether or not that is the right explanation, we may now turn to Matthew's strange story of revived saints and ask whether it alludes to or draws Ezek 37, understood as a prophecy of the eschatological revivification of the dead. My own verdict is that it does. I offer five reasons:

(1) To begin with the obvious: there is an overlap of theme. If Matt 27:51b-53 tells the tale of saints rising from the dead, ancient readers, as we have seen, could read Ezek 37:1-14 as a prophecy of eschatological resurrection. Furthermore, only a very few passages in the Hebrew Bible can be taken to prophesy resurrection[19]. If, then, one desired to borrow scriptural

---

17. See G.W.E. NICKELSBURG, Jr., *Resurrection, Immortality, and Eternal Life in Intertestamental Judaism* (HTS, 26), Cambridge, MA, Harvard University Press, 1972, pp. 17-19.

18. Cf. KOEHLER – BAUMGARTNER, s.v.: "wide U-shaped valley with gentle slopes." Within Ezekiel, according to W. ZIMMERLI, *Ezekiel: A Commentary on the Book of the Prophet Ezekiel* (Hermeneia), 2 vols., ed. F.M. CROSS – K. BALTZER, with the assistance of L.J. GREENSPOON, Philadelphia, Fortress, 1979, 1983, 1:157, it refers to "the wide alluvial plain of Babylon"; cf. Ezek 4:22; 8:4. Some rabbinic sources identify the valley with the valley of Dura, which is in fact a broad, not a steep valley: *b. Sanh.* 92b; Tg. Ps.-J. Exod 13:17; Tg. Cant 7:10; *Pirqe R. El.* 33.

19. H. BIRKELAND, *The Beliefs in Resurrection of the Dead in the Old Testa*ment, in *ST* 3 (1949) 60-78.

language to say something on that subject, Ezek 37:1-14 was one of the few options available, and certainly the only relevant passage of any length.

(2) The likelihood that one text intentionally recalls another is increased if the latter is prominent in the tradition of the former, and especially if other, related texts cite or allude to it. There is no problem on this score. Ezek 37, quoted in 2 Cor 6:16 (cf. Ezek 37:27) and clearly echoed in Rev 11:11 (cf. Ezek 37:5, 10), was not an obscure text in the early church. At least half a dozen ecclesiastical texts from the first two centuries construe that chapter as a proof text for the general resurrection[20].

(3) The Gospel and the prophetic text share several words. The most significant overlap is between Matt 27:52 (τὰ μνημεῖα ἀνεῴχθησαν . . . ἐκ τῶν μνημείων) and LXX Ezek 37:12 (ἀνοίγω ὑμῶν τὰ μνήματα . . . ἐκ τῶν μνημάτων). The parallel is forceful when one takes into account that Matthew uniformly prefers μνημεῖον over the synonymous μνῆμα[21], that ἀνοίγω + μνῆμα/μνημεῖον is hardly a common expression[22], and that Ezek 37:12 is the only LXX text to use that idiom. Beyond that are four minor links, which may or may not be significant: (a) πολύς appears in LXX Ezek 37:2 ("exceedingly πολλὰς bones") and 10 ("an exceedingly πολλη gathering") as well as in Matt 27:52 ("πολλοί bodies"). (b) LXX Ezek 37:7 speaks of the earth trembling (σεισμός) while Matt 27:51b narrates an earthquake (using the verb, σείω). (c) Whereas Ezekiel foresees God bringing the resurrected into the land of Israel (εἰσάξω ὑμας εἰς τὴν γῆν τοῦ Ἰσραήλ), Matthew writes of the saints entering into the holy city (εἰσῆλθον εἰς τὴν ἁγίαν πόλιν). (d) In Ezekiel, the bodies stand up when breath (LXX: πνεῦμα) enters them (vv.

20. Rev 20, in its account of the eschatological resurrection, also appears to draw upon Ezek 37; see I.K. BOXALL, *Exile, Prophet, Visionary: Ezekiel's Influence on the Book of Revelation*, in DE JONGE – TROMP, *Ezekiel and Its Influence*, pp. 147-164; B. KOWALSKI, *Die Rezeption des Propheten Ezechiel in der Offenbarung des Johannes* (SBS, 52), Stuttgart, Katholisches Bibelwerk, 2004, pp. 215-216, 379-90. One should note, however, that Matthew nowhere quotes from any chapter of Ezekiel, and he otherwise alludes to the prophet on one occasion only, in his version of the parable of the mustard seed (13:31-32). See D.C. ALLISON, Jr., *The Intertextual Jesus: Scripture in Q*, Valley Forge, PA, Trinity Press International, 2000, pp. 134-37. Yet, being from Q, this link is pre-Matthean. Although the Scripture index to NESTLE-ALAND[27] lists additional correlations between Ezekiel and Matthew, none of these, with the possible exception of Matt 6:9 (cf. Ezek 36:23), seems to be more than a verbal coincidence. So we cannot say that an interest in Ezekiel is a redactional trait of Matthew.

21. Matt: 0; Mark: 4; Luke: 3; cf. Matt 8:28 diff. Mark 5:3, 5; Matt 27:60 diff. Mark 15:46.

22. It does occur in *Gk. Apoc. Ezra* 4:36: "After these things a trumpet, and the graves will be opened (τὰ μνημεῖα ἀνεῴχθησαν) and the dead will rise up uncorrupted." This clearly alludes to 1 Cor 15:22, but τὰ μνημεῖα ἀνοιχθήσονται comes from either Ezekiel or Matthew. Note also the Greek frag. of *Asc. Isa* 3:16, where the language of Ezekiel refers to the resurrection of Jesus: αὐτοῦ ἀνοίξουσιν τὸ μνημονεῖον.

5. 6. 8-10. 14). In Matthew, the prodigies in chapter 27 occur immediately after Jesus breathes his last (v. 50: ἀφιῆκεν τὸ πνεῦμα)²³.

(4) The history of interpretation either enhances or diminishes the plausibility of a proposed allusion. If text A has reminded commentators of text B, the odds that it was designed to do so are increased. Conversely, if commentators have uniformly missed an allusion, doubt may be appropriate. How does it stand with Matt 27:51b-53 and Ezek 37?

As already observed, a large number of recent commentators have perceived a connection between these two texts. The pre-modern period is also not without those who move from Matt 27:51b-53 to Ezek 37:1-14 or vice versa. Ambrose follows his exposition of the resurrection in Ezek 37 with a reference to Matt 27:51b-53: "The Spirit (cf. Ezek 37:9-10.13-14) raises after the same manner as the Lord raised at the time of his own Passion, when suddenly in the twinkling of an eye the graves of the dead were opened, and the bodies living again arose from the tombs, etc."²⁴ Pseudo-Epiphanius, *Test.* 85.5, ed. R.V. Hotchkiss, Missoula, Mont., 1974, p. 66, cites Ezek 37:12-14 as a proof text ὅτι νεκροὶ ἀναστήσονται, which refers to the resurrection of the saints in Matt 27. And Albertus Magnus, *Super Mt cap. XV-XXVIII ad loc.* Opera Omnia 21/2, ed. B. Schmidt, Münster, Aschendorff, 1987, p. 649, quotes Ezek 37:12 when elucidating Matt 27:52.

The association of Matt 27:51b-53 with Ezek 37:1-14 is probably attested already in the second century. *Odes of Solomon* 22 is a first-person account of Jesus' rescue of the dead from the underworld²⁵. That its author knew Matthew seems likely enough from the final verse, which sounds like an echo of Matt 16:18: "The foundation of everything is your rock, and upon it you have built your kingdom"²⁶. Moreover, his version of the

23. But regarding this last possible parallel, BROWN, *Death*, 2:1123 n. 64, has written: "The imagery of the two passages is different. The fallen-asleep holy ones are raised in the earth-shaking moment of Jesus' death; I cannot see that Matt means that they received Jesus' released spirit…. If Matt intended a parallel to Ezek 37:6, why did he not choose a verb that would have facilitated that?"

24. *Spiritu sanc.* 30.20(149-51) (CSEL 79), ed[1]. O. Faller, Vindobanae, Hoelder – Pichler – Tempsky, 1964, pp. 214-215. Cf. Ambrose, Ps 1.54-55 (CSEL 64/6), ed. M. Petschenig, Vindobanae, Tempsky, 1919, p. 46.

25. On the date of the *Odes*, which I am inclined to place shortly before the middle of the second century, see M. LATTKE, *Dating the Odes of Solomon*, in *Antichthon* 27 (1993) 45-59.

26. Dependence upon several texts, including Matthew, seems likely. See the still useful discussion of R. HARRIS – A. MINGANA, *The Odes and Psalms of Solomon*, 2 vols., Manchester – London – New York, Manchester University Press – Longmans – Green & Co., and Bernard Quaritch, 1920, pp. 120-125. See p. 121 for *Od. Sol.* 22:12 and Matt 16:18, and cf. É. MASSAUX, *The Influence of the Gospel of Saint Matthew on Christian Literature before Saint Irenaeus, Book 2: The Later Christian Writings*, Macon, GA, Mercer – Leuven, University Press – Peeters, 1992, pp. 63-66.

descent into Sheol involves not just the freeing of souls but their return to bodies, an idea that the early church derived from Matt 27:51b-53[27], and the latter concerns "the holy ones", an expression that reappears in *Od. Sol.* 22:12 (קדישא). So it is telling for our purposes that the Odist, in recounting that liberation and resurrection, borrows from Ezekiel's vision: "And it [God's right hand] chose them from the graves (cf. Ezek 37:12-13) and separated them from the dead ones. It took dead bones (cf. Ezek 37:1-3) and covered them with flesh (cf. Ezek 37:6.8). But they were motionless (cf. Ezek 37:8), so it gave energy for life" (cf. Ezek 37:5.9-10)[28]. In other words, *Od. Sol.* 22:8-10 reveals a second-century Christian using Ezekiel's language to write about the event in Matt 27.

(5) Associating Matt 27:51b-53 with Ezek 37, understood as a prophecy of the eschatological resurrection, coheres with Matthean theology. The death and resurrection of Jesus are, in the First Gospel, eschatological motifs, and the end of Jesus is spoken of as though it coincided with the end of the age[29]. Although the consummation lies ahead, although this age is still full of tribulation, and although the faithful await the future coming of the Son of Man, eschatological prophecies have been fulfilled, Gentiles have already begun to join the congregation of the latter days, and God's Son has already been enthroned (28:20). Matthew has a form of realized eschatology, into which a claim that the vision of the dry bones has come to pass or partly come to pass fits perfectly.

II. Zechariah 14

The preceding observations establish the likelihood that Matt 27:51b-53 alludes to the resurrection in Ezek 37. Yet it is perhaps unexpected, given that 27:51b-53 draws upon Ezekiel, that the text says nothing about bones. It speaks only of σώματα, of bodies. Is this perhaps some reason to surmise

---

27. See ALLISON, *Descens ad inferos*. Given this, it is relevant that the Christian artistic tradition can conflate Ezekiel's vision with the image of Jesus rescuing the dead from the underworld; see A. GOLDSCHMIDT – K. WEITZMANN, *Die Byzantinischen Elfenbeinskulpturen des X.-XIII. Jahrhunderts. Zweiter Band: Reliefs*, Berlin, Deutscher Verlag für Kunstwissenschaft, 1979, p. 29.

28. See further HARRIS –MINGANA, *Odes*, 2:328-329.

29. See further H.-W. BARTSCH, *Die Passions- und Ostergeschichten bei Matthäus*, in *Entmythologisierende Auslegung: Aufsätze aus den Jahren 1940 bis 1960*, Hamburg, Herbert Reich, 1962, pp. 80-92; J.A. GIBBS, *Jerusalem and Parousia: Jesus' Eschatological Discourse in Matthew's Gospel*, St. Louis, Concordia, 2000, pp. 139-166; and J.P. MEIER, *Law and History in Matthew's Gospel* (AnBib, 71), Rome, Biblical Institute, 1976, pp. 30-35.

that, while Ezekiel is in the background, additional traditions may also play a role in Matthew's scene?

Despite the links between Ezek 37:12 and Matt 27:52, there is another Scripture that lays claim to bear directly on our text. This is Zech 14:4-5, which reads: "On that day his feet shall stand on the Mount of Olives, which lies before Jerusalem on the east; and the Mount of Olives shall be split in two from east to west by a very wide valley; so that half of the Mount shall withdraw northwards, and the other half southwards. And you shall flee by the valley of the Lord's mountain, for the valley between the mountains shall reach to Azal; and you shall flee as you fled from the earthquake in the days of King Uzziah of Judah. Then the Lord my God will come, and all the holy ones with him".

The affinity between this prophetic oracle and Matt 27:51b-53 may not be evident at first glance because modern readers do not typically understand Zech 14:4-5 to be an account of the resurrection, even if its eschatological character is patent[30]. But, as visitors to the Mount of Olives know, that rise is covered with Jewish graves because of the belief that, on the last day, the Messiah will return to the place, where the resurrection will commence[31]; and the proof text for this popular superstition has always been the verses just cited from Zechariah. How ancient, then, is this understanding of Zech 14:4-5?[32]

---

30. Zech 14:4-5 must be part of the reason for the eschatological associations of the Mount of Olives, which are reflected in Mark 11:1-11 (Jesus as the Son of David enters Jerusalem from the Mount of Olives); 13:1-37 (Jesus delivers his eschatological discourse from that Mount); and JOSEPHUS, *Ant.* 20.169-72; *Bell.* 2.261-63 (an Egyptian prophet marched his followers from the desert to the Mount of Olives, hoping to command the walls of Jerusalem to fall for his entrance, that he might become its ruler).

31. Cf. Z. VILNAY, *Legends of Jerusalem: The Sacred Land, Volume 1*, Philadelphia, Jewish Publication Society of America, 1973, pp. 285-287. Islamic legend has also sometimes placed the resurrection on this spot; see G. LE STRANGE, *Palestine under the Moslems: A Description of Syria and the Holy Land from A.D. 650 to 1500*, London, Alexander P. Watt, 1890, pp. 218-219.

32. If, as J.B. CURTIS, *The Mount of Olives in Tradition*, in *HUCA* 28 (1957) 137-180, has argued, the Mount of Olives was home to the cult of Nergal, the Akkadian god of death, this may well have encouraged such a reading, for in that case the mountain could have been thought of as a place of exit from and entry to the land of the dead. 2 Kings 23:13 does call the Mount of Olives הר־המשחית, "the Mount of the Destroyer" and, in Exod 12:23, המשחית is the angel of death. Further, Jews buried the dead at the foot of the Mount of Olives from olden times; see A. KLONER – B. ZISSU, *The Necropolis of Jerusalem in the Second Temple Period* (Interdisciplinary Studies in Ancient Culture and Religion, 8), Leuven – Dudley, MA, Peeters, 2007, pp. 197-230. Even apart from that, the Mount of Olives is near the Hinnom Valley, the place of the eschatological punishment of the wicked in Judaism (*1 En.* 26:1 [v. 3 refers to the Mount of Olives]; 90:24; *Sib. Or.* 1.103; 2.292; 4.186; *2 Bar.* 59:10; 85:13; *t. Sanh.* 13.3; *b. Ber.* 28b; *b. 'Erub.* 19a; *b. Pesah.* 54a; etc.), and it overlooks Jerusalem, the center of the world (Ezek 5:5; 38:12; *1 En.* 26:1; *Jub.* 8:9; *Sib. Or.* 5:250; *b. Sanh.* 37a; etc.). What site could be more appropriate for the resurrection of the dead?

The bottom left panel of the northern wall of the Dura-Europos synagogue shows that it goes back at least to the mid-third century C.E.[33]. Although most scholars have rightly looked primarily to Ezek 37 for the interpretation of this lavish, three-part fresco depicting the eschatological resurrection[34], Zech 14:4-5 is also undoubtedly reflected[35]. In the section which portrays the resurrection of the dead, the Mount of Olives (indicated by the two trees on the top of the mountain, as well as by additional trees off to the side[36]) has been split in two — precisely the event prophesied in Zech.14:4, and one without parallel in Ezekiel 37[37] — and the revived dead,

33. See below, Pictures, pp. 182-183. According to an Aramaic inscription at the site, the synagogue was completed in 245 C.E.

34. So, e.g., E.R. GOODENOUGH, *Jewish Symbols in the Greco-Roman Period: Symbolism in the Dura Synagogue*, 13 vols., Princeton, Princeton University Press, 1953-1968, pp. 179-196. See vol. XI, plate 21, for a reproduction of the panel. Although LUZ, *Matthäus*, 4:566, states, "it is not clear whether the picture of the resurrection in the Ezekiel cycle... is to be interpreted eschatologically," most interpreters have not held that Dura-Europos assumes a metaphorical understanding of Ezekiel 37. There are several good reasons for this. (a) A ceiling tile mentions the world to come and perhaps the resurrection; see J. OBERMANN, *Inscribed Tiles from the Synagogue of Dura*, in *Berytus* 7/2 (1942), p. 116 – although C.C. TORREY, *The Aramaic Texts*, in C.H. KRAELING, *The Excavations at Dura-Europos: Final Report VIII, Part 1. The Synagogue*, New Haven, Yale University Press, 1956, p. 263, offers a different reconstruction and translation. (b) Not all are raised, as one can see from the body parts to the right of the ten resurrected individuals. This reflects the belief in a resurrection of the righteous only, as in *Pss. Sol.* 3; *1 En.* 83-90; JOSEPHUS, *Bell.* 2:163; and *2 Bar.* 30:1-5. Cf. U. KELLERMANN, *Elia Redivivus und die heilszeitliche Auferweckung der Toten: Erwägungen zur ältesten Bezeugung einer Erwartung*, in K. GRÜWALDT – H. SCHROETER (eds.), *Was suchst du hier, Elia? Ein hermeneutisches Arbeitsbuch* (Hermeneutica, 4), Rheinbach – Merzbach, CMZ-Verlag, 1995, p. 76, and W.G. KÜMMEL, *Die älteste religiöse Kunst der Juden*, in *Judaica* 2 (1946), p. 53. (c) Several motifs in other panels reflect an interest in eternal life. See E. GARTE, *The Theme of Resurrection in the Dura-Europos Synagogue Paintings*, in *JQR* 64 (1973-74) 1-15. (d) Dura's split mountain comes not from Ezek 37 but from Zech 14:4-5 (see text), and must have to do with the resurrection of the dead, not the ingathering of those living in the diaspora. (e) One would expect the Dura panel to have twelve resurrected individuals if it were about the restoration of the twelve tribes; cf. C. DU MESNIL DU BUISSON, *Les Peintures de la Synagogue de Doura-Europos 245-256 après J.-C*, Rome, Pontifical Institute, 1939, p. 99, n. 2.

35. So also CURTIS, *Mount of Olives*, pp. 170-72; R.P. GORDON, *The Targumists as Eschatologists*, in *Congress Volume* (VTSupp, 29), Leiden, Brill, 1978, pp. 119-120; C.L. MEYERS – E.M. MEYERS, *Zechariah 9-14* (AB), New York, Doubleday, 1993, pp. 422-423; H. RIESENFELD, *The Resurrection in Ezekiel XXXVII and in the Dura-Europos Paintings* (UUA, 11), Stockholm, Almqvist & Wiksells, 1948, pp. 30-31; R. VON BENDEMANN, *"Lebensgeist kam in sie..."*: *Der Ezechielzyklus von Dura-Europos und die Rezeption von Eze 37 in der Apk des Johannes: Ein Beitrag zum Verhältnisproblem von Ikonizität und Narrativität*, in A. WEISSENRIEDER – F. WENDT – P. VON GEMÜNDEN (eds.), *Picturing the New Testament: Studies in Visual Images* (WUNT, 193), Tübingen, Mohr Siebeck, 2005, pp. 271-272; R. WISCHNITZER, *The Messianic Theme in the Paintings of the Dura Synagogue*, Chicago, University of Chicago Press, 1948, p. 45.

36. DU MESNIL DU BUISSON, *Peintures*, pp. 97-98: "Two isolated trees, at the summit, rather resemble the olive trees of Palestine."

37. Cf. CURTIS, *Mount of Olives*, pp. 170-71: "This cleft mountain does not fit into Ezekiel's vision in any way; thus it is necessary to explain it by external data."

or rather their body parts[38], are emerging from the crack. The fallen, castellated citadel or miniature building on the side of the mountain conveys that an earthquake has split the mountain (cf. Zech 14:4)[39], so those resurrected must be the "holy ones" of Zech 14:5. (See below, Pictures, pp. 182-183).

Rabbinic sources demonstrate that the Dura-Europos synagogue represents no idiosyncratic interpretation of Zechariah. Codex Reuchlinianus' version of the targum on Zechariah introduces 14:4 with this: "At that time the Lord will take in his hand the great trumpet and will blow ten blasts upon it to revive the dead". The targum on Cant 8:5 foretells, in obvious dependence upon Zech 14:4-5, that "when the dead rise, the Mount of Olives will split, and all of Israel's dead will come up out from it, and even the righteous who have died in exile, they will come by way of tunnels below the ground and will emerge from beneath the Mount of Olives". This incredible expectation, which presumably reflects anxiety regarding the fate of those buried outside of the land[40], appears in quite a few rabbinic texts: *Tanh.* Buber Wayehi 12:6; *y. Kil.* 32c (9:3); *y. Ketub.* 35b (12:3); *b. Ketub.* 111a; *Pesiq. R.* 1:6; 31:10 (citing Zech 14:4); etc.[41]

---

38. "One expects... Ezekiel to be surrounded by dry bones; contrary to the text he stands between heads and limbs already covered with flesh, depicting the subsequent stage. However... some bones are represented, namely, four ribs, at the foot of the mountain, out of place, next to the third Ezekiel figure. This merely means that the fresco painter fused what were originally separate scenes and set them on a continuous background, and feeling free to distribute bones and limbs at will, he gave preference to the heads and limbs already covered by flesh because they are more conspicuous and illustrate more explicitly the miracle of the reconstruction." So K. WEITZMANN, *The Frescoes of the Dura Synagogue and Christian Art*, Washington, DC, Dumbarton Oaks Research Library and Collection, 1990, p. 134.

39. The secondary literature on Dura typically pays little attention to this building. Is it perhaps an incense burner or a casket? Or might it represent the high place Solomon built on the Mount of Olives, to God's displeasure (1 Kings 11:7; 2 Kings 23:13)? DU MESNIL DU BUISSON, *Peintures*, p. 95, suggests it illustrates Ezek 35:15: "As you rejoiced over the inheritance of the house of Israel, because it was desolate, so I will deal with you; you shall be desolate, Mount Seir, and all Edom, all of it." Whatever the case may be, its position (upside down and crooked) indicates displacement as the mountain splits. Cf. WEITZMANN, *Frescoes*, p. 134: "To turn a building upside down has apparently been the artistic convention for depicting an earthquake, as may be seen in a ninth-century miniature of a GREGORY of NAZIANUS manuscript in Milan, in which the earthquake that took place in A.D. 368 in Nicaea is represented."

40. Cf. *b. Ketub.* 111a: "The dead outside the land will not be resurrected." The idea of underground tunnels served the same function as ossuaries presumably did for some: they were a way of getting the dead back to the land.

41. Partial inspiration for this belief was probably Ezek 37:12: "Therefore prophesy, and say to them, Thus says the Lord God: I am going to open your graves, and bring you up from your graves, O my people; and I will bring you back to the land of Israel." Once these words become a prophecy of the resurrection, one can understand "I will bring you back to the land of Israel" as part and parcel of the end-time resurrection: God brings the dead to the land so that they might in that place come up from their graves. This is precisely what we find in the rabbinic texts just cited, four of which refer to Ezekiel. *y. Ketub.* 35b (12:3) reads: Israel "is

It seems likely enough, moreover, that the Ezekiel panel at Dura Europos presupposes the notion of underground tunnels. As R. P. Gordon has observed: "(i) How would the bodies of the righteous who died in Israel be conducted from their graves to the Mount of Olives, if not by 'subterranean traction'? (ii) It is unlikely that a painting in Babylonia would represent the resurrection in such a way as to exclude those for whom the fresco was made. (iii) It is probable that the group of ten men in Greek garb on the right of the panel are representatives of the ten tribes of the northern kingdom"[42]. To this one may add (iv) the panel depicts the body parts emerging not from ossuaries but from the black cleft in the Mount of Olives[43] and (v) the resurrected individuals on the right side of the Ezekiel panel wear Greek garb, which may be a way of saying that they are from the diaspora, in which case, their bodies have somehow been transported to the land of Israel[44].

The painting at Dura was executed in the first half of the third century, well over a hundred years after Matthew, and one might think this too late to tell us anything about the late first century. We can, however, trace the interpretation of Zech 14:4-5 as a prophecy of the resurrection to shortly after 100 C.E., to a text often thought to be closely related to the First Gospel[45]. The closing words of the *Didache* are these: "And then there will appear the signs of truth: first the sign of an opening in heaven, then the sign of the sound of a trumpet, and third, the resurrection of the dead – but not of all; rather, as it is written, 'The Lord will come, and all his holy ones with

---

the land in which the dead will first come to life in the time of the Messiah…. If that is the case, then our rabbis in Babylon will be at a disadvantage. R. Simai said: 'The Holy One, blessed be he, will cave the ground before them, and they will roll like wines-skins. Once they reach the land of Israel, their souls are with them.' What is the scriptural basis for this?" There follows a reference to Ezek 37:14.

42. GORDON, *The Targumists as Eschatologists*, pp. 119-120. KÜMMEL, *Kunst der Juden*, p. 53; VON BENDEMANN, *"Lebensgeist"*, p. 272; and R. WISCHNITZER-BERNSTEIN, *The Conception of the Resurrection in the Ezekiel Panel of the Dura Synagogue*, in *JBL* 60 (1941) 46-47, agree with the last point. Cf. JOSEPHUS, *Ant.* 11.133 (the "ten tribes beyond the Euphrates" constitute "countless myriads whose number cannot be ascertained") and Dura's exodus panel, where the twelve male figures must represent the twelve tribes.

43. One may compare the black space from which the dead emerge in the traditional icons of the resurrection of Jesus.

44. Ezekiel's garb has also changed, from the Persian style on the left to the Greek style on the right. Presumably the switch represents the donning of eschatological garments; cf. *1 En.* 62:15-16; Rev 3:5; *4 Ezra* 2:39, 45; *Asc. Isa* 7:22; 8:14, 26; 9:9.24-26; etc. But KELLERMANN, *Elia Redivivus*, pp. 75-77, suggests that the two figures on the right might be Elijah as Jewish tradition associates him with the resurrection of the dead; see, e.g., *m. Sota* 9:15; *y. Šeq.* 47c (3:3); and perhaps already LXX Sir 48:11.

45. See the collection of essays in H. VAN DE SANDT (ed.), *Matthew and the Didache: Two Documents from the Same Jewish-Christian Milieu?*, Assen, Van Gorcum – Minneapolis, Fortress, 2005.

him'. Then the world will see the Lord coming upon the clouds of heaven"
(16:7-8). The formal quotation from Zech 14:5 is the proof that the resurrection will be not for all but only for some, because the Lord will not come
with everybody but only with "his holy ones"[46]. Because, then, the most
likely date for the *Didache* is ca. 100,[47] the *Didache*'s little apocalypse establishes that a Jewish Christian, shortly after Matthew, viewed Zech 14:4-5 as
a proof-text for the eschatological resurrection, at least of the righteous.

Although that is enough for our purposes, I should like to propose that
1 Thess 3:13 also merits mention in this connection. The verse reads: "And
may he so strengthen your hearts in holiness that you may be blameless
before our God and Father at the coming (παρουσία of our Lord (κυρίου)
Jesus with all his saints" (μετὰ πάντων τῶν ἁγίων αὐτοῦ). The appeal to Zech
14:5, with which one may compare the use of that text in *Did.* 16:7-8 (see
above) and *4 Bar.* 9:18[48], – is unmistakable, as the commentators almost
uniformly observe[49]. Paul's Lord will come "with all his saints" because
Zechariah prophesied of the Lord coming "with all his saints" (LXX: ἥξει
κύριος . . . πάντες οἱ ἅγιοι μετ᾽ αὐτοῦ).

This interests because, only a few lines later, Paul takes up the subject of
the *parousia*, and when he does so, it and the resurrection turn out to be
inextricably linked: "For since we believe that Jesus died and rose again, even
so, through Jesus, God will bring with him those who have died. For this we

46. The Dura painting appears to reflect precisely this use of Zech 14:4-5. Unconnected
body parts remain to the right of those raised from the dead. The resurrection leaves them in
their prior, disarticulated, inanimate state. Given this, one may infer that the remains at the
far left, which include four heads, are the body parts of those in the diaspora, and that only
three of them roll through underground tunnels to come out of the Mount of Olives and that
only three bodies receive the breath of life. One head—the one at the far right – remains
where it is, unresurrected. Not all are raised.

47. K. NIEDERWIMMER, *The Didache: A Commentary* (Hermeneia), Minneapolis, MN,
Fortress, 1998, pp. 52-54.

48. *4 Bar.* 9:18: "He whom I have seen adorned by his Father and coming into the world
on the Mount of Olives will satisfy the hungry souls." This is part of the Christian ending to
Paraleipomena Jeremiou and probably comes from the second century; cf. J. HERZER, *4 Baruch
(Paraleipomena Jeremiou)*, Atlanta, Society of Biblical Literature, 2005, pp. xxxiv-xxv. One
can also ask whether Acts 1:11-12 associates the *parousia* with the Mount of Olives. The
angels tell the apostles that Jesus will come as he went: ἐλεύσεται ὃν τρόπον ἐθεάσασθε αὐτὸν
πορευόμενον. Might this not embrace the place (the Mount of Olives) as well as the manner
(on clouds)? A few commentators have had this thought; see, e.g., M. BAUMGARTEN, *The Acts
of the Apostles: or The History of the Church in the Apostolic Age*, 3 vols., Edinburgh, T. & T.
Clark, 1854, 1:31-33, and GILL, *Commentary*, p. 869. Cf. J.D.G. DUNN, *The Acts of the
Apostles*, London, Epworth, 1996, p. 15: "The identification of the site of the ascension as
the Mount of Olives… may… reflect the eschatological significance attributed to the Mount
of Olives in Zech 4.4-5."

49. Cf. A. MALHERBE, *The Letters to the Thessalonians* (AB), New York, Doubleday, 2000,
p. 214.

declare to you by the word of the Lord, that we who are alive, who are left until the coming of the Lord, will by no means precede those who have died. For the Lord himself, with a cry of command, with the archangel's call and with the sound of God's trumpet, will descend from heaven, and the dead in Christ will rise first" (1 Thess 4:14-16). Although these verses do not allude to Zech 14:4-5, the phrase, "through Jesus, God will bring with him those who have died," reiterates the earlier 3:13, which does allude to it.

That Zech 14:4-5 has informed chapter 4 as well as chapter 3 of 1 Thessalonians seems to follow from one of the puzzles of 1 Thess 4:13-18. Why do the saints meet Jesus in the air when he is presumably on his way to earth?[50]. The image of Christians in the clouds with Jesus is striking and strange. Some commentaries, in accounting for it, remind us that, when a dignitary approached a city, a delegation would typically go out to meet him and then turn around and enter the gate with him[51]. But if Jesus in fact descends in order to establish his rule on the earth, why would the saints not simply meet Jesus at his landing point, wherever that may be[52], and then proceed with him to his final destination (perhaps Jerusalem proper or even the temple)? The ascent into the air up to the clouds remains odd and unexplained.

50. The commentaries discuss whether, for Paul, Jesus returns to the earth or the saints dwell with him eternally in the sky or heaven. Favoring the latter is E.J. RICHARD, *First and Second Thessalonians* (SP, 11), Collegeville, MN, Liturgical Press, 1995, pp. 238-39, 247-48. Unfortunately, the text is frustratingly silent, but S. LÉGASSE, *Les Épîtres de Paul aux Thessaloniciens* (LD Commentaires, 7), Paris, Cerf, 1999, pp. 265-267, is probably right to urge that Paul's scenario presupposes Jesus' rule with the saints on earth. (a) The scene is one of descent from heaven (καταβήσεται ἀπ' οὐρανοῦ). (b) Nothing is said of ascent to heaven, only to the air; and as AUGUSTINE, *Civ.* 20.20 (CCSL, 48), ed. B. Dombart, Turnhout, Brepols, p. 734, wrote: "We are not to take the statement that 'we will always be with the Lord' as meaning that we are to remain for ever in the air with the Lord." Paul writes not "there (ἐκεῖ) we will be with the Lord" but "thus (οὕτως) we will be with the Lord." (c) The word παρουσία itself connotes a return to and arrival at an earthly city. (d) The παρουσία involves the eschatological judgment, and as only the saints have ascended, the judge must descend to deal with the rest; so if the saints are always with him (1 Thess 4:17), they must return to earth. (e) Although Paul nowhere in his extant writings clarifies where Christians will be after the παρουσία, the earth is, more often than not in early Jewish and Christian sources, the centre of God's eschatological activities, especially Israel and Jerusalem. See further W. HORBURY, *Land, Sanctuary and Worship*, in J. BARCLAY – J. SWEET (eds.), *Early Christian Thought in Its Jewish Context*, Cambridge, Cambridge University Press, 1996, pp. 219-222, and P. STUHLMACHER, *Die Stellung Jesu und des Paulus zu Jerusalem: Versuch einer Erinnerung*, in *ZTK* 86 (1989) 148-155.

51. Cf. THEOPHYLACT, *Comm. 1 Thess* ad loc. PG 124:1313D, and L. CERFAUX, *Christ in the Theology of St. Paul*, New York – Edinburgh – London, Herder and Herder –Thomas Nelson and Sons, Ltd., 1959, pp. 41-42. For caution as to just what Paul's words imply see M.R. COSBY, *Hellenistic Formal Receptions and Paul's Use of ΑΠΑΝΤΗΣΙΣ in 1 Thessalonians 4:17*, in *BBR* 4 (1994) 15-33.

52. Paul does not specify where precisely Jesus will arrive. Either it did not matter to him or he assumed as a matter of course that it would be Jerusalem or, in accord with texts cited throughout this article, the Mount of Olives.

Zech 14:4-5 supplies an explanation. When Paul quotes that Scripture in 1 Thess 3:3, his interpretation of it is that Jesus will come "with all his saints". Since, then, the apostle envisions Jesus coming on the clouds (1 Thess 4:17; cf. Dan 7:13-14), he must likewise have the saints coming on the clouds. This, moreover, requires that the dead saints have already been raised, all of which correlates with Zech 14:4-5 when this last is taken as a prophecy of resurrection, as in *Did.*16:7-8[53]. In other words, the saints are raised (Zech 14:5) and then they come with the Lord (Zech 14:5)[54].

Whether or not one accepts this explanation of the peculiar sequence of events in 1 Thess 4, the *Didache* suffices to establish that someone, in or near Matthew's time and place, saw Zech 14:4-5 as a prophecy of the resurrection. With this in mind, parallels between the latter and Matt 27:51b-53 become manifest. In both, the dead are raised, and this takes place immediately outside of Jerusalem. (One may contrast this with Ezek 37, where the resurrection takes places in the Diaspora). In both, the resurrected ones are called οἱ ἅγιοι (LXX Zech 14:5; Matt 27:52; this word is not used of those resurrected in Ezek 37)[55]. In both, σχίζω is used in the passive, in connection with a mountain (LXX Zech 14:4: σχισθήσεται τὸ ὄρος) or rocks (Matt 27:52:αἱ πέτραι ἐσχίσθησαν). In both there is an earthquake. Matthew says that "the earth shook" (ἡ γῆ ἐσείσθη) and that the centurion and those with

53. Cf. also *Cant Rab.* 4:11:1; *Ruth Rab.* Proem 2; and *Eccles Rab.* 1:11:1: in these the prophets are the holy ones who come with God; clearly they have already been resurrected.

54. Although this is speculative, maybe Zech 14:4-5 played a role in naming "the tomb of Zechariah," the splendid monument on the foothills of the Mount of Olives. We do not know who was really buried there, nor do we know when the tomb, which was probably built in the second half of the first century B.C.E., got its current name. But according to MEYERS – MEYERS, *Zechariah 9-14*, p. 422, "the association with Zechariah may come from this very verse," 14:4. What is more appropriate than that the prophet who foretold the resurrection on the Mount of Olives should be buried there? Moreover, *Liv. Proph. Zech.* 15:6 has the prophet "buried near Haggai," and *Liv. Proph. Hag.* 14:2 has the latter buried "near the tomb of the priests," which may well refer to the first-century B.C.E. tomb of the priestly family of Bnei-Hezir, which is right next to the so-called "tomb of Zechariah." Cf. AUS, *Samuel, Saul, and Jesus*, p. 118, n. 33. To this one cannot object that the tradition concerns not the prophet Zechariah but the priest martyred in 2 Chron 24, because legend sometimes identified the two; see S. BLANK, *The Death of Zechariah in Rabbinic Literature*, in *HUCA* 13 (1938) 327-346. In any case, there is also a competing medieval Jewish legend, which holds that the so-called "Tombs of the Prophets," on the Mount of Olives, contained the grave of the prophet Zechariah.

55. One might counter that, in Zechariah, the holy ones must be celestial beings; cf. *1 En.* 1:9; 1QM 12:1-7; *Apoc. Elijah* 3:4; *Pesiq. R.* 21:9. Some rabbinic texts, however, identify them instead with the prophets; and 1 Thess 2:13 and *Did.* 16:7-8, as we have seen, equate them with the resurrected saints (perhaps under the influence of Dan 7:18.25.27, where "the holy ones of the Most High" are almost certainly the saints). Further, that humans would become angels or like angels is well-attested; see Wis 5:5 (assuming that "sons of God" = angels); 4QSb 4:25; 4Q511 fr. 35; *1 En.* 104:1-6; PHILO, *Sacr.* 5; *2 Bar.* 51:5.10; Acts 6:15; *T. Isaac* 4:43-48, etc. The MT has "and all the holy ones with you" (עמך). Although that

him "saw the earthquake" (σεισμόν, 27:54) while LXX Zech 14:5 prophesies that, after the Mount of Olives splits, people will flee as they "fled from the earthquake (σεισμοῦ) in the days of King Uzziah of Judah" (cf. Amos 1:1; Josephus, *Ant.* 9.225). In both, the immediate context reports a supernatural darkness (Zech 14:6; Matt 27:45), and from at least the time of Origen, Christian tradition associated the darkness in Zechariah with the crucifixion[56]. Finally, in both Matthew and Zechariah, Jerusalem figures prominently. In Matt 27:53, the holy ones go into "the holy city" (εἰς τὴν ἁγίαν πόλιν). In Zechariah, "Jerusalem" is named in 14:2 and 4, "the city" occurs three times in v. 2 (ἡ πόλις, τῆς πόλεως bis), and chapter 14 ends by emphasizing the holiness of Jerusalem: "On that day there shall be inscribed on the bells of the horses, 'Holy (MT: קדש; LXX: ἅγιον) to the Lord.' And the cooking-pots in the house of the LORD shall be as holy as the bowls in front of the altar; and every cooking-pot in Jerusalem and Judah shall be holy (MT: קדש; LXX: ἅγιον) to the LORD of hosts" (vv. 20-21).[57]

Do these parallels suggest the inference that Matt 27:51b-53 is partly based upon Zech 14:4-5?[58]. I believe that they do, when we keep in mind several more points.

reading may be corrupt (the LXX, the Syriac, the Vulgate, the targum, and some Hebrew mss. have "with him"), it existed in antiquity, and someone could have taken it to mean: "and all the angels with you (= Israel)." Cf. DIDYMUS the BLIND, *Comm. Zech* ad loc. (SC, 85), ed. L. Doutreleau, Paris, Cerf, 1962, pp. 1006-1008, who identifies "the holy ones" with the saints and angels.

56. Cf. ORIGEN, *Scholia Matt* PG 17.308C; *Const. Ap.* 5:14:16 ed. F. Funk, Paderborn. Schöningh 1905, p. 277; EUSEBIUS, *Dem. ev.* 10.7 (GCS, 23), ed. I.A. Heikel, Leipzig, Hinrichs, 1913, pp. 469-470; CYRIL of JERUSALEM, *Cat.* 13.24 (PG, 33), pp. 801B-C; PS.-EPIPHANIUS, *Test.* 59-60 ed. R.V. Hotchkiss, Missoula, Mont., 1974, p. 54; PS.-CHRYSOSTOM, *In sanc. pascha* 45 (SC, 48), ed. F. Floëri – P. Nautin, Paris, Cerf, 1957, p. 157; JOHN of DAMASCUS, *Sabb.* 26 (PTS, 29), ed. B. Kotter, Berlin, De Gruyter, 1988, p. 135. LXX Zech 14:6-7 was commonly understood to predict not only the darkness at the crucifixion but also the cold weather at the time, which interpreters inferred from the circumstance that Peter warmed himself by a fire (Mark 14:26; John 18:18).

57. In Ezek 37, those resurrected are brought back to "the land." Jerusalem merits no mention.

58. C.A. HAM, *The Coming King and the Rejected Shepherd: Matthew's Reading of Zechariah's Messianic Hope*, Sheffield, Phoenix, 2005, pp. 102-105, argues against finding an allusion to Zechariah. His objections fail. (a) Although he denies that Zech 14:4-5 prophesies an earthquake, how does the Mount of Olives split and the land become rearranged without one? The earthquake in the time of Uzziah presages a like event in the future. (b) It does not matter that one can find parallels outside of Zech 14:4-5 for the *topoi* of Matt 27:51b-53. What counts is their concatenation in two texts. Both Matt 27:51b-53 and Zech 14:4-5 feature an earthquake, the splitting of rocks, the appearance of holy ones, resurrection, and Jerusalem. (c) Once we read Zech 14:4-5 as a prophecy of resurrection, the conceptual parallels Matthew shares with Zech 14:4-5 are no less significant than those it shares with Ezek 37. The same observations also counter the criticism of TROXEL, *Matt 27.51-54 Reconsidered.*

(1) If the formal quotation in Matt 2:6 can juxtapose Mic 5:1.3 with 2 Sam 5:2 (= 1 Chron 11:2), so that readers are sent to two parental texts at once[59], and if Matt 3:17 can recall both Ps 2:7 and Isa 42:1[60], then nothing disallows us from thinking that, if 27:51b-53 draws upon Ezek 37, it cannot also draw upon Zech 14.

(2) Early Christian tradition was fond of Zechariah[61]. In particular, it linked Jesus' passion to texts from Zech 9-14[62]. Mark, for example, recounts the passion of Jesus as though it were the fulfillment of that scriptural apocalypse: the peaceful king enters the holy city (11:1-10; cf. Zech 9:9), he comes to the temple (11:15-17; cf. Zech 14:16, 21), he stands on the Mount of Olives (13:1; cf. Zech 14:4)[63], he establishes the new covenant in blood (14:24; cf. maybe Zech. 9:11), and he experiences a time of trial and affliction, when the shepherd is struck and his sheep scattered (14:26-52; cf. Zech 13:7-14:3)[64].

Matthew reproduced all this and even added to it[65]. In 21:4-5, he turned Mark's implicit reference to Zechariah's oracle of a meek king entering Jerusalem (Zech 9:9) into an explicit quotation. In 26:15, he specified that

59. Note also Matt 11:10 (combining Exod 23:30 and Mal 3:3); 22:24 (combining Gen 38:8 and Deut 25:5); and 27:9-10 (combining Zech 11:13 with several verses from Jeremiah: 18:2-6; 19:1, 2, 4, 6, 11; 32:6-15).

60. DAVIES and ALLISON, *Matthew*, 1:336-39.

61. Cf. M. JAUHIAINEN, *The Use of Zechariah in Revelation* (WUNT, 2/199), Tübingen, Mohr Siebeck, 2005.

62. See ALLISON, *End*, pp. 33-36; C.A. EVANS, *Zechariah in the Markan Passion Narrative*, in T.R. HATINA (ed.), *Biblical Interpretation in Early Christian Gospels, Volume 1: The Gospel of Mark* (LNTS, 304), London, T. & T. Clark, 2006, pp. 64-80; J. MARCUS, *The Way of the Lord: Christological Exegesis of the Old Testament in the Gospel of Mark*, Louisville, Westminster/John Knox, 1992, pp. 154-164; and D.J. MOO, *The Old Testament in the Gospel Passion Narratives*, Sheffield, Almond Press, 1983, pp. 173-224.

63. Many exegetes have made this intertextual connection, beginning with TERTULLIAN, *Marc.* 4.39 (OECT), ed. E. EVANS, p. 490; cf. ORIGEN, *Comm. Matt* 86 (GCS, 38), ed. E. Klostermann – E. Benz – L. Früchtel, Leipzig, Hinrichs, 1933, p. 200.

64. Modern commentators have also sometimes found in Mark 11:23 ("if you say to this mountain, 'Be taken up and thrown into the sea', and if you do not doubt in your heart, but believe that what you say will come to pass, it will be done for you") or its synoptic parallels a reference to Zech 14:4, where the Mount of Olives is split and half of it is removed πρὸς θάλασσαν; cf. W.R. TELFORD, *The Barren Temple and the Withered Tree: A Redaction-Critical Analysis of the Cursing of the Fig-Tree Pericope in Mark's Gospel and Its Relation to the Cleansing of the Temple Tradition* (JSNTSS, 1), Sheffield, JSOT Press, 1980, p. 158.

65. For an overview see J. NOLLAND, *The King as Shepherd: The Role of Deutero-Zechariah in Matthew*, in T.R. HATINA (ed.), *Biblical Interpretation in Early Christian Gospels, Volume 2: The Gospel of Matthew*, London – New York, T. & T. Clark, 2008, pp. 133-146; also MOSS, *Zechariah Tradition*. For a more skeptical view of how much Matthew employed Zechariah see P. FOSTER, *The Use of Zechariah in Matthew's Gospel*, in C. TUCKETT (ed.), *The Book of Zechariah and Its Influence*, Aldershot, UK – Burlington, VT, Ashgate, 2003, pp. 65-85.

Judas betrayed Jesus for thirty pieces of silver, an amount he took from Zech 11:12. Then, in 27:3-10, in recounting Judas's suicide, he quoted words from Zech 11:13. So finding yet one more reference to Zech 9-14 in Matthew's passion narrative can occasion no surprise. The First Evangelist made more use of that relatively short portion of Scripture than he did of the entirety of Ezekiel.

(3) To read Matt 27:51b-53 as implicitly claiming that God, at the time of the crucifixion, brought to realization or inaugurated the prophecy in Zech 14:4-5 fits Matthew's theology as well as does the allusion to Ezek 37. This is because "the second half of the Book of Zechariah, chs. ix-xiv, has the character of an apocalypse, and while its component visions (like those of many apocalypses) are not easy to bring into a consistent scheme, it can be understood as setting forth a whole eschatological programme"[66]. To relate Zech 14:4-5, which foretells end-time events, to Matt 27:52b-53, which recounts things that happened at Jesus' end, accords with Matthew's partially-realized eschatology[67].

(4) We saw, when discussing Matt 27:51b-53, that the text has reminded ancient and recent commentators of Ezek 37:1-14. How does it stand with regard to Zech 14:4-5? A number of exegetes and theologians through the centuries have moved from Matt 27:51b-53 to Zech 14:4-5 or vice versa. As for earlier times, Eusebius offers an exposition of Zech 14:1-10 which, although mostly allegorical, counts the earthquake at the crucifixion as the realization of Zech 14:5[68]. Cyril of Alexandria, in his commentary on the minor prophets, cites Matt 27:51-53 when discussing Zech 14:5 (*XII Proph.*), ed. P.E. Pusey, Bruxelles, Culture et Civilisation, 2:516. Similarly, Theodoret of Cyrus, *Comm. Zech* ad loc. (PG 81), p. 1953A, finds in Zech 14:4-5 a reference to the time when "God betrayed his anger", when the

66. C.H. DODD, *According to the Scriptures: The Sub-structure of New Testament Theology*, London: Fontana, 1965, p. 64.

67. According to P.D. HANSON, *The Dawn of Apocalyptic: The Historical and Sociological Roots of Jewish Apocalyptic Eschatology*, Philadelphia: Fortress, 1979, pp. 350-351, the use of Zechariah in the passion narratives implies that "the end-time terrors would have to befall God's son before the final glorious events could be inaugurated (even as the apocalyptic circles of Second Zechariah and elsewhere believed that the apocalyptic woes would have to befall the people before the glorious eschaton could arrive)." This may well capture Matthew's point of view.

68. In *Dem. ev.* 6.18 (GCS 23), ed. Heikel, Leipzig, Hinrichs, 1913, pp. 274-84. Earlier, if it dates from the middle of the third century, is *2 Treat. Seth* 58:20-59:11, which rewrites Matt 27:51b-53 in this fashion: "Darkness took them.... They nailed him to the tree. The veil of the temple he tore with his hands. It was a trembling which seized the chaos of the earth for the souls which were in the sleep below were released. And they arose. They went about boldly...." One wonders whether the striking expression, "chaos of the earth" reflects LXX Zech 14:4, which speaks of an exceedingly great χαός.

Romans "nailed the Lord to the cross", when "darkness was poured out over the whole world", when "creation was in turmoil at the crime of crucifixion", and when "the mountains released wings against them", that is, moved to create a rift, as in the time of king Uzziah. He goes on, as so many other church fathers, to find in Zech 14:6-7 a prophecy of the darkness at noon and Peter warming himself by the fire (cf. Mark 14:67). Isho'dad of Merv, *Comm. Matt* 22 HSem 6 ed. M.D. Gibson, pp. 191-92, records the opinion of some that the resurrected saints of Matt 27:51b-53 "assembled on the Mount of Olives", which must reflect the influence of Zechariah's oracle. And Albertus Magnus, *Super Mt cap. XV-XXVIII ad loc.* Opera Omnia 21/2, ed. B. Schmidt, Münster, Aschendorf, 1987, p. 649, cites Zech 14:4 as a parallel to the earthquake in Matt 27:51. So, as a matter of exegetical history, readers have indeed linked Matthew's account to Zechariah's prophecy[69].

Before moving to the next point, I should like to note an intriguing possibility. The eastern iconic tradition of the Anastasis may be a witness to the association of Matt 27:51b-53 and Zech 14:4-5. In one standard type, Christ rises from the underworld, which is depicted below his feet as a black space. He lifts up Adam with one hand, Eve with the other. In the background are two jagged mountain tops[70]. The land of the dead is in the valley between those two peaks which, before they split, "formed only one single mountain"[71]. In some variants, the land of the dead is clearly inside the split mountain[72]. This interests because the dominant exegetical tradition in the east understood Matt 27:51b-53 in terms of the harrowing of hell; that is, it identified the holy ones in Matthew's narrative with some of

---

69. I also suspect that this traditional association lies behind JOHN DONNE's poem, "Good Friday, 1613, Riding Westward," which at one point has these lines: "What a death were it then to see God die? // It made His own lieutenant, Nature, shrink, // It made His footstool crack, and the sun wink." In Zech 14, the mountain splits after God's feet land upon it; and tradition for that reason sometimes spoke of the Mount of Olives, or of some spot on it, as God's footstool; see J. BRASLAVI – M. AVI-YONAH, *Mount of Olives (Olivet)*, in F. SKOLNIK – M. BERENBAUM (eds.), *Encyclopedia Judaica, Volume 14. Mel-Nas*, Detroit, Thomson Gale, ²2007, p. 585.

70. For examples see figs. 80, 81, and 87 in A.D. KARTSONIS, *Anastasis: The Making of an Image*, Princeton, Princeton University Press, 1986. Also below, Pictures, pp. 186-188.

71. So KARTSONIS, *Anastasis*, p. 209. Cf. ANDREW of CRETE, *Or. 9* (PG 97), p. 1016C: when Christ suffered, "the sun was darkened, the moon became black, the earth shook, the abyss was subdued, and mountains were split" (ὄρη σχιζόμενα – is this an allusion to LXX Zech 14:4: σχισθήσεται τὸ ὄρος?). Kartsonis argues that "the rending of the mountain of earth" was "a familiar motif of the Anastasis" and "already schematized by the early eleventh century." She also finds evidence for a typological correlation between the cross of Jesus and the rod of Moses: the latter split the sea, the former the earth.

72. E.g. the mosaic diptych of the twelve feasts from Constantinople, now in the Museo dell'Opera del Duomo, France.

those rescued from the land of the dead[73]. Is it, then, only coincidence that the icon depicts the events of Matt 27:51b-53 against the backdrop of something very much like the split mountain on the Ezekiel panel at Dura Europos? Maybe both images rather go back to Zech 14:4-5, to the belief that the resurrection would involve the splitting of the Mount of Olives[74].

III. THE FUSION OF EZEKIEL 37:1-14 AND ZECHARIAH 14:4-5

Having argued that Matt 27:51b-53 implicitly refers to two biblical texts, Ezek 37 and Zech 14:4-5, I should like to return to the Ezekiel panel of the Dura Europos synagogue. As already observed, that panel depicts the eschatological resurrection and, in so doing, visually conflates two texts, Ezek 37 and Zech 14:4-5, or rather depicts the resurrection with those two passages in mind. Should we infer that those two texts were linked before the Dura mural?

I believe that we should, for several reasons. (1) A connection seems likely on the face of it because so few texts in the Tanak can be made out to prophesy the resurrection[75]. So given that some, in pre-Christian times, construed Ezek 37 as a resurrection text, and given that, as the *Didache* proves, some readers at least by Matthew's time thought of Zech 14:4-5 as being about the same subject, it would have been natural enough to associate the two[76].

It may also be relevant that Ezekiel's vision takes place in the middle of a בקעה, a broad valley (37:1-2), and that Zech 14:4-5 also features a large valley. When the Lord's feet stand on the Mount of Olives, the prophet foretells that it will be "split in two (נבקע) from east to west by a very wide (MT:

---

73. See ALLISON, *Matt 27:51-53 and the Descens ad inferos* and note *Gos. Nicod.* Latin B 10(26):1: "Then we all went forth with the Lord, leaving Satan and Hades in Tartarus. And to us and many others it was commanded that we should rise in the body to testify in the world of the resurrection of our Lord Jesus Christ and of those things which had been done in the underworld."

74. There are also parallels in ANE mythology and art, where a god emerges from the netherworld from between a split mountain. See MORGENSTERN, *King-God*, pp. 148-49, 182. Morgenstern even conjectures that Zech 14 is corrupt, and that the original text envisaged a resurrection of the dead.

75. When R. Simai, in *Sifre* 306 on Deut 32:2, declares that every Scripture lesson refers to the resurrection of the dead, he adds that "we do not know how to interpret properly." This concedes how hard it is to find resurrection in many texts.

76. It is possible that Zech 9-14 is itself dependent upon Ezek 34-48; see D.C. MITCHELL, *The Message of the Psalter: An Eschatological Programme in the Book of Psalms* (JSOTSS, 252), Sheffield, Sheffield Academic Press, 1997, pp. 146-149.

גדולה מאד) valley… and you will flee by the valley of the Lord's mountain, for the valley between the mountains shall reach to Azal"[77]. Admittedly, Zechariah uses a different noun for "valley" – גאי – than does Ezekiel, who employs בקעה. Nonetheless, MT Zech 14:4 does use the verb בקע, a relative of the noun בקעה, to refer to the splitting of the Mount of Olives, so our two passages share a linguistic link. Furthermore, both texts bring to the mind's eye the space between two widely separated mountains[78], and Zech 14:10 goes on to speak of the whole becoming a "plain" [79](בקעה). The LXX translates גאי גדולה מאד with σφόδρα χαός, which means "exceedingly vast expanse"[80].

(2) Regarding the images at the Dura-Europos synagogue, the Jewish art historian, Rachel Hachlili, has given this as her judgment:

> Pictorial formula, repetitive iconography and the stylistic details that the artists used all indicate that pattern books are the most probable source for the Dura paintings. The Dura artists possibly had sets of iconographic conventions which they used in the scenes they portrayed, as well as extensive cycles of biblical scenes which they could copy, abbreviate or even improvise according to their needs. Themes and schemes, styles and composition were probably inherited from prototypes.[81]

If this is the right inference, the depiction of Ezekiel's resurrection was not invented for the occasion but was traditional, which in turn implies that the association of Ezekiel and Zechariah was traditional. This is all the more likely given that "the Jewish population of Dura, consisting perhaps of some 65 members, was probably made up of merchants and traders stemming from Syro-Palestine and nearby Mesopotamia. Dura was not an intellectual center; no gymnasium or theatre was found there"[82]. One understands why

---

77. The meaning of "Azal" (אצל) is unknown; one guesses that it is a place name. The LXX, which has several variants – ἕως Ἰασόδ or Ἰασόλ or Ἰασσά or Ἀσαήλ – does not help.
78. Even if we do not know the meaning of "Azal", the drama and grand scope of the text imply that it is some distance away (אל אצל).
79. It is possible that the mountain to the right in the Dura panel is actually the right half of the mountain that is splitting in the left panel: in accordance with Zechariah, half of the mountain has moved to create a great plain in the middle.
80. As χαός can also mean "nether abyss" (LSJ, s.v.), maybe the word encouraged associating Zech 14:4-5 with the resurrection of the dead. Or perhaps the LXX translator already believed the text had something to do with the underworld.
81. R. HACHLILI, *Ancient Jewish Art and Archaeology in the Diaspora* (HO), Leiden – Boston – Cologne, Brill, 1998, p. 189. Cf. pp. 193-194; also M.L. THOMPSON, *Hypothetical Models of the Dura Paintings*, in J. GUTMANN (ed.), *The Dura-Europos Synagogue: A Re-evaluation (1932-1972)*, Atlanta, Scholars Press, 1992, pp. 31-52. But for caution in this matter see A.J. WHARTON, *Good and Bad Images from the Synagogue of Dura-Europos: Contexts, Subtexts, Intertexts*, in *Art History* 1 (1994) 1-25.
82. J. GUTMAN, *Early Synagogue and Jewish Catacomb Art and Its Relation to Christian Art*, in *ANRW* II/21.2 (1984), p. 1315.

"many scholars agree that the program of the synagogue paintings is unlikely to have been invented at Dura"[83].

(3) Several images at Dura have relatives in later Christian art[84]. This implies a common artistic tradition. More particularly, the left section of Dura's Ezekiel panel has a remarkable parallel in a ninth-century Christian miniature in the Bibliothèque Nationale in Paris, in a collection of homilies of Gregory Nazianzenus (Gr. 510)[85]. Here too a depiction of Ezekiel's vision features a mountain, although there is no mountain in Ezek 37; and from it, or rather from a black space in its side, disarticulated human remains are emerging, just as at Dura[86]. Moreover, the hand of God above the prophet is common to both works[87], and the two trees at the top of the split mountain in the synagogue are matched by two trees standing atop the mountain in the miniature[88]. Unless one posits that the image in a building along the Euphrates that was buried in 256 C.E. somehow inspired a much later Christian piece, one must posit that the two images go back to an ancient predecessor[89].

The antiquity of Dura's image is also supported by the earliest extant Christian representation of Ezekiel 37, a gold glass from the late third or early fourth century C.E.[90]. This features a detached head (not a skull) as well as separated, flesh-covered feet and hands to Ezekiel's right; a stylized tree serving as the border on to the viewer's left; and a slender mountain rising to his eye level – all of which more or less matches what we find at

83. GUTMAN, *Early Synagogue and Jewish Catacomb Art*, p. 1315.

84. See K. SCHUBERT, *Jewish Pictorial Traditions in Early Christian Art*, in *Jewish Historiography and Iconography in Early and Medieval Christianity* (CRINT, 3/2), Assen – Maastricht – Minneapolis, Van Gorcum – Fortress, 1992, pp. 139-260, and above all K. WEITZMANN – H.L. KESSLER, *The Frescoes of the Dura Synagogue and Christian Art* (Dumbarton Oaks Studies, 28), Washington, DC, Dumbarton Oaks Research Library and Collection, 1990.

85. The best reproduction is in Henri OMONT, *Miniatures des plus anciens manuscrits grecs de la Bibliothèque nationale du VIᵉ au XIVᵉ siècle*, Paris, Honoré Champion, 1929, plate LXVIII. See below, Picture, p. 184.

86. One cannot see this in most of the reproductions, but it is clear enough from the plate in Omont.

87. This appears elsewhere in Christian visual depictions of Ezek 37; see e.g. the prints from Ripoll and Roda Bibles referred to in n. 103.

88. Although they have lost their foliage in the later piece. – My own guess concerning the two trees on the mountain top at Dura is that, if they do not represent olive trees, they may represent the legend that there were two Cypress trees atop the Mount of Olives; see *y. Ta'an.* 60a (4:5); *Lam Rab.* 2:2.

89. See further G. WODTKE, *Malereien der Synagoge in Dura und ihre Parallelen in der christlichen Kunst*, in *ZNW* 34 (1935) 51-61; WEITZMANN, *Freskoes*, pp. 138-139.

90. See W. NEUSS, *Das Buch Ezechiel in Theologie und Kunst bis zum Ende des XII. Jahrhunderts*, Münster, Aschendorffsche Verlagsbuchhandlung, 1912, pp. 141-142, and the plate opposite p. 142. See below, reproduction, p. 185.

Dura[91]. There are, to be sure, differences; but the similarities can scarcely be deemed coincidence.

(4) Ezek 37 is, in *Tanh.* Buber Wayehi 12:6; *y. Kil.* 32c (9:3); *y. Ketub.* 35b (12:3); and *Pesiq. R.* 1:6, the exegetical basis for the tradition that bones will roll through underground tunnels on the day of resurrection. In *Pesiq. R.* 31:10, the scriptural testimony is Zech 14:4-5, and *Tg. Cant* 8:5 has this: "When the dead revive, the Mount of Olives will split apart and all the dead of Israel will issue from beneath it, and even the righteous who have died in exile will come by way of tunnels below the ground and issue from beneath the Mount of Olives"[92]. So in later rabbinic tradition at least, Ezek 37:1-14 and Zech 14:4-5 were linked to the same imaginative scenario of end-time resurrection. Further, it is suggestive that rabbinic texts often associate Zech 14:3 ("Then the Lord will go forth and fight against those nations as when he fights on a day of battle") with the battle of Gog, foretold in Ezek 38-39[93].

(5) Although the rabbinic texts just cited are late, the Dura synagogue shows that the intertextual link was made much earlier. This should not surprise. There are other images at Dura with parallels in only late rabbinic sources. For example, its depiction of the contest between Elijah and the prophets of Baal features a miniature man standing inside the altar. The Tanak holds no explanation for this. But in *Exod Rab.* 15:15 and *Yalqut Shimoni* on 1 Kings 18:26, we are told that Baal's prophets hollowed out the altar and hid therein a man, instructing him to ignite a fire when signaled to do so. God, however, sent a snake to bite him and he died[94]. The

---

91. There is also a tree in the background with two widely separated bunches of leaves. One hesitates, however, to make much of this as that motif appears elsewhere on the glass.

92. Cf. also *Ma'aseh Daniel*, ed. A. JELLINEK, Leipzig, F. Niles, 1873, 5:128, where Elijah climbs the Mount of Olives before he blows the trumpet for the resurrection. Also somehow related to these materials is *Quest. Barth.* 4:12, where Jesus leads followers "down from the Mount of Olives", Michael the archangel blows a trumpet, there is an earthquake, and then Beliar and angels ascend from the underworld.

93. *Sifre* 76 on Num 10:1-10; *ARN* A 34; *Lev Rab.* 27:11; *Est Rab.* 7:23; *Midr. Ps* 17:10; *Lekach Tob* on Num 24:17; etc. Cf. Theodoret of Cyprus, *Os.-Mal.* ad Zech 14:12. The link is natural, given the high probability that Zech 14 borrows from Ezek 38-39; see K.R. SCHAEFER, *Zechariah 14: A Study in Allusion*, in *CBQ* 57 (1995) 66-91.

94. See J. GUTMANN, *The Illustrated Midrash in the Dura Synagogue Paintings: A New Dimension for the Study of Judaism*, in *American Academy of Jewish Research Proceedings* 50 (1983) 91-104. In the rabbinic tradition, the man who conspires with the prophets of Baal is named Hiel, and the Elijah panel has an Aramaic graffito which appears to read: חיאעל; see C.H. KRAELING, *The Wall Decorations*, in *Preliminary Report on the Synagogue at Dura*, New Haven, Yale University Press, 1936, p. 56. GUTMANN, *Midrash*, and KRAELING, *Synagogue*, pp. 140-41, 351-54, offer additional examples of Dura images with their literary counterparts in later midrash. I am at a loss to explain the judgment of GOODENOUGH, *Jewish Symbols*, 10:151: "there is at least as great a chance that the story arose to explain such a painting as that the painting illustrates the story."

lesson is that the extant literary remains are not always reliable reflections of what was known when.

(6) Matthew itself should be the proof that Zech 14:4-5 and Ezek 37:1-14 were traditionally associated. It is scarcely plausible that Matthew's subtle allusion to two texts influenced subsequent Jewish tradition. It is much more reasonable to hypothesize that Matthew and the designer of the Duro-Europos synagogue were familiar with a tradition that depicted the eschatological resurrection in language drawn from Ezek 37:1-14 and Zech 14:4-5.

IV. MATTHEW'S ANTHROPOLOGY

Having established the scriptural background of Matt 27:51b-53, I should like to consider what it might mean for Matthew's anthropology. Let me begin by observing that, at first glance, our evangelist seems to have had a very literal view of the resurrection of the dead. This follows not only from the empty tombs of both Jesus and the saints but also from the use of Ezek 37:1-12 and Zech 14:4-5. The latter texts were, as we have seen, associated with the notion that, since so many Jews have been buried outside Palestine, God will, in the final day, make tunnels under the earth, through which the bones of those in the diaspora will roll into the land, where the resurrection will take place. Whether or not Matthew knew this belief or held it[95], his text does mirror the image at Dura, which visually displays a scriptural literalism. There are, moreover, related convictions in the rabbinic corpus. Some rabbis, for instance, recognizing the inevitable, namely, that human bodies, over time, become scattered and disintegrate, taught that all that needs to endure is the tip of the coccyx bone, about which the following tale is told:

> Hadrian – may his bones rot – asked R. Joshua b. Hananiah, "From what part in the body will the Holy One, blessed be he, make a person sprout up in the age to come?" He said to him, "He will make him sprout out of the nut of the spinal column". He said to him, "How do you know this?" He said to him, "Bring one to me, and I will explain it to you". He put it [the nut brought to him] into the fire, yet it did not burn up. He put it into water, yet it did not dissolve. He pulverized it between millstones, yet it was not crushed. He put it on a block and smashed it with a hammer. The block split, the hammer was cleft, yet it remained undamaged[96].

95. The evangelist may have believed, as so many of his later readers, that "the holy ones" were ancient worthies from various times and places. If so, and unless he believed them all to have been buried on the Mount of Olives, he would necessarily have had to conclude that God had somehow transported their remains to the same place – if he ever reflected on the matter, which perhaps he did not.

96. *Gen Rab.* 28:3. Cf. *Lev Rab.* 18:1; *Eccl Rab.* 12:5.

Just as literal-minded were the discussions as to whether the resurrected will appear nude or clothed[97], or whether God will start with the bones or with the flesh (e.g. *Gen Rab.* 14:5).

Matt 27:51b-53 betrays a similar understanding of resurrection: it is the reanimation of corpses[98]. Further, the holy ones are able to exit their tombs and walk about only after those tombs have been opened by the earthquake. The reader naturally infers that, had the sleepers awakened but the rocks not been split and the tombs not opened, the many bodies of the saints would have been stuck where they were.

That, however, is not the whole story, for we find something else in chapter 28, which tells of Jesus' resurrection from the dead:

> After the sabbath, as the first day of the week was dawning, Mary Magdalene and the other Mary went to see the tomb. And suddenly there was a great earthquake; for an angel of the Lord, descending from heaven, came and rolled back the stone and sat on it. His appearance was like lightning, and his clothing white as snow. For fear of him the guards shook and became like dead men. But the angel said to the women, "Do not be afraid; I know that you are looking for Jesus who was crucified. He is not here; for he has been raised, as he said. Come, see the place where he lay" (28:1-6).

What counts for our purposes is the order of events in these lines. First, the women arrive at the tomb. Second, there is an earthquake that immediately precedes or coincides with an angel descending from heaven and rolling back the stone. Third, the guards become afraid. Fourth, the angel tells the women that Jesus has been raised from the dead, and that they may see for themselves by entering his tomb.

It is clear from this sequence that Jesus has risen and gone elsewhere before the angel or the women have arrived. The stone is accordingly removed not so that Jesus can exit but so that the witnesses may enter. That is, the resurrected one has already exited before the stone falls away, which means he has somehow left a seemingly closed space[99]. So, despite the extensive parallels between the end of Matthew 27 and the beginning of Matthew 28[100], Jesus' resurrection is unlike that of those raised in 27:51b-53. In the

---

97. *b. Ketub.* 111b; *b. Sanh.* 90b; *PRE* 33. Cf. *Sem.* 9.23: "In the same clothes in which one descends to Sheol will he appear in the age to come."

98. I assume here that Matthew intended 27:51b-53 to be read not as a theological parable but as a record of what happened in the past. I have made this case elsewhere: D.C. ALLISON, Jr., *Memory and Invention: How Much History?*, in *Constructing Jesus: Memory, Imagination, and History*, Grand Rapids, MI, Baker Academic, 2010, pp. 435-462.

99. LUTHER, for theological reasons, enjoyed stressing this point: *Confession Concerning Christ's Supper* (Luther's Works, 37), St. Louis, Concordia, 1961, pp. 216-217.

100. See esp. RIEBL, *Auferstehung*, pp. 63-67.

latter passage, the tombs open so that the revived can come forth: "the tombs were opened, and many bodies of the saints who had fallen asleep were raised, and coming out of the tombs (after his resurrection) they entered the holy city and appeared to many." In chapter 28, Jesus, to the contrary, leaves his sepulcher while it is still closed.

Now I do not believe that we should ponder much these different ideas of resurrection. The evangelist may have given the topic little or no thought. Perhaps he was the unwitting victim of tradition, which handed him two stories that did not perfectly cohere. Or perhaps he recognized the tension and was indifferent, because he was uninterested in mapping the details of the eschatological future. One recalls that his Gospel contains passages in which hell brings destruction (7:13; 10:28), others in which it is "eternal" (18:8; 25:41.46). But whatever the extent of the evangelist's reflections, Matthew offers us one story in which the dead are not free to move about until their graves are opened, another in which a resurrected body can pass through solid rock. (The latter circumstance does, incidentally, cohere with other early Christian traditions, which have the resurrected Lord appearing suddenly out of nowhere and disappearing into thin air just as abruptly (Luke 24:31.36.51; John 20:19.26; Acts 1:9). One also recalls John 20:6-7: "Simon Peter... saw the linen wrappings lying there, and the cloth that had been on Jesus' head, not lying with the linen wrappings but rolled up in a place by itself". These words imply that Jesus' "body had in some way disappeared from, or passed through, the cloths and left them lying as they were"[101]).

If, giving full heed to the fact that the First Gospel is not the work of a systematic theologian, we refrain from harmonizing its two different conceptions of resurrection, we should also resist inferring that, since Matthew believed in resurrection, he could not have had a dualistic anthropology or believed in life immediately after death, that is, before the resurrection. Many ancient Jews and Christians who looked for the resurrection of the body simultaneously believed in some sort of soul that could survive physical death[102]. Even the Ezekiel panel at Dura, despite its portrayal of literal resurrection, may presuppose a dualistic anthropology. In the center panel, a winged being is conveying breath into three reconstituted corpses, in accord with Ezek 37:10: "the breath came into them, and they lived, and

---

101. C.K. BARRETT, *The Gospel according to St. John*, Philadelphia, PA, Westminster, [2]1978, p. 563. Contrast John 11:44: Lazarus is still bound in his grave clothes.

102. For a blessed interim state combined with belief in resurrection see *1 En.* 208 and 22:1-14; 60:8 and 62:15; 2 Macc 7:9 and 36; *4 Ezra* 7; JOSEPHUS, *Bell.* 3.374 (characterizing the Pharisees).

stood on their feet, a vast multitude". Above this winged being are three
more winged beings, similar to the figure next to the corpses. And yet they
are of a different size, color, and dress[103]. So instead of seeing here the four
winds (Ezek 37:9), as often suggested[104], we may have here an angelic being
on the bottom and, above the three bodies, the three souls about to enter
those bodies. This is the interpretation of Kurt Weitzmann, who remarks
that the flying psyches are "approximately the size of the figures" on the
ground, and that they will presumably enter through the mouth[105]. He
compares the San Marco mosaic in Venice, in which God holds a little
psyche to put into Adam's mouth and bring him to life[106].

Unfortunately, that must remain conjecture. But whatever the case at
Dura, Matthew's Gospel does assume a dualism of soul and body. 14:26
shows us the author's assumption that his audience was familiar with the
concept of a ghost: "But when the disciples saw him walking on the lake,
they were terrified, saying, 'It is a ghost (φάντασμα)!' And they cried out in
fear". And in 10:28, Matthew's Jesus exhorts his followers not to "fear those
who kill the body (σῶμα) but cannot kill the soul (ψυχή); rather fear him
who can destroy both soul (ψυχή) and body (σῶμα) in Gehenna". Implicit
in these words is the idea that body and soul are separated at death and
joined later for the last judgment[107]. This is exactly what one finds in the
so-called Apocalypse of Ezekiel, which teaches the resurrection of the dead
and yet is thoroughly dualistic. Again, the argument in Matt 22:29-33, that

103. The three upper figures are smaller than the standing figure below them. They are
white whereas the bottom figure is brown. As for dress, the upper figures have small hats, the
bottom figure does not; the upper figures feature small rays or decorative pins in their hair,
the bottom figure does not; and the lower figure has a black band around the chest, the
others do not..

104. And as in the stone relief on a sixth-century Christian tomb at Dara; see M.C. MUN-
DELL, A Sixth Century Funerary Relief at Dara in Mesopotamia, in Jahrbuch der österreichischen
Byzantinistik 24 (1975) 209-227. Note also the four winds at the four corners in the illustra-
tions of Ezek 37 in the Ripoll (Farfa) Bible (Cod. Vat. Lat. 5729) fol. 209 and in the Roda
Bible (Paris Bibliothèque Nationale Latin ms. 6) fol. 45b; see W. NEUSS, Die katalanische
Bibelillustration um die Wende des ersten Jahrtausends und die altspanische Buchmalerei, Bonn
– Leipzig, Kurt Schroeder, 1922, plate 31.

105. Cf. DU MESNIL DU BUISSON, Peintures, p. 97, and M. PHILONENKO, De Qoumrân
à Doura-Europos: La vision des ossements desséchés (Ézéchiel 37,1-4), in RHPR 74 (1994), p. 8;
also Gen 2:7 and the idea that the soul departs with the last breath or from the mouth: PIN-
DAR, Nem. 1.47; EG 547.7-8; LXX Job 41:13; T. Abr. 20:8; Gk. Apoc. Ezra 6:4; Apoc. Sed.
10:3; Hist. Jos. Carp. 19. Christian art can depict the soul (under the guise of an infant)
coming from the mouth of the dying (e.g. the 10th cent. fresco of the Dormition at Ayvali
Kilise, Cappadocia and Codex Dion. 65, fol. 11v).

106. WEITZMANN, Frescoes, p. 136.

107. See C. MILIKOWSKY, Which Gehenna? Retribution and Eschatology in the Synoptic
Gospels and Early Jewish Texts, in NTS 34 (1988) 238-249.

God is not the God of the dead but of the living, may well imply that Abraham, Isaac, and Jacob are still alive[108]. My guess, then, is that Matthew probably did believe in an interim period[109]; it just was not of much importance or interest to him. He was rather consumed by his vision of the end, above all the last judgment, and by the moral exhortation he thought should accompany that vision.

To sum up, then: Matthew's Gospel seems to contain more than one idea about the resurrection, and it also seems to assume that, after death, the soul continues to exist apart from the body, although there are no hints as to how or where. There is no consistent scheme or idea. The evangelist's mind was elsewhere[110].

Pittsburgh Theological Seminary   Dale C. ALLISON, Jr.
U.S.A.
616 N Highland Avenue
Pittsburgh, PA 15206
USA

---

108. See W.D. DAVIES – D.C. ALLISON, Jr., *An Exegetical and Critical Commentary on the Gospel according to St. Matthew.* Vol. 3 (ICC), Edinburgh, T. & T. Clark, 1997, pp. 231-232.

109. Contrast J. CLARK-SOLES, *Death and the Afterlife in the New Testament*, New York – London, T. & T. Clark, 2006, p. 170: Matthew "has no holding tank, purgatory, or intermediate place or state."

110. I should like to thank Ron TAPPY and Steve TUELL for conversations concerning the paintings at Dura-Europos as well as the Hebrew of Zechariah 14.

MATTHEW'S STORIES ABOUT JESUS' BURIAL AND RESURRECTION (27:55-28:20) AS THE CLIMAX OF HIS GOSPEL

INTRODUCTION

In exegetical studies on Jesus' resurrection, two extreme positions can, as a rule, be distinguished. At one end of the scale, we find the traditional view that the resurrection and the subsequent meetings with his disciples are historical events: according to this view, it is a fact that, a few days after his crucifixion, Jesus reunited himself with his physical body and has shown himself as such to his disciples[1]. The other extreme is that the resurrection is not an event in Jesus' life but in the life of believers; "Jesus is risen into the kerygma, into the proclamation of the Church"[2]. The resurrection functions here as a highly symbolic image for the revival of Jesus' disciples, shortly after his crucifixion. The antithetical concepts of "religious metaphor or bodily reality" in the title of this book reflect these two positions.

In this contribution, I will try to find a more nuanced view which unites elements of both extremes and simultaneously goes beyond them. I will do so on the basis of stories of Jesus' burial and resurrection in Matt 27:55-28:20. These stories conclude this Gospel. In section I, I will explore how the conclusion of Matthew's book relates to the rest of his Gospel. Does the end contain new perspectives or do lines that were prepared for earlier merely come together? In section II, I will pursue this theme by examining what Matthew understood by "resurrection" and how his image of Jesus' resurrection hangs together with other central concepts in his Gospel.

---

[1] Recently defended by N.T. WRIGHT, *The Resurrection of the Son of God* (Christian Origins and the Question of God, 3), Minneapolis, MN., Fortress, 2003.
[2] This formulation is derived from N. PERRIN, *The Resurrection Narratives: A New Approach*, London, SCM, 1977, p. 59.

I. PLACE AND FUNCTION OF MATT 27:55-28:20 IN THE
COMPOSITION OF THE GOSPEL AS A WHOLE

Matt 27:55-28:20 is a long narrative unit consisting of five scenes. In the first, third, and fifth scenes, Jesus' disciples appear (A); it is told how they came to dedicate themselves to continuing the innovation movement begun by Jesus. In the second and fourth scenes (B), we see how enemies of Jesus want to prevent the revival of this movement at all costs. Schematically, the structure is as follows.

A 27:55-61	B 27:62-66	A 28:1-10	B 28:11-15	A 28:16-20

This alternating pattern (A-B-A-B-A) shows that two stories are intertwined here that are in fact at right angles to each other[3]. In the A scenes, it emerges that Jesus has been resurrected from the dead and that his disciples revive as a result of this event; in the B scenes, voices from the opposite party assert that the faith in the resurrection is based on deceit by Jesus' disciples, who have hidden his body and have subsequently spread the story that he is alive again.

1. The Jesus Party

As a first step in the inquiry into the connection between 27:55-28:20 and the rest of Matthew's book, let us take a closer look at the role of the disciples in the A scenes. When Jesus is arrested, his disciples have all fled (26:56) and they do not appear again until the fifth scene, where they are reunited with him in Galilee. In the first and third scenes, other followers of Jesus appear, who have not been mentioned before: a group of women from Galilee and a man, Joseph of Arimathea. The women have followed Jesus from Galilee, but the readers do not learn this until in 27:55b through a statement by the narrator, that has the character of an internal analepsis. Joseph has not been mentioned before either; when he is introduced, he is said to have become a disciple of Jesus but when or how this has happened is not related.

---

[3] Except for a difference in demarcation, the same suggestion can be found in R.E. BROWN, *The Resurrection in Matthew (27:62-28:20)*, in *Worship* 64 (1990) 159-160, who points out, moreover, that the same alternating pattern occurs in the five scenes of Matt 1:18-2:23 and in view of this similarity he speaks of an *inclusio*. W. WEREN, *Matteüs* (Belichting van het bijbelboek), 's-Hertogenbosch, Katholieke Bijbelstichting – Brugge, Tabor, 1994, pp. 253-255, extends this to the entire overture (1:1-4:11) and finale (26:17-28:20) and presents a detailed list of correspondences. See also W. WEREN, *The Macrostructure of Matthew's Gospel: A New Proposal*, in *Bib* 87 (2006) 171-200, p. 189.

That the women have belonged to Jesus' followers since the beginning of his ministry is also implied in 28:5-6 where an angel says to two of them, both called Mary, that the crucified Jesus has been made alive as he himself had announced (ἠγέρθη καθὼς εἶπεν). The καθὼς εἶπεν refers to statements made by Jesus in 16:21; 17:22-23 and 20:18-19 in the presence of his disciples only – and apparently also in that of the Galilean women – on his suffering, death, and resurrection. The women are told by the angel that the announcements made by Jesus earlier have now become reality. In this way, it is implicitly denied that he is an impostor, as argued by the opposite party (27:63).

Furthermore, the women are told that they must communicate the message of the resurrection to the (male) disciples and that they must urge them to go Galilee, where they will see Jesus. The second part of this message anticipates the reunification of the risen Jesus with his disciples in 28:16-20. The women carry out their instructions and thus function as a link in the tradition chain of which Jesus and the angel form the beginning. After the women, the disciples will form the next link when they start to spread the message of the resurrection, not only among the people of Israel (27:64) but among all nations (28:19).

As the women hasten towards the disciples, Jesus comes to meet them. They react to this sudden meeting by kneeling down before him. In the fifth scene, the disciples will do the same. This mark of honour is the culmination of a line that runs through the entire Gospel (see προσκυνέω in 2:2.8.11; 8:2; 9:18; 14:33; 15:25; 20:20) and must not be seen as an act of blasphemy in violation of the commandment from Deuteronomy 6:13 to worship God only (4:8-10).

The fifth scene, too, is bound to the rest of Matthew's Gospel by all kinds of threads. I will limit myself here to a number of observations that relate to the role of the disciples:

- Jesus' reunification with the eleven disciples in Galilee has been announced three times (26:32; 28:7.10) and now these previous announcements are proven to be reliable. New information is that this rendez-vous takes place on "the mountain to which Jesus had directed them"(NRSV); another possible translation is "the mountain where Jesus gave them commands", in which case we have a reference to the mountain of 5:1[4].

---

[4] See W.D. DAVIES – D.C. ALLISON, *A Critical and Exegetical Commentary on the Gospel according to Saint Matthew*, Vol. 3 (ICC), Edinburgh, T&T Clark, 1997, p. 681.

- As in 14:26.33, which contains a dual reaction by the disciples to Jesus' appearance, the homage that is paid in 28:17 is also accompanied by doubt. Probably οἱ δὲ ἐδίστασαν indicates that some doubted, not the entire group. This mix of worship and doubt reflects the fact that, elsewhere in the book, Matthew lets Jesus typify the disciples as men of little faith (6:30; 8:26; 14:31; 16:8; 17:20) and that the evangelist describes especially Peter, their torch bearer and their example, as a two-faced character[5].

- From the risen one, the eleven disciples receive their mission that extends to all nations, including the people of Israel[6]. Here, the mission strategy is broadened as compared to the Mission Discourse, where the twelve apostles were sent to "the lost sheep of the house of Israel" and were not allowed to go among the gentiles or the Samaritans (10:5-6). This broadening has been prepared in the course of the book (see e.g. 15:21-28).

- While, in the course of the book, the disciples have been constantly taught by Jesus, a new situation now arises because they themselves are now going to teach. However, they do not, as a result, become teachers who are going to preach their own doctrine and establish their own schools. In their teaching, they will continue to be bound by everything that Jesus has taught them (28:20), his interpretation of the thora is the guide, he is their one teacher (23:8).

All this shows that 28:16-20 is a passage in which images of the disciples' role developed earlier culminate. In addition, innovative matters come up that have not been referred to before. There is a new initiation ritual, baptism, that is to be administered while the names of God, Jesus, and the Holy Spirit are invoked. This ritual is to be performed after a short period of elementary instruction ("make disciples of all nations"). After baptism, the new converts are to be initiated into Jesus' teaching over a longer period. This can be deduced from the order of the words in 28,19-20: "baptizing them [...] and teaching them to obey everything that I have commanded you"[7].

---

[5] K. SYREENI, *Peter as Character and Symbol in the Gospel of Matthew*, in D. RHOADS – K. SYREENI (eds.), *Characterization in the Gospels: Reconceiving Narrative Criticism* (JSNTSup, 184), Sheffield, Sheffield Academic Press, 1999, pp. 106-152; see also W. WEREN, *Steenrots en struikelblok: Petrus als leerling en leider in het evangelie van Matteüs*, in H. BECK – R. NAUTA (eds.), *Over leiden: Dynamiek en structuur van het religieus leiderschap*, Tilburg, Syntax Publishers, 1999, pp. 100-119.

[6] An important argument for this is that Matthew makes a clear distinction between τὰ ἔθνη and πάντα τὰ ἔθνη. The first term is a reference to non-Jews (4:15; 6:32; 10:5.18; 12:18.21; 20:19.25), while the second refers to all humanity, without excluding the people of Israel (24:9.14; 25:32; 28:19).

[7] See G. SCHEUERMANN, *Gemeinde im Umbruch: Eine sozialgeschichtliche Studie zum Matthäusevangelium* (FB, 77), Würzburg, Echter Verlag, 1996, p. 245.

2. Jesus' Opponents

The B scenes mainly contain matters that have not come up before. Here, Matthew describes the origin of an alternative explanation of the fact that Jesus is not found in his tomb. Matthew feels coerced to mention this interpretation, that is at odds with his own view because – as he states – it had persisted and circulated among Jews to his own day (Ἰουδαῖοι is a generalisation, born in the heat of the debate). The story of the soldiers, that is meant to discredit the belief in the resurrection, is countered by Matthew, who tries to show that the story about the disciples' theft of the body is based on deceit. Thus, the B scenes show a glimpse of a controversy from the period in which he was finalising his Gospel (ca. 80-90 C.E.).

It is striking that the views of the opponents, who are outsiders, have been formulated on a number of points from the insider perspective of Matthew and his communities.

- In the chronology of the narrative, people from the opposing party are the first to speak of Jesus' resurrection from the dead; they already do so on the day after his death; and they use exactly the same words as the angel the next day, in his meeting with the two women (ἠγέρθη ἀπὸ τῶν νεκρῶν in 27:64 and 28:7).
- The story of the theft of the body implies that Jesus' body is no longer in the tomb; this is also implied by the testimony that he has been brought back to life.
- The Pharisees and the chief priests state that they themselves have heard Jesus announce that he would rise again after three days (27:63); thus, they base the belief in the resurrection on words spoken by Jesus, as does the angel (28:6).
- On the basis of their account of what Jesus said (27:63: μετὰ τρεῖς ἡμέρας ἐγείρομαι), it seems obvious to suppose that they are referring to statements by Jesus on his stay in the grave in 12:40[8]; there, too, the time limit of "three days" is mentioned and there, too, the Pharisees are present; that they link the somewhat cryptic words from 12:40 to Jesus' resurrection (as is shown by ἐγείρομαι in 27:63) suggests that they support the christological interpretation of Jonah 2:1 offered in 12:40[9].

---

[8] There can be no connection between Matt 27:62 and the so-called passion summaries (16:21; 17:22-23; 20:18-19; 26:2) because these summaries are exclusively aimed at the disciples and consistently refer to "on the third day" rather than "after three days".

[9] According to Matt 12:40, there is a correlation between Jonah's fate (Jonah 2:1 LXX) and that of the Son of Man. Jonah's deliverance and Jesus' resurrection are not explicitly mentioned, but they do echo in the background. In Jonah 2:3, Jonah refers to his time in the

Matthew thus paints the opposing party in the image of the Jesus party. In this way, he suggests that, on a number of essential points, they have the same information as Jesus' supporters but that they deliberately misrepresent this information. The enmity of the Pharisees is one of the dominant subjects in Matthew's book. The new aspect which he adds to this is that they wanted to nip the revival of the Jesus movement in the bud by spreading the rumour that the disciples had staged the resurrection.

3. The Risen Jesus

Why did not Matthew just ignore the story of the stealing of the body? By mentioning it in his Gospel, he cannot help but propagate it. This story has not come down to us through early Jewish sources, so it may not have been as widely known among Jews as Matthew would have us think[10]. In my view, he includes the opponents' story in his Gospel because, by doing so, he renders more credibility to his conviction that Jesus was really resurrected, body and all. After all, the basis for their story about a nocturnal body theft is that Jesus' body is no longer in the tomb. Matthew also supposes that Jesus is no longer in his tomb; given this supposition, it must be concluded that he perceives Jesus' resurrection as an event in which also his body is involved.

In 27:55-28:20, consistent reference is made to Jesus' body: a) in conformity with Jewish customs[11], Joseph of Arimathea takes his body down from the cross on the day of his death, wraps it in pure linen, and places it in a new grave, which does not contain any other body, so that there can be no confusion; b) from Jesus' announcement that he will rise again after three days, the opponents deduce that something will happen with his body; c) a similar connection can be found in 28:6 where the angel first observes that Jesus is no longer in his tomb and then explains this phenomenon by

belly of the great fish as time spent in the belly of Hades. His subsequent deliverance can therefore be understood as being saved from death; within the synonymous parallellism in 12:40, Jonah's deliverance prefigures the resurrection of the Son of Man. See also the redaction-critical study by P. HOFFMANN, *Die Auferweckung Jesu als Zeichen für Israel: Mt 12,39f und die matthäische Ostergeschichte*, in K. KERTELGE – T. HOLZ – C.-P. MÄRZ (eds.), *Christus bezeugen* (ETS, 59), Leipzig, St.-Benno-Verlag, 1989, pp. 110-123.

[10] However, there is a remarkable parallel in formulation between Matt 27:64 and Gos. Pet. 30: μήποτε ἐλθόντες οἱ μαθηταὶ αὐτοῦ κλέψωσιν αὐτον. Justin, who was writing in the middle of the second century C.E., also has the story of the theft of the body (*Dial.* 108:2).

[11] See C.A. EVANS, *Jewish Burial Traditions and the Resurrection of Jesus*, in *Journal for the Study of the Historical Jesus* 3 (2005) 233-248.

claiming that he has risen from the dead; d) after his resurrection, Jesus is able to move again, his followers can see and hear him again, just like before his death; the two Marys take hold of his feet and thus come into physical contact with him.

In the light of all this, it is very strange that in the narrative about the open tomb (28:1-7), we are only told *that* Jesus is risen, but not *how and when* this has happened. This is a gap in the story. That the description is not exhaustive but selective at this point can be demonstrated as follows:

a) The angel rolls back the stone, not to make way for Jesus[12] but to be able to show the two women that Jesus is no longer in the tomb.

b) The guards fall down like dead men, but their shock reaction follows their confrontation with the angel from heaven, and is not the result of the fact that they have seen Jesus rise with their own eyes; on this point, there is a decisive difference between Matthew and the account of the guards in the Gospel of Peter (Gos. Pet. 35-44).

c) The report of the guards about "all that had happened" (ἄπαντα τὰ γενόμενα in 28:11) can relate to nothing more, given the fact that they were in a dead faint at the time, than the phenomena mentioned in 28:2-3: the earthquake, the appearance of the angel, and the stone that was rolled back.

Why does Matthew's story contain a gap just at the *moment suprême*? The usual answer to this question is that, in this way, he wants to underline that the resurrection from the dead is an act performed by God (ἠγέρθη is a *passivum divinum*)[13] and as such resists verification by eye witnesses. This is a profound explanation, but it is not at all valid: elsewhere, Matthew does speak about the dead coming out of their graves after having been raised by God (27:53, probably in the sight of a centurion and his chums). Besides, in 17:1-8, he describes the metamorphosis of Jesus' appearance without any reserve[14]

---

[12] Contra G. LÜDEMANN, *The Resurrection of Christ: A Historical Inquiry*, New York, Prometheus Books, 2004, p. 93: "Evidently the tradition used by Matthew had the angel open the tomb so that the revived Jesus could come out". He argues that Matt 28:2-4 is based on an old tradition which can (also) be found in Gos. Pet. 35-44.

[13] O. HOFIUS, *"Am dritten Tage auferstanden von den Toten": Erwägungen zum Passiv ἐγείρεσθαι in christologischen Aussagen des Neuen Testaments*, in R. BIERINGER – V. KOPERSKI – B. LATAIRE (eds.), *Resurrection in the New Testament* (BETL, 165), Leuven, University Press – Peeters, 2002, pp. 93-106, however, claims that the passive reading of ἐγείρεσθαι is not at all certain.

[14] According to 17:2, Jesus' face shone like the sun (cf. Dan 10:6) and his clothes became dazzling white (cf. Dan 7:9); the word order is the same as in 28:3, where the appearance of the angel is described and then his clothes.

and three disciples are present to witness this scene. The transfiguration on the mountain prefigures Jesus' new existence after his death[15]. It can therefore be regarded as a predated resurrection story. Many other examples can be added because, to a certain extent, Matthew's story about Jesus' earthly life is pervaded with the belief in his resurrection. This is one of the reasons why it is continually about things that are only fully accessible from a perspective of belief.

An appeal to the idea that the resurrection, as an act performed by God, resists objectifying descriptive language therefore does not offer a conclusive explanation of the fact that 28:1-7 does not contain a description of the way in which Jesus left his tomb. Only one explanation remains, namely, that historically, there is simply no one who has been an eye witness to his resurrection. If there had been any, Matthew would have presented these eyewitnesses: there would hardly have been a better way to refute the body theft story spread by the opponents[16]. It is to the evangelist's credit that he did not bend the facts at such a crucial moment in his Gospel and has not, in an imaginative way, filled the gap in his narrative.

I end this section with the conclusion that the end of Matthew's Gospel is firmly grounded in the book as a whole. The end of this Gospel does not confront the reader with any great surprises for two reasons. Firstly because, what will happen to Jesus after his death has been prepared for in various ways beforehand and, secondly, because after his death, he continues to be actively involved with his people – in an almost physically tangible way, as he used to do before his crucifixion. The emphasis on the physical aspects of the resurrection are reinforced by the controversy with the competing interpretation suggested by the opposing party, which also centres on what might have happened with Jesus' dead body.

---

[15] There are more similarities between Matt 28 and 17:1-12: a) in both cases, a mountain serves as the place of the action (17:1; 28:16); b) there is a shock reaction (17:6.7; 28:4.5.10); c) προσέρχομαι, one of Matthew's favourite words (51 occurrences in Matthew, 5 in Mark, 10 in Luke), only occurs in 17:7 and 28:18 with Jesus as the subject: he makes his way to his disciples, in both cases from an exalted position; elsewhere in Matthew, this verb generally indicates the movement of an individual or group into the direction of Jesus (usually with the disciples or with people in distress as the subject).

[16] I found this argument – which I think is very plausible – in A.F. SEGAL, *Life after Death: A History of the Afterlife in the Religions of the West*, New York etc., Doubleday, 2004, p. 448: "The fact is: No one actually saw Jesus arise. This is a difficulty for the early mission of the church. [...] Had there been witnesses they would not have been left out". Like Mark, with his story about the open tomb, Matthew tries to soften the difficulty pointed out here.

II. MATTHEW'S INTERPRETATION OF JESUS' RESURRECTION

In this second section, I will explore how Matthew interprets the concept of "resurrection" and how his picture of Jesus' resurrection is fitted within other issues in his Gospel[17].

1. What Does Matthew Mean by "Resurrection"?

In some ways, in interpreting Jesus' resurrection, Matthew emphasises the same things as the other New Testament authors:

- The power of God is manifested in this event (cf. 22:29); God is the agent behind the risen Jesus: the *passivum divinum* ἠγέρθη indicates that it is God who has caused him to live again.
- This act performed by God must not be exclusively perceived as a meta-historical event (which is a contradiction in terms): because this act involves the crucified Jesus, there is already a link with history[18].
- That Matthew attaches a great deal of importance to the fact that the risen one and the crucified one are identical is shown by his particular attention to the bodily aspects of the resurrection.
- Nevertheless, there would be too much *continuity* if the resurrection merely constituted the coming to life of a dead body or the return of a dead person to earthly life.
- Conversely, there would be too much *discontinuity* if the new existence of the risen one should be understood as only a spiritual reality.
- There is also lack of continuity if the body of the risen one should be a totally new body to replace the earlier body.

In other ways, however, Matthew has an interpretation of his own: he understands the resurrection of Jesus as an event that has a strong impact on the life of the religious community[19], and not merely as an individual

---

[17] I try to apply to Matthew the point of departure formulated by Claudia Setzer at the beginning of her book: "Early Jews and Christians who believed in the bodily resurrection did not accept it as an isolated tenet, but as part of a constellation of beliefs. Belief in resurrection carried with it a set of other tenets, some explicit, some implicit". See C. SETZER, *Resurrection of the Body in Early Judaism and Early Christianity: Doctrine, Community, and Self-Definition*, Boston – Leiden, Brill, 2004, p. 1.

[18] LÜDEMANN, *Resurrection*, p. 14.

[19] In 27:51-53, he links – in a rather badly concealed way? – Jesus' resurrection to the raising of other dead people. For the question of whether Israel's saints or Christian believers are referred to here, see W. WEREN, *Human Body and Life beyond Death in Matthew's Gospel*, in T. NICKLAS – F.V. REITERER – J. VERHEYDEN (eds.), *The Human Body in Death*

event. With their statement that Jesus lives again, the disciples mean that
he is there again and continues to be actively involved with them. Matthew
lets Jesus express this idea in the final sentence of this Gospel: "And remember, I am with you always, to the end of the age" (28:20).

That Jesus will remain permanently with his own is a favourite theme in
Matthew. After all, his name is Emmanuel (1:23) and he himself states that
he will be present where two or three are gathered in his name (18:20). Still,
he cannot only be found in the religious community. This appears from the
passage on the final judgement (25:31-46), where, in his role as judge at the
end of time, he speaks about his presence in the world in all history before
the end of the age. At that ultimate moment, he explains, to everyone's
surprise, that he has always been there with those who suffered hunger or
thirst, were naked or roamed around as strangers, and with those who were
sick or in prison. Exactly those suffering people he then calls his brothers
and sisters. This statement lends special colour to his promise in the final
sentence of Matthew: Jesus is indeed with his disciples, who are his brothers
and sisters (12:49-50; cf. 28:7.10), but then they have to be where he can
be found, with those who are in distress, whom he also looks upon as his
brothers and sisters (25:40).

After his resurrection, the matthean Jesus is not taken up into heaven but,
endowed with all power in heaven and on earth, he is the driving force in
the lives of his disciples. Therefore it could rightly be said that he comes to
life again in their midst but, according to Matthew, it should be added
immediately that it is not the disciples who make Jesus live again, but that
it is Jesus who brings his church to life.

Within the temporal organisation of Matthew's Gospel, the resurrection
is not the end point and not even the high point, but the beginning of a
"new age", namely, the period between his resurrection and the parousia,
which can also be referred to as the time of the community[20]. The final
sentence in 28:20 ("always, until the end of the age") brings the entire
future history into view. It is this long period, starting when the book
breaks off, that Matthew anticipates in earlier parts of his Gospel when his
main character, Jesus, holds long discourses that contain a lot of information on the things that will befall the disciples in the years after Jesus'

---

and Resurrection (Deuterocanonical and Cognate Literature, Yearbook 2009), Berlin – New
York, De Gruyter, 2009, pp. 267-283. For more information see Dale ALLISON'S contribution in this volume.

[20] Already found in PERRIN, *Resurrection*, p. 56: "Matthew sees the resurrection of Jesus
as inaugurating a new age in the history of mankind [...], the age of the church, an age to be
brought to an end by the parousia".

death. In this way, he has integrated later experiences of the disciples into his story on Jesus' ministry. Thus, the theological idea that Jesus belongs to his church and that the church belongs to Jesus is expressed on a narrative level.

This theological idea can be made more concrete: the members of the community share in Jesus' authority on earth to forgive sin (9:8) and to continue his preaching of God's kingdom and his messianic deeds (10:1.8; cf. 11:5; 10:7; cf. 4:17)[21]; in their teaching, they consider themselves bound to his interpretation of the thora; in their way of life, they model themselves on their master, who is their ethical paradigm (e.g. 5:3-12); in the field of ethics, they are inspired by the expectation that, at the final judgement, Jesus will definitively separate the righteous from the wicked, richly rewarding the one party and gruesomely punishing the other (e.g. 25:31-46). Through its proclamation and the way it expresses its faith in practical behaviour, the community makes its claim that Jesus is truly risen a reality.

We see here how narrowly the resurrection concept in Matthew is linked to other concepts and ideas that are related to God, the community's self-image, the world surrounding it, and the history of salvation.

III. Conclusion: Body and Resurrection

I have now established that Matthew – among other things, because of a false interpretation of the resurrection by opponents of his community – places great emphasis on Jesus' body. He does so to underline that the risen Lord is none else than the crucified Jesus; what also plays a role is that, in Matthew's opinion, a person is incomplete without a body. The question is now what Matthew understands by "body".

This discussion is usually marred by the assumption that Matthew equals "bodily" with "physical". This view forms the background to a book by Simcha Jacobovici and Charles Pellegrino from 2007 on a first century tomb discovered in Talpiot, which they believed to be Jesus' family tomb[22]. They argue that his remains were stored in an ossuary found there, because it bore an epitaph with the name of Yeshua bar Yosef. Would this be the deathblow of the Christian belief in the resurrection if this was indeed the case?

---

[21] These acts include raising the dead (11:5; cf. 10:8).

[22] S. JACOBOVICI – C. PELLEGRINO, *The Jesus Family Tomb: The Discovery That Will Change History Forever*, San Franciso, Harper, 2007.

No, not necessarily, because a body is more than a physical reality.[23] Especially for human beings, the body is a gateway to others: thanks to my body, I am someone with an identity and am I able to communicate with the people around me. The body represents the ability to interact and can therefore be seen as equivalent to the person to the extent that he lives and acts in this world. This idea is also found in Matthew's Easter stories: after his death, Jesus continues to be present on the earth, where he is very closely connected with his disciples and with people in distress. Matthew is not out to make us believe that corporality must be identified with bones, flesh, and blood. He is very close to our idea that the human body stands for the person, is linked to someone's identity, and enables someone to communicate and interact. And this is exactly what we see the risen Jesus do in Matthew's stories: he is involved with his own people – even more than before his death – and he himself gives them the power to continue his cause.

The antithesis between bodily and spiritual breathes an anthropological dualism that is alien to Matthew's way of thinking. With his emphasis on the bodily aspects of the resurrection, he wants to honour its reality (resurrection happened not only in the heads or hearts of Jesus' disciples), but first and foremost, in this way, Matthew wants to show that Jesus' exalted existence is meaningful for the salvation of the world. Or in Segal's words: "His resurrection not only should be bodily, it must be bodily or it is not significant for the salvation of the world"[24].

Tilburg University   Wim J.C. WEREN
School of Humanities
P.O. Box 90153
NL-5000 LE Tilburg
The Netherlands

---

[23] I agree with the portrait of the human person in J.B. GREEN, *Body, Soul, and Human Life: The Nature of Humanity in the Bible*, Grand Rapids, MI, Baker Academic, 2008, p. 179: "[...] who we are, our personhood, is inextricably bound up in our physicality, and so is inextricably tied to the cosmos God has created, and in the sum of our life experiences and relationships". The consequences of this view are that "there is no part of us, no aspect of our personhood, that survives death" and that "belief in life-after-death requires embodiment – that is, re-embodiment. And this provides the basis for relational and narrative continuity of the self".

[24] SEGAL, *Life After Death*, p. 451.

THE GREAT ESCAPE: SOME COMMENTS ON A CONTROVERSIAL SUGGESTION FOR EXPLAINING MATT 28:2-4

Matthew's version of the Empty Tomb story builds on Mark's, but at the same time in a significant way also goes beyond it. He does so most dramatically at the end of the story when rewriting Mark's last verse, adding joy to the women's fear, informing the reader that they indeed went to inform the disciples of what had happened, and on their way have them meet with the Risen Lord who repeats to them, almost verbatim, the command of the angel (28:9-10). And he does so, almost as dramatically, in the opening lines when describing how an angel descending from heaven rolls back the stone that closed off the tomb (28:2-4) and by framing the whole with a double side-story about the guards that had been posted at the tomb (27:62-66; 28:11-15). It is this latter part I wish to look at.

I. The Hypothesis

Almost forty years ago, in 1973, in a now famous essay on Matthew's Empty Tomb narrative and the traditions it has incorporated, Nikolaus Walter argued that this narrative contains elements that are characteristic of a certain type of rescue miracle[1]. As a matter of fact, Matthew would have combined three types of "Easter narratives": the "empty tomb" version, which he found in Mark, the "appearance" version, which he took from tradition and by which he continued the story beyond Mark's, and the "rescue" version, which he likewise took from the tradition. Traces of this latter version can be found in the motifs of an angel opening the entrance to the tomb and of the soldiers' guard (watching helplessly), but in the form in which this variant on a resurrection story came to Matthew it also contained

---

[1] N. WALTER, *Eine vormatthäische Schilderung der Auferstehung Jesu*, in *NTS* 19 (1972-1973) 415-429, esp. pp. 419-425 (p. 419: "Befreiungswundererzählung").

a description of Jesus actually leaving the tomb[2]. Matthew changed this version quite drastically[3]. He gave rather more emphasis to the apologetic aspects by elaborating upon the motif of the guards[4]. More importantly, he just cut out the heart of the story, and dropped the description of the liberation altogether. A reason is easy to find: "Er hat offenbar empfunden, dass die naive Übertragung des Türöffnungs-Befreiungs-Topos auf die Osterdarstellung sich theologisch nicht durchhalten lässt, weil das Ostergeschehen alle denkbaren Analogien irdischen Geschehens, einschliesslich solcher wunderhafter Vorgänge, ..., überschreitet. Matt. meint vielmehr, dass der Vorgang der Auferstehung Jesu als solcher erzählerisch nicht dargestellt werden kann"[5]. It is just "not done". It is also possible that Matthew did not wish to grant the enemy guard the privilege of being the first ones to "see" the risen Lord[6]. This "rescue" version would be a relatively recent one compared to the other two, because of its interest in describing the resurrection[7]. Walter argues it is definitely younger than the "appearance" version. It is more difficult to establish its relation to the "empty tomb" version, but Walter suspects these may be two different and independent ways of reformulating the *kerygma* about the resurrection in a narrative form[8]. The "rescue" version left traces also outside Matthew's gospel. The author of the *Gospel of Peter* was less scrupulous about such things and copied more extensively from the same tradition that Matthew had used, including the account of a resurrection from the tomb[9]. Contrary, then, to what many have said or suspected, Matthew's is not the first step towards an account like the one in the *Gospel of Peter*, but rather the first step away from such a tradition[10].

---

[2] "in Matt. xxvii. 62-6/xxviii. 2-4/xxviii. 11-15 (ist uns) der Rest einer Ostererzählung erhalten, die neben den Erzählungen von Ostererscheinungen und der Erzählung von der Auffindung des leeren Grabes einen dritten Typ, eben den einer Erzählung vom Auferstehungsvorgang selbst, belegt" (*ibid.*, p. 421). Compare the description of the contents of this traditional story on p. 423: "Es ist also anzunehmen, dass die vormatthäische Fassung erzählte, das sein Engel ... vom Himmel herabkam, unter Erdbeben den Stein wegwälzte und den Gekreuzigten und Begrabenen herausführte und mit ihm zum Himmel zurückkehrte, während die eigens dazu bestellten Wächter von alledem nichts merkten geschweige die Befreiung verhindern konnten".

[3] *Ibid.*, p. 423: "An einer solchen Vorlage hätte dann Matt. entschieden geändert".

[4] WALTER finds evidence of this in the tension between 28:4 (the guards are "like dead") and 28:11 (they claim they have seen everything); cf. *ibid.*, p. 421 n. 1.

[5] *Ibid.*, p. 423.

[6] *Ibid.*, p. 423: "Weniger dürfte eine Rolle spielen ...".

[7] *Ibid.*, p. 425: "(gehört) einem relativ jungen Typ von Ostererzählungen an, bei dem der Vorgang der Auferweckung selbst Gegenstand des Berichts war".

[8] *Ibid.*, p. 425.

[9] *Ibid.*, pp. 424 and 426-429. The quite singular reading of Mark 16:3 in codex *k* would be another witness to a similar, though not identical, tradition (*ibid.*, p. 422).

[10] *Ibid.*, p. 425: "kein 'erster Schritt' ..., sondern Ergebnis bewusster Reduktion".

Walter does not cite any predecessors for his interpretation. He refers to Otto Weinreich's brilliant monograph on rescue stories, including the opening of doors, but he correctly points out that Weinreich explicitly declined commenting on the empty tomb and appearance stories in the gospels, because he thought the rescue motifs were not an integral and necessary part of the story[11]. "Auf die Auferstehungsberichte selbst gehe ich nicht ein. … Nicht das 'Wie', sondern die Tatsache der Auferstehung ist das Entscheidende für die Evangelienberichte"[12]. Walter begs to differ, at least for Matthew: "Doch scheint mir, dass die Dinge für Matt. xxviii. 2-4 sofort anders liegen, wenn man diese Verse mit xxvii. 62-6 und xxviii. 11-15 zusammennimmt"[13]. Walter also points out that H. Grass had already "suspected" that the pre-Matthean version might have contained an account of the resurrection itself. But Grass did not go beyond a mere suggestion.

In the same year as Walter, and independently from him, the same suggestion about Matthew having used a "rescue" version was argued in great detail by Reinhard Kratz in a monograph on epiphany and rescue stories in biblical and extra-biblical tradition that culminated in a chapter on Matthew's version of the tomb and resurrection story[14]. Kratz's work was highly praised by his promoter, Rudolf Pesch, who saw in it an excellent specimen of the kind of exegetical work that was being done in Frankfurt at that time[15]. Pesch took up the suggestion and applied it to Mark's story of the empty tomb[16], which Kratz in turn picked up in his Habilitationsschrift of 1979, in which

---

[11] O. WEINREICH, *Gebet und Wunder: Zwei Abhandlungen zur Religions- und Literaturgeschichte*, in F. FOCKE *et al.* (eds.), *Genethliakon Wilhelm Schmid zum siebzigsten Geburtstag am 24. Februar 1929* (Tübinger Beiträge zur Altertumswissenschaft, 5), Stuttgart, Kohlhammer, 1929, 169-464. The first essay is on "Primitive Gebetsegoismus" (169-199); the second, much longer one, and the one that interests us here, is entitled "Türöffnung im Wunder-, Prodigien- und Zauberglauben der Antike, des Judentums und Christentums" (pp. 200-464). Weinreich gave quite some attention to the "escape-from-prison" stories in the Acts of the Apostles, comparing these to a similar story in Euripides' *Bacchantes* (576-637) and even concluding that Luke depended upon the latter (pp. 314-341; on Luke and Euripides, pp. 332-341). See A. VÖGELI, *Lukas und Euripides*, in *TZ* 9 (1953) 415-438.

[12] WEINREICH, *Gebet und Wunder*, p. 311 n. 48a. For an interpretation of the gospel stories, Weinreich refers to E. BICKERMANN, *Das leere Grab*, in *ZNW* 23 (1924) 281-293 (see below).

[13] WALTER, *Schilderung*, p. 420.

[14] R. KRATZ, *Auferweckung als Befreiung: Eine Studie zur Passions- und Auferstehungstheologie des Matthäus (besonders Mt 27,62-28,15)* (SBS, 65), Stuttgart, KWB Verlag, 1973, esp. pp. 57-83.

[15] "Ich freue mich, dass mit dieser Studie erstmalig ein Stück der im jungen Frankfurter Fachbereich Religionswissenschaften betriebenen exegetischen Forschung dokumentiert werden kann" (from the "Vorwort", p. 5).

[16] R. PESCH, *Das Markusevangelium* (HTKNT, 2/2), Freiburg – Basel – Wien, Herder, 1977, pp. 522-527.

he also incorporated a slightly revised version of the chapter on Matthew from his earlier book and included a comment on Walter[17]. A nice example indeed of a most fruitful cooperation between "master and student"[18]!

Kratz agrees with Walter that the whole complex of Matt 27:62-28:15 can only be satisfactorily explained (and indeed, "relativ leicht", as Kratz adds rather optimistically) if one accepts that the two guard stories that frame the tomb story cannot be disconnected from it and help to make sense of it, and that Matthew's account shows traces of the genre of the "rescue" and "door opening" stories[19]. He also agrees that the complex is pre-Matthean, though he also shows in his analysis, which is far more detailed than Walter's, that it has been thoroughly reworked by the evangelist. "Dies darf jedoch nicht dazu verleiten, Mattäus von vornherein auch als Verfasser des Sondergutes anzusehen"[20]. He further agrees that it is Matthew who combined the tradition with the Markan account and thereby strengthened the apologetic and polemical tone (and also added some elements in the epiphany)[21]. He finally also agrees with Walter that Matthew refrained from taking the last step and from explicitly describing the resurrection, but this agreement at the same time points to a major difference between the two authors. Indeed Kratz is most critical of the suggestion that Matthew would have relied on the same tradition as the *Gospel of Peter*, hence would have omitted a crucial element that was already found there[22]. Instead he thinks it is possible that the tradition hinted at Jesus' rescue without also explicitly describing it. "Wie Mattäus selbst (und eigentlich auch die vormarkinische Passionsgeschichte) beweist, kann eine Ostergeschichte auch unter Verwertung von Türöffnungs- und Befreiungswundertraditionen sehr wohl ohne anschauliche Schilderung der Auferstehung selbst auskommen"[23]. The argument is a bit shaky, because it relies on the

---

[17] R. KRATZ, *Rettungswunder: Motiv-, traditions- und formkritische Aufarbeitung einer biblischen Gattung* (Europäische Hochschulschriften, 23/123), Frankfurt – Bern, Lang, 1979, pp. 500-510 (Mark 16:1-8) and 511-541 (Matt 27:62-28:15). As a rule I will cite from this second version.

[18] For another example of their cooperation, see the series of volumes entitled *So liest man synoptisch: Anleitung und Kommentar zum Studium der synoptischen Evangelien*, 7 vols., Frankfurt, Knecht, 1975-1980.

[19] KRATZ, *Rettungswunder*, p. 511: "Der gordische Knoten der Mattäus-Fassung lässt sich relativ leicht lösen, wenn man zum einen den Zusammenhang der Wächterszenen mit der Grabesgeschichte erkennt, zum anderen, dass der mattäische Kontext deutliche Berührungen mit der Gattung der Türöffnungs- und Befreiungswundergeschichten aufweist".

[20] *Ibid.*, p. 512.

[21] *Ibid.*, p. 533.

[22] *Ibid.*, p. 534: "kaum plausibel".

[23] *Ibid.*, p. 534.

same texts for which the hypothesis is to be proven. Unlike Walter, Kratz does not have to assume that Matthew changed the original purpose of the motif of the angel opening the tomb turning him into an *angelus interpres*[24]. But it cannot be denied that the angel in Matthew's version is not said to have "liberated" Jesus from the grave. In any case, Kratz follows E. Schweizer, against Walter, in concluding that Matthew's version is a first step towards a representation of the resurrection, rather than a reduction from a tradition that already contained such a description[25]. Matthew's decision to incorporate this kind of tradition into his account of the tomb story served the double purpose that he could enrich his version with elements known from biblical – the epiphany – and from the broader Greco-Roman tradition – the rescue theme. Apologetics and polemics played a crucial role in this, but beyond that Kratz also points to a theological purpose. Matthew has turned the empty tomb story he received from Mark into a prototypical illustration of ancient Jewish expectations about an afterlife, and on an even broader scale, of the more general theme dear to Matthew and known from biblical tradition as well, of God's reign and power and of God assisting man (i.c., Jesus) all through his life, and beyond. "Es ist wohl angezeigt bei der Befreiung Jesu aus dem Grab an eine Befreiung vom Tode zu denken. Somit wäre die Auferstehung Jesu als Überwindung des Todes die konsequente Folge seines irdischen Auftretens und insbesondere auch prototypische Erfüllung des alttestamentlichen Auferstehungshoffnungen"; and: "Die Heraufführung der Gottesherrschaft in Wort und Tat bedeutet Überwindung Satans und des Todes, Aufbruch eines neuen Lebens"[26].

All this enthusiasm apparently yielded little success. Walter nor Kratz seem to have managed to convince many. J. Gnilka mentions the hypothesis in two brief comments; both are critical, though not without any opening towards a more positive interpretation. The motifs of the guard and the sealing of the tomb are known from rescue stories, "doch ist zu beachten, dass in 28,1ff mehr erzählt wird als seine Befreiung aus dem Gefängnis. Die

---

[24] WALTER, *Schilderung*, p. 423.

[25] KRATZ, *Rettungswunder*, p. 535; with reference to E. SCHWEIZER, *Das Evangelium nach Mattäus* (NTD, 1), Göttingen, Vandenhoeck & Ruprecht, [13]1973, p. 344. Walter was familiar with Schweizer's critique of his position, which he had first presented in a paper he had given in Vienna on October 2, 1972, but unfortunately preferred not to respond to it "aus Raumgründen" (WALTER, *Schilderung*, p. 425 n. 3). KRATZ' further conclusion that this interest in representing the resurrection as a "rescue" finds its climax in medieval texts such as the twelfth-century *Christus patiens* (he takes the reference from WEINREICH, *Gebet und Wunder*, p. 338), may be one step too far. The section that is quoted from this work is a mere pastiche of Matthew's account, but does not go beyond it (KRATZ, *Rettungswunder*, pp. 536-537).

[26] KRATZ, *Rettungswunder*, p. 538 and 540.

Öffnung des Grabes durch den Engel hat mit der Auferweckung Jesu unmittelbar auch nichts zu tun"[27]. But while taking his distance from Walter,
Gnilka nevertheless also allows for 28:2-4 to be read as an indirect hint to the
resurrection. Matthew does not correct his tradition, but keeps to what he
found in it: "Wahrscheinlicher ist, dass in der Vorlage – wie bei Mt – der
Engel nur das Grab öffnete, der Auferstehungsvorgang aber damit angedeutet
sein sollte"[28]. Yet, the phrasing itself already indicates that there is a problem
with Matt 28:2-4. Commenting on Matt 28:2, W.D. Davies and D.C. Allison wonder "whether in the background of our story is the belief that angels
guide the righteous to heaven" and cite the "rescue" passages in the *Gospel of
Peter* and in codex *k* as evidence ("strongly recalls that belief"), but they do
not refer to Walter or Kratz and do not use the term "rescue miracle" or the
like[29]. Walter and Kratz (1973) figure in the bibliography of R.E. Brown's
The Death of the Messiah, but they hardly make it into the notes and their
hypothesis is not discussed for itself[30]. Ulrich Luz refers to the hypothesis in
a note and compares it to Bickermann's "Entrückungshypothese", and neither
of the two finds mercy in his eyes. The major objection is easy to guess: "Der
entscheidende Unterschied besteht darin, dass Mt 28,2 die 'Befreiung' des im
Grab eingeschlossenen Jesus gar nicht erwähnt. In V 6f ist sie lediglich voraus-
gesetzt. Die Berührungen zwischen Mt 28,1-8 und anderen Befreiungswun-
dern beschränken sich auf die VV 2-4 und auf Einzelmotive (Erdbeben, 'Tod'
der Wächter)"[31]. I am afraid it might not be that easy.

---

[27] J. GNILKA, *Das Matthäusevangelium*, vol. 2 (HKTNT, 1/2), Freiburg – Basel – Wien,
Herder, 1988, p. 486. The episodes with the guard that frame the empty tomb story are
"apologetische Tendenzgeschichten".

[28] *Ibid.*, p. 492, while repeating in n. 10 that this is not a "rescue/release story", because
it is about resurrection from death, not escaping from prison. But it is precisely the point
whether Matthew may have paralleled the two, or somehow brought them together.

[29] DAVIES – ALLISON, *The Gospel according to Saint Matthew*, vol. 3 (ICC), Edinburgh,
T&T Clark, 1997, p. 665.

[30] R.E. BROWN, *The Death of the Messiah: From Gethsemane to the Grave*, II, New York,
Doubleday, 1994, p. 1204; see also p. 1305 n. 44 (Kratz on the motif of the frustrated guard
in Acts) and p. 1306 n. 47 (Walter on the structure of the *Gospel of Peter*), and p. 1310 n.
56 (Kratz on apologetic tendencies in Matt).

[31] U. LUZ, *Das Evangelium nach Matthäus (Mt 26-28)* (EKK, 1/4), Düsseldorf – Zürich
– Neukirchen-Vluyn, Benziger – Neukirchener Verlag, 2002, p. 396 n. 8. – The major problem with Bickermann's thesis is equally "simple": the motif of "Entrückung" is usually not
connected with that of the tomb, but rather functions in such instances in which the tomb
is said to be unknown. Exceptions to this are late, all Christian and hence most probably
influenced by the tomb stories in the gospels, or in the case of Chariton's hero visiting the
tomb of his beloved Callirhoe, a matter not of the body been "rapt away", but stolen. The
latter is true; the former at least demonstrates that authors were capable of introducing the
motif also in combination with, or while being influenced by the gospels stories in which the
location of the tomb is not an issue.

II. A COMMENT

On the one hand, one might conclude that the fact that the suggestion does not seem to have been formulated before pleads against it being an "obvious" interpretation[32]. On the other hand, it is always puzzling to note how serious scholars (like Kratz and Walter) sometimes apparently "see" something that others claim is not there. But most puzzling perhaps, actually the core of the problem, is the observation that Matthew's story does indeed contain a good number of motifs and features that are characteristic for a "release story". It poses the double problem of how motif and genre relate to each other, and also of how to explain that the similar, or even the same motifs can apparently occur in different genres (or be transferred from one genre to another) without "affecting" the particular genres.

Kratz has drawn the long list of motifs that are (also) characteristic for a "release story": the presence of a guard; the sealing or otherwise securing of the prison/tomb; the setting by night; the earthquake; the appearance of an angel / divine messenger; the guard made helpless and eventually being punished[33]. In the section on Mark, he draws a slightly different list, and maybe the two should be combined: the closing and/or sealing of the door, witnessed by others (the women); the observation upon returning to the tomb early in the morning that the door is opened, which therefore must have happened at night (or early morning); the (implicit reference to the) opening of the door, not witnessed by anyone; the interpretation of what happened; searching in vain for the body; a number of epiphany motifs[34]. These lists are quite impressive in themselves.

But it is not just a matter of listing motifs. It is also about their role and function. It is true, of course, that some of these features are originally at home in a different genre, that of the epiphany, but this does not automatically turn the whole story into that genre. The whole issue is to determine what is the purpose of the motif within the story. Thus, the epiphany

---

[32] It would take a long search to document this any further, but Walter and Kratz do not seem to know of any predecessors, and nothing of this kind is found in the more important commentaries on Matt they may have consulted (see, e.g., H.A.W. Meyer, B. Weiss, T. Zahn, E. Lohmeyer). The latter cites Greco-Roman parallels for the motifs of the earthquake and the sleeping guard as part of epiphany stories: E. LOHMEYER, *Das Evangelium des Matthäus*, ed. W. SCHMAUCH (KEK), Göttingen, Vandenhoeck & Ruprecht, p. 405 n. 2 (Philostratus) and 406 n. 1 (Lucian).

[33] KRATZ, *Rettungswunder*, p. 532. The opening of the tomb is remarkably missing from this list!

[34] *Ibid.*, p. 501. It should be pointed out that this second list is perhaps slightly more "heterogeneous" than the former one.

motifs are not introduced, or certainly not primarily, to explain something on the one who is revealed. It is rather the opposite: an epiphany is needed to make other things happen; it is crystal clear, I would say, that this is the case also in Matthew. The angel has not come to tell the women about his person, but about another one and about what happened to that other one. The epiphany serves a purpose other than identifying the subject who is revealed as a divine being.

But there is more to the issue. As Luz correctly points out, a formal clearly identifiable description of the "release" is missing. This cannot be denied. Is it lethal to the suggestion? Walter and Kratz, even though they have come up with quite different explanations, did not think so. Two further comments may be helpful.

It is important to note that passages that can be classified under the heading of "release stories" show some flexibility in presenting and handling this motif. In two of the three stories in Acts the prisoners are said also actually to leave prison after the angel has opened the door (5:19; 12:8.10). Here, one could say, the motif is used "properly". But in the third story the angel works in vain, for the prisoners simply stay where they are until they are finally led out of prison by the jailer himself (16:30), and the next day they even insist that they be led out of the town, which is like a prison at large, by the authorities who had locked them in (16:37.39)[35]! If one and the same author can play with the motif in such a free way … The passage in Chariton's *Callirhoe* (3.3.3) in which the hero visits the tomb of his beloved only to find out that she is no longer in it, which I take as a specimen of the genre of the "release story", rather than of an "Entrückungswunder" (*pace* Luz), flexibility is infused with a touch of irony: the one who is thought to have been "rapt away" actually is merely stolen, hence brought out of the tomb. The same Chariton elsewhere most emphatically likens imprisonment to death: "It is your death that the chains signify" (*Call.* 3.7). Weaver follows up with the comment, "Correspondingly, escape from the bars of prison is used to symbolize restored or rescued life"[36]. Prison and

---

[35] Scholars have drawn attention to this difference and argued that it turns the story into a different genre; see, e.g., E. HAENCHEN, *The Acts of the Apostles: A Commentary*, Philadelphia, Westminster John Knox, 1971, p. 501 (a conversion story); but not so for one of the latest commentators of these passages: "The shift to the jailor and his point-of-view is better understood, however, not as a displacement, but rather as a reformulation of the prison-escape *topos* observed in Acts 5, 12, and elsewhere" (J.B. WEAVER, *Plots of Epiphany. Prison-Escape in Acts of the Apostles* [BZNW, 131], Berlin, De Gruyter, 2004, p. 274).

[36] WEAVER, *Plots*, p. 113. There are also some very convincing references to ancient and modern literature on the same theme. Perhaps most telling is Plutarch in his *Lucullus*: "In capturing Cabira and most of the other strongholds, [Lucullus] found great treasures, and

death do equal also in Acts 22:4 and Luke 22:33; that one could easily lead
to the other had been demonstrated by the tragic fate of John the Baptist
(Matt 14:10 par. Mark), and indeed by that of Jesus himself who instead
of being released from prison is led away to be crucified (see the outcome
of Pilate's final attempt in Matt 27:15-23 and v. 26). Prison and death also
stand close to each other in the way Philostratus presents Apollonius' escape
from prison and "escape into death" in *Vit. Apoll.* 7.38 and 8.30. The first
story is about Apollonius' miraculous "self-escape" from prison, which to
his disciple reveals his divine nature[37]; the other lists three reports about his
death, from dying a natural death, to a miraculous disappearance in the
temple of Athena on Lindos, to an even more miraculous fate in which the
hero, of his own accord, first escapes a temple-prison on the island of Crete
and is taken up in heaven[38]. Again, if so much freedom is allowed in using
the "escape" motif, how can Matthew be blamed for being perhaps a bit too
scrupulous?

But to take this one step further, one might even question whether
scrupulous is the right term. Matthew is desperately vague (or confusing)
on what happened in 28:2-4, and when. It seems to have become common
opinion in modern commentaries to conclude that Matthew has the
women witness the descend of the angel and all that comes with it. The
reasoning is as follows: The women "see" everything, and yet no resurrection is described; hence that is not what Matthew had in mind. Luz is
quite confident about this: "V 1 führt die Frauen ein, denen die Erscheinung zuteil wird"[39]. Davies and Allison are somewhat more cautious:
"Commentators are divided over whether the women witness the descent

---

many prisons, in which many Greeks and many kinsfolk of the king were confined. As they
had long been given up for dead, it was not so much a rescue as it was a resurrection and a
sort of second birth, for which they were indebted to the favour of Lucullus" (p. 113 n. 68).
A good general formulation in H.S. VERSNEL, *Ter Unus: Isis, Dionysus, Hermes: Three Studies in Henotheism* (Inconsistencies in Greek and Roman Religion, 1), Leiden, Brill, 1990,
p. 84: "Chains or fetters are common symbols of death or any misfortune leading to or
similar to death".

[37] Τότε πρῶτον ὁ Δάμις φησὶν ἀκριβῶς ξυνεῖται τῆς ἀκριβῶς ξυνεῖναι τῆς Ἀπολλωνίου
φύσεως, ὅτι θεία τε εἴη καὶ κρείττων ἀνθρώπου, μὴ γὰρ θύσαντα, πῶς γὰρ ἐν δεσμωτηρίῳ, μηδ᾽
εὐξάμενόν τι, μηδὲ εἰπόντα καταγελάσαι τοῦ δεσμοῦ καὶ ἐναρμόσαντα αὖ τὸ σκέλος τὰ τοῦ
δεδεμένου πράττειν.

[38] Οἱ μὲν δὴ τοῦ ἱεροῦ προϊστάμενοι ξυλλαβόντες αὐτὸν ὡ γόητα καὶ λῃστὴν δῆσαι, μείλιγμα
τοῖς κυσὶ προβεβλῆσθαί τι ὑπ᾽ αὐτοῦ θάσκοντες ὁ δ᾽ ἀμφὶ μέσας νύκτας ἑαυτὸν λῦσαι, καλέσας
δὲ τοὺς δήσαντας, ἐτάσθησαν, παρελθόντος δὲ ἔσω τὰς μὲν θύρας ξυνελθεῖν, ὥσπερ ἐκέκλειτο,
βοὴν δὲ ἀδουσῶν παρθένων ἐκπεσεῖν. τὸ δὲ ᾆσμα ἦν· στεῖχε γᾶς, στεῖχε ἐς οὐρανόν, στεῖχε. οἷον·
ἴθι ἐκ τῆς γῆς ἄνω. On these two texts, see WEINREICH, *Gebet und Wunder*, pp. 295-298 and
KRATZ, *Rettungswunder*, pp. 389-391.

[39] LUZ, *Matthäus*, p. 396.

of the angel and its consequences or only come along later. But given the introduction of the women before v. 2, it seems better to think of them seeing everything"[40]. This may be correct; yet Davies and Allison remind us that the other option has also been defended. Indeed it once was a rather popular view among commentators that Matthew may have been playing with the time perspective and that what is told in vv. 2-4 actually happens when the women are on their way to the tomb, but before they have arrived there[41]. The fact that Matthew mentions the women in v. 1 already is then just "part of the game". The objection that Matthew's ἦλθεν + infinitive cannot be understood in this way and rather points to the women having arrived has more weight; in any case more than the fact that otherwise Matthew would not have mentioned that the women actually have arrived[42]. It should further also be noted that in Mark the angel clearly is waiting for them to arrive. If Matthew wished to counter this he could at least have been more pronounced on it and formulate more clearly that the women have first arrived and then witness the angel descending. As it is formulated now he has at the least created a possibility for assuming that there was a time gap between the arrival of the angel and that of the women.

But more vagueness is to be noted. Matthew substitutes for Mark's rather implicit picture a whole long and detailed description of the angel's arrival and what it causes or what accompanies it. An earthquake had been mentioned before in 27:51.54, at the hour of Jesus death, which caused great damage and distress; in the way it is formulated in vv. 51-52 (parataxis) the opening of the tombs is one of the things to happen. Not so in 28:2-4, where it is explicitly said that it is the angel who opens the tomb. Only, is it all so evident and, more importantly, it is not said for what purpose the tomb is opened. The reappearance of the earthquake motif, shortly after

---

[40] DAVIES – ALLISON, *Matthew*, p. 665.

[41] See, e.g., T. ZAHN, *Das Evangelium des Matthäus* (Kommentar zum Neuen Testament), Leipzig, Deichert, 1903,, p. 708: "Das ἦλθεν nicht die Ankunft am Grabe, sondern auch hier das Hingehen zu den genannten Ziel bezeichnet, ergibt sich aus θεωρῆσαι τὸν τάφον, was nur den Zweck ihres Hingehens, nicht eine Folge ihres Ankommens am Ziel angeben kann". Zahn finds a further argument for his position in Matt 19:1 (see p. 579). Cf. already H. GROTIUS, *Annotationes in Novum Testamentum*, II, Groningen, Ex officina W. Zuidema, 1827, p. 389: "Putem autem hoc, ut & lapidis devolutionem, sed & fugam custodum, evenisse dum mulieres in itinere essent. ... Argumento est quod Marcus de mulieribus narrat [16,4]".

[42] Both arguments in B. WEISS, *Das Matthäus-Evangelium* (KEK), Göttingen, Vandenhoeck & Ruprecht, [8]1890, p. 492. The latter argument is less important, as the reader knows from v. 1 that the women are "on their way". A further possible objection could be that otherwise the epiphany occurs for the guard only; but that may be less of a problem.

27:51.54, may not be the most elegant feature[43]. In any case, it has led scholars to wonder who does what. Thus, R.H. Gundry tries to make sense of all the elements and comments as follows on v. 2: "Since the earthquake in 27:51-54 split open the rock tombs at the moment of the saints' resurrection, we are probably meant to understand that the angel's rolling away the stone has the purpose of letting him out of the tomb (though he remains unobserved for the time being)"[44]. This may be too sophisticated a reading, but it is one that has a certain claim in the history of exegesis[45]. As for the purpose of the angel opening the tomb, Matthew has dropped the whole scenery and dialogue of Mark 16:3-4 and he has changed the reason for the women visiting the tomb. They clearly have no hope of getting in (diff. Mark). They knew it was closed off "with a big stone" (27:60; Matthew imports the size of the stone from Mark 16:3). They merely want "to see the tomb", just as they had been sitting in front of it (and watching it) in 27:61. When in 28:6 they are given the opportunity to check what the angel has been telling them (it is not clear whether they also enter the tomb), it is the consequence of something that had happened before; in any case it is not said either that inviting the women in was the purpose for opening the tomb.

That something has happened to Jesus is clear to see for everyone present (and awake!). Matthew says this in various forms. The women are invited to check the tomb and they find it empty. They are told that Jesus is risen (28:6) and going before them to Galilee, obviously to meet with them there (28:7). In other words, the angel tells them that he is not (yet) taken up

---

[43] Cf. LOHMEYER's comment: "Dies Erdbeben in der Osternacht stösst sich ein wenig mit dem anderen in der Todesstunde; das ist wohl ein Zeichen für den Wandel der Überlieferung, welcher das Ereignis der Auferstehung bedeutsamer geworden ist als der Tod" (LOHMEYER, *Matthäus*, p. 405 n. 2). That may be so, but on the other hand, the first earthquake certainly is impressive enough to provoke the great confession of 27:54; and if Matthew was responsible for adding in both motifs (or if they stem from tradition he at least prefers to keep them in his text), he did little to avoid this kind of unnecessary complications.

[44] R.H. GUNDRY, *Matthew: A Commentary on His Literary and Theological Art*, Grand Rapids, MI, Eerdmans, 1982, p. 587.

[45] GROTIUS (*Annotationes*, II, p. 376) at 27:52 cites Aristides for the fact that an earthquake can open tombs ("Notat Aristides in descriptione terrae motus quo Rhodus eversa est: [*Monumenta dirupta sunt*]: et mox: [*Monumenta foras eiiciebant mortuos*]"). But in 28:2 the earthquake can have all possible other meanings and functions, but apparently not that of opening the tomb: "ut indicaretur commovendum esse totum orbem praedicatione Christi" (Munsterus); "ut custodes qui dormiebant, excitarentur, & resurrectionis Christi cogerentur esse testes" (Maldonatus); "ut constaret, hos Angelos esse" (Maldonatus again); "praesentemque esse Dei virtutem" (Lucas Brugensis); "ut signum esset secuturae ὀπτασίας satis notum Judaico populo" (Grotius). References cited from the *Critici Sacri*, IV, ed. P. POLUS, London, 1708, p. 654.

into heaven, but still present among them, only not in the near vicinity.
Matthew does not have him say that Jesus "escaped" from the tomb, or
was "freed" from it, but that would have been a good way of putting it.
In his efforts to "say the unspeakable", Matthew even seems to have wan-
dered off into un-trodden ground, indeed to have gone to the verge of
abyss itself, when at times he somehow seems to fuse together the angel
and the risen Lord, a quite dangerous experiment! This has been noted
already by Kratz: "Die Ankündigung der Erscheinung des Auferstandenen
in Galiläa entspricht wörtlich der bei Markus. Doch behauptet der Engel
hier von sich, 'siehe, ich habe es euch gesagt', während bei Markus sinn-
voller 'wie er (Jesus) euch gesagt hat' zu lesen ist. Das Engelwort klingt
wie ein Wort aus dem Munde Jesu selbst, es hätte auch nur dann eigentlich einen Sinn. … Überhaupt wird der Engel bei Matthäus so sehr sou-
verän geschildert (vgl. auch οἶδα: V 5), dass man fast an ein Ineinander-
fliessen der Gestalt des Engels und des Auferstandenen denken könnte.
Auch die unmittelbar anschliessende Erscheinung Jesu vor den Frauen am
Grab, die wie eine Dublette zur Engelerscheinung anmutet, legt dies
nahe"[46]. This comment may seem to be a bit "over the top", but it is not
completely wrong. In the same v. 7 where the angel speaks "as Jesus", he
also repeats the same words that had been used by the high-priests and the
Pharisees in 27:64 to refer to the resurrection, but that does not count
against the observation of Kratz; it would rather support the idea that
Matthew is "fusing things together".

   Kratz concludes his analysis with a rather broad and general reference to
the importance of the theme of God's reign and power in Matthew's gospel,
and what this power can do to human beings. This is correct, and the motif
can well have played a role in Matthew's understanding of what happens to
Jesus in the tomb[47]. But maybe the theme can also be narrowed a bit, just
to make it look "sharper" still. All the gospel authors are interested in how

---

[46] KRATZ, *Rettungswunder*, pp. 526-527. On the parallel in v. 7, see LUZ: "Der Engel
unterstreicht … nicht mehr die Ankündigung Jesu, nach Galiläa zu gehen, sonder seine ganze,
mit göttlicher Autorität gesprochene Botschaft" (*Matthäus*, p. 405). Luz compares it to Matt
24:25 ("die einzige mt Par."), where Jesus is speaking. On v. 10, cf. the succinct comment of
DAVIES – ALLISON: "The content again repeats the angelic message, v. 7" (*Matthew*, p. 670).
Actually, it is more than about content only; part of the wording is identical in both passages.
At times the angel even seems to be more confident than Jesus himself: see "I know" in v. 5
and compare with "Whom do you seek?" in John 20:14. On the possibility that John 20:11-
18 depends on Matt, see the detailed analyses by F. NEIRYNCK, *Les femmes au tombeau*, in
NTS 15 (1968) 168-190 and *John and the Synoptics: The Empty Tomb Stories*, in *NTS* 30
(1984) 161-187.
   [47] KRATZ, *Rettungswunder*, pp. 537-541 ("Auferweckung als Befreiung vom Tod").

Jesus sees himself in relation to the Father. Yet it would seem that Matthew is particularly interested in this motif when it comes to "rescuing" Jesus from any kind of danger, including imprisonment and death. In 4:6 Matthew agrees with Luke in quoting from the Psalm about how angels will assist and protect an endangered Christ threatened by the devil and balancing on the pinnacle of the Temple. In 26:53 he is the only one to insert in the story of the arrest of Jesus a verse that has him express his confidence that all this can be avoided, with the help of "legions of angels" God willing. The verse only underscores what the reader can sense about the outcome of the arrest that is to follow, and indeed already knows from 26:4 (par. Mark 14:2) and even long before that (Matt 12:14 par. Mark 3:6). It is when catastrophe has struck and all seems hopeless that the "rescue" finally happens, with an angel assisting. It all must have made sense for Matthew, and probably also for his readers[48].

III. TELLING THE WHOLE STORY – OR ALMOST SO

Walter and Kratz concluded that Matthew did not wish, or did not dare, to go "this one step too far"[49]. As said above, for the one, Matthew backs off from what he found in his tradition; for the other, he has set the first step towards such a description[50]. I would rather say that he tells it all, except for the final word, that the angel of the Lord has rescued or liberated Jesus from the tomb. Why does he not also take the last step? Was it really all so threatening or debilitating for the *kerygma* also to "visualise" the idea that God saves from beyond the tomb? But how that? Would it have been a weakness in the polemics with opponents? But again, how that? Describing God liberating his Beloved One from the death is hardly a weakness. It may be a somewhat underdeveloped or folkloristic way of pronouncing or representing the *kerygma*, but it is a way that many others have gone, already relatively soon after Matthew (the

[48] On purpose I have refrained from going into the difficult question of distinguishing between tradition and the part of Matthew's redaction in this whole section of 27:62-28:15. That there may well be a significant portion of redaction in the text has been argued by many. See NEIRYNCK (above n. 46); cf. also I. BROER, *Die Urgemeinde und das Grab Jesu: Eine Analyse der Grablegungsgeschichte im Neuen Testament* (SANT, 31), München, Kösel, 1972, pp. 69-79. If so, this obviously has a direct impact on the role such "broader" interests of Matthew may have played in composing the end sequence of his gospel.

[49] See KRATZ's "an die Grenzen des Erlaubten" (*Rettungswunder*, p. 534).

[50] "einen ersten Schritt in Richtung auf eine direkte Schilderung der Auferstehung Jesu" (*ibid.*).

Gospel of Peter!) and all through the history of art. It was not Matthew's
nor any other of the gospel accounts that have prevented this development. Moreover, with regard to Matthew, one would think it certainly is
less of a weakness in a text that is replete with "legendary" motifs and that
had just "described" how the dead come out of their tombs at the blast of
an earthquake.

I am afraid I do not have a ready-made answer for why Matthew refrained
from describing the resurrection itself. But I can point out one or two
things. There is quite some polemics and apologetics and quite some irony,
good and strong polemics and apologetics and irony, in the stories about
the guards. They seem to draw themselves ever deeper into trouble and all
they try to do as a cover-up is doomed to fail. Yet they escape punishment
and instead are even rewarded for their clumsiness, a motif that commentators have linked to Judas handling Jesus' arrest (accepting money!) or have
understood as a kind of parody of what it means to obey to a command[51].
There is irony all over here.

But the question remains: why go all the long way and then stop short
before the end? It looks as if Matthew has not spared his efforts to provide
the reader with all s/he needs to read the text as a rescue/release story; but
then he leaves it to the reader to fill in the full picture. Is not this also a
kind of irony? In any case, it works well within the larger framework of Matt
27:62-28:15. On the one hand, there are those who claim to have "seen all
that happened", but they have seen nothing and they do not know or
understand anything. On the other hand, there are those women who come
and see beyond their own expectation what has happened, but they are not
granted the privilege of explicitly being promoted to witnesses of Jesus' rescue from the tomb. And then there is also the reader, as a third party, who
is led by Matthew to expect that s/he will be rewarded with such a description – it is all carefully prepared for: the scene with the guard in 27:62-66,
the angel descending and opening the tomb in 28:2-4 –, but then the story
breaks off, or takes another turn, when the angel addresses the women and
informs them of what happened to Jesus. The break is between 28:4 and
28:5, and the hopes that might have been created about also hearing of the
rescue itself are shattered. And is not this again what irony is about: not to
tell the things that everyone expects you to tell, creating an expectation and

---

[51] For the first suggestion, see DAVIES – ALLISON, *Matthew*, p. 672. Pesch has qualified
the phrase ὡς ἐδιδάχθησαν in 28:15 as a " 'verstümmelte' Ausführungsformel" or a "defekte
Ausführungsformel"; see R. PESCH, *Eine alttestamentliche Ausführungsformel im Matthäus-
Evangelium*, in *BZ* 10 (1966) 220-245; 11 (1967) 79-95, pp. 91 and 94.

"deluding" the reader, almost till the very last moment, and then … leave it there? Matthew plays with motifs and tools that are at home in the genre of the rescue miracle; but the resurrection itself is not described, and should not be. Yet it must have "happened".

KU Leuven   Joseph Verheyden
Faculty of Theology
St-Michielsstraat 4/3101
B-3000 Leuven
Belgium

"BODILY RESURRECTION" OF JESUS IN MATTHEW?[1]

In the description of the conference to whose proceedings this paper wishes to contribute we find a phraseology that is very common when it comes to discussing "resurrection". The straightforward alternative "Religious Metaphor" *or* "Bodily Reality" seems to imply that one either has to accept that resurrection means a person coming back to life in the literal sense of a body of flesh and blood coming out of a tomb which in turn is left behind empty, or that one merely uses a metaphor without any background in life and human experience[2]. I think this alternative is flawed, it neither does justice to the complexity of the textual evidence nor to the metaphorical character of language in general.

There is not much in Matthew that provides information about the *anthropological* aspects of what the evangelist calls "resurrection" (27:53 ἔγερσις; 28:6.7 ἠγέρθη). In this paper we want to concentrate on the question of how Matthew pictures the resurrected Jesus. The few passages available provide us at least with some information to assess the proposed alternative "religious metaphor" or "bodily reality".

I. RESURRECTION IN MATTHEW OUTSIDE THE PASSION NARRATIVE

Before we examine the passion and resurrection narrative and deal with the question of the resurrected Jesus, we need to view three texts that are of particular interest.

1. I thank Wim Weren and Huub van de Sandt for a fruitful period in Tilburg studying Matthew together and for inviting me to this conference. I am also grateful to my Leiden colleagues Henk Jan de Jonge and Johannes Magliano-Tromp for their helpful comments.
2. Wim Weren, *Human Body and Life beyond Death in Matthew's Go*spel, in T. NICKLAS, – F.V. REITERER – J. VERHEYDEN (eds.), *The Human Body in Death and Resurrection* (Deuterocanonical and Cognate Literature, Yearbook 2009), Berlin – New York, De Gruyter, 2009, 267-283, pp. 267-268 starts with the same question but follows a different path and arrives at different conclusions than the ones proposed here.

1. Matt 10:28: Killing Body or Soul

Καὶ μὴ φοβεῖσθε ἀπὸ τῶν ἀποκτεννόντων τὸ σῶμα, τὴν δὲ ψυχὴν μὴ δυναμένων ἀποκτεῖναι· φοβεῖσθε δὲ μᾶλλον τὸν δυνάμενον καὶ ψυχὴν καὶ σῶμα ἀπολέσαι ἐν γεέννῃ.

This verse, part of a long instruction to the disciples in Matt 10:16-39 envisioning the possibility of martyrdom for members of the community (see also 5:11-12; 22:6; 23:34-36), represents one of the few passages that allow a glimpse into the evangelist's anthropological assumptions[3].

Although often seen as result of influence of Greek "dichotomic" popular philosophy[4], the short passage is witness of the age-old conviction that a person does not totally cease to exist in the moment of death, but that "something" survives to continue in a somewhat "lesser" form of existence in the underworld. This, of course is not exclusively "Greek", but can be found in the Hebrew Bible, too[5]. Matthew's use of σῶμα and ψυχή is in agreement with traditional, widely accepted popular belief and with language occurring in the Hebrew Bible about נֶפֶשׁ, just like naming the underworld γεέννα which obviously is not merely the place of temporal judgment but the final abode of all[6].

Matthew obviously sees a person as a combination of σῶμα *and* ψυχή. In our passage, σῶμα is seen as that aspect of a person which perishes when a person passes away. Σῶμα is left in the tomb to decay, adversaries have power over it and can kill it (ἀποκτεῖναι), all in contrast to ψυχή. Ψυχή, namely, remains, but it is not simply a separate part of the person, nor inherently immortal as in the Platonic tradition. It is not so much the "soul" in the traditional sense of a separate entity, but the person itself in its ability to continue its existence beyond the grave. As ψυχή, a person cannot be destroyed by humans, but it can be made accountable for its deeds and judged by God. Ψυχή carries the identity of the person on from his or her earthly existence until it comes to hover around in the underworld awaiting

---

3. I do not see why Luz thinks that the passage does not intend to make statements about anthropological matters or about life after death (U. Luz, *Das Evangelium nach Matthäus*, 2 Teilband [EKKNT, 1/2], Zürich, Benziger Verlag – Neukirchen-Vluyn, Neukirchener Verlag, 1990, p. 127).

4. E.g. Luz, *Das Evangelium nach Matthäus*, vol. 2, p. 126.

5. On how careful one has to be when it comes to classifying what "the" Greeks said about "resurrection" see S.E. Porter, *Resurrection. The Greeks and the New Testament*, in S.E. Porter – M.A. Hayes – D. Tombs (eds.), *Resurrection* (JSNTSup, 186), Sheffield, Sheffield University Press, 1999, pp. 52-81.

6. Luz, *Das Evangelium nach Matthäus*, vol. 2, p. 126.

and being confronted by divine judgment. Ψυχή means the same person, but in a different form of existence.

In the second half of the passage, Matthew warns the readers to fear "the one" (singular δυνάμενον in place of plural ἀποκτενόντων) who has the power to destroy both σῶμα and ψυχή in the underworld. Luz emphasizes that "the one" is nobody else but God himself[7] who in the end will judge all persons and send those who did not fear him to eternal destruction (what might happen to the other persons is not mentioned here). The change in verb marks an important difference: while "killing" in the first half of 10:28 only affects the σῶμα, but not the ψυχή, the second half of the sentence, however, clearly affects both σῶμα and ψυχή and implies a final, definitive extinction of a person's *entire* existence. This second, ultimate extinction is expressed with the term ἀπολέσαι. The fact that σῶμα is mentioned once more in the context of γέεννα emphasizes the totality of annihilation of a person, an event that also affects the body which was left in the tomb. The text, therefore, only distinguishes two phases, a temporal death through killing, and a final destruction in γέεννα.

2. Matt 14:26: Seeing Jesus on the Lake of Galilee

Οἱ δὲ μαθηταὶ ἰδόντες αὐτὸν ἐπὶ τῆς θαλάσσης περιπατοῦντα ἐταράχθησαν λέγοντες ὅτι φάντασμά ἐστιν, καὶ ἀπὸ τοῦ φόβου ἔκραξαν.

Another relevant passage is Matt 14:26. When the disciples saw Jesus walk across the Lake of Galilee they took him for a ghost (φάντασμα). A φάντασμα is a supernatural figure, dangerous, with blurred contours and unclear intentions (cf. Josephus, *Ant.* 1.131-133)[8]. It is no surprise to see the disciples react as they do: with panic (ταράττω) and screaming out in fear (ἀπὸ τοῦ φόβου ἔκραξαν). Jesus immediately answers the disciples' panic by talking to them (14:27) and assuring them that it is actually himself (ἐγώ εἰμι) and no apparition. It is the words Jesus speaks which convince the disciples of the identity of the one who has walked on the Lake a moment ago.

Of course, this is not a resurrection story, nor does the term σῶμα play any direct role in it. Instead, Matthew plays with literary elements of an

---

7. Luz, *Das Evangelium nach Matthäus*, vol. 2, p. 127.
8. W.D. Davies – D.C. Allison, *A Critical and Exegetical Commentary on the Gospel According to Saint Matthew.* Vol 2 (ICC), Edinburgh, T&T Clark, 1991, p. 505 propose the disciples might have thought they saw the "ghost of a dead Jesus", in any case φάντασμα "underlines the note of fear in the face of the extraordinary, the numinous".

epiphany[9]: the disciples see a supernatural figure, fall in panic and the situation is resolved by Jesus' self-revelation. The passage nevertheless adds to our inquiry because it demonstrates how Matthew reflects about the fact how easily humans can be led astray by their visual senses. Apparitions could easily confuse and betray those who are confronted with them. People could take for reality what in fact only deceives their senses. Jesus' appearance is not enough to confirm who he is, the disciples only recognize him and dispel their fear when he reveals himself and they hear his *words*. This is a topic that will later reappear in the post-resurrection encounters between Jesus and some of his disciples.

3. Matt 22:29-32: Post-Resurrection Existence is Being like Angels

Ἐν γὰρ τῇ ἀναστάσει οὔτε γαμοῦσιν οὔτε γαμίζονται, ἀλλ᾽ ὡς ἄγγελοι ἐν τῷ οὐρανῷ εἰσιν.

Matt 22:30 – embedded in a dispute about resurrection between Jesus and the Sadducees – is one of the few passages in Matthew where the evangelist makes a more explicit statement about the way and form in which the resurrected exist after resurrection. The text, therefore, reveals an important element of Matthew's "anthropology", even though the term σῶμα does not occur.

The unusual singular οὐρανός (cf. 28:2; 24:30; 26:64) – in difference to the typically Matthean plural (cf. 18:10; 24:36 and, e.g., wherever the "Father" is connected to οὐρανός) – is "outsider language" and also corresponds to the singular ἐν ἀναστάσει[10]. Its rhetorical purpose is to contrast the earthly existence with the life "in" the resurrection when the resurrected will no longer marry nor be married but still remain under God's power (δύναμις τοῦ θεοῦ). Resurrection is understood as an act of God's power and his loyalty to the descendants of Abraham, Isaac and Jacob, coupled with a transformation of the resurrected person (note that σῶμα is not mentioned!) into a form of existence that is *like* (ὡς) that of "angels in heaven". Just as God has the power to finally destroy a ψυχή (10:28), he is able to raise the dead into a new existence. Not to marry nor be married can be taken as *pars pro toto* underlining the fundamental difference between pre- and post-resurrection existence. Jesus' opponents are wrong to assume that post-resurrection existence will be nothing else than a continuation of the earthly way of life, it is

9. J. GNILKA, *Das Matthäusevangelium* (HTKNT, 1/2), vol. 2, Freiburg – Basel – Wien, Herder, 1988, p. 13; DAVIES – ALLISON, *Matthew*, vol 2, p. 506 on epiphany.

10. J.T. PENNINGTON, *Heaven and Earth in the Gospel of Matthew* (NovTSup, 126), Leiden – Boston, Brill, 2007, pp. 144-146.

their position that is absurd[11]. All earthly needs and dealings will be over ἐν ἀνάστασιν[12]. In any case, the resurrected will have been transformed into an existence which for Matthew can only be compared to that of heavenly angels. Nothing explicit is said about the corporeal implications of this transformation – apart from the fact that angels do not marry[13]. It is likely to assume, but nowhere directly expressed in Matthew, that the resurrected Jesus also shares an angelic way of existence.

To sum up: Matthew only allows short glimpses into how he pictured the existence of persons that were resurrected. He is convinced that resurrection is an act of God's unlimited power, only parallel to God's ability to annihilate a person in judgment (10:28), and that resurrection implies some kind of transformation of the resurrected. What this implies exactly, Matthew is only able to express with the help of an analogy that emphasizes the difference to pre-resurrection existence more than the continuity (22:30). Matthew also indicated how his disciples were able to identify a person as "authentic Jesus" in dubious situations: by hearing his voice and recognizing his message (14:26).

II. The Resurrection Narratives

In the narratives about Jesus' passion and resurrection (Matt 26-28), a couple of features reappear that already were present in other contexts in the gospel. So, even if Matthew does not present a comprehensive anthropology and does not even come close to the degree of reflection apparent in Paul (esp. in 1Cor 15), his statements on resurrection can be expected to have a certain consistency and cohesion[14]. Let us take a closer look at some relevant passages and start with how Matthew deals with the empty tomb of Jesus.

11. Luz, *Das Evangelium nach Matthäus*, vol. 3, p. 264.
12. Davies – Allison, *Matthew*, vol. 3, p. 227 rightly see ἐν as not referring to the moment when this happens, but as expressing the modality of the new existence "in the resurrected condition (of the just)".
13. On the aspect of angelic sexuality see Davies – Allison, *Matthew*, vol. 3, pp. 227-230. Parallels like *2 Bar* 51:10 suggest, however, that an existence "like angels" implies the ability to travel freely and change one's shape at will, see D.J. Harrington, *Afterlife Expectations in Pseudo-Philo, 4Ezra, and 2Baruch, and Their Implications for the New Testament*, in R. Bieringer – V. Koperski – B. Lataire (eds.), *Resurrection in the New Testament* (BETL 165), Leuven – Paris – Dudley MA, Peeters, 2002, 21-34, pp. 30-32. Jesus' change of place from Jerusalem to the Galilee seems to fit into this pattern, the change of shape of course not.
14. See Weren, *Human Body*, p. 281.

1. Matt 27:62-66; 28:11-15: The Empty Tomb

In this passage of "apologetics and polemics at the same time"[15], Matthew is witness of the fact that the tomb – a heirloom of pre-Matthean tradition – has itself become a problem (27:62-66; 28:11-15). Matthew demonstrates that the empty tomb by no means was a self-evident phenomenon, nor was it regarded as proof of a particular way or type of resurrection[16]. Matthew does not explicitly call the tomb "empty", rather do the angels turn the readers' attention to the spot "where he had been laid" (28:6 ἔκειτο) and thus confirm that "he is no longer there" (28:6 οὐκ ἔστιν ὧδε). But how could that happen? The dispute among the high priests, Pharisees and elders (27:62; 28:11-12) demonstrates that the fact that Jesus was "no longer here" could be explained and interpreted in various ways. The tomb narrative provides no information about *how precisely* Jesus resurrected nor about *how* we have to perceive the resurrected Jesus. Matthew, it seems, is not interested in these questions, very much unlike Paul, who – in response to a totally different debate in his own community and on the basis of a different cultural background – is pushed by his Corinthian opponents to develop the concept of "pneumatic corporeality" of the resurrected (1Cor 15, speaking about σάρξ and πνεῦμα etc.). Nothing of that kind of reflection is apparent in Matthew, it should therefore not be read into his narrative either.

And still, Jesus' "body" *does* play a role in Matthew. For the first time in the passion narrative, Matthew in 27:58 uses this word when he describes Joseph of Arimathaea asking Pilate to get permission to bury the σῶμα of Jesus. This usage resembles what we have already seen in 10:28 where Matthew makes a distinction between σῶμα which is perishable and can be killed, and ψυχή which will not suffer this fate before the final judgment. In 27:58 ψυχή is not mentioned, because the text is not interested here in discussing what "element" of Jesus should be taken to continue after death. The focus is on the burial, and it is nothing but the σῶμα which could be buried to eventually decay in the grave. It is clear, therefore, that in 27:58 σῶμα refers to *Jesus as corpse*, the more so, since Matthew already stressed how Jesus – after crying out for the last time – has "given up" the spirit (27:50 ἀφῆκεν τὸ πνεῦμα), his vitality, his life. The fact that Matthew demonstrates that the tomb was empty can only mean that Jesus took his σῶμα with him when he resurrected: it did not decay, otherwise it could still have been seen resting at the place where he had been buried (28:6).

---

15. DAVIES – ALLISON, *Matthew*, vol. 3, p. 652.
16. According to WEREN, *Human Body*, p. 274 an "ambiguous phenomenon".

The dead Jesus *is* σῶμα – but the resurrected, what is he? Matthew doesn't tell. We can only note that the term σῶμα is no more used after 27:58 and draw our conclusions from it. Though it can be assumed by implication that Jesus took his body with him when he rose from the grave, nowhere is the resurrected Jesus explicitly called σῶμα; instead Matthew identifies him in his narrative only by *his name* or uses a *pronoun*. And further: Nowhere does Matthew use a single, particular noun to describe the resurrected Jesus, he rather *narrates* what the resurrected Jesus did and how people reacted towards him. But before we examine that, we need to take a look at a passage that adds to our picture of how Matthew uses σῶμα.

2. Matt 27:52-53: The Dead Coming out of their Graves

An interesting contrast to Jesus as σῶμα is presented by the Matthean *Sondergut* tradition about the appearance of many (πολλά, not all!) bodies (σώματα) of deceased saints (κεκοιμημένοι ἅγιοι) coming out of their graves (27:52-53)[17]. Davies and Allison rightly call this episode an "explosion of the supernatural"[18]. The resurrection of the "many bodies of the holy ones" is joined together in a list with other cosmic portents, such as the rending of the temple veil, the shaking of the earth or the splitting of the rocks (Matt 27:51). That the resurrection of the σώματα was seen as precisely such a cosmic portent and manifestation of God's power, but not as the beginning of the eschatological resurrection (which is in the background of, e.g., 22:30) is stressed by the fact that it is taken up into the immediate context of Jesus' death[19], although according to Matthew it happened chronologically *after* Jesus' resurrection (27:53 μετά). The text is a purposeful commentary of the evangelist and should not be interpreted away as a later gloss. It probably indicates more than a *chronological* relationship between the resurrection of Jesus and that of the σώματα. Referring to various allusions in the rest of the gospel, Gurtner sees the opening of the graves as demonstration of the life-giving power of Jesus' death and emphasizes the visionary character of the

---

17. WEREN, *Human Body*, pp. 275-277; LUZ, *Das Evangelium nach Matthäus*, vol. 4, pp. 364-371; DAVIES – ALLISON, *Matthew*, vol. 3, pp. 633-635; D.M. GURTNER, *The Torn Veil: Matthew's Exposition of the Death of Jesus* (SNTSMS, 139), Cambridge, Cambridge University Press, 2007, pp. 144-152; C. McAFEE MOSS, *The Zechariah Tradition and the Gospel of Matthew* (BZNW, 156), Berlin – New York, De Gruyter, 2008, pp. 197-201.

18. DAVIES – ALLISON, *Matthew*, vol. 3, p. 639.

19. Cf. GURTNER, *The Torn Veil*, p. 145 who also prefers a "theophanic reading" as portent over an "apocalyptic" one, but see his definition of "apocalyptic" (*Ibid.*, pp. 152-160). On the visionary character of the passage and its implied sequence of events see GURTNER, *The Torn Veil*, pp. 160-169.

narrative (with reference to Ezek 37LXX; Zech 14LXX) which makes trans-
cendent realities behind the scenes of tragic events evident to the reader[20].
Luz rightly points out that only *many* of the "holy ones" raise from their
graves, but not *all*, and concludes from this phrasing that the passage should
not be understood "direkt in apokalyptischem Sinn als Schilderung der
endzeitlichen Auferstehung *der* Gerechten"[21]. Matthew does not look to the
future in 27:52-53, but shows with the help of Ezek 37LXX; Zech 14LXX how
Jesus' crucifixion can be understood as the crucial turning point of the eschatological ages *now*[22].

Although Matthew uses the word ἐγείρω for both resurrections, and
despite the fact that both "resurrected" are said to have appeared to others
(27:53 φαινίζειν; 28:7 ὄψεσθε; 28:17 ἰδόντες), there still are notable differences:

- Unlike in the case of Jesus, Matt 27:52-53 describes *that* the graves
  opened and the σώματα ἁγίων climbed out, thereby going further in
  detail than later in his own narrative about Jesus. Here, we *do* have a
  description of how Matthew pictured resurrection. But why does Matthew later refrain from such a detailed description when it comes to Jesus?
- Unlike in the case of Jesus, Matt 27:52-53 speaks about the σώματα even
  after their resurrection, i. e. when they entered the Holy City and were
  seen by many. We just saw that Matthew does not name the resurrected
  Jesus σῶμα. Why such a distinction?
- Unlike in the case of Jesus, no angel appears in the context of Matt
  27:52-53. The angel, therefore, is not necessary to accomplish "resurrection". He is not the initiator of Jesus' resurrection, but has a different
  role: he is the messenger of the fact that Jesus is not longer in the tomb.

The differences can be explained and the questions above answered by
looking at the tradition-historical setting of the passage[23]. Although the text
speaks of "holy ones" and their resurrection in time, nothing is said that they
were murdered and that their resurrection was the way how God vindicated

20. GURTNER, *The Torn Veil*, pp. 150-151. Weren, on the other hand, sees Matt 27:51-
54 as a "preparation for the story in Matt 28:1-10 about Jesus' own resurrection" (*Human
Body*, p. 283); DAVIES – ALLISON, *Matthew*, vol. 3, pp. 640-641.
    21. LUZ, *Das Evangelium nach Matthäus*, vol. 4, pp. 365-366 who interprets the appear-
ance of the holy ones in the holy city as prediction of punishment for the fact that they have
crucified the righteous Jesus (see Matt 23:37-39; 27:25), an observation I find convincing.
Cf. Gurtner's careful discussion (*The Torn Veil*, pp. 152-160).
    22. See DAVIES – ALLISON, *Matthew*, vol. 3, p. 639.
    23. See LUZ, *Das Evangelium nach Matthäus*, vol. 4, pp. 364-371 and Dale Allison's
article in this volume.

them. The passage, therefore, lacks much of the common martyrological connotations. At the same time, there is no mention of transformation like in 22:30 either, being only the bodies that rose, and one has difficulties to imagine how Matthew wanted this surrealistic scenery to be pictured. Rending of the veil in the Temple[24], earthquake and splitting of rocks are part of the cosmic, supernatural dimensions of Jesus' death illustrating its turning-point character, although they do not immediately usher in a wider, cosmic catastrophe of the world as we know it[25]. To the contrary: the Holy City still stands and people (πολλοί) seem to go about their business, as well as the centurion and his soldiers (27:54), when they encounter the resurrected σώματα. Matthew leaves the question open what happened with the resurrected σώματα after they were seen: did he think they would die again and wait until the final resurrection[26]? No matter what answer one might prefer, I am inclined to suspect that their σώματα are not different from the bodies they had before[27].

Lacking explicit martyrological and immediate eschatological connotations, Matt 27:54-55 can only be understood as portent whose surreal and supernatural character underline the divine nature of the crucifixion[28] which impresses the centurion and his guards so much that they acknowledge the divine nature of the person who died such a death under such terrible circumstances[29].

24. On this motif see GURTNER, *The Torn Veil*, pp. 97-202.
25. Much to the contrary to how I read the text, DAVIES – ALLISON, *Matthew*, vol. 3, p. 639, see these portents as evidence that "the Day of the Lord dawns on Golgotha: the divine judgment descends and the first-fruits of the resurrection are gathered. The end of Jesus is the end of the world in miniature". Apart from the fact that I am at a loss to grasp how the world can end "in miniature", I only find in Matthew that the eschatological judgment takes place when Jesus returns as Son of Man (and then not only in miniature, but certainly also inaugurated by cosmic portents similar to the ones mentioned in context with crucifixion). Jesus' crucifixion is Jesus' "darkest hour" (cf. LUZ, *Das Evangelium nach Matthäus*, vol. 4, p. 347), only to be vindicated by God himself who raises Jesus from his grave and enthrones him as ruler of the world for all times. It is in this function in which he will later return as judge. To connect crucifixion with eschatological judgment seems to me more a fruit of later Christian reflection than Matthew's own understanding.
26. DAVIES – ALLISON, *Matthew*, vol. 3, p. 634.
27. Different with interesting arguments WEREN, *Human Body*, p. 277.
28. LUZ, *Das Evangelium nach Matthäus*, vol. 4, p. 365.
29. R. BAUCKHAM, *Descents to the Underworld*, in ID. (ed.), *The Fate of the Dead: Studies on the Jewish and Christian Apocalypses* (NovTSup, 93), Leiden – Boston – Köln, Brill, 1998, 9-48, p. 39 sees the passage as related to "the widespread early extra-canonical tradition that Christ released the Old Testament saints from Hades", but states that it "makes no explicit reference to Christ's activity in Hades". He therefore concludes that the passage "was used to express the eschatological significance of the death of Christ, by which the power of death has been broken".

3. Conceptualizing the Resurrected Jesus

Let us move one step further. Even if Matthew *was* of the opinion that Jesus' bones were no longer present in the tomb after his resurrection, he obviously did not suppose that Jesus had returned to life as we know it and in a body that we all share. But how then? A couple of observations about Jesus' post-resurrection existence might help answer this question:

According to Matthew, the angel only descended from heaven and removed the capstone precisely at the moment when the women were arriving at the tomb (28:2). This is odd and notably in contrast to what we can read in Mark: Here, the stone *had* already been removed *before* the women had arrived, and it is very plausible that Mark implies that Jesus had risen and was gone long before the women reached the tomb (Mark 16:4 κεκύλισται). Not so in Matthew. If we assume that the Matthean construction implies a chronology of events, we are led to believe that the grave was opened *when* the women arrived, but that Jesus had risen and left the tomb *before* the stone was removed and *before* the women arrived (28:2)! This *is* odd, but not impossible and in line with Jewish traditions about the death of martyrs[30]. They, too, are *directly* resurrected to heaven as an act of vindication. At the same time, the resurrection directly out of the grave is Jesus' first step to his inthronization[31]. Many texts also indicate that these martyrs

---

30. DAVIES – ALLISON, *Matthew*, vol. 3, p. 638 might be right in their opinion that Jesus did not die a "noble death", but I do not accept their verdict: "Of Jesus' heroic valour and faith we hear nothing". More balanced LUZ, *Das Evangelium nach Matthäus*, vol. 4, p. 347: "Jesus wird in den Farben eines biblischen Gerechten dargestellt, der leidet, mit seinem Gott ringt und ihn sogar anklagt". The centurion's reaction (Matt 27:54), e.g., would not be understandable if he had not seen Jesus' "heroic valour and faith" behind Jesus' terrible *Gottverlassenheit* on the cross. GURTNER, *The Torn Veil*, p. 128 rightly points out that Jesus' death carries a positive value for Matthew "as an act of willing obedience to his father". On the Jewish martyr tradition which is behind Matthew's narrative see esp. J.W. VAN HENTEN, *The Maccabean Martyrs as Saviours of the Jewish People* (JSJSup, 57), Leiden, Brill, 1997; J.W. VAN HENTEN – B.A.G.M. DEHANDSCHUTTER – H.J.W. VAN DER KLAAUW (eds.), *Die Entstehung der jüdischen Martyrologie* (StPB, 38), Leiden, Brill, 1989; H.J. DE JONGE, *De opstanding van Jezus: De joodse traditie achter een christelijke belijdenis*, in T. BAARDA – H.J. DE JONGE – M.J.J. MENKEN (eds.), *Jodendom en vroeg christendom: Continuïteit en discontinuïteit*, Kampen, Kok, 1991, pp. 47-61; H.J. DE JONGE, *Visionary Experience and the Historical Origins of Christianity*, in BIERINGER – KOPERSKI – LATAIRE, *Resurrection in the New Testament*, 35-53, pp. 46-48; M. DE JONGE, *Jesus' Death for Others and the Death of the Maccabean Martyrs*, in ID., *Jewish Eschatology, Early Christian Christology and the Testaments of the Twelve Patriarchs. Collected Essays* (NovTSup, 63), Leiden, Brill, 1991, pp. 125-134; U. KELLERMANN, *Auferstanden in den Himmel. II Makkabäer 7 und die Auferstehung der Märtyrer* (SBS, 95), Stuttgart, Katholisches Bibelwerk, 1979.

31. Cf. also A.Y. Collins' important study on Jesus' apotheosis and his empty tomb in Mark (*Ancient Notions of Transferral and Apotheosis in Relation to the Empty Tomb Story in Mark*, in T.K. SEIM – J. ÖKLAND [eds.], *Metamorphoses: Resurrection, Body and Transformative Practices in Early Christianity* [Ekstasis, 1], Berlin – New York, De Gruyter, 2009, pp. 41-57).

are transformed when taken up into heaven: most expressing the new way of existence after vindication by using a terminology connected to light (Matt 13:43; Dan 23:3; *L.A.B.* 33:5; *4 Ezra* 7:97-98.125; *2 Bar* 51:5.10), others imply that the body is also affected (2 Macc 7)[32]. From there they can (but need not) return to earth and appear to humans. It is this pattern that forms the background of Matthew's narrative.

- In this context, the difference between Jesus and the σώματα ἁγίων is important to note. The σώματα ἁγίων only rose and climbed out of their graves *as* their graves opened (27:52-53). In 27:52-53, the open graves were the prerequisite of the dead coming out and being able to walk around. Jesus, however, has obviously risen *before* the grave opened. In his case, the opening of the grave does not make way for the resurrected to leave the place of burial, but rather allows access for the women to let them see the place where Jesus rested before he rose and left (28:6). The open grave proves that the grave was empty and that Jesus had risen. How exactly Jesus *managed* to rise and leave a closed grave is not explained. This is clearly not *Matthew's* question, no matter how odd *we* might find that, and his silence should make us careful not to apply our own categories and concepts to an event that Matthew himself has no words or wish to explain.
- Neither the author nor the women or, therefore, the readers are presented as witnesses of Jesus' resurrection. The women witness the angel, not Jesus at the grave. Only the guards commissioned at the request of the High Priests and Pharisees were present (27:65), but they have no role in the drama of Jesus' resurrection (28:13) and were terrified to death when the angel appeared (28:4). Matthew does present them as liars and participants of the deceit of the High Priests and the elders (28:12-15)[33].

---

32. J. ZANGENBERG, *Trockene Knochen, himmlische Seligkeit: Todes- und Jenseitsvorstellungen in Qumran und im Alten Judentum*, in A. BERLEJUNG – B. JANOWSKI (eds.), *Tod und Jenseits im Alten Israel und in seiner Umwelt: Theologische, religionsgeschichtliche, archäologische und ikonographische Aspekte* (FAT, 64), Tübingen, Mohr Siebeck, 2009, 655-689, pp. 676-677. The relatively high interest in the corporeality of the resurrected martyrs and epiphanies of heroes in 2 Macc might indeed also partly result from the text's critique of Greek ideals of body and masculinity and the strong motif of recompense which also includes the restoration of the body, see B. SCHMITZ, *Auferstehung und Epiphanie: Jenseits- und Körperkonzepte im Zweiten Makkabäerbuch*, in NICKLAS – REITERER – VERHEYDEN – BRAUN, *The Human Body*, 105-142, pp. 132-36.

33. W.J.C. WEREN, *"His Disciples Stole Him Away" (Mt 28,13): A Rival Interpretation of Jesus' Resurrection*, in BIERINGER – KOPERSKI – LATAIRE, *Resurrection in the New Testament*, pp. 147-163.

– This is in marked contrast to the role of the guards under the command of the centurion who watched Jesus' crucifixion. It was these guards who saw the earthquake and the subsequent "events" (27:54: τὰ γενόμενα): earthquake, splitting of rocks and resurrected σώματα and – unlike their counterparts commissioned at the request of the High Priests and Pharisees (28:11 τὰ γενόμενα) – understood the proper meaning of them, drew the right conclusion and confessed that Jesus indeed was God's Son (27:54), thereby not only underlining the portent character of the cosmic events described before, but also functioning as welcome model to be imitated by the readers. Negative examples are the passers-by (27:39-40), chief priests and elders (27:41-43), as well as the bandits who were crucified with him (27:44) who all ridiculed Jesus. It seems that such contrasting types are much more important for Matthew than previously noted. With the centurion and his guards (and others) as witnesses, the crucifixion is a public event, while the resurrection is not.

– Matthew does not know of any apparition of Jesus at the grave itself, he will be seen only later "on the way" when the women hurried to the disciples (28:9-10). Jesus' connection to the grave, therefore, is definitively over.

– When the resurrected Jesus encounters people, their reaction is straightforward: they can see him, hear him, even touch him and obviously recognize him, but it is equally clear that this new existence is not a mere continuation of the old. In both cases Jesus responds with a command (28:9.19). Once the women recognize Jesus, they prostrate before him and embrace his feet – a gesture of submission and the clear proof that Jesus, despite the fact that he as an executed person now talking to them, is not a φάντασμα: the women recognize Jesus immediately. Moreover, ghosts have no feet[34]. Allison may be right that this passage also contains an apologetic moment: the fact that Jesus has feet clearly shows that he is really risen, but how much that says about his "corporeality" is not further explained. The fact that the resurrected Jesus "appeared" and "was seen" by others does in itself not tell anything about the way in which he was resurrected[35].

34. On the background and purpose of the motif see D.C. ALLISON, *Touching Jesus' Feet (Matt 28:9)*, in ID. (ed.), *Studies in Matthew: Interpretation Past and Present*, Grand Rapids, MI, Baker Academic, 2005, pp. 107-116.

35. Cf. D. ZELLER, *Erscheinungen Verstorbener im griechisch-römischen Bereich*, in BIERINGER – KOPERSKI – LATAIRE, *Resurrection in the New Testament*, 1-19, p. 19.

— When the eleven disciples see Jesus in Galilee, they also prostrate before him, but some have doubts. The question is not why some disciples came to doubt[36], but why the women did *not*: because of the angel who explained to them what had happened. On the mountain in Galilee, however, there was no angel, only the resurrected Jesus himself. It is very plausible that the disciples express doubts of Matthew's own audience about how one is to understand that Jesus resurrected. No matter what people found problematic, all questions of identity and continuity are settled once Jesus starts *talking* in a very similar way as on the Lake in 14:27: θαρσεῖτε (cf. 28:9 χαίρετε; 28:10 μὴ φοβεῖσθε). It is the continuity of the teaching from one mountain to the other, from the mountain of the Sermon to the one of the Commission, and the command to make all peoples Jesus' disciples and baptize them, nothing else, which answers the question about the identity of the preacher and the continuity of the resurrected. This is also the way how the readers are to picture the resurrected Jesus and how they should understand that he will not depart from his followers again.

III. The Resurrection of Jesus in Matthew: "Bodily", "Metaphorical" or What?

The Matthean perception of the resurrected Jesus is probably not so different from that of Paul. True, Paul says explicitly that the risen one had a body, although a spiritual one, whereas Matthew does not speak about σῶμα in connection to the resurrected Jesus, let alone about the nature of that body. However, just like Paul, Matthew must have thought of Jesus after resurrection as a person living with God in heaven (24:30), i.e. in some heavenly existence and form, who later appeared to his disciples from heaven. What is clear is that Jesus' form of existence, while still being "the same person" as before his crucifixion, has changed. How we have to conceptualize this existence is not fully explained: He is not a σῶμα as before, nor a ψυχή of the kind that exists in γεέννα, nor a φάντασμα. The real difference between Matthew and Paul lies in their idea about what happened to Jesus' *earthly* body after he had risen. Paul does not say and probably did not think it to have left the tomb (1Cor 15:3)[37]; Matthew, on the other hand, believed that

36. Weren might well be right when he draws a line to Matt 14:26 and writes that the doubts resulted from the fact that some disciples did not immediately recognize Jesus (*Human Body*, p. 273).
37. Contrary to this M. HENGEL, *Das Begräbnis Jesu bei Paulus und die leibliche Auferstehung aus dem Grabe*, in F. AVEMARIE – H. LICHTENBERGER (eds.), *Auferstehung – Resurrection*.

it *had* left the tomb and had been taken up unto heaven. But according to Matthew, Jesus' σῶμα does not come back on earth in a way described in 27:52-53, but he appears in a "supernatural" existence for which the term σῶμα, as Matthew uses it elsewhere, is no longer fully appropriate.

The direction of Jesus' change of existence becomes clear if one looks at the end of the gospel. The resurrected Jesus exists in a form that makes clear that he is still the same who has taught the disciples before crucifixion (contrary to φάντασμα, a mere "as if"-resurrection) and that he, although being recognizable and touchable, will not perish anymore (denying the possibility to call him σῶμα). Jesus has attained that form of existence which enables him to remain with his disciples until the consummation of the world (28:20). It is a unique form, entirely subject to the one purpose of Jesus' resurrection that Matthew envisioned. Functionally, Jesus is now enthroned as universal ruler, bestowed with the power over heaven and earth, and whose message is now carried around the world.

Matthew's last sentence clarifies a second point: The end of the world has not yet come with Jesus' resurrection (or the one of the σώματα). Nowhere do we find anything that suggests that Matthew perceived Jesus' resurrection as the first, initiating step of the final, eschatological resurrection. Nor is Jesus' resurrection in Matthew connected to the coming resurrection of the believers. Matthew's focus is entirely on the fact that Jesus is enthroned as ruler of the world who – after his resurrection – is now able to remain "with you all days" (ἐγὼ μεθ' ὑμῶν εἰμι πάσας τὰς ἡμέρας), making the announcement of the Immanuel at the beginning of the gospel (1:22-23) a reality for all time, and emphasizing that Jesus will be present and recognizable when and as long as his disciples follow his word (18:20; 28:20). I agree with Wim Weren when he writes: "(A)fter his death, Jesus is present in the circle of his followers. His renewed life is bestowed on him by God, who has called people into being and who has the creative power of making human beings rise up from dust and ashes"[38]. But I cannot see that Matthew connects these expectations to Jesus' bodily existence *post resurrectionem*, nor does the evangelist take recourse to statements about Jesus' corporeality to counter suspicions that the resurrected might not be the crucified, did not really die or was only reanimated[39]. None of these

---

The Fourth Durham-Tübingen Research Symposium Resurrection, Transfiguration and Exaltation in Old Testament, Ancient Judaism and Early Christianity (Tübingen, September 1999) (WUNT, 135), Tübingen, Mohr Siebeck, 2001, pp. 79-91.

38. WEREN, *Human Body*, p. 282.

39. DAVIES – ALLISON, *Matthew*, vol. 3, p. 650 see the phrasing of Matt 27:58 as indication that Matthew "was not much concerned with the objection that Jesus did not die on the cross".

issues seems to be Matthew's concerns. I rather suspect that Weren reads modern concepts of "body" into the gap that opens up for modern readers because of the simple fact that the resurrected Jesus is never called σῶμα. But there *is* no "gap", and we should be cautious here and ask ourselves if our own questions really were Matthew's[41]. For Matthew, σῶμα is a term of the *pre*-resurrection Jesus, he has other means to explain how the *post*-resurrection Jesus exists.

Matthew's narrative has its own profile and presents its own view of the resurrected Jesus. It is but one voice in the early Christian choir about how to picture Jesus' resurrection, which in itself is only one part of a vast and polyphone symphony of Jewish concepts about the so-called "resurrection of the dead". Each singer in this choir emphasizes what is important for him. The alternative "bodily" or "metaphorical" does not quite hit the point of what Matthew has to say, both concepts and especially the way they are contrasted with each other are modern and as a whole miss the mark[42]. For Matthew it suffices that his readers know that Jesus really rose from the grave, that he is enthroned as ruler over the world and that his followers know that he will be with them whenever they meet in his name.

Institute of Religious Studies   Jürgen K. Zangenberg
Faculty of Humanities
Matthias de Vrieshof 1
2311 BZ Leiden
The Netherlands

40. Weren admits that fact himself: "That the human body is also involved in this resurrection is not explicitly stated", but then continues to search for implications that it nevertheless was (*Human Body*, p. 281). I agree with D.C. Allison on how to deal with such difficulties and see the problem "in the eye of the beholder" (*Deconstructing Matthew*, in Id. (ed.), *Studies in Matthew. Interpretation Past and Present*, Grand Rapids, MI, Baker Academic, 2005, 237-249, p. 249).

41. Weren speaks of a "doctrine about bodily resurrection" of which only elements were used by Matthew (*Human Body*, p. 281). I doubt that such a "doctrine" ever existed, see Zangenberg, *Trockene Knochen, himmlische Seligkeit*.

42. On the hermeneutical aspects see also Claudia Setzer's article in this volume.

BIBLIOGRAPHY

ALEXANDER, P.S., *Jesus and the Golden Rule*, in J.H. CHARLESWORTH – L.L. JOHNS (eds.), *Hillel and Jesus: Comparative Studies of Two Major Religious Leaders*, Minneapolis, MN, Fortress, 1997, pp. 363-388.

ALLEN, W.C., *A Critical and Exegetical Commentary on the Gospel according to St Matthew* (ICC), Edinburgh, T&T Clark, 1907.

ALLISON, D.C., JR., *Deconstructing Matthew*, in ID. (ed.), *Studies in Matthew: Interpretation Past and Present*, Grand Rapids, MI, Baker Academic, 2005, pp. 237-249.

——, *Did the Evangelists Believe Their Own Stories?*, in ID., *Constructing Jesus: Memory and Imagination*, Grand Rapids, MI, Baker Academic, 2010.

——, *The End of the Ages Has Come: An Early Interpretation of the Death and Resurrection of Jesus* (Studies on the New Testament and Its World), Edinburgh, T. & T. Clark, 1987.

——, *The Intertextual Jesus: Scripture in Q*, Valley Forge, PA, Trinity Press International, 2000.

——, *Matt 27:51-53 and the Descent ad inferos* in P. LAMPE – M. MAYORDOMO – M. SATO (eds.), *Neutestamentliche Exegese im Dialog: Hermeneutik – Wirkungsgeschichte – Matthäusevangelium*, Neukirchen, Neukirchener Verlag, 2008, pp. 335-355.

——, *Memory and Invention: How Much History?*, in ID., *Constructing Jesus: Memory, Imagination and History*, Grand Rapids, MI, Baker Academic, 2010, pp. 435-462.

——, *The New Moses: A Matthean Typology*, Minneapolis, MN, Fortress, 1993.

——, *Resurrecting Jesus: The Earliest Christian Tradition and Its Interpreters*, New York, T & T Clark, 2005.

——, *Touching Jesus' Feet (Matt 28:9)*, in ID. (ed.), *Studies in Matthew: Interpretation Past and Present*, Grand Rapids, MI, Baker Academic, 2005, pp. 107-116.

AMIR, Y., *Die Zehn Gebote bei Philon von Alexandrien*, in ID. (ed.), *Die Hellenistische Gestalt des Judentums bei Philon von Alexandrien* (Forschungen zum Jüdisch-Christlichen Dialog, 5), Neukirchen-Vluyn, Neukirchener Verlag d. Erziehungsvereins, 1983, pp. 131- 163.

AUS, R.D., *The Death, Burial, and Resurrection of Jesus, and the Death, Burial, and Translation of Moses in Judaic Tradition* (Studies in Judaism), Lanham, University Press of America, 2008.

——, *Samuel, Saul and Jesus: Three Early Palestinian Jewish Christian Haggadoth* (SFSHJ, 105), Atlanta, Scholars Press, 1994.

BACHER, W., *Die Agada der Tannaiten*, Vol. 1, Strassburg, Trübner, 1884; repr. Berlin, De Gruyter, 1965-1966.

BARRETT, C.K., *The Gospel according to St. John*, Philadelphia, PA, Westminster, ²1978.

BARTSCH, H.-W., *Die Passions- und Ostergeschichten bei Matthäus*, in ID. (ed.), *Entmythologisierende Auslegung: Aufsätze aus den Jahren 1940 bis 1960*, Hamburg, Herbert Reich, 1962, pp. 80-92.

BAUCKHAM, R., *Descents to the Underworld*, in ID. (ed.), *The Fate of the Dead: Studies on the Jewish and Christian Apocalypses* (NovTSup, 93), Leiden – Boston – Köln, Brill, 1998, pp. 9-48.

BAUMGARTEN, M., *The Acts of the Apostles: Or the History of the Church in the Apostolic Age*, Vol.1, Edinburgh, T. & T. Clark, 1854.

BAXTER, W.S., *Mosaic Imagery in the Gospel of Matthew*, in *Trinity Journal* 20 (1999) 69-83.

BEARD, M., *The Roman Triumph*, Cambridge, MA, Harvard University Press – London, Belknap Press, 2007.

BEARE, F.W., *The Gospel according to Matthew*, Oxford, Blackwell, 1981.

BENDEMANN, R. von, *"Lebensgeist kam in sie…": Der Ezechielzyklus von Dura Europos und die Rezeption von Eze 37 in der Apk des Johannes: Ein Beitrag zum Verhältnisproblem von Ikonizität und Narrativität*, in A. WEISSENRIEDER – F. WENDT – P. VON GEMÜNDEN (eds.), *Picturing the New Testament: Studies in Visual Images* (WUNT, 193), Tübingen, Mohr Siebeck, 2005, pp. 253-286.

BERGER, K., *Die Gesetzesauslegung Jesu: Ihr historischer Hintergrund im Judentum und im Alten Testament*, Vol.1 (WMANT, 40/1), Neukirchen, Neukirchener Verlag, 1972.

BETZ, H.D., *The Sermon on the Mount: A Commentary on the Sermon on the Mount, Including the Sermon on the Plain (Matthew 5:3-7:27 and Luke 6:20-49)* (Hermeneia), Minneapolis, MN, Fortress, 1995.

BICKERMANN, E., *Das leere Grab*, in *ZNW* 23 (1924) 281-292.

BIRKELAND, H., *The Beliefs in Resurrection of the Dead in the Old Testament*, in *ST* 3 (1949) 60-78.

BLACK, M.C., *The Rejected and Slain Messiah Who is Coming with His Angels: The Messianic Exegesis of Zechariah 9-14 in the Passion Narratives*, PhD Thesis, Emory University, 1991, Ann Arbor, MI, University Microfilms, pp. 222-226.

BLANK, S., *The Death of Zechariah in Rabbinic Literature*, in *HUCA* 13 (1938) 327-346.

BLENKINSOPP, J., *Isaiah 1-39* (AB, 19), New York, Doubleday, 2000.

BLOCK, D.I., *The Book of Ezekiel: Chapters 25-48*, Grand Rapids, MI, Eerdmans, 1998.

BONNARD, P., *L'Évangile selon Saint Matthieu* (CNT, 1), Genève, Labor et Fides, ³2002.

BONSIRVEN, J., *Le Judaïsme Palestinien au temps de Jésus-Christ: Sa théologie. I. La théologie dogmatique* (Bibliothèque de théologie historique), Paris, G. Beauchesne & Fils, 1934.

BORNKAMM, G., *Der Aufbau der Bergpredigt*, in *NTS* 24 (1978) 419-432.

BORRET, M., *Origène: Contre Celse*, Vol. 3: livres V et VI (SC, 147), Paris, Cerf, 1969.

BOXALL, I.K., *Exile, Prophet, Visionary: Ezekiel's Influence on the Book of Revelation*, in H.J. DE JONGE – J. TROMP (eds.), *The Book of Ezekiel and Its Influence*, Aldershot – Burlington, VT, Ashgate, 2007, pp. 147-164.

BRADY, M., *Biblical Interpretation in the 'Pseudo-Ezekiel' Fragments (4Q383-391) from Cave Four*, in M. HENZE (ed.), *Biblical Interpretation at Qumran*, Grand Rapids, MI – Cambridge, UK, Eerdmans, 2005, pp. 88-109.

BRANDENBURGER, E., *Fleisch und Geist: Paulus und die dualistische Weisheit* (WMANT, 29), Neukirchen-Vluyn, Neukirchener Verlag, 1968.

BRASLAVI, J. – M. AVI-YONAH, *Mount of Olives (Olivet)*, in F. SKOLNIK – M. BERENBAUM (eds.), *Encyclopedia Judaica, Volume 14. Mel-Nas*, Detroit, Thomson Gale, 2007, p. 585.

BRAUMANN, G., *Zum Traditionsgeschichtlichen Problem der Seligpreisungen Mt V 3-12*, in *NovT* 4 (1960) 253-260.

BROER, I. *Die Urgemeinde und das Grab Jesu: Eine Analyse der Grablegungsgeschichte im Neuen Testament* (SANT, 31), München, Kösel, 1972.

BROOKE, G.J., *Ezekiel in Some Qumran and New Testament Texts*, in J.T. BARRERA – L.V. MONTANER (eds.), *The Madrid Qumran Congress: Proceedings of the International Congress on the Dead Sea Scrolls Madrid 18-21 March, 1991* (STDJ, 11), Vol.1, Leiden, Brill – Madrid, Editorial Complutense, 1992.

BROWN, R., *The Death of the Messiah: From Gethsemane to the Grave: A Commentary on the Passion Narratives in the Four Gospels*, 2 vols. (ABRL), New York, Doubleday, 1994.

——, *The Gospel of Peter and Canonical Gospel Priority*, in *NTS* 33 (1987) 321-343.

——, *The Resurrection in Matthew (27:62-28:20)*, in *Worship* 64 (1990) 157-170.

BRUNER, F.D., *Matthew: A Commentary. Volume 2: The Churchbook. Matthew 13-28*, Grand Rapids, MI – Cambridge, UK, Eerdmans, 2004.

BUCHANAN, G.W., *The Gospel of Matthew*, 2 vols. Lewiston – Queenston – Lampeter, Mellen Biblical Press, 1996.

BUCHHOLZ, D.D., *Your Eyes Will Be Opened: A Study of the Greek (Ethiopic) Apocalypse of Peter* (SBLDS, 97), Atlanta, Scholars Press, 1988.

BULTMANN, R., *Die Geschichte der synoptischen Tradition* (FRLANT, 12), Göttingen, Vandenhoeck & Ruprecht, 1921; repr. 1970.

BURKERT, W., *Ancient Mystery Cults* (Carl Newell Jackson Lectures), Cambridge MA, Harvard University Press, 1987.

BURNETT, F.W., Παλιγγενεσία in Matt. 19:28: *A Window on the Matthean Community?*, in *JSNT* 17 (1983) 60-72.

CARTER, W., *Households and Discipleship: A Study of Matthew 19-20* (JSNTSup, 103), Sheffield, JSOT, 1994.

——, *Matthew and the Margins: A Sociopolitical and Religious Reading* (The Bible and Liberation Series), Maryknoll, NY, Orbis, 2000.

CAVALLIN, H.C.C., *Life After Death: Paul's Argument for the Resurrection of the Dead in 1 Cor 15, Part I. An Enquiry into the Jewish Background*, Lund, CWK Gleerup, 1974.

CERFAUX, L., *Christ in the Theology of St. Paul*, New York – Edinburgh – London, Herder and Herder – Thomas Nelson and Sons, Ltd., 1959.

CHADWICK, H., *Origen: Contra Celsum*, Cambridge, University Press, 1953; repr. 1965.

CHARLESWORTH, J.H., (ed.), *The Old Testament Pseudepigrapha*, 2 Vols., London, Darton, Longman & Todd, 1983-1985.

——, *Where Does the Concept of Resurrection Appear and How Do We Know That?*, in J.H. CHARLESWORTH – C.D. ELLEDGE (eds.), *Resurrection: The Origin and Future of a Biblical Doctrine* (Faith and Scholarship Colloquies Series), New York – London, Continuum – Clark, 2006, pp. 1-21

CIRILLO, L., *Livre de la révélation d'Elkasaï*, in F. BOVON – P. GEOLTRAIN (eds.), *Écrits apocryphes chrétiens I* (Bibliothèque de la Pléiade), Paris, Gallimard, 1997, pp. 829-872.

CLARK-SOLES, J., *Death and the Afterlife in the New Testament*, New York, – London, T. & T. Clark, 2006.

COHEN, A., *The Symbolic Construction of Community* (Key Ideas), Chichester, Horwood – London, Tavistock,1985.

COLLINS, J.J., *Daniel* (Hermeneia), Minneapolis, MN, Fortress, 1993.

——, *The Sibylline Oracles*, in J.H. CHARLESWORTH (ed.), *The Old Testament Pseudepigrapha*, Vol.1, London, Darton, Longman & Todd, 1983.

COLLINS, A.Y., *Ancient Notions of Transferral and Apotheosis in Relation to the Empty Tomb Story in Mark*, in T.K. SEIM – J. ÖKLAND (eds.), *Metamorphoses: Resurrection, Body and Transformative Practices in Early Christianity* (Ekstasis, 1), Berlin – New York, De Gruyter, 2009, pp. 41-57.

——, *The Beginning of the Gospel: Probings of Mark in Context*, Minneapolis, MN, Fortress, 1992.

COSBY, M.R., *Hellenistic Formal Receptions and Paul's Use of ΑΠΑΝΤΗΣΙΣ in 1 Thessalonians 4:17*, in *BBR* 4 (1994) 15-33.

COULOT, C., *La Structuration de la péricope de l'homme riche et ses différentes lectures (Mc 10,17-31; Mt 19, 16-30; Lc 18, 18-30)*, in *RSR* 56 (1982) 240-252.

CROSSAN, J.D., *The Cross That Spoke: The Origins of the Passion Narrative*, San Francisco etc., Harper, 1988.

——, *Four Other Gospels: Shadows on the Contours of Canon*, Minneapolis, MN, Fortress, 1985.

——, *The Gospel of Peter and the Canonical Gospels*, in T.J. KRAUS – T. NICKLAS (eds.), *Das Evangelium nach Petrus: Text, Kontexte, Intertexte* (TU, 158), Berlin – New York, De Gruyter, 2007, pp. 117-134.

CURTIS, J.B., *The Mount of Olives in Tradition*, in *HUCA* 28 (1957) 137-180.

DANBY, H., *The Mishnah*, Oxford, University Press, 1977.

DAUTZENBERG, G., *Sein Leben bewahren: Psyché in den Herrenworten der Evangelien* (SANT, 14), München, Kösel, 1966.

DAVIES, W.D. and D.C. ALLISON, JR., *A Critical and Exegetical Commentary on the Gospel according to Saint Matthew*, Vol. 1. *Introduction and commentary on Matthew I-VII* (ICC), Edinburgh, T. & T. Clark, 1988.

——, *A Critical and Exegetical Commentary on the Gospel according to Saint Matthew*, Vol. 2. *Commentary on Matthew VIII-XVIII* (ICC), Edinburgh, T&T Clark, 1991.

——, *A Critical and Exegetical Commentary on the Gospel according to Saint Matthew*, Vol. 3. *Commentary on Matthew XIX-XXVIII* (ICC), Edinburgh, T. & T. Clark, 1997.

DAY, J., *The Development of Belief in Life After Death in Ancient Israel*, in J. BARTON – D.J. REIMER (eds.), *Essays in Honour of Rex Mason*, Macon, GA, Mercer University Press, 1996, pp. 231- 257.

DENAUX, A., *Matthew's Story of Jesus' Burial and Resurrection*, in R. BIERINGER – V. KOPERSKI – B. LATAIRE (eds.), *Resurrection in the New Testament* (BETL, 165), Leuven, Leuven University Press – Peeters, 2002, pp.123-145.

DENKER, J., *Die theologiegeschichtliche Stellung des Petrusevangeliums: Ein Beitrag zur Frühgeschichte des Doketismus* (Europäische Hochschulschriften, Reihe 23, Band 36), Bern, Lang, 1975.

DERRETT, J.D.M., *PALINGENESIA (Matthew 19.18)*, in *JSNT* 20 (1984) 51-58.

DEUTSCH, C., *Hidden Wisdom and the Easy Yoke: Wisdom, Torah and Discipleship in Matthew 11.25-30* (JSNTSup, 18), Sheffield, Sheffield Academic Press, 1987.

DE VAUX, R., *Rapport préliminaire sur la deuxième campagne*, in *RB* 61 (1954) 206-236.

DÍEZ-MACHO, A., *Un Segundo fragmento del Targum Palestinese a los Profetas*, in *Bib* 39 (1958) 198-205.

DIHLE, A., *Die Goldene Regel: Eine Einführung in die Geschichte der antiken und frühchristlichen Vulgärethik* (Studienhefte zur Altertumswissenschaft, 7), Göttingen, Vandenhoeck & Ruprecht, 1962.

DIMANT, D., *Qumran Cave 4. XXI: Parabiblical Texts, Part 4: Pseudo-Prophetic Texts* (DJD, 30), Oxford, Clarendon Press, 2001.

——, *Resurrection, Restoration, and Time-Curtailing in Qumran, Early Judaism, and Christianity*, in *RevQ* 19 (2000) 527-548.

DODD, C.H., *According to the Scriptures: The Sub-structure of New Testament Theology*, London, Fontana, 1965.

DONALDSON, T.L., *Jesus on the Mountain: A Study in Matthean Theology* (JSNTSup, 8), Sheffield, JSOT Press, 1985.

DREYFUS, F., *L'argument scripturaire de Jésus en faveur de la résurrection des morts*, in *RB* 66 (1959) 213-224.

DU MESNIL DU BUISSON, C., *Les peintures de la synagogue de Doura-Europos 245-256 après J.-C.*, Rome, Pontifical Institute, 1939.

DUNN, J.D.G., *The Acts of the Apostles*, London, Epworth, 1996.

DUPONT, J., *Les Béatitudes 1: Le problème littéraire* (ÉBib), Paris, Gabalda, 1969.

——, *Die individuelle Eschatologie im Lukasevangelium und in der Apostelgeschichte*, in P. HOFFMANN (ed.), *Orientierung an Jesus*, Freiburg, Herder, 1973, pp. 37-47.

——, *Le logion des douze thrônes (Mt 19,28; Lc 22,28-30)*, in *Bib* 45 (1964) 355-392.

EBNER, M., *Jesus – ein Weisheitslehrer?: Synoptische Weisheitslogien im Traditions-prozess* (Herders Biblische Studien, 15), Freiburg, Herder, 1998.

EDWARDS, C., *Incorporating the Alien: The Art of Conquest*, in C. EDWARDS – G. WOOLF (eds.), *Rome the Cosmopolis*, Cambridge, Cambridge University Press, 2003, pp. 44-70.

EDWARDS, C. – G. WOOLF (eds.), *Rome the Cosmopolis*, Cambridge, Cambridge University Press, 2003.

EISENBAUM, P., *A Speech Act of Faith: The Early Proclamation of the Resurrection of Jesus*, in V.WILES – A.BROWN – G.SNYDER (eds.), *Putting Body and Soul Together: Essays in Honor of Robin Scroggs*, Valley Forge, Trinity, 1997, pp. 24-45.

ELLEDGE, C.D., *Resurrection of the Dead: Exploring Our Earliest Evidence Today*, in J.H. CHARLESWORTH (ed.), *Resurrection: The Origin and Future of a Biblical Doctrine* (Faith and Scholarship Colloquies Series), New York, – London, Continuum – Clark, 2006, pp. 22-52.

——, *The Resurrection Passages in the Testaments of the Twelve Patriarchs: Hope for Israel in Early Judaism and Christianity*, in J.H. CHARLESWORTH (ed.), *Resurrection: The Origin and Future of a Biblical Doctrine* (Faith and scholarship colloquies series), New York, – London, Continuum – Clark, 2006, pp. 79-103.

ENGEMANN, J., *Auf die Parusie Christi hinweisende Darstellungen in der frühchristlichen Kunst*, in *JAC* 19 (1976) 139-156.

EVANS, C.A., *Jewish Burial Traditions and the Resurrection of Jesus*, in *Journal for the Study of the Historical Jesus* 3 (2005) 233-248.

——, *Zechariah in the Markan Passion Narrative*, in T.R. HATINA (ed.), *Biblical Interpretation in Early Christian Gospels, Volume 1: The Gospel of Mark* (LNTS, 304), London, T. & T. Clark, 2006, pp. 64-80.

FIEDLER, P., *Das Matthäusevangelium* (TKNT, 1), Stuttgart, Kohlhammer, 2006.

FILSON, F.V., *A Commentary on the Gospel According to St. Matthew* (BNTC), London, ²1971.

FLEDDERMANN, H.T., *Q: A Reconstruction and Commentary* (Biblical Tools and Studies, 1), Leuven, Peeters, 2005.

FLUSSER, D., *Johanan ben Zakkai and Matthew*, in ID. (ed.), *Judaism and the Origins of Christianity*, Jerusalem, Magnes, 1988, pp. 490-493.

——, *A Rabbinic Parallel to the Sermon on the Mount*, in D. FLUSSER, *Judaism and the Origins of Christianity* (Collected Articles), Jerusalem, Magnes, 1988, pp. 494-508.

——, *Die Tora in der Bergpredigt*, in H. KREMERS (ed.), *Juden und Christen lesen dieselbe Bibel* (Duisburger Hochschulbeiträge, 2), Duisburg, Braun, 1973, pp. 102-113.

——, *Two Anti-Jewish Montages in Matthew*, in D. FLUSSER (ed.), *Judaism and the Origins of Christianity*, Jerusalem, Magnes, 1988, pp. 552-560.

FOSTER, P., *The Gospel of Peter*, in ID. (ed.), *The Non-Canonical Gospels*, London – New York, Continuum, 2008, pp. 30-42.

——, *The Use of Zechariah in Matthew's Gospel*, in C. TUCKETT (ed.), *The Book of Zechariah and Its Influence*, Aldershot, UK – Burlington, VT, Ashgate, 2003, pp. 65-85.

FRIEDMAN, R. and S. OVERTON, *Death and Afterlife: The Biblical Silence*, in A.J. AVERY-PECK – J. NEUSNER (eds.), *Judaism in Late Antiquity: Part Four: Death, Life after Death, Resurrection, and the World to Come in the Judaism of Antiquity* (HO, 1. Abt., Bd. 49), Leiden, Brill, 2000, pp. 35-59.

FUNK, F.X., *Doctrina duodecim apostolorum: Canones apostolorum ecclesiastici ac reliquae doctrinae de duabus viis expositiones veteres*, Tübingen, Laupp, 1887.

GARCÍA MARTÍNEZ, F. – E.J.C. TIGCHELAAR, *The Dead Sea Scrolls Study Edition*, Vol 1, Leiden – Grand Rapids, MI, Brill – Eerdmans, ²2000.

GARCÍA MARTÍNEZ, F., *The Apocalyptic Interpretation of Ezekiel in the Dead Sea Scrolls*, in J. LUST – F. GARCÍA MARTÍNEZ – M. VERVENNE (eds.), with the collaboration of B. DOYLE, *Interpreting Translation: Studies on the LXX and Ezekiel in Honour of Johan Lust* (BETL, 142), Leuven – Paris – Dudley, MA, Leuven University Press – Peeters, 2005, pp. 163-176.

GARROW, A.J.P., *The Gospel of Matthew's Dependence on the Didache* (JSNTSup, 254), London – New York, T&T Clark, 2004.

GARTE, E., *The Theme of Resurrection in the Dura-Europos Synagogue Paintings*, in *JQR* 64 (1973-74) 1-15.

GEOLTRAIN, P., *Le traité de la vie contemplative de Philon d'Alexandrie: Introduction, traduction et notes* (Semitica, 10), Paris, Librairie d'Amérique et d'Orient Adrien- Maisonneuve, 1960.

GIBBS, J.A., *Jerusalem and Parousia: Jesus' Eschatological Discourse in Matthew's Gospel*, St. Louis, Concordia, 2000.

GIET, ST., *L'Énigme de la Didachè* (Publications de la Faculté des Lettres de l'université de Strasbourg, 149), Paris, Ophrys,1970.

GILL, J., *Gill's Commentary*, 5 vols., Grand Rapids, MI, Baker Academic, 1980.

GNILKA, J., *Das Matthäusevangelium*, vol. 1 (HTKNT, 1/1), Freiburg – Basel – Wien, Herder, 1986.

——, *Das Matthäusevangelium*, vol. 2 (HTKNT, 1/2), Freiburg – Basel – Wien, Herder, 1988.

GOLDINGAY, J., *Daniel* (WBC, 30), Dallas, Word, 1989.

GOLDSCHMIDT, A. – K. WEITZMANN., *Die Byzantinischen Elfenbeinskulpturen des X.-XIII. Jahrhunderts. Zweiter Band: Reliefs*, Berlin, Deutscher Verlag für Kunstwissenschaft, 1979.

GOLDSTEIN, J.A., *II Maccabees* (AB, 41A), New York, Doubleday, 1983.

GOODENOUGH, E.R., *Jewish Symbols in the Greco-Roman Period: Symbolism in the Dura Synagogue*, 13 vols., Princeton, Princeton University Press, 1953-1968, Vol X, XI.

GOPPELT, L., *Christentum und Judentum im ersten und zweiten Jahrhundert* (BFCT, Reihe 2, Bd. 55), Gütersloh, Bertelsmann, 1954.

GORDON, R.P., *The Targumists as Eschatologists*, in *Congress Volume* (VTSup, 29) Leiden, Brill, 1978, pp. 113-130.

GOUNELLE, R., *La descente du Christ aux enfers: Institutionnalisation d'une croyance* (Collection des Études Augustiniennes, Série Antiquité, 162), Paris, Institut d'Études Augustiniennes, 2000.

GRASSI, J., *Ezekiel XXXVII.1-14 and the New Testament*, in *NTS* 11 (1965) 162-164.

GREEN, J.B., *Body, Soul, and Human Life: The Nature of Humanity in the Bible*, Grand Rapids, MI, Baker Academic, 2008.

GRUNDMANN, W., *Das Evangelien nach Matthäus* (THNT, 1), Berlin, Evangelische Verlagsanstalt, 1968.

GUELICH, R.A., *The Sermon on the Mount: A Foundation for Understanding*, Waco, TX, Word Publishing, ²1983.

GUNDRY, R.H., *Matthew: A Commentary on His Handbook for a Mixed Church under Persecution*, Grand Rapids, MI, Eerdmans, 1994.

——, *Matthew: A Commentary on His Literary and Theological Art*, Grand Rapids, MI, Eerdmans, 1982.

GURTNER, D.M., *The Torn Veil: Matthew's Exposition of the Death of Jesus* (SNTSMS, 139), Cambridge, Cambridge University Press, 2007.

GUTMANN, J., *Early Synagogue and Jewish Catacomb Art and Its Relation to Christian Art*, in *ANRW* II/21.2 (1984) 1313-1342.

——, *The Illustrated Midrash in the Dura Synagogue Paintings: A New Dimension for the Study of Judaism*, in *American Academy of Jewish Research Proceedings* 50 (1983) 91-104.

HACHLILI, R., *Ancient Jewish Art and Archaeology in the Diaspora* (HO, 1. Abt., Bd. 35), Leiden – Boston – Cologne, Brill, 1998.

HAENCHEN, E., *The Acts of the Apostles: A Commentary*, Philadelphia, PA, Westminster John Knox, 1971.

HAM, C.A., *The Coming King and the Rejected Shepherd: Matthew's Reading of Zechariah's Messianic Hope*, Sheffield, Phoenix, 2005.

HAMILTON, N.G., *Resurrection Tradition and the Composition of Mark*, in *JBL* 84 (1965) 415- 421.

HÄNLEIN-SCHÄFER, H., *Die Iconographie des Genius Augusti im Kapital und Hauskult der frühen Kaiserzeit*, in A.M. SMALL (ed.), *Subject and Ruler: The Cult of the*

Ruling Power in Classical Antiquity (Journal of Roman Archaeology. Supplementary Series, 17), Ann Arbor, JRA, 1996, pp. 73-98.

——, *Veneratio Augusti. Eine Studie zu den Tempeln des ersten römischen Kaisers* (Archaeologica, 39), Rome, Bretschneider, 1985.

HANSON, K.C., *Transformed on the Mountain: Ritual Analysis and the Gospel of Matthew*, in *Semeia* 67 (1994/1995) 147-170.

HANSON, P.D., *The Dawn of Apocalyptic: The Historical and Sociological Roots of Jewish Apocalyptic Eschatology*, Philadelphia, PA, Fortress, 1979.

HARL, M. (ed.), *La Bible d'Alexandrie: La Genèse*, Paris, Cerf, 1986.

HARRINGTON, D.J., *Afterlife Expectations in Pseudo-Philo, 4 Ezra, and 2 Baruch, and Their Implications for the New Testament*, in R. BIERINGER – V. KOPERSKI – B. LATAIRE (eds.), *Resurrection in the New Testament* (BETL, 165), Leuven – Paris – Dudley, MA, Peeters, 2002, pp. 21-34.

——, *The Gospel of Matthew* (SP, 1), Collegeville, MN, Liturgical Press – Michael Glazier, 1991.

——, *The Rich Young Man in Matthew 19,16-22: Another Way to God for Jews?*, in F. VAN SEGBROECK – C.M. TUCKETT – G. VAN BELLE – J. VERHEYDEN (eds.), *The Four Gospels 1992*, Vol. 2, Leuven, University Press – Peeters, 1992, pp. 1425-1432.

HARRIS, R. – A. MINGANA, *The Odes and Psalms of Solomon*, 2 vols, Manchester – London – New York, Manchester University Press – Longmans – Green & Co., and Bernard Quaritch, 1920.

HARTAL, M., *The Land of the Itureans: Archaeology and History of the Northern Golan in the Hellenistic, Roman and Byzantine Periods* (Golan Studies, 2), Qazrin, Golan Research Institute, 2005.

HARTENSTEIN, J., *Das Petrusevangelium als Evangelium*, in T.J. KRAUS – T. NICKLAS (eds.), *Das Evangelium nach Petrus: Text, Kontexte, Intertexte* (TU, 158), Berlin – New York, De Gruyter, 2007, pp. 159-181.

HECKEL, T.K., *Vom Evangelium des Markus zum viergestaltigen Evangelium* (WUNT, 120), Tübingen, Mohr, 1999.

HEINEMANN, J., *Prayer in the Talmud* (SJ, 9), Berlin, De Gruyter, 1977.

HELDERMAN, J., *Die Engel bei der Auferstehung und das lebendige Kreuz: Mk 16,3 in k, einem Vergleich unterzogen*, in F. VAN SEGBROECK – C.M. TUCKETT – G. VAN BELLE – J. VERHEYDEN (eds.), *The Four Gospels 1992* (BETL, 100), Leuven, Leuven University Press – Peeters, 1992, pp. 2321-2342.

HENGEL, M., *Das Begräbnis Jesu bei Paulus und die leibliche Auferstehung aus dem Grabe*, in F. AVEMARIE – H. LICHTENBERGER (eds.), *Auferstehung – Resurrection. The Fourth Durham-Tübingen Research Symposium Resurrection, Transfiguration and Exaltation in Old Testament, Ancient Judaism and Early Christianity (Tübingen, September 1999)* (WUNT, 135), Tübingen, Mohr Siebeck, 2001, pp. 79-91.

HENTEN, J.W. VAN, *The Maccabean Martyrs as Saviours of the Jewish People* (JSJSup, 57), Leiden, Brill, 1997.

HENTEN, J.W. VAN, with the collaboration of B.A.G.M. DEHANDSCHUTTER and H.J.W. VAN DER KLAAUW (eds.), *Die Entstehung der jüdischen Martyrologie* (StPB, 38), Leiden, Brill, 1989.

HERZER, J., *4 Baruch (Paraleipomena Jeremiou)*, Atlanta, Society of Biblical Literature, 2005.

HIEKE, T., *Das Petrusevangelium vom Alten Testament her gelesen*, in T.J. KRAUS – T. NICKLAS (eds.), *Das Evangelium nach Petrus: Text, Kontexte, Intertexte* (TU, 158), Berlin – New York, De Gruyter, 2007, pp. 91-115.

HILL, L., *The Two Republicae of the Roman Stoics: Can a Cosmopolite be a Patriot?*, in *Citizenship Studies* 4 (2000) 65-79.

HITCHNER, R.B., *Globalization Avant La Lettre: Globalization and the History of the Roman Empire*, in *New Global Studies* 2 (2008) 1-16.

HOFFMANN, P., *Die Auferweckung Jesu als Zeichen für Israel: Mt 12,39f und die matthäische Ostergeschichte*, in K. KERTELGE – T. HOLZ – C.-P. MÄRZ (eds.), *Christus bezeugen* (ETS, 59), Leipzig, St.-Benno-Verlag, 1989, pp. 110-123.

——, *Die Toten in Christus: eine religionsgeschichtliche und exegetische Untersuchung zur paulinischen Eschatologie* (NTAbh NF, 2), Münster, Aschendorff, 1966.

HOFFMANN, P. – CH. HEIL, *Die Spruchquelle Q*, Darmstadt, Wiss. Buchgesellschaft – Leuven, Peeters, 2002.

HOFIUS, O., *"Am dritten Tage auferstanden von den Toten": Erwägungen zum Passiv ἐγείρεσθαι in christologischen Aussagen des Neuen Testaments*, in R. BIERINGER – V. KOPERSKI – B. LATAIRE (eds.), *Resurrection in the New Testament* (BETL, 165), Leuven, University Press – Peeters, 2002, pp. 93-106.

HOGETERP, A.L.A., *Expectations of the End: A Comparative Traditio-Historical Study of Eschatological, Apocalyptic and Messianic Ideas in the Dead Sea Scrolls and the New Testament* (STDJ, 83), Leiden, Brill, 2009, pp. 258- 259.

——, *Resurrection and Biblical Tradition: Pseudo-Ezekiel Reconsidered*, in *Bib* 89 (2008) 59- 69.

HOLLANDER H.W. – M. DE JONGE, *The Testaments of the Twelve Patriarchs: A Commentary* (SVTP, 8), Leiden, Brill, 1985.

HOLTZ, G., *Der Herrscher und der Weise im Gespräch: Studien zu Form, Funktion und Situation der neutestamentlichen Verhörgespräche und der Gespräche zwischen jüdischen Weisen und Fremdherrschern* (ANTZ, 6), Berlin, Institut Kirche und Judentum, 1996.

HOPKINS, K., *Death and Renewal* (Sociological Studies in Roman History, 2), Cambridge, Cambridge University Press, 1983.

HORBURY, W., *Land, Sanctuary and Worship*, in J. BARCLAY – J. SWEET (eds.), *Early Christian Thought in Its Jewish Context*, Cambridge, Cambridge University Press, 1996, pp. 219-222.

HORST, P. VAN DER, *Ancient Jewish Epitaphs: An Introductory Survey of a Millennium of Jewish Funerary Epigraphy (200 B.C.E.-700 C.E.)* (CBET, 2), Kampen, Pharos, 1991.

HOWIE, J.G., *The Evangelist and the Revisers: Revision and Counter-Revision in Matthew 27 and 28*, in *Hyperboreus* 13 (2007) 209-242.

HULTGREN, A.J., *Jesus and His Adversaries: The Form and Function of the Conflict Stories in the Synoptic Tradition*, Augsburg, MN, Augsburg Publishing House, 1979.

HULTGREN, S., *1Q521, the Second Benediction of the* Tefilla, *the* Hăsîdîm, *and the Development of Royal Messianism*, in *RevQ* 91 (2008) 313-340.

——, *4Q521 and Luke's Magnificat and Benedictus*, in F. GARCÍA MARTÍNEZ (ed.), *Echoes from the Caves: Qumran and the New Testament* (STDS, 85), Leiden, Brill, 2009, pp. 119-132.

JACOBOVICI, S. – C. PELLEGRINO, *The Jesus Family Tomb: The Discovery That Will Change History Forever*, San Francisco, Harper, 2007.

JANZEN, J.G., *Resurrection and Hermeneutics: On Exodus 3.6 in Mark 12.26*, in *JSNT* 23 (1985) 43-58.

JARICK, J., *Questioning Sheol*, in S.E. PORTER – M.A. HAYES – D. TOMBS (eds.), *Resurrection* (JSNTSup, 186), Sheffield, Sheffield Academic Press, 1999, pp. 22-32.

JAUHIAINEN, M., *The Use of Zechariah in Revelation* (WUNT, 2/199), Tübingen, Mohr Siebeck, 2005.

JEFFORD, C.N., *The Sayings of Jesus in the Teaching of the Twelve Apostles* (VCSup, 11), Leiden – New York, – København – Köln, Brill, 1989.

JEREMIAS, J., *Neutestamentliche Theologie 1: Die Verkündigung Jesu*, Gütersloh, Mohn, 1971.

——, πύλη, πυλών, in *TWNT* 6 (1990) 920-927.

JOBES, K.H. – M. SILVA, *Invitation to the Septuagint*, Grand Rapids, MI, Baker Academic, 2000.

JONGE, H.J. DE, *De opstanding van Jezus: De joodse traditie achter een christelijke belijdenis*, in T. BAARDA – H.J. DE JONGE – M.J.J. MENKEN (eds.), *Jodendom en vroeg christendom: Continuïteit en discontinuïteit*, Kampen, Kok, 1991, pp. 47-61.

——, *Visionary Experience and the Historical Origins of Christianity*, in R. BIERINGER – V. KOPERSKI – B. LATAIRE (eds.), *Resurrection in the New Testament* (BETL, 165), Leuven, Leuven University Press – Peeters, 2002, pp. 35-53.

JONGE, M. DE, *Jesus' Death for Others and the Death of the Maccabean Martyrs*, in ID. (ed.), *Jewish Eschatology, Early Christian Christology and the Testaments of the Twelve Patriarchs. Collected Essays* (NovTSup, 63), Leiden, Brill, 1991, pp. 125-134.

JUNOD, É., *Évangile de Pierre*, in F. BOVON – P. GEOLTRAIN (eds.), *Écrits apocryphes chrétiens I* (Bibliothèque de la Pléiade), Paris, Gallimard, 1997, pp. 241-254.

——, *Polymorphie du Dieu Sauveur*, in J. RIES (ed.), *Gnosticisme et monde hellénistique* (Publications de l'Institut Orientaliste de Louvain, 27), Louvain-la-Neuve, Institut Orientaliste, 1982, pp. 38-46.

JUNOD, É. – J.D. KAESTLI, *Acta Iohannis: Praefatio – Textus* (C.Chr. Series Apocryphorum, 1), Turnhout, Brepols, 1983.

KARTSONIS, A.D., *Anastasis: The Making of an Image*, Princeton, Princeton University Press, 1986.

KELLERMANN, U., *Auferstanden in den Himmel: II Makkabäer 7 und die Auferstehung der Martyrer* (SBS, 95), Stuttgart, Katholisches Bibelwerk, 1979.

——, *Elia Redivivus und die heilszeitliche Auferweckung der Toten: Erwägungen zur ältesten Bezeugung einer Erwartung*, in K. GRÜWALDT – H. SCHROETER (eds.), *Was suchst du hier, Elia? Ein hermeneutisches Arbeitsbuch* (Hermeneutica, 4), Rheinbach – Merzbach, CMZ-Verlag, 1995, pp. 75-77.

KIEFFER, R., *"Mer-än"-kristologin hos synoptikerna ("More-than" Christology in the Synoptics)*, in *Svensk Exegetisk Årsbok* 44 (1979) 134–147.

KILPATRICK, G.D., *The Origins of the Gospel According to St. Matthew*, Oxford, University Press, 1946.

KIRK, A., *Tradition and Memory in the Gospel of Peter*, in T.J. KRAUS – T. NICKLAS (eds.), *Das Evangelium nach Petrus: Text, Kontexte, Intertexte* (TU, 158), Berlin – New York, De Gruyter, 2007, pp. 135-158.

KLAUCK, H.-J., *Apokryphe Evangelien: Eine Einführung*, Stuttgart, Katholisches Bibelwerk, 2002.

——, *4. Makkabäerbuch* (JSHRZ, 3, Lfg. 6), Gütersloh, Mohn, 1989.

KLONER, A. – B. ZISSU., *The Necropolis of Jerusalem in the Second Temple Period* (Interdisciplinary Studies in Ancient Culture and Religion, 8), Leuven – Dudley, MA, Peeters, 2007.

KLOPPENBORG VERBIN, J.S., *Excavating Q: The History and Setting of the Sayings Gospel*, Minneapolis, MN, Fortress, 2000.

KÖHLER, W.-D., *Die Rezeption des Matthäusevangeliums in der Zeit vor Irenäus* (WUNT, 2/24), Tübingen, Mohr, 1987.

KOESTER, H., *Ancient Christian Gospels: Their History and Development*, Philadelphia, PA, Trinity Press International – London, SCM, 1990.

——, *Apocryphal and Canonical Gospels*, in *HTR* 73 (1980) 105-130.

KONRADT, M., *The Love Command in Matthew, James, and the Didache*, in H. VAN DE SANDT – J. ZANGENBERG (eds.), *Matthew, James and Didache: Three Related Documents in Their Jewish and Christian Settings* (Symposium Series, 45), Atlanta, SBL, 2008, pp. 271-288.

KOWALSKI, B., *Die Rezeption des Propheten Ezechiel in der Offenbarung des Johannes* (SBS, 52), Stuttgart, Katholisches Bibelwerk, 2004.

KRAELING, C.H., *The Wall Decorations*, in *Preliminary Report on the Synagogue at Dura*, New Haven, Yale University Press, 1936.

KRATZ, R., *Auferweckung als Befreiung: Eine Studie zur Passions- und Auferstehungstheologie des Matthäus (besonders Mt 27,62-28,15)* (SBS, 65), Stuttgart, KWB Verlag, 1973.

——, *Rettungswunder: Motiv-, traditions- und formkritische Aufarbeitung einer biblischen Gattung* (Europäische Hochschulschriften, 23/123), Frankfurt – Bern, Lang, 1979.

KRAUS, T.J. – T. NICKLAS (eds.), *Das Petrusevangelium und die Petrusapokalypse: Die griechischen Fragmente mit deutscher und englischer Übersetzung* (GCS NF, 11; Neutestamentliche Apokryphen, 1), Berlin – New York, De Gruyter, 2004.

KRAUS, T.J. – T. NICKLAS (eds.), *Das Evangelium nach Petrus: Text, Kontexte, Intertexte* (TU, 158), Berlin – New York, De Gruyter, 2007.

KÜMMEL, W.G., *Die älteste religiöse Kunst der Juden*, in *Judaica* 2 (1946) 1-56.

LANG, B., *Street Theater, Raising the Dead, and the Zoroastrian Connection in Ezekiel's Prophecy*, in J.LUST (ed), *Ezekiel and His Book: Textual and Literary Criticism and their Interrelation* (BETL, 74), Leuven, Leuven University Press – Peeters, 1986, pp. 307-314.

LAPHAM, F., *Peter: The Myth, the Man and the Writings: A Study of Early Petrine Text and Tradition* (JSNTSupp, 239), Sheffield, Academic Press, 2003.

LATTKE, M., *Dating the Odes of Solomon*, in *Antichthon* 27 (1993) 45-59.

LÉGASSE, S., *L'appèl du riche (Marc 10,17-31 et parallèles): Contribution à l'étude des fondements scripturaires de l'état religieux* (VS), Paris, Beauchesne, 1966.

——, *Les Épîtres de Paul aux Thessaloniciens* (LD Commentaires, 7), Paris, Cerf, 1999.

LE MOYNE, J., *Les Sadducéens* (ÉBib), Paris, Gabalda, 1972.

LENTZEN-DEIS, F., *Das Motiv der Himmelsöffnung in verschiedenen Gattungen der Umweltliteratur des Neuen Testaments*, in *Bib* 50 (1969) 301-327.

LEVENSON, J., *Resurrection and the Restauration of Israel: The Ultimate Victory of the God of Life*, New Haven, CT, Yale University Press, 2006.

LICHTENBERGER, H., *Auferstehung in den Qumranfunden*, in F. AVEMARIE – H. LICHTENBERGER (eds.), *Auferstehung – Resurrection* (WUNT, 135), Tübingen, Mohr Siebeck, 2001.

LILJE, H., *Die Lehre der zwölf Apostel: Eine Kirchenordnung des ersten christlichen Jahrhunderts*, Hamburg, Furche-Verlag, 1956.

LOADER, W.R.G., *Jesus' Attitude towards the Law: A Study of the Gospels* (WUNT, 2/97), Tübingen, Mohr Siebeck, 1997.

LOHMEYER, E., *Das Evangelium des Matthäus*, ed.,W.SCHMAUCK (KEK), Göttingen, Vandenhoeck & Ruprecht, [2]1958.

LUCK, U., *Die Frage nach dem Guten: Zu Mt 19,16–30 und Par.*, in W. SCHRAGE (ed.), *Studien zum Text und zur Ethik des Neuen Testaments*, Berlin – New York, De Gruyter, 1986, pp. 282-297.

LÜDEMANN, G., *The Resurrection of Christ: A Historical Inquiry*, New York, Prometheus Books, 2004.

——, *Resurrection of Jesus: History, Experience, Theology*, transl. J.Bowden, Minneapolis, MN, Fortress, 1994.

LUST, J., *Ezekiel 36-40 in the Oldest Greek Manuscript*, in *CBQ* 43 (1981) 517-533.

——, *Ezekiel's Utopian Expectations*, in A. HILHORST – É. PUECH – E.J.C. TIGCHELAAR (eds.), *Flores Florentino: Dead Sea Scrolls and Other Jewish Studies in Honour of Florentino García Martínez* (JSJSup, 122), Leiden, Brill, 2007, pp. 403-419.

LUZ, U., *Das Evangelium nach Matthäus*, 1. Teilband, Mt 1-7 (EKKNT, I/1), Zürich, Benziger Verlag – Neukirchen-Vluyn, Neukirchener Verlag, 1985.

——, *Das Evangelium nach Matthäus*, 2. Teilband, Mt 8-17 (EKKNT, I/2), Zürich – Braunschweig – Neukirchen-Vluyn, Benziger – Neukirchener Verlag, 1990.

——, *Das Evangelium nach Matthäus*, 3. Teilband, Mt 18-25 (EKKNT, I/3), Zürich, Benziger Verlag – Neukirchen-Vluyn, Neukirchener Verlag, 1997.

——, *Das Evangelium nach Matthäus*, 4. Teilband, Mt 26-28 (EKKNT, I/4), Düsseldorf – Zürich, Benzinger – Neukirchen-Vluyn, Neukirchener Verlag, 2002.

MACNEILE, A.H., *The Gospel according to St Matthew*, London, Macmillan, 1915.

MAGNESS, J., *The Archaeology of Qumran and the Dead Sea Scrolls*, Grand Rapids, MI, Eerdmans, 2002.

MALANDRA, W.W., *Zoroastrianism: Holy Text, Beliefs and Practices*, in *Encyclopedia Iranica* Online Edition.

MALHERBE, A., *The Letters to the Thessalonians* (AB), New York, Doubleday, 2000.

MANSON, T.W., *The Sayings of Jesus as Recorded in the Gospels according to St. Matthew and St. Luke*, London, SCM, 1949.

MARA, M.G., *Évangile de Pierre* (SC, 201), Paris, Cerf, 1973.

——, *Il Vangelo di Pietro* (Scritti delle origini cristiane, 30), Bologna, Dehoniane, 2002.

MARCUS, J., *The Way of the Lord: Christological Exegesis of the Old Testament in the Gospel of Mark*, Louisville, Westminster/John Knox, 1992.

MARTIN-ACHARD, R., *De la mort à la résurrection d'après l'Ancien Testament* (Bibliothèque théologique), Neuchâtel, Delachaux et Niestlé, 1956.

MARTIN-ACHARD, R. – G.W.E. NICKELSBURG, *Resurrection*, in D.N. FREEDMAN (ed.), *ABD*, Vol. 5, New York, Doubleday, 1992, pp. 681-691.

MASON, S., *Flavius Josephus on the Pharisees: A Composition-Critical Study*, Boston – Leiden, Brill, 2001.

MASSAUX, É., *Influence de l'évangile de saint Matthieu sur la littérature chrétienne avant saint Irénée*, Leuven – Gembloux, Leuven University Press, 1950; repr. (BETL, 75), Leuven, Peeters, 1986.

——, *The Influence of the Gospel of Saint Matthew on Christian Literature before Saint Irenaeus, Book 2: The Later Christian Writings*, Macon, GA, Mercer – Leuven, University Press – Peeters, 1992.

MACNEILE, A.H., *The Gospel according to St Matthew* London, Macmillazn, 1915.

MCAFEE MOSS, C., *The Zechariah Tradition and the Gospel of Matthew* (BZNW, 156), Berlin – New York, De Gruyter, 2008.

MEIER, J.P., *The Debate on the Resurrection of the Dead: An Incident From the Ministry of the Historical Jesus*, in *JSNT* 77 (2000) 8-14.

——, *Law and History in Matthew's Gospel* (: A Redactional Study of Mt. 5:17-48 AnBib, 71), Rome, Biblical Institute, 1976.

——, *Matthew* (NTM, 3), Wilmington, DE, Michael Glazier, 1980.

MELLO, A., *Évangile selon Saint Matthieu: Commentaire midrashique et narratif* (LD, 179), Paris, Cerf, 1999.

MENKEN, M.J.J., *Matthew's Bible: The Old Testament Text of the Evangelist* (BETL, 173), Leuven, University Press – Peeters, 2004.

MEYERS, C.L. – E.M. MEYERS, *Zechariah 9-14* (AB), New York, Doubleday, 1993.

MILIKOWSKY, C., *Which Gehenna? Retribution and Eschatology in the Synoptic Gospels and Early Jewish Texts*, in *NTS* 34 (1988) 238-249.

MITCHELL, D.C., *The Message of the Psalter: An Eschatological Programme in the Book of Psalms* (JSOTSup, 252), Sheffield, Sheffield Academic Press, 1997.

MOO, D.J., *The Old Testament in the Gospel Passion Narratives*, Sheffield, Almond Press, 1983.

MOORE, G.F., *Judaism in the First Centuries of the Christian Era*. Vol. 2 (1930), New York, Schocken Books, 1971.

MORETTI, L., *Inscriptiones Graecae Urbis Romae* III (Studi pubblicati dall'Istituto italiano per la storia antica, 28), Rome, Istituto italiano per la storia antica, 1979.

MORGENSTERN, J., *The King-God*, in *VT* 10 (1960) 148-182.

MORTLEY, R., *The Idea of Universal History from Hellenistic Philosophy to Early Christian Historiography* (Texts and Studies in Religion, 67), Lewiston, NY, Edwin Mellen, 1996.

MOSS, C.M., The *Zechariah Tradition and the Gospel of Matthew* (BZNW, 156), Berlin – New York, De Gruyter, 2008.

MOUNCE, R.H., *Matthew* (NIBC, 1), Peabody-Carlisle, Hendrickson – Paternoster Press, 1991.

MUILENBURG, J., *The Literary Relations of the Epistle of Barnabas and the Teaching of the Twelve Apostles*, Marburg, n.p., 1929.

MÜLLER, J.R., *The Five Fragments of the Apocryphon of Ezekiel: A Critical Study* (JSPSup, 5), Sheffield, Sheffield Academic Press, 1994.

MUNDELL, M.C., *A Sixth Century Funerary Relief at Dara in Mesopotamia*, in *Jahrbuch der österreichischen Byzantinistik* 24 (1975) 209-227.

MUSSNER, F., *Das 'Gleichnis' vom gestrengten Mahlherrn (Lk 13,22-30): Ein Beitrag zum Redaktionsverfahren und zur Theologie des Lukas*, in *TTZ* 65 (1956) 129-143.

MYLLYKOSKI, M., *What Happened to the Body of Jesus?*, in I. DUNDERBERG – C. TUCKETT – K. SYREENI (eds.), *Fair Play: Diversity and Conflicts in Early Christianity*, Leiden – Boston – Köln, Brill, 2002, pp. 43-82.

NAST, W., *A Commentary on the Gospels of Matthew and Mark: Critical, Doctrinal, and Homiletical*, Cincinnati, Poe & Hitchcock, 1864.

NEIRYNCK, F., *Les femmes au tombeau*, in *NTS* 15 (1968) 168-190.

——, *John and the Synoptics: The Empty Tomb Stories*, in *NTS* 30 (1984) 161-187.

——, *Q-Synopsis: The Double Tradition Passages in Greek* (SNTA, 13), Leuven, University Press – Peeters, 1988.

NEUSS, W., *Das Buch Ezechiel in Theologie und Kunst bis zum Ende des XII. Jahrhunderts*, Münster, Aschendorffsche Verlagsbuchhandlung, 1912.

——, *Die katalanische Bibelillustration um die Wende des ersten Jahrtausends und die altspanische Buchmalerei*, Bonn – Leipzig, Kurt Schroeder, 1922.

NICKELSBURG, G.W., *1 Enoch 1: A Commentary on the Book of 1 Enoch, Chapters 1-36; 81-108* (Hermeneia), Minneapolis, MN, Fortress, 2001.

———, *Resurrection*, in L.H. SCHIFFMANN – J.C. VANDERKAM (eds.), *Encyclopedia of the Dead Sea Scrolls*, Vol. 2, Oxford, University Press, 2000.

———, *Resurrection, Immortality, and Eternal Life in Intertestamental Judaism* (HTS, 26), Cambridge, MA, Harvard University Press, 1972.

NICKLAS, T., *Angels in Early Christian Narratives of the Resurrection of Jesus: Canonical and Apocryphal Texts*, in F. REITERER – T. NICKLAS – K. SCHÖPFLIN (eds.), *Angels: The Concept of Celestial Beings – Origins, Development and Reception* (ISDCL Yearbook), Berlin – New York, De Gruyter, 2007, pp. 293-311.

———, *Die 'Juden' im Petrusevangelium (PCair 10759): Ein Testfall*, in *NTS* 46 (2000) 206-221.

———, *Die Leiblichkeit der Gepeinigten: Das Evangelium nach Petrus und antike Märtyrerakten* in J. LEEMANS (ed.), *Martyrdom and Persecution in Late Antique Christianity* (BETL, 241), Leuven, Peeters, 2010.

———, *Ein "neutestamentliches Apokryphon"? Zum umstrittenen Kanonbezug des sog. "Petrusevangeliums"*, in *VigChr* 56 (2002) 260-272.

———, *Zwei petrinische Apokryphen im Akhmim-Codex oder eines? Kritische Anmerkungen und Gedanken*, in *Apocrypha* 16 (2005) 75-96.

NIEBUHR, K.-W., *Gesetz und Paränese: Katechismusartige Weisungsreihen in der frühjüdischen Literatur* (WUNT, 2/28), Tübingen, Mohr, 1987.

NIEDERWIMMER, K., *Die Didache* (KAV, 1), Göttingen, Vandenhoeck & Ruprecht, ²1993.

———, *The Didache: A Commentary* (Hermeneia), Minneapolis, MN, Fortress, 1998.

NOLLAND, J., *The Gospel of Matthew: A Commentary on the Greek Text*, Grand Rapids, MI – Cambridge, UK, Eerdmans, 2005.

———, *The King as Shepherd: The Role of Deutero-Zechariah in Matthew*, in T.R. HATINA (ed.), *Biblical Interpretation in Early Christian Gospels, Volume 2: The Gospel of Matthew*, London – New York, T. & T. Clark, 2008, pp. 133-146.

OBERMANN, J., *Inscribed Tiles from the Synagogue of Dura*, in *Berytus* 7/2 (1942) 89-138.

OLLEY, J.W., *Righteousness in the Septuagint of Isaiah: A Contextual Study* (Society of Biblical Literature Septuagint and Cognate Studies, 8), Missoula, MT, Scholars Press, 1978.

OMONT, H., *Miniatures des plus anciens manuscrits grecs de la Bibliothèque nationale du VIᵉ au XIVᵉ siècle*, Paris, Honoré Champion, 1929.

OVERMAN, J.A., *Between Rome and Parthia: Galilee and the Implications of Empire*, in Z. ROGERS (ed.), *A Wandering Galilean: Essays in Honour of Sean Freyne*, Leiden, Brill, 2009, pp. 279-300.

———, *Matthew's Gospel and Formative Judaism: The Social World of the Matthean Community*, Minneapolis, MN, Fortress, 1990.

PANNENBERG, W., *Jesus, God and Man*, transl. L.L.Wilkins and D.A.Priebe, Philadelphia, PA, Westminster Press, ²1977.

PARAMBI, B., *The Discipleship of the Women in the Gospel according to Matthew: An Exegetical Theological Study of Matt 27:51b-56, 57-61 and 28:1-10* (Tesi Gregoriana Serie Teologia, 94), Rome, Gregorian University Press, 2002.

PARK, J.S., *Conceptions of Afterlife in Jewish Inscriptions: With Special Reference to Pauline Literature* (WUNT, 122), Tübingen, Mohr, 2000.

PATTE, D., *The Gospel according to Matthew: A Structural Commentary on Matthew's Faith*, Philadelphia, PA, Fortress, 1987.

PAUL, D. J., *'Untypische' Texte im Matthäus? Studien zu Charakter, Funktion und Bedeutung einer Textgruppe des Matthäischen Sonderguts* (NTAbh, 50), Münster, Aschendorff, 2004.

PENNINGTON, J.T., *Heaven and Earth in the Gospel of Matthew* (NovTSup, 126), Leiden – Boston, Brill, 2007.

PERES, I., *Griechische Grabinschriften und neutestamentliche Eschatologie* (WUNT, 157), Tübingen, Mohr Siebeck, 2003.

PÉRÈS, J-N., *L'Épître des Apôtres accompagnée du Testament de notre Seigneur et notre Sauveur Jésus Christ* (Apocryphes. Collections de Poche de l'AELAC), Turnhout, Brepols, 1994.

PERRIN, N., *The Resurrection Narratives: A New Approach*, London, SCM, 1977.

PESCH, R., *Eine alttestamentliche Ausführungsformel im Matthäus-Evangelium*, in *BZ* 10 (1966) 220-245.

——, *Eine alttestamentliche Ausführungsformel im Matthäus-Evangelium*, in *BZ* 11 (1967) 79- 95.

——, *Das Markusevangelium. II.Teil: Kommentar zu Kap. 8,27-16,20* (HTKNT, 2/2), Freiburg, Herder, 1977.

PESCH, R. – R. KRATZ, *So liest man synoptisch: Anleitung und Kommentar zum Studium der synoptischen Evangelien*, 7 vols., Frankfurt, Knecht, 1975-1980.

PHILONENKO, M., *De Qoumrân à Doura-Europos: La vision des ossements desséchés (Ézéchiel 37, 1-4)*, in *RHPR* 74 (1994) 1-12.

POOLE, M., *Annotations on the Holy Bible*, Vol. 3, London, Henry G. Bohn, 1846.

POPKES, W., *Die Gerechtigkeitstradition im Matthäus-Evangelium*, in *ZNW* 80 (1989) 1-23.

PORTER, S.E., *Resurrection: The Greeks and the New Testament*, in S.E. PORTER – M.A. HAYES – D. TOMBS (eds.), *Resurrection* (JSNTSup, 186), Sheffield, University Press, 1999, pp. 52- 81.

PORTON, G.G., *Sadducees*, in D.N. FREEDMAN (ed.), *ABD*, Vol. 5, New York, Doubleday, 1992.

PRICE, S., *Rituals and Power: The Roman Imperial Cult in Asia Minor*, Cambridge, Cambridge University Press, 1984.

PUECH, É., *La croyance des Esséniens en la vie future: Immortalité, résurrection, vie éternelle?* Vol. 1: *La résurrection des morts et le contexte scripturaire*, Paris, J. Gabalda, 1993.

——, *La croyance des Esséniens en la vie future: Immortalité, résurrection, vie éternelle?* Vol. 2: *Les données Qumraniennes et classique*, Paris, J. Gabalda, 1993.

——, *Hodayot*, in L.H. SCHIFFMANN – J.C. VANDERKAM (eds.), *Encyclopedia of the Dead Sea Scrolls*, Vol. 1, Oxford, Oxford University Press, 2000.

——, *Qumrân grotte 4. XVIII: Textes hébreux (4Q521-4Q528, 4Q576-4Q579)* (DJD, 25), Oxford, Clarendon Press, 1997.

RAHMANI, L.Y., *A Catalogue of Jewish Ossuaries in the Collection of the State of Israel*, Jerusalem, The Israel Antiquities Authority/The Israel Academy of Sciences and Humanities, 1994.

RÄISÄNEN, H., *Matthäus und die Hölle: Von Wirkungsgeschichte zur ethischen Kritik*, in M. MAYORDOMO (ed.), *Die prägende Kraft der Texte: Hermeneutik und Wirkungsgeschichte des Neuen Testaments* (SBS, 199), Stuttgart, Kath. Bibelwerk, 2005, pp. 103-124.

——, *The Rise of Christian Beliefs: The Thought World of Early Christians*, Minneapolis, MN, Fortress, 2010.

REYDAMS-SCHILS, G., *The Roman Stoics: Self, Responsibility, and Affection*, Chicago, University of Chicago Press, 2005.

RICHARD, E.J., *First and Second Thessalonians* (SP, 11), Collegeville, MN, Liturgical Press, 1995.

RIEBL, M., *Auferstehung Jesu in der Stunde seines Todes? Zur Botschaft von Mt 27,51b-53* (SBS), Stuttgart, Katholisches Bibelwerk, 1978.

RIESENFELD, H., *The Resurrection in Ezekiel XXXVII and in the Dura-Europos Paintings* (UUA, 11), Stockholm, Almqvist & Wiksells, 1948.

ROBINSON, J.M. – P. HOFFMANN – J.S. KLOPPENBORG (eds.), *The Critical Edition of Q* (Hermeneia), Minneapolis, MN, Fortess, 2000.

ROETZEL, C., *OIKOUMENE and the Limits of Pluralism in Alexandrian Judaism and Paul*, in J. A. OVERMAN – R. S. MACLENNAN (eds.), *Diaspora Jews and Judaism*, Atlanta, Scholars Press, 1992, pp. 163-182.

RORDORF, W. – A. TUILIER , *La Doctrine des douze Apôtres (Didachè)* (SC, 248 bis), Paris, Cerf, 1998.

SALDARINI, A., *Matthew's Christian-Jewish Community* (CSJH), Chicago, The University of Chicago Press, 1994.

——, *Pharisees, Scribes and Sadducees in Palestinian Society: A Sociological Approach*, Grand Rapids, MI, Cambridge, U.K., Eerdmans – Livonia, MI, Dove Booksellers, 1988.

SAMPSON, G., *The Defeat of Rome in the East: Crassus, the Parthians, and the Disastrous Battle of Carrhae, 53 BC*, Philadelphia, PA, Casemate, 2008.

SANDT, H. VAN DE, *The Didache Redefining its Jewish Identity in View of Gentiles Joining the Community*, in A. HOUTMAN – A. DE JONG – M. MISSET-VAN DE WEG (eds.), *Empsychoi Logoi: Religious Innovations in Antiquity* (AJEC, 73), Leiden – Boston, Brill, 2008, pp. 246-265.

——, (ed.), *Matthew and the Didache: Two Documents from the Same Jewish-Christian Milieu?*, Assen, Van Gorcum, 2005.

SANDT, H. VAN DE, – D. FLUSSER, *The Didache: Its Jewish Sources and Its Place in Early Judaism and Christianity* (CRINT, 3/5), Assen, Van Gorcum – Minneapolis, MN, Fortress, 2002.

SCATOLINI APÓSTOLO, S. S., *Ezek 36, 37, 38, and 39 in Papyrus 967 as Pre-Text for Re-Reading Ezekiel*, in J.LUST – F.G. MARTÍNEZ – M. VERVENNE (eds.), *Interpreting Translation: Studies on the LXX and Ezekiel in Honour of Johan Lust* (BETL, 142), Leuven – Paris – Dudley, MA, Leuven University Press – Peeters, 2005, pp. 331-357.

SCHAEFER, K.R., *Zechariah 14: A Study in Allusion*, in *CBQ* 57 (1995) 66-91.

SCHAFF, PH., *The Oldest Church Manual, Called the Teaching of the Twelve Apostles*, New York, Funk & Wagnalls, 1886.

SCHENK, W., *Der Passionsbericht nach Markus: Untersuchungen zur Überlieferungsgeschichte der Passionstraditionen*, Gütersloh, Gütersloher Verlagshaus Mohn, 1974.

——, *Die Sprache des Matthäus*, Göttingen, Vanderhoeck & Ruprecht, 1987.

SCHEUERMANN, G., *Gemeinde im Umbruch: Eine sozialgeschichtliche Studie zum Matthäusevangelium* (FB, 77), Würzburg, Echter Verlag, 1996.

SCHLOSSER, J., *Le logion de Mt 10,28 par. Lc 12,4-5*, in F. VAN SEGBROECK – C.M. TUCKETT – G. VAN BELLE – J. VERHEYDEN (eds.), *The Four Gospels 1992*, (BETL, 100), Leuven, University Press – Peeters, 1992, pp. 621-631.

SCHMID, J., *Das Evangelium nach Matthäus* (RNT,1), Regensburg, Friedrich Pustet, 1965.

SCHMITZ, B., *Auferstehung und Epiphanie: Jenseits- und Körperkonzepte im Zweiten Makkabäerbuch*, in T. NICKLAS – F.V. REITERER – J. VERHEYDEN (eds.), in collaboration with H. BRAUN, *The Human Body in Death and Resurrection*, Berlin, De Gruyter, 2009, pp.105-142.

SCHRAGE, W., *Die Elias-Apokalypse* (JSHRZ, V.3), Gütersloh, Gütersloher Verlagshaus, 1980.

SCHUBERT, K., *Jewish Pictorial Traditions in Early Christian Art*, in *Jewish Historiography and Iconography in Early and Medieval Christianity* (CRINT, 3/2), Assen – Maastricht – Minneapolis, MN, Van Gorcum – Fortress, 1992, pp. 139-260.

SCHULZ, S., *Q Die Spruchquelle der Evangelisten*, Zürich, Theologischer Verlag, 1972.

SCHÜRER, E., *The History of the Jewish People in the Age of Jesus Christ (175 B.C. – A.D. 135): A New English Version Revised and Edited by* G. VERMES – F. MILLAR – M. BLACK, Vol. 2, Edinburgh, Clark, 1979.

SCHWANKL, O., *Die Sadduzäerfrage (Mk. 12,18-27 par.): Eine exegetisch-theologische Studie zur Auferstehungserwartung* (BBB, 66), Frankfurt am Main, Athenäum, 1987.

——, *Die Sadduzäerfrage (Mk 12.18-27) und die Auferstehungserwartung Jesu*, in *Wissenschaft und Weisheit* 50 (1987) 81-92.

SCHWEIZER, E., *Das Evangelium nach Mattäus* (NTD, 1), Göttingen, Vandenhoeck & Ruprecht,1973.

——, *The Good News according to Matthew*, Atlanta, John Knox, 1975.

——, *The Good News according to Matthew*, London, SPCK, 1978.

——, *Matthäus and seine Gemeinde* (SBS, 71), Stuttgart, Katholisches Bibelwerk, 1974.

——, σῶμα κτλ, in *ThWNT* 7 (1964) 1024-1091.

SEELIGMANN, I.L., *The Septuagint Version of Isaiah: A Discussion of Its Problems* (Mededeelingen enVerhandelingen van het Vooraziatisch-Egyptisch Genootschap "Ex Oriente Lux", 9), Leiden, Brill, 1948.

SEGAL, A.F., *Life after Death: A History of the Afterlife in the Religions of the West*, New York etc., Doubleday, 2004.

SENIOR, D.P., *The Death of God's Son and the Beginning of the New Age*, in A. LACOMARA (ed.), *The Language of the Cross*, Chicago, Franciscan Herald Press, 1977, pp. 31-59.

——, *The Death of Jesus and the Resurrection of the Holy Ones (Mt 27:51-53)*, in *CBQ* 38 (1976) 312-329.

——, *The Passion According to Matthew: A Redactional Study* (BETL, 29), Leuven, University Press, 1975.

SETZER, C., *Excellent Women: Female Witness to the Resurrection*, in *JBL* 116 (1997) 259-272.

——, *Resurrection of the Body in Early Judaism and Christianity: Doctrine, Community, and Self-definition*, Boston – Leiden, Brill, 2004.

SIM, D.C., *Apocalyptic Eschatology in the Gospel of Matthew* (SNTSMS, 88), Cambridge, University Press, 1996.

——, *The Gospel of Matthew and Christian Judaism: The History and Social Setting of the Matthean Community* (Studies of the New Testament and Its World), Edinburgh, T&T Clark, 1998.

——, *The Meaning of* παλιγγενεσία *in Matthew 19.28*, in *JSNT* 50 (1993) 3-12.

SMITH, D.A., *The Post-Mortem Vindication of Jesus in the Sayings Gospel Q* (Library of New Testament Studies, 338), London, T&T Clark, 2006.

——, *Revisiting the Empty Tomb: The Post-Mortem Vindication of Jesus in Mark and Q*, in *NT* 45 (2003) 123-137.

SMITH, R.R.R., *The Imperial Reliefs from the Sebasteion at Aphrodisias*, in *JRS* 77 (1987) 88- 138.

SONNEMANS, H., *Seele: Unsterblichkeit, Auferstehung: zur griechischen und christlichen Anthropologie und Eschatologie*, (Freiburger theologische Studien, 128), Freiburg – Basel – Wien, Herder, 1984.

SPARKS, L., *Gospel as Conquest: Mosaic Typology in Matthew 28:16-20*, in *CBQ* 68 (2006) 651- 663.

STÄHLIN, O. – L. FRÜCHTEL, (eds.), *Clemens Alexandrinus*, vol 3: *Stromata Buch VII und VIII, Excerpta ex Theodoto, Eclogae propheticae, Quis dives salvetur, Fragmente*, Berlin, Akademie-Verlag, ²1970.

STANTON, G.N., *A Gospel for a New People: Studies in Matthew*, Edinburgh, T&T Clark, 1992; Repr., 1993.

STENDAHL, K., *Matthew*, in M. BLACK – H. H. ROWLEY (eds.), *Peake's Commentary on the Bible*, Sunbury-on-Thames Middlesex, Nelson, 1962.

STEWART, R.B. (ed.), *The Resurrection of Jesus: John Dominic Crossan and N.T. Wright in Dialogue,* Minneapolis, MN, Fortress, 2006.

STRACK, H.L. – P. BILLERBECK, *Kommentar zum Neuen Testament aus Talmud und Midrasch.* 6 vols., Munich, Beck, 1922-1961.

STRANGE, G. LE, *Palestine under the Moslems: A Description of Syria and the Holy Land from A.D. 650 to 1500,* London, Alexander P. Watt, 1890.

STUHLMACHER, P., *Die Stellung Jesu und des Paulus zu Jerusalem: Versuch einer Erinnerung,* in *ZTK* 86 (1989) 148-155.

SYREENI, K., *Between Heaven and Earth: On the Structure of Matthew's Symbolic Universe,* in *JSNT* 40 (1990) 3-13.

—, *Incarnatus est? Christ and Community in the Johannine Farewell Discourse,* in J. MRÁZEK – J. ROSKOVEC (eds.), *Testimony and Interpretation: Early Christology in Its Judeo-Christian Milieu,* London – New York, T&T Clark, 2004, pp. 247-263.

—, *The Making of the Sermon on the Mount: A Procedural Analysis of Matthew's Redactorial Activity 1: Methodology & Compositional Analysis* (Annales Academiae Scientiarum Fennicae Diss., 44), Helsinki, Suomalainen Tiedeakatemia, 1987.

—, *Peter as Character and Symbol in the Gospel of Matthew,* in D. RHOADS – K. SYREENI (eds.), *Characterization in the Gospels: Reconceiving Narrative Criticism* (JSNTSup, 184), Sheffield, Academic Press, 1999, pp. 106-152.

—, *Testament and Consolation: Reflections on the Literary Form of the Johannine Farewell of Jesus,* in J. PAKKALA – M. NISSINEN (eds.), *Houses Full of Good Things. Essays in Memory of Timo Veijola* (Publications of the Finnish Exegetical Society, 95), Helsinki, Finnish Exegetical Society – Göttingen, Vandenhoeck & Ruprecht, 2008, pp. 573-590.

—, *The Witness of Blood: The Narrative and Ideological Function of the 'Beloved Disciple' in John 13-21,* in A. MUSTAKALLIO – H. LEPPÄ – H. RÄISÄNEN (eds.), *Lux Humana, Lux Aeterna: Essays on Biblical and Related Themes in Honour of Lars Aejmelaens* (Publications of the Finnish Exegetical Society, 89), Helsinki, Finnish Exegetical Society – Göttingen, Vandenhoeck & Ruprecht, 2005, pp. 164-185.

—, *Working in the Daylight: John 9:4-5 and the Question of Johannine "Literary Archaeology",* in *Svensk Exegetisk Årsbok* 70 (2005) 265-279.

TELFORD, W.R., *The Barren Temple and the Withered Tree: A Redaction-Critical Analysis of the Cursing of the Fig-Tree Pericope in Mark's Gospel and Its Relation to the Cleansing of the Temple Tradition* (JSNTSup, 1), Sheffield, JSOT Press, 1980.

TERMINI, C., *Philo's Thought within the Context of Middle Judaism,* in A. KAMESAR (ed.), *The Cambridge Companion to Philo,* Cambridge, Cambridge University Press, 2009, pp. 108.

THEISSEN, G. – A. MERZ, *Der historische Jesus: ein Lehrbuch,* Göttingen, Vandenhoeck & Ruprecht, 1996.

THOMPSON, M.L., *Hypothetical Models of the Dura Paintings*, in J. GUTMANN (ed.), *The Dura- Europos Synagogue: A Re-evaluation (1932-1972)*, Atlanta, Scholars Press, 1992, pp. 31- 52.

TILBORG, S. VAN – P. CHATELION COUNET, *Jesus' Appearances and Disappearances in Luke 24* (Biblical Interpretation, 45), Leiden – Boston – Köln, Brill, 2000.

TILLICH, P., *Symbol und Wirklichkeit* (Kleine Vandenhoeck-Reihe, 151), Göttingen, Vandenhoeck & Ruprecht, 1966.

TORREY, C.C., *The Aramaic Texts*, in C.H. KRAELING, *The Excavations at Dura-Europos: Final Report VIII, Part 1. The Synagogue*, with contributions by C.C. TORREY – C.B. WELLES – B. GEIGER, New Haven, Yale University Press, 1956.

——, *The Lives of the Prophets: Greek Text and Translation*, Philadelphia, PA, Society of Biblical Literature, 1946.

TRICK, B.R., *Death, Covenants, and the Proof of Resurrection in Mark 12:18-27*, in *NovT* 49 (2007) 232-256.

TROMP, J., *"Can These Bones Live?" Ezekiel 37:1-14 and Eschatological Resurrection*, in H.J. DE JONGE – J. TROMP (eds.), *The Book of Ezekiel and Its Influence*, Aldershot – Burlington, VT, Ashgate, 2007, pp. 61-78.

TROXEL, R.L., *Matt 27.51-54 Reconsidered: Its Role in the Passion Narrative, Meaning and Origin*, in *NTS* 48 (2002) 41-47.

URO, R., *Apocalyptic Symbolism and Social Identity in Q*, in ID. (ed.), *Symbols and Strata: Essays on the Sayings Gospel Q* (Publications of the Finnish Exegetical Society, 65), Helsinki, Finnish Exegetical Society, 1996, pp. 67-118.

VAGANAY, L., *L'Évangile de Pierre* (ÉBib), Paris, Gabalda, 1930.

VANDEN HOWE, I., *Het verrijzenisverhaal in het Petrusevangelie*, in G. VAN OYEN – P. KEVERS (eds.), *De apocriefe Jezus*, Leuven, Vlaamse Bijbelstichting, 2006, pp. 93-121.

VANDERKAM, J.C., *The Dead Sea Scrolls Today*, Grand Rapids, MI, Eerdmans, ²2010.

——, *An Introduction to Early Judaism*, Grand Rapids, MI, Eerdmans, 2002.

VERSNEL, H.S., *Ter Unus: Isis, Dionysus, Hermes: Three Studies in Henotheism* (Inconsistencies in Greek and Roman Religion, 1), Leiden, Brill, 1990.

VILNAY, Z., *Legends of Jerusalem: The Sacred Land, Volume 1*, Philadelphia, PA, Jewish Publication Society of America, 1973.

VIVIANO, B.TH., *Study as Worship: Aboth and the New Testament* (SJLA, 26), Leiden, Brill, 1978.

VOGELI, A., *Lukas und Euripides*, in *TZ* 9 (1953) 415-438.

VOKES, F.E., *The Riddle of the Didache: Fact or Fiction, Heresy or Catholicism?* (The Church Historical Society, 32), London, SPCK – New York, Macmillan, 1938.

——, *The Ten Commandments in the New Testament and in First Century Judaism*, in *SE* 5 (1968) 146-154.

WALBANK, F.W., *Polybius*, Berkeley, University of California Press, 1972.

WALTER, N., *Eine vormatthäische Schilderung der Auferstehung Jesu*, in *NTS* 19 (1972/1973) 415- 429.

WASSERMAN, E., *The Death of the Soul in Romans 7: Sin, Death, and the Law in Light of Hellenistic Moral Psychology* (WUNT 2/256), Tübingen, Mohr Siebeck, 2008.

WEAVER, J.B., *Plots of Epiphany. Prison-Escape in Acts of the Apostles* (BZNW, 131), Berlin, De Gruyter, 2004.

WEINRICH, W.C. (ed.), *Revelation* (Ancient Christian Commentary on Scripture NT, XII), Downers Grove, IL, InterVarsity Press, 2005.

WEINREICH, O., *Gebet und Wunder: Zwei Abhandlungen zur Religions- und Literaturgeschichte*, in F. FOCKE – J. MEWALDT *et al.* (eds.), *Genethliakon Wilhelm Schmid zum siebzigsten Geburtstag am 24. Februar 1929* (Tübinger Beiträge zur Altertumswissenschaft, 5), Stuttgart, Kohlhammer, 1929, pp. 169-464.

WEISS, B., *Das Matthäus-Evangelium* (KEK), Göttingen, Vandenhoeck & Ruprecht,1890.

WEITZMANN, K. – H.L. KESSLER, *The Frescoes of the Dura Synagogue and Christian Art* (Dumbarton Oaks Studies, 28), Washington, DC, Dumbarton Oaks Research Library and Collection, 1990.

WELLHAUSEN, J., *Das Evangelium Matthaei*, Berlin, Georg Reimer, 1914.

WENGST, K., *Ostern – Ein wirkliches Gleichnis, eine wahre Geschichte: Zum neutestamentlichen Zeugnis von der Auferweckung Jesu*, Munich, Christian Kaiser, 1991.

WEREN, W., *'His Disciples Stole Him Away' (Mt 28,13): A Rival Interpretation of Jesus' Resurrection*, in R. BIERINGER – V. KOPERSKI – B. LATAIRE (eds.), *Resurrection in the New Testament* (BETL, 165), Leuven, University Press – Peeters, 2002, pp.147-163.

——, *Human Body and Life beyond Death in Matthew's Gospel*, in T. NICKLAS – F.V. REITERER – J.VERHEYDEN (eds.), *The Human Body in Death and Resurrection* (Deuterocanonical and Cognate Literature, Yearbook 2009), Berlin – New York, De Gruyter, 2009, pp. 267-283.

——, *The Ideal Community according the Matthew, James, and the Didache*, in H. VAN DE SANDT – J. ZANGENBERG (eds.), *Matthew, James and Didache: Three Related Documents in Their Jewish and Christian Settings* (Symposium Series, 45), Atlanta, SBL, 2008, pp. 177-200.

——, *The Macrostructure of Matthew's Gospel: A New Proposal*, in *Bib* 87 (2006) 171-200.

——, *Matteüs* (Belichting van het bijbelboek),'s-Hertogenbosch, Katholieke Bijbelstichting – Brugge, Tabor, 1994.

——, *Steenrots en struikelblok: Petrus als leerling en leider in het evangelie van Matteüs*, in H. BECK – R. NAUTA (eds.), *Over leiden: Dynamiek en structuur van het religieus leiderschap*, Tilburg, Syntax Publishers, 1999, pp. 100-119.

——, *The Use of Isaiah 5,1-7 in the Parable of the Tenants (Mark 12,1-12; Matthew 21,33-46)*, in *Bib* 79 (1998) 1-26.

WESTERMANN, C., *Genesis 12–36: A Commentary* (trans. J.J. SCULLION), Minneapolis, MN, Augsburg, 1985.

WHARTON, A.J., *Good and Bad Images from the Synagogue of Dura Europos: Contexts, Subtexts, Intertexts*, in *Art History* 1 (1994) 1-25.

WIEFEL, W., *Das Evangelium nach Matthäus* (THKNT, 1), Leipzig, Evangelische Verlagsanstalt, 1998.

WILLIAMS, F., *The Panarion of Epiphanius of Salamis: Book I (Sects 1-46)* (NHS, 35), Leiden – Boston, Brill, 1987.

WILSON, J.F., *Caesarea Philippi: Banias, the Lost City of Pan*, London, Tauris, 2004.

WINKLHOFER, A., *Corpora Sanctorum (Mt 27,51ff)*, in *TQ* 133 (1953) 30-67.

WINSTON, D., *The Wisdom of Solomon* (AB, 43), New York, Doubleday, 1978.

WISCHNITZER-BERNSTEIN, R., *The Conception of the Resurrection in the Ezekiel Panel of the Dura Synagogue*, in *JBL* 60 (1941) 43-55.

WISCHNITZER, R., *The Messianic Theme in the Paintings of the Dura Synagogue*, Chicago, University of Chicago Press, 1948.

WITHERINGTON III, B.F., *Matthew* (Smyth & Helwys Bible Commentary), Macon, GA, Smyth & Helwys, 2006.

WODTKE, G., *Malereien der Synagoge in Dura und ihre Parallelen in der christlichen Kunst*, in *ZNW* 34 (1935) 51-61.

WRIGHT, B.G., *The Apocryphon of Ezekiel and 4QPseudo-Ezekiel*, in L.H. SCHIFF-MAN – E. TOV – J.C. VANDERKAM (eds.), *The Dead Sea Scrolls: Fifty Years After Their Discovery 1947– 1997. Proceedings of the Jerusalem Congress, July 20–26, 1997*, Jerusalem, Israel Exploration Society in Cooperation with the Shrine of the Book – Israel Museum, 2000, pp. 462–480.

WRIGHT, N.T., *The Resurrection of the Son of God* (Christian Origins and the Question of God, Volume 3), Minneapolis, MN, Fortress, 2003.

YARNOLD, E., Τέλειος *in St. Matthew's Gospel*, in F.L. CROSS (ed.), *Studia Evangelica IV* (TU, 102), Berlin, Akademie-Verlag, 1968, pp. 269-273.

ZAHN, T., *Das Evangelium des Matthäus* (Kommentar zum Neuen Testament), Leipzig, Deichert, 1903.

ZANKER, P., *The Power of Images in the Age of Augustus*, Ann Arbor, University of Michigan Press, 1988.

ZANGENBERG, J., *Trockene Knochen, himmlische Seligkeit: Todes- und Jenseitsvorstellungen in Qumran und im Alten Judentum*, in A. BERLEJUNG – B. JANOWSKI (eds.), *Tod und Jenseits im Alten Israel und in seiner Umwelt: Theologische, religionsgeschichtliche, archäologische und ikonographische Aspekte* (FAT, 64), Tübingen, Mohr Siebeck, 2009, pp. 655-689.

ZELLER, D., *Erscheinungen Verstorbener im griechisch-römischen Bereich*, in R. BIERINGER – V. KOPERSKI – B. LATAIRE (eds.), *Resurrection in the New Testament* (BETL, 165), pp. 1-19.

——, *Jesus und die Philosophen vor dem Richter (zu Joh 19,8 11)*, in ID. (ed.), *Neues Testament und hellenistische Umwelt* (BBB, 150), Hamburg, Philo, 2006, pp. 123-127.

——, *The Life and Death of the Soul in Philo of Alexandria*, in *The Studia Philonica Annual* 7 (1995) 19-55.

——, *Die weisheitlichen Mahnsprüche bei den Synoptikern* (FB, 17), Würzburg, Echter, ²1983.

ZIMMERLI, W., *Ezekiel: A Commentary on the Book of the Prophet Ezekiel*, Vol. 1 (Hermeneia), eds. F.M. CROSS – K. BALTZER, with the assistance of L.J. GREENSPOON, Philadelphia, PA, Fortress, 1979.

INDEX OF SOURCES

HEBREW BIBLE / OLD TESTAMENT

GENESIS
2:7	180
5:24	7, , 46, 131
15:15	5
15:18	5
17:17-19	146
23:2	5
23:4	5
23:20	5
25:8	5
29:1-14	67
29:3	67
29:8	67
29:10	67
29:31	146
30:22-23	146
35:27	5
35:28-29	5
37:35	6
38:8	143, 170
42:38	6
44:29	6
44:31	6

EXODUS
2:24	147-148
3:1-15	148
3:6	5, 136, 146-148, 151
3:15	147
3:16	147
4:4	147
9:23	32
9:29	32
9:33-34	32
12:23	162
19:16	32
19:19	32
19-23	73
23:30	170
25:5	143

LEVITICUS
18:5	116
19:18	112, 116

NUMBERS
16:33	6
21:18	65
21:20	66
23:14	66

DEUTERONOMY
3:17	66
3:27	66
4:12	32
4:33	32
4:36	32
5:22	32
5:23	32
6:13	191
8:11-20	120
11:26	112
18:15	12
25:5	143, 170
28:1-14	120
28:11	120
30:15-20	116
31:23	73
32:39	12
34:1	66

34:5	66		14:30	116
34:5-6	65			
34:6	66		JOB	
			5:26	5
JOSHUA			14:7-12	139
1:1-9	73		14:14	133, 137
			17:16	10
JUDGES			19:25-27	133, 137
5:20	145		26:14	32
			28:7	145
1 SAMUEL			37:4	32
2:1-10	137		41:13	180
2:6	137		42:17	12, 133, 137
2:10	32			
7:10	32		PSALMS	
12:23	44		1:5	12, 133, 137
			2:7	170
2 SAMUEL			6:6	6
5:2	170		6:9	124
22:7-8	154		16:10	7
22:13	33		21:30	12
22:14	32		22	69
			22:29	12
1 KINGS			30:3	7
11:7	164		30:18	6
17	44		48:15	6
17:17-24	7, 130-131		49:16	7
18:26	176		73:17	11
			73:21-28	11
2 KINGS			73:24	7
2:1-11	8		86:13	7
2:1-15	7, 131		88:13	131
2:12	62		89	72
4	44		89:48	6
4:31-37	7, 130-131		117:26	62
13	44		139:8	7
13:20-21	7, 130-131		141:7	6
23:13	162, 164			
			PROVERBS	
1 CHRONICLES			6:23	116
11:2	170			
22:1-16	73		QOHELETH/ECCLESIASTES	
			3:19-21	131, 139
			9:3-5	139
2 CHRONICLES			9:5-10	131
24	168		9:10	7
EZRA			ISAIAH	
1:2-4	3			

2:2-3	72	32:27	7
2:19	155	34-48	173
5:1-7	87	35:15	164
14:9	7	36:23	159
14:11	7	37	20, 44, 132-133, 135,
14:15	7		163, 168-170, 174, 224
24-27	9, 132	37:1-2	158, 173
25-26	136	37:1-3	161
25:6	8	37:1-10	136, 157
25:8	8, 44, 132	37:1-12	130, 177
26:14	44	37:1-14	19, 131, 156, 158-160,
26:19	8, 10-12, 44, 131-133,		171, 176-177
	136-137, 155, 158	37:2	159
42:1	170	37:5	156, 159-161
42:1-4	89	37:6	160-161
52-53	69	37:7	159
53:8	7	37:7-10	156
53:9	65	37:8	161
60:21	140	37:8-10	160
61	136	37:9	180
63:19	32	37:9-10	160-161
		37:10	155, 159
JEREMIAH		37:11-14	155
1:1-10	73	37:12	154-155, 159-160, 162,
1:4	50		164
2:1	50	37:12-13	136, 161
18:2-6	170	37:12-14	160
19:1	170	37:13-14	160
19.2	170	37:14	160, 165
19:4	170	37:27	159
19:6	170	38-39	176
19:11	170	38:12	162
21:8	112	39	157
32:6-15	170	39:1-20	157
		39:21-29	157
EZEKIEL		40	72
1	46	40:1-48:35	157
1:1	32	43:2	33
1:4	33		
1:13	33	DANIEL	
1:27	33	1	9
1:28	33	5-7	73
3:22-23	158	7	73
4:22	158	7:9	195
5:5	162	7:13-14	73, 168
8:4	158	7:18	168
10:4	33	7:25	168
32:21	7	7:27	168

8:10	132, 145
8-12	9
10:6	195
11:31-35	9
12	136
12:1	10
12:1-3	9
12:2	9-11, 13, 16, 19, 24, 146, 155, 158
12:2-3	10-11, 44, 102, 131, 145, 155
12:3	9, 155
23:3	227

HOSEA
6:1-3	131
6:6	91
13:14	136

AMOS
1:1	169

JONAH
2:1	193
2:2	7
2:3	193

MICAH
5:1	170
5:3	170

NAHUM
1:6	155

HABAKKUK
2:3	136
3:4	33

ZEPHANIAH
3:8	155

ZECHARIAH
9-14	170-171, 173
9:9	170
9:11	170
11:12	171
11:13	170-171
13:7-14:3	170

14	161, 224
14:1-10	171
14:2	169
14:3	176
14:4	163-164, 168, 170, 172-174
14:4-5	154-155, 162-169, 174, 176-177
14:5	164, 166, 168-169, 171
14:6	169
14:6-7	169, 172
14:10	174
14:12	176
14:16	170
14:20-21	169
14:21	170

MALACHI
2:4-5	116
3:3	170
4:5	7

APOCRYPHA AND SEPTUAGINT

BARUCH
3:9	116

JUDITH
9:11	147
9:12	147
9:14	147

1 MACCABEES
	88
7	54

2 MACCABEES
	22, 97, 136-137, 142
6:12-17	134
6:26	104
6:30	98, 103
7	13-14, 16, 24, 227
7:9	13, 98, 133, 146, 179
7:11	133
7:14	13, 133
7:23	13
7:25	133

7:29	133
7:36	13, 133, 146, 179
9	14
12:43	142
12:43-46	133
12:44	142
14:37-46	133

3 MACCABEES

7:16	147

4 MACCABEES

1:20	98
1:28	98
6:29	98
7:18	149
7:18-19	149
9:7	98-100
9:25	98
10:4	99, 101
11:7	98
12:20	98
13:13	99
13:14	99
13:15	99
13:20	98
16:24	149
16:24-25	149
17:5	145
17:12	45
18:17	132, 157

18:23	99

SIRACH/ECCLESIASTICUS

10:11	139
30:17	139
38:21-23	139
48:11	165
49:8	157

WISDOM OF SOLOMON

1:1-6:21	14, 16
1:12	14
1:16-2:24	14
2:1	14
2:1-3	15
2:10-20	69
2:23	14, 99
2:24	14
2:24b	15
3:1	14-15, 99, 104
3:1-4	15
3:1-10	15-16
3:1-4:16	129
3:4	99
3:4-5	15
3:5-6	15
3:7-10	15
5:5	145, 168
9:15	99
15:8	99
15:11	99

OLD TESTAMENT PSEUDEPIGRAPHA

Apocalypse of Elijah

3:4	168
31:15-16	38
34:6	101
34:33-36	101
35:4-6	101

Apocalypse of Sedrach

10:3	180

Assumption of Moses

3:9	147
10:9	145

2 Baruch

13:1-2	32
22:1	32
30:1	138
30:1-5	163
42:8	138
51:5	145, 168, 227
51:10	138, 145, 168, 221, 227
59:10	162
85:13	162

4 Baruch (Paraleipomena Jeremiou)

9:18	166

1 Enoch
1:9   168
18:15   132
20:8   146
22-27   132, 138
22:1-14   146, 179
22:13   138
25:6   156
26:1   162
26:3   162
37-71   18
43:1-4   145
51:1-2   19
58:2-3   132
60:8   146, 179
61:5   19
62:15   146, 179
62:15-16   165
70-71   145
83-90   163
86:1-6   145
90:20-27   145
90:21   132
90:24   162
92-104   97
92-105   138
93:6   155
103:3   138
103:7   138
104:1-6   146, 168
104:2-7   145
208   179

2 Enoch
1:2   36
1:8   130
18:1   36
22:4-11   145
29   145

4 Ezra
2:39   165
2:45   165
7   146, 179
7:32   138
7:37   38
7:78   101
7:97-98   227

7:125   227
14:30   116

Greek Apocalypse of Ezra
4:36   159
6:4   180

History of Joseph
19   180

Joseph and Aseneth
14   145

Jubilees
8:9   162
45:3   147

Liber antiquitatum biblicarum
(Pseudo-Philo)
3:10   138
19:12   138
25:7   138
32:15   145
33:5   145, 227

Life of Adam and Eve
41:2-3   138

Lives of the Prophets
Haggai 14:2   168
Zechariah 15:6   168
Ezekiel 2:15 137, 142
Ezekiel 3:11-12   132, 138
Ezekiel 3:12 156
Ezekiel 13   157

Martyrdom and Ascension of Isaiah
3:16   159
5:10   98
7:22   165
8:14   165
8:26   165
9:9   165
9:24-26   165

Odes of Solomon
22:8-10   161
22:12   160

42:11   130

Pseudo-Phocylides
Sentences
3-7   116
3-8   117
97-115   138
103-104   138
104   138
105   101
105-108   138
106   101
108   101
111   138
115   138

Psalms of Solomon
3   138, 163
3:11-12   138
3:12   132
13   138
14   138
14:2   116
15   138

Revelation of Ezra
4:36   159

Sibylline Oracles
1.103   162
2.221-26   132, 157
2.292   162
4.179-82   157
4.186   162
5.250   162
6.26-27   39

Testaments of the Twelve Patriarchs
Benj. 10:6-10   138
Jud. 25:1   138
Jud. 25:4   138
Reu. 5:7   36
Sim. 6:7   138
Zeb. 10:1-4   138

Testament of the Three Patriarchs
Ab. 20:8   180
Isaac 4:43-48   145, 168

Testament of Job
2:6   101
20:3   101

Testament of Solomon
20:14-17   145

DEAD SEA SCROLLS

1QM / War Scroll
XII, 1-7   168

1QS / Rule of the Community
IV   81
IV, 2-8   81
IV, 11-14   81
IV, 6-8   130

1QH / Thanksgiving Hymns
XI, 12   20
XI, 19   20
XI, 19-23   20
XI, 21-22   20
XIII   20
XIV   20

XIX   20
XIX, 10-14   20

1QHᵃ / Thanksgiving Hymnsᵃ
XX, 9-14   130
XI, 19-20   130
XIV, 29-30   130
XVI   130
XVI, 5-6   130
XVII, 4-12   130
XIX, 12-14   130

1QpHab VII, 7-8   136
4QMᵃ   145
4QSb IV, 25   145, 168
4Q201-4Q212   18

4Q245	134	4Q388	135
4Q385	132, 135-136	4Q391	135
4Q385-386	20	4Q434a	134
4Q385-388	135	4Q511 fr. 35	145, 168
4Q385b	135	4Q521	19, 135, 137
4Q385c	135	4Q548	134
4Q386	135-136	11QPsᵃ XIX, 10-11	130

GREEK JEWISH WRITERS

JOSEPHUS		2.165	140
Against Apion		3.372-375	140
2.217	140	3.374	146, 179
Jewish Antiquities			
1.131-133	219	PHILO	
9.225	169	*Creation*	
11.133	165	154	22
13.380-383	102	*Good Person*	
17.349-354	140	109	100
18.11-25	139	*Heir*	
18.14	140	275-283	81
18.16	23, 140	*Moses 1*	
20.169-72	162	156-157	86
Life		*Posterity*	
1.10	23	11.39	22
Jewish War		*Providence*	
1.97-98	102	2.11	100
1.113	102	*QE*	
2.119-166	139	2.39	22
2.154-155	17	*Sacrifices*	
2.154-158	140	1.5	145
2.157	140	2.5	21
2.165	23, 140	2.7	22
2.261-63	162	5	168
2.163	140, 163		

NEW TESTAMENT

MATTHEW		2:6	170
1:1-4:11	190	2:8	191
1:18-2:23	190	2:11	191
1:22	76	3:10	124
1:22-23	75, 230	3:17	170
1:23	198	2:20	96
2:2	191	4:1-12	71

4:6	213	8:28	159
4:8-10	191	9:8	199
4:15	88, 192	9:18	191
4:17	199	9:18-26	8
4:23	82	9:35	82
4:25-8:1	71	10	96
5:1	191	10:1	199
5:3-12	199	10:5	84, 192
5:7	71-72	10:7	199
5:11-12	218	10:8	199
5:14-16	91	10:5	84
5:17	113	10:5-6	192
5:17-20	73	10:16-39	218
5:17-48	109, 114	10:17	82
5:17-7:12	113, 118	10:17-22	90
5:20	82, 117	10:18	192
5:21-48	73, 117, 124-126	10:19-20	95
5:29	96	10:22	90
5:29-30	125	10:23	123
5:48	114, 117	10:28	95, 97-100, 102-103,
6:9	159		105, 179-180, 218-222
6:10	82	10:29-31	97
6:19	114	10:39	96
6:19-21	114	11:5	199
6:24	114	11:10	170
6:25	96	11:14	8
6:30	192	11:21-24	151
6:32	192	11:25-30	76
7:12	73, 113, 118	11:27	126
7:12-14	109	11:28	72
7:13	111, 179	11:29	76, 96
7:13-14	108, 110, 113, 119, 120,	12:1-14	125
	124-125	12:9	82
7:13-27	73, 108-110, 119, 124-	12:14	89, 213
	125	12:16	89
7:15-23	119-120	12:18	86, 192
7:19	124	12:18-21	88-89
7:21	124	12:21	192
7:21-23	119	12:30	83
7:24-27	119, 124-125	12:31-32	83
7:28	72	12:40	193-194
8:1	73	12:41-42	151
8:2	191	12:49-50	198
8:5-12	89	13:41-43	123
8:11	151	13:43	227
8:11-12	9	13:54	82
8:12	13	14:2	127
8:26	192	14:10	209

14:26	180, 192, 219, 221, 229	19:24	107-108, 120-121
14:27	219, 229	19:25	108, 119, 121
14:31	192	19:26	119
14:33	191-192	19:27	107, 121, 125
15:21-28	192	19:27-30	107, 110, 120, 125
15:25	191	19:28	108-109, 121-124, 127
15:29-31	71	19:28-30	121
16:8	192	19:28	121-123
16:13-20	88	19:29	107-108, 121-122
16:16	126	20:1	107
16:18	160	20:18-19	191, 193
16:21	191, 193	20:19	192
16:25-26	96	20:20	191
16:26	120	20:25	192
16:27	123	20:28	96
17:1	196	21:4-5	170
17:1-8	71, 195	21:33-46	87
17:1-12	196	22:6	218
17:2	195	22:23	141, 143-144, 149
17:2-13	8	22:23-33	5, 23, 52, 129-130, 136,
17:5	32		141
17:6	196	22:23-28	141
17:7	196	22:23-24	149
17:9	127	22:24	143-170
17:20	192	22:25-27	143-144
17:22-23	191, 193	22:25	149
18:8	125, 179	22:26	149
18:9	125	22:27	149
18:10	220	22:28	25, 141-144, 149
18:18	126	22:29	137, 141-142, 144, 197
18:20	198, 230	22:29-32	141, 220
19:1	210	22:29-33	180
19:16	107-108, 110, 114-116	22:30	141-142, 144, 149, 220-
19:16-22	107, 110, 118, 127		221, 223, 225
19:16-30	107-109, 114	22:31	142-143, 146, 149
19:17	107-108, 114, 114-116,	22:31-32	141, 144, 146
	116, 120-121	22:32	6, 149
19:18	116	22:33	141-142
19:18-19	116, 118	22:37	96
19:18-22	118	23:8	76, 192
19:19	109, 116	23:13-15	82
19:20	109, 114, 118	23:27-28	82
19:21	107-108, 114, 117-121	23:34	82
19:22	107, 114, 119,	23:34-36	218
19:23	107-108, 119, 121	23:37-39	224
19:23-26	107, 110, 118, 120	23:39	62
19:23-27	127	24-26	90
19:23-30	124	24:9	90, 192

24:13	90		227, 230
24:14	90, 192	27:53	169, 195, 217, 223-224
24:25	212	27:54	32, 169, 210-211, 225,
24:27-31	123		228
24:30	220, 229	27:54-55	225
24:36	220	27:55-28:20	189-190, 194
24:36-44	123	27:55-61	190
25:26	81	27:55	190
25:31-32	123	27:58	222-223, 230
25:31-46	123, 198-199	27:60	67, 211
25:32	192	27:61	48, 211
25:40	198	27:62	193, 222
25:41	25, 179	27:62-66	190, 201-203, 214, 222
25:46	25, 179	27:62-28:15	204, 213-214
26	50	27:63	70, 191, 193
26-28	221	27:64	51, 70, 191, 193-194,
26:2	193		212
26:4	213	27:65	227
26:15	170	27:66	70
26:17-28:20	190	28	179
26:32	191	28:1	31, 48, 210
26:38	96	28:1-3	31
26:53	213	28:1-6	178
26:56	190	28:1-7	195-196
26:64	123, 220	28:1-8	206
27	50, 54	28:1-10	31, 190, 224
27:3-10	171	28:2	32-33, 69-70, 206, 210-
27:9-10	170		211, 220, 226
27:15 23	209	28:2-3	69, 195
27:25	224	28:2-4	195, 201-203, 206, 209-
27:26	209		210, 214
27:34	68	28:3	33, 195
27:35	68	28:4	30-31, 196, 202, 214,
27:39-40	228		227
27:41-43	228	28:5	35, 196, 212, 214
27:44	228	28:5-6	191
27:43	68	28:6	193-194, 211, 217, 222,
27:45	169		227
27:50	160, 222	28:6-7	48
27:51	32, 159, 172, 210-211,	28:7	127, 191, 193, 198,
	223		211-212, 217, 224
27:51-52	210	28:7-10	198
27:51-53	54, 69, 153-154, 158,	28:9	36, 228-229
	160-162, 168-173, 177-	28:9-10	70, 201, 228
	178, 197	28:10	191, 196, 198, 212, 229
27:51-54	211, 224	28:11	30, 195, 202, 228
27:52	159-160, 162, 168, 211	28:11-12	222
27:52-53	8, 39, 41, 171, 223-224,	28:11-15	190, 201, 203, 222

28:12-15	227	13:13	90
28:13	70, 227	14:2	213
28:15	46, 50	14:24	170
28:16	196	14:25	151
28:16-20	71, 73, 190-192	14:26	169
28:17	192, 224	14:26-52	170
28:18	50, 196	14:27-28	59
28:19	76, 191-192, 228	14:67	172
28:19-20	84, 192	15:23	68
28:20	75, 161, 192, 198, 230	15:24	68
		15:32	68
MARK		15:42-47	65
2:20	63	15:43	66
3:6	213	15:46	48, 67, 159
5:3	159	16:1	48
5:5	159	16:1-8	60, 204
5:21-43	130	16:3	202, 211
8:32	59	16:3-4	211
9	59	16:4	35, 226
9:2-10	66	16:6	34, 59-60
9:7	32	16:7	59-60
9:10	66	16:8	48
9:13	60		
9:38-41	83	LUKE	
9:43-47	125, 151	2:17	90
9:45	96	6:43-44	125
9:47	96	6:47-49	125
9:48	103	9:34-35	32
10	59	9:49-50	83
10:17	121	10:25	114
10:17-31	108-109	11:23	83
10:19	116	12:2-9	95
10:20	114	12:4-5	95
10:21	120	12:4-7	95-96
10:23	119	12:4	95
10:24	109, 119, 127	12:5	95
10:30	121, 123	12:6	96
11:1-10	170	12:7	96
11:1-11	62, 162	12:11-12	95
11:5-17	170	13:23-24	110-111
11:23	170	13:28-29	89
12:18	143	14:14	142, 151
12:18-27	5, 52, 136	18:18	114, 121
12:24	144	18:20	116
12:26	146	20:27-40	5, 52, 136
12:28	140	21:17	90
13:1	170	22:27	122
13:1-37	162	22:29	122

22:30	122		2:31-36	58
22:33	209		5:19	208
23:46	104		6:15	168
24:31	179		7:56	32
24:36	179		12:8	208
24:42-43	48		12:10	208
24:51	179		16:30	208
			16:37	208
JOHN			16:39	208
1-12	63		22:4	209
1:51	32		23:8	23, 140
2:21	72			
3:14	63		ROMANS	
4	67		1:3-4	58
4:21	72		7:10	116
5:25	130		8:29	63
6	67		8:34	58
7:37-38	67		13:8-10	116
8:21	63			
8:28	63		1 CORINTHIANS	
9	63		10:1-4	67
11	130		10:2	67
11:24	142		15	48, 221-222
11:44	179		15:3	229
12:16	63		15:3-7	49, 60, 77
12:23	63		15:20	58, 63
12:32	63		15:22	159
12:34	63		15:54	136
12:36	63			
13-14	63		2 CORINTHIANS	
13:1	63		6:16	159
13:33	63		12:1-3	130
14:22	63			
17:1	63		EPHESIANS	
17:5	63		5:14	130
18:18	169			
19:34	67		COLOSSIANS	
20:6-7	179		1:18	63
20:11-18	212			
20:15	48		1 THESSALONIANS	
20:19	179		2:13	168
20:26	179		3:3	168
20:27-28	48		3:13	166-167
			4:13-18	167
ACTS			4:14-16	167
1:9	179		4:17	167-168
1:11-12	166			
4:2	140			

REVELATION

1:10	32
1:15b	32
1:20	145
3:5	165
4:1	32, 130
7:2	32
8:5	32
9:1	145
10:1-3	36

10:3-4	32
10:4	32
11:11	156, 159
11:19	32
12:4	145
12:10	32
14:2	32
16:18	32
20	159

SAYINGS "SOURCE" (Q)

3:16	62
6:22-23	61
7:19	62
7:35	61
10:21-22	61
11:31-32	61
11:47-51	61
12:22-31	96

12:39-49	62-63
13:34-35	61
13:35	62
13:35b	62-63
14:27	61
17:23-24	63
19:12-13	63
19:42-46	63

DIDACHE

1-4	108
1-6	111
1:1	109
1:1-2	109
1:2	112, 118
1:2-4:14	118
1:3a	112
1:3a-2:1	111
1:3b-2:1	111, 117
1:4	117

2:2-7	112, 116
3:1-6	109
5	108
5:2	120
6:2a	117
6:2-3	111, 117
7:1	112-113
14:1	31
16:7-8	166, 168

OTHER EARLY CHRISTIAN WRITINGS*Acts of John*

Acts of John
| 98:1-6 | 37 |

CLEMENT OF ROME
1 Clement
| 50:4 | 156 |

CLEMENT OF ALEXANDRIA
Quis dives salvetur
| 26:7 | 120 |
Stromata
| 4.11.80.4 | 100 |

CYRIL OF ALEXANDRIA
XII Prophets
2.516   171

Epistle to the Apostles
16   38

EPIPHANIUS OF SALAMIS
Panarion
19:4:1   37

EUSEBIUS OF CAESAREA
Demonstratio evangelica
6.18   171

Gospel of Nicodemus
Latin B 10(26):1   173

Gospel of Peter
19   35
21   32
28-35a   30
30   194
32-42   30
34-42   30
35-37   31
35-44   195
35a   31
35b-42   30
36   32-33
37   33
38   30, 34
39   35, 37
39-41   38
39-42   34
40   36
41   39
42   37
43   30
44   32
45-49   30
50-57   30
56   35
56b   35

HIPPOLYTUS OF ROME
Refutation of all Heresies
9:13:1-3   37
9:22   18

IGNATIUS OF ANTIOCH
Magnesians
9:1   31

JUSTIN MARTYR
I Apology
2.4   100
45.6   100
Dialogue
32.3-6   49
80:3-5   52
106-108   49
108.2   49, 194

Letter of Barnabas
12:1   132
18-20   111

PSEUDO-EPIPHANIUS
Testimony
85.5   160

ORIGEN
Contra Celsum
2.55   48
2.77   49
6.16   120
7.53   100

Questions of Bartholomew
4:12   176

TERTULLIAN
De Resurrectione Carnis
29-30   132
De Spectaculis
30.6   132

RABBINC LITERATURE

MISHNAH
m.Avot
2:7   116
m.Sanhedrin
10:1   52, 140
m.Sotah
9:15   165

TOSEFTA
t.Sanhedrin
13:3   162
13:3-5   52
13:5   142

PALESTINIAN TALMUD
y.Ketubbot
35b   164, 176
y.Kil'ayim
32c   156, 164, 176
y.Shabbat
3c   156
y. Sheqalim
47c   156, 165
y. Ta'anit
60a   175

BABYLONIAN TALMUD
b.Berakot
28b   103, 162
b.Eruvin
19a   162
b.Ketubbot

111a   164
111b   178
b. Pesahim
54a   162
b. Sanhedrin
19b   178
37a   162
90a-92b   149, 151
90b   178
90b-92A   143
90b-92b   146
91ab   96
92b   156, 158
b.Shabbat
31a   112
88b   53
152b   156
b Ta'anit
2b   156

TARGUMIC TEXTS
Targum Jonathan
Zechariah 14:4   164
Targum Ketuvim
Canticles 8:5   164, 176
Canticles 7:10   156, 158
Targum Neofiti 1
Numbers 21:19-20   66
Targum Pseudo-Jonathan
Exod 13:17   156, 158
Lev 19:18   112
Lev 19:34   112

OTHER RABBINIC WORKS

Avot of Rabbi Natan
A5   24
A34   176
Mekilta
on Exod 20:7   156
Sifre
76 on Num 10:1-10   176
306 on Deut   156
306 on Deut 32:2   173
Midrash Psalms
17:10   176

Pesiqta Rabbati
1:6   164, 176
21:9   168
31:10   164, 176
Pirqe Rabbi Eliezer
31   53
33   156, 158
Gen Rabbah
13:6   156
14:5   156, 158
28:3   177

96:5	156	3:15:1	156
Exod Rabbah.		12:5	177
15:15	176	Cant Rabbah	
Lev Rabbah		4:11:1	168
14:9	132, 156	7:9	156
18:1	177	Lam Rabbah	
27:11	176	2:2	175
Deut Rabbah		Midrash Tanhuma	
7:6	156	Bereshit 5	140
Ruth Rabbah		Buber Wayehi 12:6	164, 176
Proem 2	168	Buber Wayeshev 9:8	156
Esth Rabbah		Yalqut Shim'oni	
7:23	176	1Kings 18:26	176
Eccl Rabbah			
1:11:1	168		

NAG HAMMADI CODICES

Second Treatise of the Great Seth		Apocalypse of Peter	
58:20-59:11	171	1:6	38
		4	156
		4:7-9	132

PAGAN GREEK AND LATIN AUTHORS

ARISTOTLE		EPICTETUS	
De Anima I		Discourses	
2 405a 29-33	101	1.29.16	100
De Anima II		1.29.18	100
4 415b 8	104	2.2.15	100
		3.23.21	100
CHARITON OF APHRODISIAS		Enchiridion	
Chaereas and Callirhoe		53.4	100
3.3	59, 206		
3.7	206	MAXIMUS OF TYRUS	
CICERO		12.8.1	100
De Legibus			
1.28-29	86	PHILOSTRATUS	
1.53	86	Vita Apollonii	
De Officiis		7.38	209
3.69	91	8.5	101
		8.30	209
DIOGENES LAERTIUS			
9.28	100	PLATO	
9.59	100	Apology	
		30C	100

Phaedo

70c-d	139
72a	139
77e	100
84b-e	100
106a-d	100
113d-114b	102

Timaeus

41d-42b	132
42b	101

PLUTARCH
Moralia

475e	100

INDEX OF MODERN AUTHORS

Alexander, Ph. S. 112
Allen, W.C. 123
Allison Jr., D. C. 8, 40, 45, 50, 69, 72-74, 82, 107, 111, 114-117, 120, 124, 126, 141-142, 145-146, 153-154, 159, 161, 170, 173, 178, 181, 191, 198, 206, 209-210, 212, 214, 219-226, 228, 230-231
Amir, Y. 116
Aus, R.D. 57, 64-68, 70, 75, 154, 168
Avi-Yonah, M. 172
Bacher, W. 112
Barrett, C.K. 179
Bartsch, H.-W. 161
Bauckham, R. J. 225
Baumgarten, M. 166
Baxter, W.S. 73
Beard, M. 87
Beare, F. W. 107, 123
Bendemann, R. von 163, 165
Berger, K. 116
Betz, H. D. 109, 113
Bickermann, E. 59, 149, 203, 206
Birkeland, H. 158
Black, M.C. 154
Blank, S. 168
Blenkinsopp, J. 11
Block, D.I. 154
Bonnard, P. 107, 115-116
Bonsirven, J. 130
Bornkamm, G. 109
Borret, M. 120
Boxall, I.K. 159
Brady, M. 157
Brandenburger, E. 101
Braslavi, J. 172
Braumann, G. 113
Broer, I. 213
Brooke, G.J. 154

Brown, R.E. 29, 43, 74, 154, 160, 190, 206
Bruner, F.D. 154
Buchanan, G.W. 154
Buchholz, D.D. 38
Bultmann, R. 150
Burkert, W. 79
Burnett, F.W. 121-123, 126
Carter, W. 107, 117, 120-121
Cavallin, H.C.C. 12, 130, 138-139, 141
Cerfaux, L. 167
Chadwick, H. 120
Charlesworth, J. H. 129, 132, 134, 137-138
Chatelion Counet, P. 59
Cirillo, L. 37
Clark-Soles, J. 127, 181
Cohen, A. 54
Collins, J.J., 9, 157
Collins, A.Y. 60, 64, 226
Cosby, M.R. 167
Coulot, C. 119
Crossan, J. D. 27-28, 38-39, 46, 50
Curtis, J.B. 162-163
Danby, H. 140
Dautzenberg, G. 104
Davies, W. D. 8, 69, 82, 107, 111, 114-117, 120, 124, 126, 141-142, 145-146, 170, 181, 191, 206, 209-210, 212, 214, 219-226, 230
Day, J. 8
Dehandschutter, B.A.G.M. 226
Denaux, A. 49
Denker, J. 27, 38
Derrett, J.D.M. 123, 126
Deutsch, C. 126
De Vaux, R. 18
Díez-Macho, A. 156

Dihle, A.   112
Dimant, D.   135, 156
Dodd, C.H.   171
Donaldson, T.L.   72
Donne, J.   172
Dreyfus, F.   146-148
Du Mesnil du Buisson, C.   163-164, 180
Dunn, J.D.G.   166
Dupont, J.   96, 111, 122-123, 126
Ebner, M.   96
Edwards, C.   85
Eisenbaum, P.   50
Elledge, C.D.   132, 134, 136-139
Engemann, J.   38
Evans, C.A.   170, 194
Fiedler, P.   154
Filson, F.V.   124, 126
Fleddermann, H.T.   96
Flusser, D.   89-90, 108-109, 111-113
Foster, P.   28, 36, 170
Friedmann, M.   117
Friedman, R.   44
Funk, F. X.   109
García Martínez, F.   136, 156
Garrow, A. J.P.   116
Garte, E.   163
Geoltrain, P.   115
Gibbs, J.A.   161
Giet, St.   109
Gill, J.   155, 166
Gnilka, J.   102, 115-117, 123-124, 154, 205-206, 220
Goldingay, J.   9
Goldschmidt, A.   161
Goldstein, J.A.   13-14
Goodenough, E. R.   163, 176
Goppelt, L.   109
Gordon, R.P.   163, 165
Gounelle, R.   39
Grassi, J.   154
Green, J.B.   199
Grundmann, W.   153
Guelich, R. A.   113, 117
Gundry, R. H.   154, 211
Gurtner, D.M.   154-155, 223-226
Gutmann, J.   174-176
Hachlili, R.   174
Haenchen, E.   208

Ham, C.A.   169
Hamilton, N.G.   59-60
Hänlein-Schäfer, H.   85, 87
Hanson, K.C.   71
Hanson, P.D.   136, 171
Harl, M.   88
Harrington, D. J.   107, 117, 138, 154, 221
Harris, R.   160-161
Hartal, M.   88
Hartenstein, J.   29
Heckel, T.K.   27
Heil, Ch.   96
Heinemann, J.   137, 147
Helderman, J.   39
Hengel, M.   229
Henten, J.W. van   45, 226
Herzer, J.   166
Hieke, T.   35
Hill, L.   85
Hitchner, R.B.   85
Hoffmann, P.   96, 101, 194
Hofius, O.   195
Hogeterp, A.L.A.   133-134, 136, 156
Hollander H.W.   138
Holtz, G.   97-98
Hopkins, K.   80
Horbury, W.   167
Horst, P.W. van der   138
Howie, J.G.   47, 50
Hultgren, A.J.   150
Hultgren, S.   137, 150
Jacobovici, S.   199
Janzen, J.G.   141, 144, 148
Jarrick, J.   6
Jauhiainen, M.   170
Jefford, C.N.   109, 116
Jeremias, J.   111
Jobes, K.H.   11, 12
Jonge, H.J. de   51, 226
Jonge, M. de   138, 226
Junod, É.   36-37
Kaestli, J.D.   37
Kartsonis, A.D.   172
Kellermann, U.   163, 165, 226
Kessler, H.L.   175
Kieffer, R.   74
Kilpatrick, G.D.   83
Kirk, A.,   29

Klauck, H.-J.   29, 99
Klaauw, H.J.W. van der   226
Kloner, A.   162
Kloppenborg Verbin, J.S.   61-62
Köhler, W.-D.   28
Koester, H.   27
Konradt, M.   117
Kowalski, B.   159
Kraeling, C.H.   176
Kratz, R.   203-209, 212-213
Kraus, T.J.   27, 35
Kümmel, W.G.   163, 165
Lang, B.   156
Lapham, F.   36
Lattke, M.   160
Légasse, S.   115, 167
Le Moyne, J.   139-141
Lentzen-Deis, F.   32
Levenson, J.   53-54
Lichtenberger, H.   134-135
Lilje, H.   109
Loader, W.R.G.   115
Lohmeyer, E.   207, 211
Luck, U.   112
Lüdemann, G.   49, 51, 195, 197
Lust, J.   157
Luz, U.   96, 107, 111, 115, 117, 154, 163, 206, 208-209, 212, 218-219, 221, 223-224, 226
MacNeile, A.H.   123
Magness, J.   18
Malandra, W.W.   4
Malherbe, A.   166
Manson, T.W.   111, 123
Mara, M.G.   32, 36-37
Marcus, J.   170
Martin-Achard, R.   3, 7, 130-131
Mason, S.   139
Massaux, É.   28, 160
McAfee Moss, C.   223
Meier, J.P.   117, 146, 150, 154, 161
Mello, A.   154
Menken, M.J.J.   115, 143, 146
Merz, A.   29
Meyer, H.A.W.   207
Meyers, C.L.   163, 168
Meyers, E.M.   163, 168
Milikowsky, C.   180

Mitchell, D.C.   173
Mingana, A.   160-161
Moo, D.J.   170
Moore, G.F.   130
Moretti, L.   80
Morgenstern, J.   155, 173
Mortley, R.   85
Moss, C.M.   155, 170
Mounce, R.H.   126
Muilenburg, J.   109
Müller, J.R.   157
Mundell, M.C.   180
Mussner, F.   111
Myllykoski, M.   65
Nast, W.   153
Neirynck, F.   95, 212-213
Neuss, W.   175, 180
Nickelsburg, G.W.   10, 14, 18, 20, 130, 156, 158
Nicklas, T.   27-28, 35, 41
Niebuhr, K.-W.   116
Niederwimmer, K.   108, 166
Nolland, J.   155, 170
Obermann, J.   163
Olley, J.W.   88
Omont, H.   175
Overman, J.A.   83, 88
Overton, S.   44
Pannenberg, W.   43
Parambi, B.   154
Park, J.S.   139
Patte, D.   107
Paul, D. J.   154
Pellegrino, C.   199
Pennington, J.T.   220
Peres, I.   101
Pérès, J-N.   38
Perrin, N.   189, 198
Pesch, R.   150, 203, 214
Philonenko, M.   180
Poole, M.   153
Popkes, W.   113
Porter, S.E.   218
Porton, G.G.   24
Price, S.   87
Puech, É.   15, 19-21, 134-135, 139, 156
Rahmani, L.Y.   80
Räisänen, H.   103

Reydams-Schils, G.   85-86
Richard, E.J.   167
Riebl, M.   154, 178
Riesenfeld, H. 163
Robinson, J.M.   96
Roetzel, C.   86, 88
Rordorf, W.   108
Saldarini, A.   43, 140
Sampson, G.   88
Sandt, H. van de   108-109, 111-113, 117
Scatolini Apóstolo, S. S.   157
Schaefer, K.R.   176
Schaff, Ph.   109
Schenk, W.   123, 154
Scheuermann, G.   192
Schlosser, J.   96, 103
Schmid, J.   155
Schmitz, B.   227
Schrage, W.   38
Schubert, K.   175
Schulz, S.   96
Schürer, E.   139, 141
Schwankl, O.   130, 143-144, 146, 149
Schweizer, E.   83, 101, 123, 154-155, 205
Seeligmann, I.L.   88
Segal, A.F.   195, 199
Senior, D.P.   154-155
Setzer, C.   44, 47, 197, 231
Silva, M.   11, 12
Sim, D.C.   112-113, 123
Smith, D.A.   57-63, 68
Smith, R.R.R.   87
Sonnemans, H.   104
Sparks, L.   73-74
Stählin, O.   120
Stanton, G.N.   113
Stendahl, K.   155
Stewart, R.B.   46, 54
Strange, G. le   162
Stuhlmacher, P.   167
Syreeni, K.   63, 80-81, 113, 192
Telford, W.R.   170
Termini, C.   22
Theißen, G.   29
Thompson, M.L.   174
Tigchelaar, E.J.C.   136
Tilborg, S. van   59
Tillich, P.   49

Torrey, C.C.   142, 163
Trick, B.R.   144-146, 148-149
Tromp, J.   156
Troxel, R.L.   155, 169
Tuilier, A.   108
Uro, R.   61
Vaganay, L.   32-33, 39
Vanden Howe, I.   29
VanderKam, J.C.   17-18, 23
Versnel, H.S.   209
Vilnay, Z.   162
Viviano, B.Th.   126
Vögeli, A.   203
Vokes, F.E.   109, 116
Walbank, F.W.   86
Walter, N.   28, 201-208, 213
Wasserman, E.   102
Weaver, J.B.   208
Weinrich, W.C.   36
Weinrich, O.   203, 205, 209
Weiss, B.   207, 210
Weitzmann, K.   161, 164, 175, 180
Wellhausen,   J.   153
Wengst, K.   154
Weren, W.   46-47, 50, 87, 117, 190, 192, 197, 217, 221-222, 224-225, 227, 229-231
Westermann, C.   5
Wharton, A.J.   174
Wiefel, W.   124
Williams, F.   37
Wilson, J.F.   88
Winklhofer, A.   155
Winston, D.   14-15
Wischnitzer, R.   163, 165
Witherington III, B.F.   154
Wodtke, G.   175
Woolf, G.   85
Wright, B.G.   157
Wright, N.T.   8, 12, 15, 46, 54, 155, 189
Yarnold, E.   115
Zahn, T.   207, 210
Zanker, P.   85
Zangenberg, J.   227, 231
Zeller, D.   62, 97-98, 102, 228
Zimmerli, W.   158
Zissu, B.   162

INDEX OF SUBJECTS

Abaddon 20

Abel 21

Abraham 5, 21, 53, 138, 145-150, 220

Adam 138, 172, 180

Afterlife / life after death 3-4, 11, 13-14, 16-18, 21-25, 42, 44-46, 49, 99, 108-109, 127, 129-131, 139-140, 143-145

Age to come/coming age 108, 121, 123, 138, 157, 177-178

Amidah /Eighteen Benedictions 137, 147

analepsis 190

Anastasis 172

Angel 21, 25, 33-36, 41, 50, 53, 65, 70, 123, 132, 138, 140, 145, 166, 168, 176, 178, 191, 193-195, 201, 205-214, 220-222, 224, 226-228

   The angel of death 162

   Angel of the Lord 32-33, 178, 213

Anthropological dualism 200

Anthropology 95, 101, 104, 177, 179, 217-218, 220-221

Antiochus IV 11, 13, 133

Antitheses of Matthew 76, 82, 114, 126

Apocalypse 132-133, 166, 170-171

   Apocalyptic 10, 32, 45, 55, 89, 101, 103, 125, 223

   Apocalypticism 81, 95, 136

Appearance 8, 50-51, 54-55, 58-59, 63, 69-70, 76, 169, 178, 192, 195, 201-203, 220, 223-224

Archangel Michael 44, 167, 176

Arise 12, 19, 45, 138, 192, 196

Ascend 35, 37, 39, 66, 153, 167, 176

   Ascension 71, 76, 166

   Ascension of Jesus 63, 76

   Ascension of Moses 75

Assumption 35, 57-60, 62-64, 68, 70-71, 75

   Assumption of Enoch 131

Assumption of Jesus 64, 71

Belief in life-after-death/afterlife 3, 5, 17-18, 24, 129, 200

   Belief in post-mortem existence 10-11

   Belief in resurrection 9-10, 13, 18-20, 24-25, 44-46, 51-52, 55, 70, 75-77, 130, 132-134, 137, 141-142, 144, 151, 163, 179, 193, 196-197, 199

Blessing 5, 10, 12, 53, 67, 70, 81, 120, 145

   Gevurah /Power blessing 53

   Mechayeh hametim blessing 53

Bodily existence 40-41, 230

Bodily resurrection 8-9, 12, 15-16, 18, 20, 22, 25, 45, 47, 49, 51-52, 57, 70, 76, 129, 132-134, 136-137, 141-143, 197, 200, 231

Body and soul 45, 51, 95-96, 98, 101, 103, 129, 157, 180

Body-soul dualism 98, 101, 180

Bone 6, 19-20, 44, 80, 132, 135-136, 138, 155, 157-159, 161, 164, 176-178, 200, 226

Breath of God 99, 166

Bringing back (in) to the land 154-155, 159, 164

Burial 5-6, 43, 48, 50, 65-66, 73, 189, 222

Burial customs / practices 5, 18, 194

Burial place/site / cemetry 64-65, 17-18, 227

Catechesis / Catechism 113, 115-116, 126

Centurion 30, 34, 69, 89, 195, 225-226, 228

Christology 36, 61-62, 67, 74-75

Command / Commandments 14, 72-74, 76, 99, 107, 109, 112-118, 127, 138, 149, 162, 167, 191-192, 201, 214, 228-229

Consummation of the world   126, 230
Continuance of being / existence   12, 23, 57, 146, 148
Convert   115, 120
Corporal / corporality   41, 200
Corporeal / corporeality   15-16, 23, 40, 44-47, 49-50, 54, 221-222, 228, 230
Corpse   18, 47, 178-180, 222
Covenant   5, 13, 145, 147-150
Creation theology   45, 51-52
Creator   13, 53-54, 103, 105, 147
Cross   32, 34-41, 43, 48, 50, 61, 63, 172, 194, 226, 230
Crucify   35-41, 49, 65, 178, 191, 197, 199, 209, 224, 228, 230
Crucifixion   40-41, 68-69, 169, 171-172, 189, 196, 224-225, 228-230
Daniel   10, 13, 132, 137
Darkness   3, 9, 50, 81, 138, 169, 171-172
Death   3, 5-8, 10, 13-15, 19, 22-25, 44-45, 50, 53-54, 61-67, 69-70, 73, 75, 79-81, 96, 98-104, 108, 110-111, 120, 124-125, 127, 129, 131, 139-141, 145-146, 148-150, 179-180, 191, 193-196, 199-200, 206, 208-210, 213, 218, 222-223, 225-226
    The dead   5, 7-9, 12-13, 19-20, 23, 44, 49, 51-55, 63-64, 66, 69, 80, 127, 129-132, 134-137, 140, 142-143, 147-148, 153, 156, 158-161, 163-165, 167-168, 172-173, 176-181, 190, 193, 195, 197, 199, 214, 220, 227, 231
    Death and resurrection   53, 70, 148, 161
Decalogue / Ten Commandments   112, 115-116, 118, 127
Descend   32-34, 40, 50, 53, 167, 178, 201, 209-210, 214, 225-226
Descensus ad inferos   37, 39
Descent   3, 40, 50, 153, 161, 167, 209
Destruction   81, 97, 99, 102-103, 108, 110, 119, 123, 157, 179
Diaspora   103, 163, 165, 168, 177
Dichotomy of body and soul   96, 98, 101
Die   8, 12-13, 22-23, 25, 35, 49, 54, 58, 65, 69, 75, 79-81, 101, 104, 127, 134, 143-144, 149, 153, 164-167, 176, 225-226, 230
Disappearance   58-60, 62-63, 209

Disembodied   15-16, 24-25
Doctrine   100-101, 103, 112, 143, 151, 192
    Doctrines on afterlife   24, 139-140
    Doctrine of resurrection   9, 17, 146, 231
    Doctrine of the Sadducees   23
Doubt (about resurrection)   50-51, 55, 192, 229
Dura / Dura Europos   158, 163-165, 173-177, 179
Dust   10, 44, 131, 138, 158
Earthquake   32, 50, 53, 69-70, 159, 162, 164, 168-169, 171-172, 178, 195, 207, 210-211, 214, 225, 228
Easter narratives   30, 41, 60, 200, 201
Egypt   51, 54, 138, 148
Eleazar   98, 104, 157
Elijah   7-8, 33, 62, 66, 74, 165, 176
End   70, 72, 75, 80, 99, 110, 123, 127, 219, 225, 230
End of time(s)   70, 72, 75, 80, 134, 148, 198
End-time resurrection   164, 176
Enoch   7, 45-46, 63, 131-132, 138, 145
Entering (a new) life   114-116, 118, 125, 127
Epiphany   32, 60, 71, 203-205, 207-208, 210, 220, 227
Epitaph   138, 199
Escape   203, 208-209, 212, 214
Eschatological resurrection   98, 133, 157-158, 161, 163, 166, 173, 177
Eschatology   10, 12, 21, 54, 99, 102, 104, 127, 130, 136, 161, 171
Eschaton   109, 123, 171
Eternal life   13, 20, 81, 95, 102, 107-108, 114, 118-119, 121, 125, 127, 129, 145, 163
Eternal death   102-103
Ethics   81-82, 125, 199
Everlasting life   9, 13, 22, 44, 131-132, 158
Exaltation   58, 132, 145
Expectations on life after death   43, 46, 49, 205
Ezekiel   6, 19-20, 46, 132, 135, 138, 154-157, 159, 161-162, 165, 171, 173-175, 179

Fate 7, 10, 13-16, 23, 55, 57-58, 65, 79-81, 85, 90-92, 110, 124

Fear 31, 41, 48, 50, 53, 95, 97-98, 103, 178, 180, 201, 219-220

Flesh 17, 44, 52-53, 155, 157, 161, 164, 175, 178, 200

Funerary inscriptions 79-80

Funerary practices 5

Gehenna 95, 180

Ghost 48, 55, 180, 219, 228

God of life / the living 11, 54, 148, 181

God of the dead 148, 162, 181

Grave 11, 14, 18, 47, 59-60, 65-66, 68-69, 153-156, 161-162, 165, 193-195, 205, 218, 222-224, 226-228, 231

    Empty grave 66, 227

    Open(-ed) graves 154, 160, 179, 226-227

Guard 30-31, 34, 40, 46-51, 53-54, 70, 76, 178, 195, 201-202, 204-205, 207, 214, 225, 227-228

Hades 23, 40, 139, 173, 194, 225

Heal / healings 8, 19, 71, 81, 89, 131, 133, 135, 137

Heaven 31-39, 50, 55, 66-67, 75-76, 81-84, 101, 108, 114, 119-121, 124, 127, 131-132, 134, 144, 147, 165-167, 178, 195, 198, 201, 206, 209, 212, 220, 226, 229-230

    Heavenly existence 229

    Heavenly Father 117, 151

    Heavenly figure/creature 36, 61, 70

Hell 19, 22, 95-96, 102, 119, 125, 127, 172, 179

Hinnom Valley 162

Holy ones 8, 20, 69, 160-162, 164, 166, 168-169, 172, 177-178, 223-224

Holy One 165, 177

Hope 4-5, 8, 10, 12, 14-15, 20, 44, 53, 79, 101, 134-136, 138, 144, 157

Identity 145, 200, 218-219, 229

Immanuel / Emmanuel 75, 198, 230

Immortality 14-16, 21-22, 24, 45, 95, 99, 120, 140, 218

    Astral immortality 44-45, 145

    Spiritual immortality 45, 47, 50

    Immortality of the soul 15-17, 21-23, 45, 99-101, 104, 129, 138-140

Interim period/state 104, 146, 179, 181

Intermediary/intermediate state 102, 127, 181

Isaac 5, 53, 138, 146-150, 220

Jacob 5-6, 67, 70, 138, 146-150, 220

Jerusalem 61-62, 83, 91, 129, 155, 162, 167-170, 221

    Holy city 69, 153, 159, 169-170, 179, 224-225

Jesus' death 50, 61-63, 67, 69-70, 73, 75, 160, 191, 193-196, 198, 200, 210

John the Baptist 8, 62, 66, 124, 209

Jonah 7, 193-194

Joseph of Arimathea 65-68, 190, 194, 222

Judaism 44, 46, 54, 64, 67, 112, 118, 129-130, 139, 150

    and afterlife 4, 11-12, 22, 130

    and resurrection 46, 49, 132, 231

Judge 95, 97, 99, 101, 120, 126, 167, 198, 218-219, 222

Judgment 6, 10, 12, 14, 18-19, 25, 51, 61, 81, 122-127, 137, 140, 167, 157, 176, 198, 218-219, 221-222

    Divine judgment 6, 81, 102, 124, 219, 225

    Judgment day 126

    Judgment at the End (of Days) 53, 127

    The final judgement 12, 22, 123-125, 140, 180-181, 198-199, 222

Kingdom 90, 107-108, 114, 119, 122-123, 160, 165

Kingdom of God/heaven 65-66, 82-84, 108-109, 119, 121, 124-125, 151, 199

Law 73-74, 76, 108, 118, 125, 134, 140-144, 150

Legend 70, 153, 162, 168, 175

Levirate law 141, 143-145

Life 3-7, 9-11, 13-14, 18, 20, 22, 24-25, 29, 59, 69, 74, 79-81, 91, 95-96, 98-99, 101-102, 104, 107-108, 110-121, 124-125, 127, 129-133, 135, 139, 149, 151, 161, 179, 189, 196-198, 200, 205, 208, 217, 220, 222, 230

    Bring (back) to life 54, 133, 135, 180, 193, 198

    Come (back) to life 44, 153, 155, 165, 197-198, 217

    Restore (to) life 53-54, 208

Life and death   22, 25, 44, 54, 125, 127
The Lord's Day   31, 35
Love commandment   109, 113, 118, 127
Martyr   8-9, 13, 16, 22, 25, 45, 97-99,
   102, 104, 133, 218, 226-227
Mary   48, 178, 191, 195
Mary Magdalene   30, 35, 178
Messiah   19, 49, 65, 74, 135, 162, 165
Metaphor   8, 20-21, 43-44, 49, 76, 102,
   108, 125, 189, 217, 221
Mortal   10, 21, 59, 120, 129
Mortality 5, 53, 144, 148
Moses   8, 33, 64-67, 73-76, 138, 146,
   148, 172
Moses typology   64-65, 68-69
Mount of Olives   155, 162-165, 169-170,
   172-174, 176
Mount Sinai   74, 138, 143
National restoration   8, 10, 19, 44, 132
Near-death   7, 104
Necromancy   44
Nergal   162
Netherworld   37, 173
New age   55, 126, 198
Ossuary   80, 165, 199
Outsiders   17, 47, 54, 193, 220
Parable of the reunion of body and
   soul   157
Parousia   38-39, 62, 104, 123, 166
Passion   29, 38, 43, 48, 59-61, 98, 160,
   170-171, 193, 204, 222
Passion and resurrection narrative 27-28,
   60, 63, 217, 221
Patriarchal narratives   4-6, 10, 22
Perfect   114, 117-118, 121
Pharisees   9, 23, 45, 48, 52, 81, 83, 89,
   117, 124, 129, 137, 139-140, 150, 179,
   193-194, 212, 222, 227
Physical body   22, 134, 189
Physical death   15, 22, 179
Physical resurrection   14-15, 24-25, 48
Pilate   41, 47, 209, 222
Pneumatic   72, 222
Post-mortem existence   3, 57, 76
Post-resurrection existence   220, 226
Pre-existence   15, 23
Prison and death   207, 209, 213
Prodigies   138, 160

Promise   5, 8-11, 13, 19, 44, 52, 91, 138,
   147-149
Prophet of the resurrection   157, 168
Psyche 180
Punishment   6, 9, 13-14, 23, 25, 44, 48,
   81, 99, 102-103, 125, 132, 139-140,
   162
Purgatory   181
Purification   16, 81, 100
Raise (up)   8-9, 12, 19-20, 44-46, 51-54,
   59, 61, 69, 75, 127, 134-135, 138, 144,
   147, 153, 157, 160, 168, 178-179, 195
Reanimation of corpses   178
Reincarnation   45, 139
Relationship (humans)   144-145, 149,
   -150, 200
Relationship (God/heaven – humans) 5-6,
   21, 82, 149-150
Rescue stories   203-205, 214
Restoration   22, 44, 54, 136, 227
   National restoration   8, 10, 20, 44, 132
   Restoration of Israel   54, 131, 136
   Restoration of Judah   131
The resurrected   58, 70, 159, 164-165,
   168, 172, 178-179, 220-224, 227, 229-
   230
Resurrected Jesus/Lord   76, 179, 190, 194,
   217, 221-224, 228-231
Resurrection   8-21, 23-25, 29-31, 34, 36,
   40-41, 43-55, 57-61, 64, 68-70, 73-77,
   95-96, 98, 102, 104, 123, 127, 129-150,
   153, 156-158, 160-163, 165-166, 168,
   173, 176-181, 189-200, 201-206, 209,
   212, 214-215, 217, 219-231
   Final resurrection   139, 225, 230
   General resurrection   58, 70, 96, 102,
   135, 143, 148, 150-151, 159
   Second resurrection   153
Resurrection of the body   9, 12, 15-16, 18,
   20-21, 23, 25, 45, 47, 49, 51-52, 57, 70,
   76, 99, 132-134, 136-137, 139, 141-
   143, 179, 197, 200, 223, 225, 228, 230
Resurrection of saints   38, 40-41, 160, 211
Return to life/earth   132, 156, 167, 197,
   226
Revival   189-190, 194
The revived   54, 155, 158, 163, 179, 190,
   195

Revivification 4, 7-8, 19, 136

The righteous 9-10, 12, 14-16, 19, 21-22, 24-25, 44-45, 55, 63, 69, 81, 91, 123-124, 131-136, 138-139, 149, 156, 164-166, 176, 199, 206

Righteousness 9, 117, 127, 132, 135

Rise 12, 17, 19-20, 35, 39, 44, 49, 158-159, 164, 167, 172-173, 178, 194-195, 227-230

Risen Jesus 34-41, 48-49, 59, 70, 76, 122, 178, 189, 191-192, 195, 197, 199-202, 211-212, 226-229

Roman funerary inscription 79-80

Sadducees 23- 25, 52-53, 124, 129-130, 139-151, 220

Saints 38-39, 41, 50, 54, 139, 145, 153, 155, 158-160, 166-168, 172, 177-179, 197, 222

Salvation 19-21, 41, 58, 84, 119, 135, 137, 199-200

Satan 173, 205

Self 96, 98, 100

Separation of body and soul 101, 180

Sepulchre 31, 33-36, 179

Sermon on the Mount 108-109, 113-114, 119

Sheol 3-4, 6-7, 9-10, 14, 19-20, 23-24, 38, 44, 130-131, 161, 178

Sinews 136, 155, 157

Skin 98, 136, 155, 157

Soul *Passim*
    The soul departs 53, 81
    The soul dying 101
    Permanency of the soul 103
    Ruin of the soul 102
    Soul continues to exist 179, 181
    Soul return to body 53, 161
    Soul and body 95

Splitting of the mountain(s)/Mount of Olives 155, 162-164, 169, 172-176

Splitting of rocks 69, 153, 169, 211, 223, 225, 227

Spirit 13, 44-45, 69, 81, 101, 138, 140

Stone 12, 47, 67, 70, 211
    Removing the stone 33, 47, 67, 70, 178, 226
    Roll away/back the stone 31, 33-34, 47, 53, 67, 178, 195, 201, 211

Supernatural 50, 132, 169, 219-220, 223, 225, 230

Survive 99, 143, 218

Symbol 43, 49, 52, 54, 71-72

Symbolism 71-72

Tartarus 173

Temple 23, 69, 72, 91, 137, 157, 167, 170-171, 209, 213, 225

Theodicy 20, 24, 134-135

Theology
    Assumption theology 62, 64, 71
    Resurrection theology 75

Tomb 12, 30-31, 35, 40-41, 44, 46-50, 54, 69-70, 133, 138, 153, 160, 168, 178, 193-196, 199, 201-205, 207-208, 210-214, 217-219, 222, 224, 226, 229
    The closing of/sealing of the tomb 47-48, 201
    Empty tomb 28, 43, 47-48, 50-51, 53, 55, 57, 59-60, 64-65, 67-68, 76-77, 177, 201-203, 205, 221-222
    open(-ed) tomb 35, 153, 178-179, 195-196, 205, 210-211, 214
    rock tomb 67-68, 211

Torah 13, 53, 72-73, 113, 117-118, 125-126, 141, 143, 146, 192, 199

Touch 48, 50, 98-100, 228, 230

Transfiguration 8, 32-33, 50, 58, 66, 75, 196

Transform 16, 24, 221, 227

Transformation 9, 55, 71-72, 132, 136, 141, 145, 220-221, 225

Translate (person) 7-8, 58-59, 65, 75-76

Transmigration 101, 139

Tremble 70, 159, 171

Trumpet 164-165, 176
    God's trumpet 167

Underworld 6, 44, 101, 140, 160-161, 172-174, 176, 218-219

Veil of the temple 171, 223, 225

Vindication 57-58, 61, 67, 70, 75, 124, 224, 226-227

Vision 4, 8-9, 19, 25, 30, 34, 46-47, 50, 84, 132, 135-136, 155-158, 161, 171, 173, 175, 181

Wisdom 7, 15, 81, 131-132

Witness 20, 30, 50, 58-59, 69, 140, 178, 196, 202, 207, 227-228

Eye witnesses   195-196

Witness (text-)   27-28, 111, 218, 222

Women witness   47-48, 207, 209-210, 214, 227

Women at the tomb   35, 47-48, 59, 67, 70, 76, 178, 191, 195, 210-211, 226

World to come   52, 81, 91, 140, 145, 163

PRINTED ON PERMANENT PAPER • IMPRIME SUR PAPIER PERMANENT • GEDRUKT OP DUURZAAM PAPIER - ISO 9706

N.V. PEETERS S.A., WAROTSTRAAT 50, B-3020 HERENT